D1590798

After the Golden Age

# AFTER the GOLDEN AGE

## Romantic Pianism and Modern Performance

KENNETH HAMILTON

OXFORD
UNIVERSITY PRESS
2008

# OXFORD
## UNIVERSITY PRESS

Oxford University Press, Inc., publishes works that further
Oxford University's objective of excellence
in research, scholarship, and education.

Oxford   New York
Auckland   Cape Town   Dar es Salaam   Hong Kong   Karachi
Kuala Lumpur   Madrid   Melbourne   Mexico City   Nairobi
New Delhi   Shanghai   Taipei   Toronto

With offices in
Argentina   Austria   Brazil   Chile   Czech Republic   France   Greece
Guatemala   Hungary   Italy   Japan   Poland   Portugal   Singapore
South Korea   Switzerland   Thailand   Turkey   Ukraine   Vietnam

Published by Oxford University Press, Inc.
198 Madison Avenue, New York, New York 10016

www.oup.com

Library of Congress Cataloging-in-Publication Data

Hamilton, Kenneth, 1963–
After the golden age : romantic pianism and modern performance / Kenneth Hamilton.
p.   cm.
Includes bibliographical references (p. ) and index.
ISBN 978-0-19-517826-5
1. Piano—Performance—History.   I. Title.
ML700.H26 2007
786.2'14309—dc22          2007002202

5   7   9   8   6

Printed in the United States of America
on acid-free paper

For Monika

# Preface

I recently, regrettably, attended a recital of four Beethoven sonatas given by an internationally lauded player in a large hall. The artist was unexpectedly preceded by a herald with frowning brow and solemn countenance. His function was to admonish the audience that they should not cough or make any noise whatsoever during the performance, owing to the supposedly fatal effect this would have on the pianist's laserlike but evidently precarious concentration. With the vulgar multitude suitably chastised and a stunned atmosphere created, the grim visage of the great player consented to appear before his unworthy auditors. He predictably proceeded to perform with all the spontaneity of a tenth take in the recording studio—and the program featured the supposedly improvisatory "Quasi una fantasia" sonatas (op. 27) too. It was a miserable experience.

To what extent did this funereal occasion, this reverential disinterring of musical masterpieces relate to any type of concert Beethoven might have known? Hardly at all. We would have had to wait for many decades after the composition of the relevant sonatas regularly to encounter such an event. And what of the manner of performance, with its ultra-scrupulous adherence to the letter of the score, even down to the almost exact observation of the pedal instructions in the first movement of the *Moonlight* Sonata? The audience was understandably surprised at the murky fog of sound that arose from this, for if the pedal directions were Beethoven's, the piano certainly was not, but rather a modern concert Steinway as similar to an early instrument as a biplane to a jumbo jet. The resulting musical effect was, predictably, vastly different, and turned what was probably intended to be a subtle merging of mild dissonances into a more strident cacophony. It made Beethoven seem daringly iconoclastic, but also incomprehensible.

How did we end up here from the much more varied, spontaneous, and improvisatory piano culture of the nineteenth century—when, ironically, most of our repertoire was actually composed? What lessons can the historical record teach us that might be applied again to modern performance? This book attempts to answer these questions by tracing traditions of piano playing and concert programming from the early romantic era to the early twentieth century, from Chopin and Liszt to Paderewski and Busoni. In the process it touches upon why we now play differently from players on early recordings—recordings still so avidly admired by many modern pianists—and on the elusive concept of a "Golden Age of the Piano" itself. It ends with a plea not to sideline completely the performance traditions of the great pianists of the past through a too rigorous—and again unhistorical—obsession with urtext editions and urtext playing. Dare we say that the composer need not always have the final word?

Many piano students accept more or less unquestioningly the structure and etiquette of the standard modern piano recital, but our concert decorum was for a long time far from the received norm. From the perspective of earlier eras, we might ask ourselves why we hush people who clap between movements of a piece, why we usually expect pianists to perform from memory, and why we are so worried about wrong notes—the last an especially recent psychosis that scarcely troubled Anton Rubinstein or Eugen d'Albert, only two of the most illustrious splashy players of the past. Elucidation of these issues and others equally pertinent not only points up the inevitable transience of our own customs, but provides food for thought should we wish to change our own practices in a classical music world that so often seems deliberately distant from its own audience.

This book was written because I remain fascinated by the piano and piano music. Custom has, for me at any rate, not staled their infinite variety. Yet my pleasure in the piano is matched by frustration at many of the fusty rituals of modern concert-giving, in which the music is served up with the superciliousness of a sneering sommelier offering overpriced wine at a too-long-established restaurant. In the hope that a more vivid historical awareness might actually help to clear a few of the cobwebs away, I originally suggested this project to Bruce Phillips, doyen of music editors, who commissioned it with encouraging conviction. The book was subsequently cajoled along with charming urgency by Kim Robinson, and efficiently ushered into print by Suzanne Ryan, ably assisted by Norman Hirschy and Lora Dunn. The immediately brightened tone of Suzanne's voice when I—instead of proffering the usual litany of increasingly bizarre excuses—actually told her the book was finished was indeed heart-warming.

During the writing process, a welcome grant from the British Arts and Humanities Research Board enabled me to concentrate on the task in hand, while the initial draft benefited enormously from the wisdom and perspicacity of friends and colleagues who were kind enough to take time out of their own activities constructively to criticize mine. In particular, Jonathan Bellman and Larry Todd waded dauntlessly through an entire earlier version of the book, offering in the process quite indispensable encouragement and counsel. William Weber, the generally acknowledged guru of the study of concert history, very generously allowed me access to his forthcoming work and made many welcome and apt suggestions regarding my own. Jim Samson, allegedly having had his printout of various chapters confiscated "for reasons of national security" at an airport checkpoint, nevertheless was able to make many detailed and thought-provoking comments, reconstructed impressively from memory and delivered subtly in a surveillance-eluding whisper during an intermittently dull concert. Back at Oxford University Press, the finely tuned production and copyediting talents of Christi Stanforth and Barbara Norton ensured that the book now before the public is considerably more consistent than the one that first landed on their desks. Finally, for other advice and general morale-boosting it is my pleasure to acknowledge that I owe more than one drink to Hugh Macdonald, Roger Parker, Robert Philip, Valerie Woodring-Goertzen, and Colin Lawson.

# Contents

# Figures and Music Examples

# After the Golden Age

# 1

# Great Tradition, Grand Manner, Golden Age

Much have I travelled in the realms of gold
And Many goodly states and kingdoms seen;
Round many Western islands have I been
Which Bards in Fealty to Apollo hold.
Oft of one wide expanse had I been told...
—John Keats, "On First Looking
into Chapman's Homer"

I have just performed Chopin's concerto (a work I once studied with Paderewski himself) with the newly formed orchestra in New York City, mindful of the fact that, to some extent, I represent a great tradition that I now pass on to younger generations in turn.

—Sigismund Stojowski, 1935

## A Realm of Gold...

References to a golden age of pianism, a "Great Tradition" of piano playing, still abound in books, broadcasts, and concert reviews the world over. Quotation marks around the terms are less often seen, for many writers who habitually use them seem to be convinced that they require no explanation, or at the very worst they are—like "love" or "strong leadership"—too difficult to define without recourse to awkwardly contentious examples. Unlike love, however, which all but the most misanthropic joyfully regard as alive and well in the world today, the Great Tradition is, supposedly, largely lost. Audiences can only hope to be granted a shimmering glimpse of it—like Sir Galahad of the Holy Grail—from the odd inspired performance by a dwindling handful of elderly pianists, or perhaps from their students, who—like Ignacy Jan Paderewski's colleague and pupil Sigismund Stojowski, quoted in the second epigraph[1]—thought of themselves as carrying the apostolic flame to subsequent generations. The term was given particularly frequent exposure in publicity surrounding the final recordings and performances of Vladimir Horowitz—the "Last Romantic," no less, according to his breathlessly adulatory press releases—who was very effectively promoted as the last scion of a noble breed. When Horowitz himself went the way of all flesh a little while later, the august lineage was, at least as represented by that particular master's publicity agents, no more, although the superb recordings of course remain. The Horowitz case is a good stepping-off point for discussion of a Great Tradition of pianism, because it illustrates two basic things about it. First, that it is chiefly now associated with performers of the mid-to-late romantic era. Secondly, that it always is, or is just about to be, extinct.

In 1961, more than twenty years before Horowitz became by default the "Last Romantic," the pianist and critic Abram Chasins—composer of the once famed piece of chinoiserie "Rush Hour in Hong Kong"—produced the second edition of his well-known reminiscences, *Speaking of Pianists*. There captivating memories of great performers of the past jostled with more sober assessments of the younger generation of contemporary players, including Sviatoslav Richter, Emil Gilels, and even a promising newcomer called Maurizio Pollini.[2] The book was justly popular. Chasins, no dilettante himself, had known personally a surprising number of the master pianists of the early twentieth century and was in an excellent position to evaluate their styles, strengths, and weaknesses. Horowitz was treated admiringly, even at times gushingly, but he could not equal the impact of the great players of the previous era, in particular Josef Hofmann (Chasins's own teacher), Sergei Rachmaninoff, and Leopold Godowsky. Their superlative artistry—even Rachmaninoff's—was only partially and imperfectly preserved on disc. They were also, by 1961, all dead.

Chasins's view of contemporary performers was thus explicitly colored by a sense of loss, of a tradition in decline, and of a continuing, perhaps inevitable degeneration from the incomparable achievements of the past to a more humdrum present. As he put it himself, "No one who lives in the real world, no one who has observed the course of piano-playing, expects or demands today the

---

[1] A student and friend of Paderewski's, Stojowski was a relatively well-known composer in his day. His master even thought of him as one of the leading composers of the modern era, an assessment that posterity has, as yet, not validated. The winsome *Chant d'Amour* was recorded by Paderewski himself.

[2] Abram Chasins, *Speaking of Pianists* (New York: Knopf, 1961–62).

luminous standards of individuality and conceptual grandeur of other days when pianistic giants roamed the earth."[3]

This "conceptual grandeur" sounds eerily reminiscent of another term often bandied around when talking of romantic pianism: the "grand manner." It was a favorite expression of Franz Liszt's student Moriz Rosenthal, who used it when contrasting his preferred style of playing with that of some supposedly more inhibited youngsters. In a 1937 interview for the music magazine *Etude* he waxed lyrical: "The grand manner is, very simply—a grand manner. A manner of playing which forms itself upon grand concepts, makes such concepts personal by grand enthusiasms, and paints its pianistic pictures in bold, brilliant, grand strokes." Though intelligent enough to realize that such a broadly defined concept could hardly be confined to any particular musical era, he was in no doubt that the style was rarely to be found among current performers: "The more typical representatives of this modern day seem less concerned with a free outpouring of generous enthusiasms, than with the practical means of achieving some goal. It is not considered "smart" to give unfettered expression to one's deepest emotions."[4]

It was no doubt in this spirit that Jeffrey Johnson chose to title his highly useful collection of *Etude* excerpts *Piano Lessons in the Grand Style from the Golden Age of "The Etude" Music Magazine, 1913–40.*[5] Typically, he linked "grand style" with "golden age" in a manner hinted at by Rosenthal and stated explicitly by many other authors and critics, especially writers of liner notes for historical recordings,[6] for whom the golden age was not simply that of *Etude*, but of pianism itself. The most recent history of piano playing has turned out pretty badly from this viewpoint. Even a writer as distinguished as Allan Evans, whose splendid work in unearthing many almost forgotten recordings deserves the sincere gratitude of all pianophiles, implicitly if (one hopes) unintentionally damned all later performers when he claimed in liner notes that certain elements of Frederic Lamond's Liszt recordings "attest to a level of musicianship no longer heard."[7] Rosenthal sought to pass on some inkling of his own grand

[3] Chasins, 152.

[4] Moriz Rosenthal (in conference with R. H. Wollstein), "The 'Grand Manner' in Piano Playing," *Etude* (May 1937). Quoted from Mark Mitchell and Allan Evans, eds., *Moriz Rosenthal in Words and Music* (Bloomington: Indiana University Press, 2006), 6.

[5] New York: Dover, 2003.

[6] And indeed narrators of DVDs such as David Dubal's *The Golden Age of the Piano* (Decca DVD, 2003): "The History of the Piano with archival photographs and film clips of the Great Pianists of the Golden Age."

[7] Cited from http://www.arbiterrecords.com/musicresourcecenter/lamond.html (accessed January 2006).

manner by contributing several "master lessons" to *Etude*, though they are not featured in Johnson's compilation. He was in distinguished company that included Mark Hambourg, Percy Grainger, Wilhelm Backhaus, and Isidor Philipp. The Polish pianist and composer Sigismund Stojowski was particularly assiduous in attempting to hand down aspects of his "great tradition" to the tyro readers of the magazine, prolifically penning master lessons, yet apparently all for nought, if the gospel of decline is accepted.

The diminutive genius Josef Hofmann, for Abram Chasins the tallest of pianistic giants, shared the view that the present was indeed unworthy of comparison with the past, but it was ironically his own playing he found wanting, claiming that it was a mere shadow of the titanic force of his teacher's— Anton Rubinstein. Some of Rubinstein's gargantuan concerts in 1884 had been perceptively reviewed by the powerful Viennese critic Eduard Hanslick. Though complaining about the sheer length of the recitals—some lasted nigh on three hours—the critic was full of praise for the performer. Here was a player who genuinely had the grand manner. Hanslick's swipes at those who lacked this quality uncannily anticipate Rosenthal's comments of more than fifty years later; perhaps the latter's detested "modern" performance style was not quite so modern after all. The much-feared critic noted that a certain emotional detachment was sadly common among players of his day, from Hans von Bülow down:

> Why does he [Rubinstein] exert such a singular fascination upon his listeners? I believe it is because his virtues arise from a source rapidly drying up—and not only in Germany—robust sensuality and love of life. That is an artistic endowment in which one is only too happy to pardon many a defect, because, among the moderns, it is so rare. Our composers and virtuosos have little of that naïve, elemental force which would rather dare than brood and which, in passion, acts impulsively and without thought of the consequences. They are dominated by the intellect, by education, by refined and more or less profound reflection. . . . Bülow may be regarded as their most distinguished representative. Compared with him, Rubinstein is a naïve, lusty nature. And that is why we listen to him with untroubled ears and uninhibited pleasure.[8]

Hanslick also reviewed one of Rosenthal's concerts that same year but failed to notice any emotional reticence here either. On the contrary, despite the astonishing virtuosity on display, he complained of "too frequent recourse to the

[8] Henry Pleasants, ed. and trans., *Hanslick's Music Criticisms* (New York: Dover, 1988), 229–30.

pedals and . . . the unlovely violence with which the keys were pounded in fortissimo passages." He signed off with a prediction that one can hear fulfilled in Rosenthal's mature recordings: "Such impetuosity may well subside with the years, as it did with Liszt and Tausig, and make way for more tenderness and warmth."[9]

Despite near-unanimous praise from Hanslick and his contemporaries, Rubinstein—and by now the tale is perhaps beginning to appear predictable—had been only too aware of his own inadequacies. He duly idolized his most celebrated predecessor. In 1873, in the midst of the frenzied adulation his playing had provoked in America, he told William Steinway, "Put all the rest of us together, and we would not make one Liszt."[10] William Mason,[11] the former student of Liszt who reported this remark in his autobiography, concurred fully with its content if not its manner of expression:

> This was doubtless hyperbole, but nevertheless significant as expressing the enthusiasm of pianists universally conceded to be of the highest rank. There have been other great pianists, some of whom are now living, but I must dissent from those writers who affirm that any of these can be placed upon a level with Liszt. Those who make this assertion are too young to have heard Liszt other than in his declining years, and it is unjust to compare the playing of one who has long since passed his prime with one who is still in it.[12]

There were some, however, who thought that Rubinstein's respect toward Liszt owed as much to generosity, modesty, and nostalgia as to a hard-headed evaluation of their respective talents. Rubinstein had certainly been bowled over in the 1840s when he first heard the man the acerbic Heinrich Heine would describe joshingly as "Der Franz" (Our Franz).[13] In his autobiography he tells us that he became at that time "a devoted imitator of Liszt, of his manners and

---

[9] Pleasants, *Hanslick's Music Criticisms*, 237.

[10] William Mason, *Memories of a Musical Life* (New York: Century, 1902), 111.

[11] The American William Mason (1829–1908) is now best known as one of Liszt's pupils in 1850s Weimar. He had a moderately successful performing career on his return to the United States but achieved more renown teaching, to which activity he dedicated the last decades of his life.

[12] Mason, 111.

[13] See Heine's poem "Im Oktober 1849" (from *Romanzero*, 1851), written in the wake of the failed Hungarian war of independence. Heine's sarcasm was directed at the notorious Hungarian "saber of honor" that Liszt occasionally sported at his concerts. He had originally received it with a somewhat rash speech promising to "let our blood be shed to the last drop for freedom." His subsequent absence from any scene where the saber might genuinely have had a use was notable.

movements, of his trick of tossing back his hair, his way of holding his hands, of all the peculiar movements of his playing."[14] Yet some who heard both Liszt and Rubinstein in the 1870s and 1880s thought that the Russian, at least by this time, distinctly surpassed the Hungarian. Emil von Sauer, a pupil of the aged Liszt and of Nikolas Rubinstein,[15] believed that Anton was not to be taken seriously in his extravagant self-deprecation—"For me, to whom it was unfortunately not given to hear Liszt in his prime, Rubinstein's reproductive art [*Reproductionskunst*] appears to be the absolute peak of piano-playing."[16] Ferruccio Busoni as a child was also more impressed by the verve of Rubinstein's playing than by Liszt's, although he later became a fervent admirer of the latter's compositions and keyboard idiom. Busoni, Sauer, and Rosenthal, in fact, all concurred that one of the major causes of Liszt's success in the 1840s was the sheer novelty of his playing compared to what had gone before.[17] To the generation growing up in the 1870s and 1880s, that novelty was more difficult to perceive. The old, increasingly ailing Liszt of these years was, at least in terms of strength and agility, no longer the man who from the 1830s to the 1850s had been unquestionably the foremost keyboard technician of his time.

But after more than a century, without even the most primitive recordings to guide us, we are severely hampered in our assessment of Liszt and Rubinstein. There can hardly be, moreover, such a thing as an "objective" view in this area, whatever some promoters of piano competitions might think. Mason did indeed hear Liszt in his prime, and Rubinstein in his glory days too, but his autobiographical *Memories of a Musical Life* partakes a little of Chasins's "good old days" approach, however much we might respect his authority. Like Chasins, Mason was a professional—he believed himself to be the first pianist to tour America exclusively as a solo artist in the 1850s[18]—who had been in personal contact

---

[14] Anton Rubinstein, *Autobiography*, trans. Aline Delano (1890; reprint, Honolulu: University Press of the Pacific, 2005), 19.

[15] Brother of Anton, no mean performer in his own right, and head of the Moscow Conservatory, where he ran a famous class for pianists.

[16] Emil von Sauer, *Meine Welt: Bilder aus dem Geheimfache meiner Kunst* (Stuttgart: Spemann Verlag, 1901), 54 (see also 103–4); my translation.

[17] Von Sauer, 104. For Busoni, see Antony Beaumont, trans. and ed., *Ferruccio Busoni: Selected Letters* (New York: Columbia University Press, 1987), 113. For Rosenthal, see Moriz Rosenthal, "If Franz Liszt Should Come Back Again," *Etude* 42, no. 4 (April 1924): 223.

[18] Mason did not quite get round to mentioning in his autobiography that the tour was not a success. See the erudite and entertaining book by R. Allen Lott, *From Paris to Peoria: How European Piano Virtuosos Brought Classical Music to the American Heartland* (New York: Oxford University Press, 2003), 111.

with many of the greatest musicians of his century. Although the performers mentioned in the two books are naturally quite different, there is some significant overlap. Both authors, for example, heard Paderewski play, Mason when Paderewski was undoubtedly in his prime, Chasins when he was a venerable and aged patriarch of the concert platform. Their very differing assessments reflect this—the first enormously enthusiastic, the second respectful of Paderewski as a "grand old man" but distinctly lukewarm about his playing.[19]

Liszt was only in his early forties and a few years into his official "retirement" as a touring pianist when Mason studied with him: "Time and again in Weimar I heard Liszt play. There is absolutely no doubt in my mind that he was the greatest pianist of the nineteenth century. Liszt was what the Germans call an *Erscheinung*—an epoch-making genius. Carl Tausig is reported to have said 'Liszt dwells alone upon a solitary mountain-top, and none of us can approach him.'"[20] But Mason grounded his praise with at least one reasoned argument: Liszt supposedly achieved superiority over Rubinstein through a greater long-range stamina and focus that would certainly have had more than musical uses:

> Rubinstein . . . had transcendent ability, accompanied, however, by certain limitations. By nature impulsive and excitable, he often lost self-control, and in consequence he frequently anticipated his climax. He was like a general who excelled in a brilliant sortie, but who had not the dogged persistence necessary to a long-sustained battle, and at the critical points he was constantly losing his self-poise. When, however, he did effect a climax, it was apt to be a great one, a jubilee. Liszt, on the other hand, was remarkable for his reserve force and for the discretion with which he made use of it; for if, perchance, he missed a climax he immediately made preparation for a new one, and was always sure to reach the zenith at precisely the right moment.[21]

Liszt himself, with the confidence of one who could so usefully time his climaxes, did not share the nostalgia potentially regressing back to Bartolomeo

---

[19] One must also remember that Mason, like Paderewski, had a very close association with the Steinway firm. The never less than cynical Bülow thought him absolutely in the pocket of Steinway when he was making a tour of the United States sponsored by the rival firm Chickering. In praising Paderewski, Mason was praising a fellow "Steinway artist."

[20] Mason, 110–11.

[21] Mason, 224. Mason's argument and evaluation are echoed almost exactly by August Stradal, who repeatedly heard both Liszt and Rubinstein (see Stradal, *1860–1930: Erinnerungen an Franz Liszt* [Bern: Paul Haupt Verlag, 1929], 160). Paderewski's view of Rubinstein (he never heard Liszt) also concurred with Mason's. See Ignacy Paderewski with Mary Lawton, *The Paderewski Memoirs, Including Letter from Bernard Shaw* (London: Collins, 1939), 112–13.

Cristofori for a pianistic golden age that was always recently over, or the reverence for a great predecessor whose achievements vastly surpassed his own. He was grateful to Carl Czerny for his essential piano teaching and he admired Frédéric Chopin as a unique talent, but of the significance of his own achievements he seems to have had little doubt. Even those who abominated Liszt's music, such as Johannes Brahms or Clara Schumann, could become almost hyperbolic in praise of Liszt the player. The former told Arthur Friedheim that Liszt represented "the classicism of piano technique."[22] When it came to evaluating pianists, he thought, "anyone who has not heard Liszt has simply no right to an opinion." Most ideas of a Great Tradition of piano playing seem indeed to have Liszt—more rarely Chopin, whose rarified style was deliberately less suited to the larger halls that became the norm for later players—as the fountainhead.[23]

The Great Tradition started with Liszt, fostered not only by his own performances, but also through the unsurpassed keyboard imagination of his compositions. Their sonorities, textures, and figurations would remain as a model of writing for the grand piano for subsequent generations who had been born long after the heyday of his virtuoso career, and whose musical interests would explore radically different paths. Just as Maurice Ravel used Liszt's *Transcendental Studies* as a reference guide to pianistic possibilities when composing *Gaspard de la nuit*, Busoni used the works of Liszt to remodel his entire keyboard technique in the 1890s.[24] He found his thoughts turning to the master when working on his edition of J. S. Bach's *Well-Tempered Clavier*, the first book of which was intended to be a "pianistic testament." As he remarked: "We have often mentioned Liszt—perhaps not often enough, for contemporary pianism owes him almost everything."[25]

Subsequent chapters of this book will discuss Liszt's playing and teaching in detail, for if the idea of a Great Tradition goes back no further than Liszt, we

[22] Arthur Friedheim, "Life and Liszt," in *Remembering Franz Liszt* (New York, 1986), 138.

[23] I do not intend to underestimate Chopin's importance here, or to slight his contribution and that of his pupils such as Matthias and Mikuli to piano teaching and performance, especially in the quest for a "singing tone" (see chapter 5). But he recoiled with revulsion from many of the big declamatory effects cultivated by Liszt and other virtuosi, which were especially suited for performances on sonorous instruments in large halls. Chopin largely remained a salon performer (in the best and most refined sense of this term).

[24] Ferruccio Busoni, *The Essence of Music*, trans. Rosamond Ley (London: Rockliff, 1957), 86.

[25] Ferruccio Busoni, ed., *The Well-Tempered Clavichord by Johann Sebastian Bach: Revised, Annotated, and Provided with Parallel Examples and Suggestions for the Study of Modern Pianoforte Technique* (New York: Schirmer, 1894), 1:154.

must ask how far his actual performance practice remained a significant and coherent influence on subsequent generations. We must also ask how much of this reverence for Liszt is enhanced by the fascination of his compositions and try to give due place to the legacy of those whose own works are now half forgotten, but whose pianistic influence remained potent, especially Sigismond Thalberg (who usually languishes in Liszt's shadow), Anton Rubinstein, von Bülow, and Theodor Leschetizky. Many aspects of later performance approaches certainly owed as much to them as to the master of Weimar.

## Great Traditions?

But is there really any such thing as a unified and coherent Great Tradition? Does it exist at all except as a picturesque shorthand for "the past" and as a warm glow of respectful nostalgia? We could ask the same question of violin playing, or singing, or acting—areas that also seem blessed or cursed with a Great Tradition—even without touching upon F. R. Leavis's famously contentious claim for one in the English novel.[26] Surely one of the most striking things about the playing of the so-called pianistic golden age is the diversity of performance styles. Rachmaninoff could hardly be mistaken for Paderewski, any more than Bülow could—one imagines—have been mistaken for Rubinstein. We might think it self-evident that there are a number of divergent traditions in any era, some of which are of larger practical influence on the next than others. The next era is itself, of course, not unified and also evolving. This worldview would be unexceptionable to Buddhists but is passionately resisted by some musicians who feel naturally more confident onstage if they can believe their performance decisions are the only "right" ones and stem from a unimpeachable ancestry.

Then there is the question of the tradition of national styles, or schools. This is particularly prominent in discussions of romantic violin playing—the "Belgian school" of Eugène Ysaÿe, the "German school" of Joachim. Similar terms are still bandied around the piano world today.[27] We have all heard of the Russian school (deriving from Anton Rubinstein—supposedly virtuosic and passionate) and the French school (partially deriving from Louis Adam and his Paris Conservatory successors—supposedly clean and precise). Even the English

[26] F. R. Leavis, *The Great Tradition: George Eliot, Henry James, Joseph Conrad* (London: Chatto and Windus, 1948).

[27] For a concise summary of this see the section titled "National Schools of Performance Teaching" in Janet Ritterman, "On Teaching Performance," in Rink, *Musical Performance*, 79–81.

school sometimes crops up (deriving from Tobias Matthay and from Clara Schumann pupils such as Mathilde Verne). The Anglified attitude allegedly promoted structurally clear, "faithful," but perhaps ever so slightly dull playing (to quote W. S. Gilbert, it "did nothing in particular, and did it very well!").[28] Of course, in the early nineteenth century the English school was associated with those players (ironically, rarely English) whose style was suited to the heavier London pianos (among them Jan Ladislav Dussek and Muzio Clementi) in contrast to the agile Viennese instruments preferred by J. N. Hummel. At that time there were easily identifiable contrasts between national schools. But when the differences between pianos began somewhat to lessen as the century progressed, national schools became a much more nebulous matter of collective taste—if there is such a thing—rather than a practical response to differing instruments. Admittedly, the French bravely—or chauvinistically—resisted the domination of the Steinway-style instrument into the early twentieth century, hanging on to the Érards that suited the nimble style of players such as Camille Saint-Saëns and François Planté. Yet the primarily Viennese-trained Paderewski often preferred an Érard for his European concerts (albeit one with specially hardened hammers), and where does Cortot—surely the most admired of all French late-romantic players—fit into the "national style"? Precision was, it has to be said, not a particularly notable quality of his playing, for all its nobility and tonal beauty. Even national schools themselves are hardly unified, with Russian musicians often drawing a sharp distinction between the styles of Moscow (overwhelmingly virtuosic) and St. Petersburg (rather more contemplative and intimate). After one of my own recitals in St. Petersburg, a lugubrious gentleman came backstage to tell me, "You play like someone from the Moscow Conservatory." I replied with effusive thanks, flattered at being considered an honorary offspring of the distinguished institution. But a Russian friend quickly whispered in my ear, "That—was not a compliment!"

The great tradition that Stojowski felt honored to be passing on in the remark quoted in the epigraph—that of Paderewski and by implication Leschetizky—was not specifically a national one, having elements that could be described as Polish, Viennese, and even Russian (Leschetizky was for a good while a colleague of Anton Rubinstein's at the St. Petersburg Conservatory). It was also not universally admired—indeed it was abhorred by some younger performers. They would in their turn become figures of influence, and partly responsible for the development of a more objective and less indulgent—or more inhibited and less

---

[28] A gibe against the British House of Lords from Gilbert and Sullivan's *Iolanthe*.

interesting, depending on your point of view—style of performance in the second half of the twentieth century. As a boy prodigy Artur Rubinstein was given the opportunity of some lessons with Paderewski. Although not insensible of the honor, he found some of the master's advice questionable, and uncomfortably at odds with his own taste: "On the last evening he sat down at one of the pianos in the salon and played for me for about two hours, showing me all sorts of pianistic difficulties, pointing out brilliant fingerings, tricky pedaling, and other interesting sidelights. From time to time he enchanted me by a beautifully played phrase, or a lovely production of tone, which could be even moving, but he discouraged me a little by an exaggerated rubato and frequently broken chords. I became aware that my musical nature was far apart from his."[29] Although it is indeed rather strange that so many distinguished rival performers, including Hambourg and Vladimir de Pachmann as well as Paderewski, come out badly from Rubinstein's reminiscences, numerous performances and recordings testified that his preferred manner of playing was radically different from Paderewski's—in a nutshell, more modern.

Any discussion of the evolution of these and other stylistic differences will, however, only be useful to current players, and only be credible to musicologists, insofar as they focus on practical and verifiable issues of performance practice rather than on the wistful "there were giants in those days" attitude that Abram Chasins strikingly shared with Homer and the authors of the Old Testament. When we read in Chopin's letters of the primly egotistical Friedrich Kalkbrenner, who claimed in 1831 that "after his [Kalkbrenner's] death, or when he completely gives up playing, there will be no representative of the great school of piano playing left," we smile at his self-satisfaction, since Kalkbrenner is virtually forgotten now, in stark contrast to Chopin.[30] Yet he was no doubt perfectly sincere—if perhaps a trifle deluded—in his remarks. Virtually every era is golden to someone. "Everybody loves somebody sometime," as Dean Martin used to sing. For Friedrich Wieck, writing in his *Clavier und Gesang* of 1853, "the golden age of the piano," unsurprisingly just recently over, was the era of W. A. Mozart, Dussek, Hummel, Ignaz Moscheles, Carl Maria von Weber, and Felix Mendelssohn—in other words, the past eighty years or so (Mendelssohn died in 1847).[31] For

[29] Arthur Rubinstein, *My Young Years* (London: Jonathan Cape, 1973), 78.

[30] Arthur Hedley, ed., *Fryderyck Chopin: Selected Correspondence* (New York: McGraw Hill, 1963), 98. Kalkbrenner's pupil Camille Stamaty was the teacher of Saint-Saëns, so in this respect Kalkbrenner's "great school" did have something of an afterlife.

[31] Friedrich Wieck, *Piano and Song: Didactic and Polemic*, trans. Henry Pleasants (Stuyvesant, N.Y.: Pendragon Press, 1988), 157.

Czerny the golden years of music in Vienna were more circumscribed—roughly the first decade of the nineteenth century (suspiciously coinciding with his student days). When Henry Pleasants collected and translated some of Hanslick's music criticism into English, the neutral titles of the original compilations (*Concerte, Componisten und Virtuosen der letzten fünfzehn Jahren*, for example) became subsumed into the nostalgic *Vienna's Golden Age of Music, 1850–1900*. No sooner do you get one golden age than a whole bundle come along together.

But the golden-age attitude does not just point up our forgivable fondness for reminiscing warmly over the departed. It places the playing of Liszt, Anton Rubinstein, Busoni, and others of their era into a mystical category of its own, by its very nature resistant to analysis, and both unapproached and unapproachable by present-day performers. It also can turn biography into scarcely credible hagiography. This is a particular problem with Liszt, exacerbated no doubt even further by the fact that, unlike Wagner or Bülow, he seems genuinely to have been a "nice guy." Legions of grateful pupils were happy to testify to this.

The issue of credibility already worried some of those students more than a century ago. When William Mason wrote his memoirs, he was obviously concerned that the praise he had given his master's talents would seem exaggerated to readers who had not known the man or ever heard his playing. His slightly simplistic response was that if it was possible to believe Mozart could compose better than anyone who had ever lived, then why should one not believe Liszt could play better than anyone who had ever lived? We do not have to agree or disagree with Mason's assumptions here to realize that such an attitude takes us beyond the bounds of practical inquiry, though we should also mention that "playing better," just like "composing better," can mean vastly different things to different tastes and eras. After all, Beethoven seemed distinctly unimpressed by Mozart's "choppy" (*gehackt*) performance style, despite his admiration for his music (excusing his lack of enthusiasm with the comment "The piano was in its infancy in those days"),[32] and Busoni, the only time he ever heard Liszt play, found the legendary pianist's performance of Beethoven's *Emperor* Concerto passionless and uninspiring.[33] Sauer regarded Rubinstein's performances in his

---

[32] According to Czerny, at any rate. See Sandra Rosenblum, *Performance Practices in Classic Piano Music: Their Principles and Applications* (Bloomington: Indiana University Press, 1988), 23–24, for these and related remarks.

[33] Busoni was only ten years old at the time. He was later taken to see Liszt at his Viennese residence at the Schottenhof. It should be mentioned that Liszt had badly cut the second finger of his left hand while being shaved earlier on the day of the concert, and it is quite possible that Busoni's disappointment with his playing could at least partly be attributed to this accident. At

final concerts technically unreliable, marred by memory lapses, and often so chaotic that it was almost impossible for a conductor to follow him.[34] Pachmann's comment on the elderly Clara Schumann's playing was yet more concise: "Awful!"[35] Most dyspeptically of all, Claudio Arrau cut much of the glitter off "the golden age" with a series of comprehensive condemnations: "This worship young people are taught today for these pianists, it's so unhealthy. It has nothing to do with reality. Paderewski was not a great pianist. A very famous one, but not great. Hofmann was another—I heard him many times. [Leopold] Godowski was one of the greatest technicians, but his playing was boring. He never played very loudly—never above mezzo forte."[36] Arrau did have a good word to say for Horowitz, but just when we might think that Rachmaninoff's reputation also might be pumped up a little ("A really great pianist . . ."), we get some speedy deflation (". . . but not a great interpreter").[37]

   Whether we agree with them or not, we must concede that these were not simply ignorant comments by pontificating reviewers who would have difficulty distinguishing Bach from Offenbach, but sincere assessments of great musicians by great musicians. You cannot, to paraphrase Abraham Lincoln, please all of the people all of the time. We can scarcely deny that the players of the past had remarkable talents, remarkable gifts, and unique personalities, but we should

---

any rate, however true Alan Walker's description of this performance as "an impressive feat" might be, his declaration that "no-one was aware of the injury he had sustained" (*Franz Liszt: The Virtuoso Years* [London: Faber and Faber, 1983], 299) requires some modification in the light of Busoni's response. Liszt's appearance on this occasion received the usual glowing review from most critics, and his friend Count Apponyi did indeed say that the effects of the injury were not noticeable, but Hanslick (normally an immense admirer of Liszt's playing even if he hated his music) was of roughly the same opinion as the juvenile Busoni and felt that Liszt's performance at his previous Viennese concert three years before (1874) had been "much more fiery and brilliant." He elaborated, "It was above all his closest friends who were the first to deny his old strength of attack, the stamina and bold certainty which Liszt had previously shown in playing bravura passages." Eduard Hanslick, *Concerte, Componisten and Virtuosen, 1870–1885* (Berlin: Allgemeiner Verein für Deutsche Literatur, 1886), 202–3. See also Deszo Legany, *Franz Liszt: Unbekannte Presse und Briefe aus Wien, 1822–86* (Vienna: Verlag Hermann Böhlaus, 1984), 204 n.1. Liszt had already given two tiring "open rehearsals" for this occasion, which may also have had a deleterious effect on the final evening's achievement. See, in addition, chapter 3, p. 93.

   [34] Von Sauer, 110.
   [35] Mark Mitchell, *Vladimir de Pachmann: A Piano Virtuoso's Life and Art* (Bloomington: Indiana University Press, 2002), 7.
   [36] Joseph Horowitz, *Arrau on Music and Performance* (Mineola, N.Y.: Dover, 1999), 92.
   [37] Horowitz, 93.

doubt that they had ethereally unapproachable talents and unequaled gifts. It is merely a counsel of despair that claims we needs must live in a silver or even a bronze age after the fabled age of gold.

## The Legacy of Liszt and Thalberg

Liszt was both an initiatory and a transitional figure as a piano virtuoso, but on his death some modern concert practices that we unwisely take for granted were far from established. The initiatory aspects of his career—heavily stressed in the first full-scale biography, Lina Ramann's *Franz Liszt als Künstler und Mensch*—have been further emphasized in scholarly and not-so-scholarly literature. There has been less focus on Liszt as a figure of transition, especially in the more hagiographic studies, and the vast distance that separates his era from ours in performance-practice terms has as a result sometimes been underestimated. We still, after all, have performers who are fond of "tracing their lineage to Liszt" through lessons from pupils of pupils.[38] I recall once hearing a miserable recording made by a pianist (who will remain anonymous) ludicrously described as "a last living link with Liszt" owing to lessons taken from Liszt's pupil Frederick Lamond. The playing did little to enhance the reputation of the glorious lineage. Here was a student of a student who thought a good pedigree was a substitute for talent.

Discussions of Liszt's playing and technique have often shared more with the world of fable than that of practical performance and can stretch credulity long past the breaking point. "Liszt's playing" itself is also frequently treated as a unified entity rather than a development over time. The performances of the aged Liszt seem to have been remarkably different from the younger—less flashy, contemplative, restrained. We can quite reasonably highlight certain common features if we wish, but whether these are more important than the differences is open to question. At any rate, Liszt's teaching in his later years was frequently at variance with his verifiable practice earlier, as indeed was the musical world. He made his reputation, in other words, with a performance approach at odds in significant aspects with the one he taught toward the end of his life.

[38] Forgivable vanity, one hopes. I remember how pleased I was myself as a piano student when I realized that I could "trace my lineage to Liszt" through lessons with Lawrence Glover, who studied with Claudio Arrau, who was a pupil of Martin Krause, who was a pupil of the great man himself. The slightly later realization that I could also trace my music teaching to Busoni (through Ronald Stevenson) added to the warm glow of belonging. Now, even if I were playing badly, I would be playing badly with authority.

Amongst the common misconceptions are the assertions that Liszt developed a fully modern piano technique and that he effectively established the piano recital in more or less its current form. At best these are partial truths. According to Moriz Rosenthal and other pupils, Liszt's was largely a wrist and finger technique. He quite deliberately eschewed the active use of arm weight in the modern fashion even on the heavier instruments he met with in his declining years.[39] This is, perhaps, hardly surprising. The pianos Liszt grew up on and played during his virtuoso heyday required far less strength of attack than the cast-iron-framed leviathans familiar to later concert audiences. Declaiming his virtuoso music at full volume on a modern Steinway requires the participation of virtually every muscle group anatomically available, but the enthusiastic employment of arm weight on an 1840s Érard merely forces the tone and strains the action. Liszt thundered with ease on an Érard and could do so at times on a heavier instrument, but it was later generations that were forced to respond fully to a piano with a heart of steel.

Liszt's initial recitals in the late 1830s were also very different from what we know today. He continued to share the stage regularly with other artists, to prelude before pieces, and to showcase improvisations on themes provided by the audience as the climax of the event. Our current standard recital is, in terms of programming, performance style, and etiquette, very much a product of the twentieth century. Though familiar repertoire in a familiar order is found increasingly from the 1850s onward, the "variety" concert maintained its popularity for decades yet, and improvisation, at least as enshrined in the almost ubiquitous custom of preluding, remained in rude health even longer.

In terms of his performance aesthetic, the highly individual, spontaneously re-creative Liszt can be hardly regarded as a pattern for the modern era, other than

---

[39] Rosenthal, "If Franz Liszt Should Come Back Again," 222. Similar comments are found in the reminiscences of, for example, Stradal, 159. Stradal also mentions that even Anton Rubinstein's cyclopean playing style was largely centered on finger and wrist action—as, again, one might expect given the types of pianos he used in his early-middle years. Liszt's basic technique seemed always to have been the wrist action he taught to Valerie Boissier in the early 1830s (see Elyse Mach, ed., *The Liszt Studies* [New York: Associated Music Publishers, 1973], xvii), though he must surely have adapted it when necessary to the demands of later, heavier instruments. This issue is discussed at length in Bertrand Ott, *Lisztian Keyboard Energy: An Essay on the Pianism of Franz Liszt* (Lewiston, N.Y.: Edwin Mellen Press, 1992), virtually *passim*. Despite Ott's impressively thorough research, it seems to me that he stretches his argument a little too far in the detail he claims to be able to recover about Liszt's technical practices. One must not forget, too, that every player uses the arm muscles to some extent. They are, after all, unavoidably connected to the hand.

as an icon. Our practical view of what a "pianist" should be like today is ironically rather closer to the model of his great rival Thalberg. Thalberg abhorred the then common requirement of improvising in public as much as any modern player seems to, but nevertheless, according to Mendelssohn in 1840, he was "just perfect; he plays the pieces he has mastered, and there he stops."[40] Of course many of the pieces he played so well were of his own composition, but for a long time Thalberg was considered to be the most satisfying player on the current scene (Mendelssohn and George Bernard Shaw's mother were not the only two to think this).[41] To a certain degree the future belonged to his interpretatively consistent and visually unostentatious aesthetic—he would probably have made a very reliable recording artist. His obsession with producing a "singing" tone on the piano was one that he shared with many of his era, but his achievements in that regard were both original and enduring. In this respect Liszt and many others openly learned from him. In fact, the aged Liszt's almost static demeanor at the keyboard—what Sauer called his "classic pose"[42]—had more in common with Thalberg's majestically upright posture, allegedly developed by smoking a Turkish pipe while practicing,[43] than with that of his own younger self. We may be hearing one of Liszt's innovations when a virtuoso fires out a dazzling passage in alternating chromatic octaves, but when a lounge pianist wreathes a slow popular tune in arpeggios, we are hearing the legacy not of Liszt but of Thalberg, even if many musicians now scarcely recognize the latter's name. The reticent Thalberg was indeed "the creator of a new school"—as Fétis famously put it—as much as Liszt was, but in ways that could not then have been entirely anticipated. In terms of concert decorum and etiquette, Thalberg's modest triumph was virtually complete by the second half of the twentieth century.

Liszt's career, longer as it was than Thalberg's, did, however, see the development of the piano from the instrument familiar to Beethoven almost to what it is today, even if some aspects of his technique remained wedded to the needs of a mid-century Érard. The last major addition to the concert grand as we know it— the middle pedal—was introduced by Steinway and Sons during the final years

---

[40] Felix Moscheles, ed., *Letters of Felix Mendelssohn* (Boston: Ticknor, 1888), 203.

[41] See Shaw's "Letter" in the preface to Paderewski, 16.

[42] Von Sauer, 175.

[43] According to Moscheles, at any rate, who taught Thalberg for a time and gave this as the reason for his "extremely military posture" while playing. See Emil F. Smidak, *Ignaz Moscheles: The Life of the Composer and his Encounters with Beethoven, Liszt, Chopin and Mendelssohn* (Aldershot: Scholar Press, 1989), 114.

of his life.[44] It is a measure of Liszt's enduring prestige, and of his receptivity to new ideas, that at the time of writing Steinway is still using in its publicity one of his letters, dated 1883, praising the invention. Liszt suggested its employment in his D♭ *Consolation* and in his transcription of the "Danse des sylphes" from Hector Berlioz's *Damnation de Faust*—both pieces which make extensive use of long-held pedal basses.[45] Liszt was one old dog who really could, when he was inclined, learn new tricks. His last decades were, moreover, substantially devoted to teaching some of the finest players of the early recording era and witnessed the gradual supplanting of the composer-performer in favor of today's interpreter-performer. It is nevertheless likely that Liszt would have been surprised at just how complete the triumph of the latter was to be.

Liszt's so-called pianistic duel with Thalberg in 1837 is a memorable, if slightly arbitrary, starting point in dating any alleged pianistic Great Tradition and its performance practice. The death of Paderewski (the most financially successful pianist ever, and as prime minister of Poland, the only one to become quite literally an elder statesman) in 1941 is a possible ending point.[46] But we could just as reasonably choose other boundaries, such as the success of Érard's double-escapement action in the early 1820s and the routine use of easily editable recording technology by the late 1940s—both of which had a fundamental impact on piano performance—as equally valid if less picturesque chronological markers. At any rate we are talking here of a period lasting not much more than a hundred years, the first decades of which were already being looked upon with nostalgia long before the final decades were out, and the passing of which has prompted poignant lamentations of loss, of reminiscences of a vanished golden age, from critics up to the present day.

The pieces composed for the piano during these 120 years or so even now make up the bulk of the standard concert repertory, but the music written

[44] There were, of course, many attempts at modifications that were not widely adopted, such as Blüthner's "aliquot" stringing system (involving the addition of an extra, unstruck string to provide sympathetic resonance), Emmanuel Moor's double-keyboard piano (D. F. Tovey was an enthusiastic advocate of this), or the supposedly ergonomically advantageous Janko keyboard.

[45] Michael Short, ed. and trans., *Liszt Letters in the Library of Congress* (Hillside, N.Y.: Pendragon Press, 2003), 236.

[46] See also Kenneth Hamilton, "The Virtuoso Tradition," in David Rowland, ed., *The Cambridge Companion to the Piano* (Cambridge: Cambridge University Press, 1998), 57–74. The world of singing, among others, also has a frequently discussed Great or Grand Tradition; see, for example, J. B. Steane, *The Grand Tradition: Seventy Years of Singing on Record* (London: Duckworth, 1974), and John Rosselli, *Singers of Italian Opera: The History of a Profession* (Cambridge: Cambridge University Press, 1992).

before 1867, when Steinway and Sons scored an overwhelming success in the Paris International Exhibition with its iron-framed, overstrung grand, was originally intended for instruments significantly different from the modern concert piano (here defined for convenience, though tendentiously, as a Hamburg or New York Steinway Model D). Those who have played on a range of well-maintained late-nineteenth-century pianos, both European and American, even here often notice a more mellow tone and slightly lighter action. A fine example is Paderewski's 1892 Steinway on display at the Smithsonian National Museum of American History in Washington, D.C., which—not surprisingly—must have been one of the finest instruments of the era. Leaving aside for the moment the question of the action modifications routinely demanded by Paderewski and the deterioration of the soundboard after more than a century, when this piano was played all too briefly by the present author in 2001 the velvety beauty and flexibility of the tone quality were still quite glorious and put to shame the unpleasantly metallic clang of some much more recent instruments.[47] Of course, Steinway must really have pulled out all the stops for Paderewski.

It was not only the instrument that was different. Piano music was performed by nineteenth-century players in a variety of venues and contexts, only some of which exist today. Semi-private "salon" recitals, for example, are now hardly a major part of most pianists' concert diaries, yet they were vastly preferred by Chopin to public concerts, (which he described as "never real music. You have to give up the idea of hearing in them all the most beautiful things in art")[48] and of great importance in establishing such reputations as those of Thalberg and Clara Schumann. As dead as the aristocratic salon is the concert between acts of a theatrical production, or the private concert before an audience of connoisseurs (*Kenner*), which, despite its intimate—and usually unpaid—nature, could be reported in the press and was often the necessary groundwork for a successful round of public concert engagements. All of these contexts demanded now-

---

[47] Steinway concert grand no. 71227, carrying the inscription "This piano has been played by me during the season 1892–1893 in seventy-five concerts. I. J. Paderewski." Admittedly, the instrument does not now seem capable of producing a particularly large volume of tone, and of course it is impossible to tell exactly how the piano sounded in the 1890s. Many thanks to Edwin Good, co-organizer of the Smithsonian piano exhibition, and author of *Giraffes, Black Dragons and Other Pianos: A Technological History from Cristofori to the Modern Concert Grand* (Stanford: Stanford University Press, 2002), for taking the time to give me a fascinating private tour of this exhibition.

[48] Jean-Jacques Eigeldinger, *Chopin: Pianist and Teacher* (Cambridge: Cambridge University Press, 1986), 5.

FIGURE 1.1. "At Steinway Hall, 1872," by Joseph Keppler (1838–94). Courtesy International Piano Archives, University of Maryland, College Park. In this caricature from Anton Rubinstein's American tour, the great pianist listens to himself distractedly while the frenzied audience behaves with less than modern decorum. On the right is Rubinstein's seemingly bored touring partner, the violinist Wieniawski.

ignored skills of preluding and improvisation, sometimes even more so than a fully public performance.[49]

The spectrum of attitudes in the nineteenth and early twentieth centuries to the interpretation of the written score was weighted very differently from modern standard practice, although the implications of this have often not been looked squarely in the face. In a similar fashion, systems of keyboard tuning and what was considered to be "equal temperament" were often at considerable variance with those today.[50] "Strict adherence to the letter of the score" likely

---

[49] Carl Czerny, *A Systematic Introduction to Improvisation on the Pianoforte*, trans. Alice Mitchell (New York: Longman, 1983), 6.

[50] See, on this topic, Jonathan Bellman, "Toward a Well-Tempered Chopin," in Artur Szklener, ed., *Chopin in Performance: History, Theory, Practice* (Warsaw: Narodowy Instytut Fryderyka Chopina, 2005). I should also sound a warning here regarding Smidak's misleading translation of Moscheles's comments on Chopin: "His piano is tuned in such a way that he does not need to play with much forte to produce the contrasts he desires" (116). The original German reads "Sein Piano ist so hingehaucht, dass er keines kräftigen Forte bedarf, um die gewünschten Contraste

meant something very much more flexible to a nineteenth-century (or earlier) musician and critic—even to the most literal-minded—than its broadly accepted meaning nowadays, and descriptions of performances, and performance practice, have to be evaluated with that in view. Indeed, it is sometimes only when one reads a genuinely detailed account of a performance, written by an outstandingly talented and perceptive musician—such as Moriz Rosenthal's thought-provoking reminiscences of Anton Rubinstein's 1885 concert in Pressburg[51]— that one realizes just how many liberties with the score must have either gone unnoticed by other nineteenth-century reviewers or, if noticed, were scarcely regarded as liberties at all. A much earlier report in the London *Times* of a Liszt performance of Handel in 1840 either was written with a fine feeling for sarcasm (evident nowhere else in the review) or simply showed a vastly different understanding of the term "scarcely any additions" from that of critics today: "His performance commenced with Handel's Fugue in E-minor, which was played by Liszt with an avoidance of everything approaching to meretricious ornament, and indeed scarcely any additions, except a multitude of ingeniously contrived and appropriate harmonies, casting a glow of color over the beauties of the composition, and infusing into it a spirit which from no other hand it ever before received."[52]

The reviewer gushed on: "The next piece was the overture to William Tell, which brought all the performer's power at once into action. In this overture, as in the fugue, Liszt with exquisite taste and tact confined his additions to the harmonies; and though this composition is one of the fullest scores that Rossini ever wrote, yet the most complete orchestra by which we have ever heard it performed never produced a more powerful effect, and certainly was far behind Liszt in spirit and unity of execution."

Liszt's arrangement of the *William Tell* Overture is indeed a fairly faithful, if pianistically treacherous, transcription (with a few slightly freer *ossia* passages).

---

hervorzubringen." C. A. Moscheles, *Aus Moscheles Leben* (Leipzig: Duncker und Humblot, 1873), 2:39. Smidak's version is simply a mistranslation. The passage should read in English, "His piano [i.e., soft dynamic range] is so whispering that he does not need a powerful forte to bring out the desired contrasts."

[51] Originally published in the *Neue Freie Presse*, 23 April 1933. An English translation appears in Mitchell and Evans, 97–103. Rosenthal's comments are backed up by an independent account of the same concert by August Stradal. See Stradal, 84–87.

[52] Adrian Williams, *Portrait of Liszt: By Himself and His Contemporaries* (Oxford: Clarendon Press, 1990), 135.

He later published his own edition of the Handel fugue (a favorite also of Anton Rubinstein's "historical" recital programs)[53] that is also reasonably sober, but with some octave doubling of the bass suggested toward the end and fingering and phrasing added. Liszt played the fugue to his pupils a few years before his death, when he was still impressively "thundering the ending in octaves."[54] The "additions to the harmonies" commented upon in the *Times* may have mostly consisted of such doubling, indeed constituting the aforementioned "exquisite tact" in an era where wholesale recomposition would not necessarily be unexpected.

## The "Continuous Performance Tradition"

But there are still some modern pianists who think attention to historical performance practice is quite superfluous for the romantic period, an attitude ably fostered by cohorts of conservative teachers in conservatories. One cannot help noticing this when giving master classes. Problems are exacerbated by a Montague-and-Capulet attitude of mutual contempt between faculty musicologists, who despise the players as historically ignorant, and faculty performers, who ridicule the musicologists as practically inept. Both clans usually have a point, and the gulf can be wide indeed. I personally witnessed a class of piano majors in one of the most prestigious U.S. conservatories come swiftly to a unanimous decision that a late-nineteenth-century, heavily edited, and highly misleading version of the Beethoven sonatas was preferable to an urtext on the grounds that "it gives you more idea how to play them." However appalling this view might be to musicologists, it was certainly the opinion of many nineteenth-century editors, who were usually, after all, themselves primarily performers. Late in life, Liszt was dismissive of a "clean" edition of Palestrina that he had just come across. He argued that most choirmasters would simply not have the time to undertake the "load of preliminary study" needed to use it. "Practical! It must all be practical!" he asserted irritably.[55]

But it is not only players who have been sceptical of the value of research into romantic performance practice. It is only in recent decades that performance

---

[53] Indeed, one reprint of the Liszt edition was prompted by the appearance of the fugue in Rubinstein's programs.

[54] Alan Walker, ed., *Living with Liszt: From the Diary of Carl Lachmund, an American Pupil of Liszt, 1882–84* (Stuyvesant, N.Y.: Pendragon Press, 1995), 62.

[55] Lina Ramann, *Lisztiana*, ed. Arthur Seidl (Mainz: Schott, 1983), 292.

from this era has been regarded as a useful subject for such studies even by musicologists, who are usually keen to discover hitherto unnoticed problems that urgently await publishable solutions. The alleged existence of a "continuous performance tradition"—a less flashy version of the Great Tradition—implies that we all really know how to play romantic, and even classical music in roughly the way its composers envisaged it. As late as 1980, Howard Mayer Brown in the notorious "performing practice" article of the penultimate edition of *The New Grove Dictionary of Music and Musicians*—for twenty subsequent years the first, and sometimes the only, port of call for English-speaking music students in search of a quick infusion of historical wisdom—declared emphatically "there is no lost tradition"; commenting further: "Individual masterpieces have often been neglected for long periods, but there has been no severance of contact for post-Baroque music as a whole, nor with the instruments used in performing it. Interest in the authentic manners of performing medieval, Renaissance and Baroque Music has followed as a logical consequence of the rediscovery in modern times of the music itself. In the case of Classical and Romantic music, no such rediscovery has been necessary."[56] After all, if Beethoven taught Czerny, Czerny taught Liszt, Liszt taught Rosenthal, Rosenthal taught Charles Rosen, and Rosen is giving a master class on Beethoven at your university, then how distant can we really be from a valid and unbroken apostolic succession?

The most recent edition (1994) of the German equivalent of the *Grove Dictionary, Die Musik in Geschichte und Gegenwart*, adopted a related point of view, admittedly with slightly different emphases. Its article "Aufführungspraxis," by Dieter Gutknecht, concentrates almost entirely on music from the Middle Ages to the baroque. In the embarrassingly slender section on music of the nineteenth century to the present day it merely comments: "The performance of music since the beginning of the nineteenth century, the contemporary included, is a problem of interpretation, whose goal ideally is best described by the term *Werktreue* [being true or faithful to the work], if we understand by this only the reproduction of those performance suggestions of the composer included in the score."[57] According to Gutknecht, then, if we just stick to the score, there should be no problem.

[56] Howard Mayer Brown, "Performing Practice," in Stanley Sadie, ed., *The New Grove Dictionary of Music and Musicians*, 20 vols. (London: Macmillan, 1980), 14:388.

[57] "Die Darstellung der Musik seit Beginn des 19. Jh., die zeitgenössische inbegriffen, ist ein interpretatorisches Problem, dessen höchste Maxime der Terminus Werktreue benennt, wenn darunter verstanden wird, nur das wiederzugeben, was vom Komponisten der Partitur an Aufführungshinweisen hinzugefügt wurde." Dieter Gutknecht, "Aufführungspraxis," in Ludwig Finscher, ed., *Die Musik in Geschichte und Gegenwart*, Sachteil 1 (Kassel: Bärenreiter, 1994), 980.

It is difficult to know where to begin here. Almost all of Gutknecht's assumptions have been significantly challenged by other scholars. To perform
convincingly from any score we need our fair share of stylistic awareness, even if
the score genuinely does "faithfully" represent the composer's performance
"intentions" at one time, which is far from always the case (the scare quotes are
regrettable but unavoidable). There are also a vast number of performance
features, including rubatos, chordal balances, half-pedalings—the list goes on—
that cannot be more than vaguely indicated by any type of notation at our
disposal without ludicrously overloading the text and the performer. As for
the composer's "intentions" themselves, Peter Stadlen's astonishing edition of
Webern's Variations—annotated by him after lessons on the piece from the
composer—or Messaien's performances of his own organ music, or Rachmaninoff's recordings of his concertos should make us realize how awkward this
superficially simple issue can really be. Quite simply, they often don't play what
they've written.

And then there are the wider issues surrounding *Werktreue*. Some of them are
certainly not new, even if the terminology occasionally is, and most of them are
as familiar to translators of works of literature as they are to musicians "interpreting" a score. Should we be true to the literal meaning of the text (if it can be
established), whatever the effect on present-day instruments and audiences? Or
should we strive to re-create, however imperfectly, what we think the original
impression might have been—that is, favor the spirit over the letter? Busoni
strongly argued the latter (as I will discuss in more detail later); critics, audi-
tioners, and examiners often need to promote the former. After all, it supposedly allows us to evaluate a performance in a more "objective" way. But even the
primacy of "the work itself" in an aesthetic sense has been called into question
by Lydia Goehr and others and treated as a contingent—and emphatically
transient—historical construct concomitant with the nineteenth-century development of a canon of masterpieces.[58] Richard Taruskin, in a typically trenchant and amusing review of the recent Cambridge University Press histories of
nineteenth- and twentieth-century music, regards present-day historical writings
as showing a struggle between an implicitly old-fashioned work-centered view of
history as a chain of canonic great masterpieces bestowed on us from Parnassus
by the muse of music, which he labels "the Romantic position," and a "realist

[58] Lydia Goehr, *The Imaginary Museum of Musical Works: An Essay in the Philosophy of Music* (New
York: Oxford University Press, 1992).

position" that conceives the past as a chain of interacting contingencies, many of them economic and social as much as artistic.[59]

The unresolved scholarly debate has, admittedly, had little impact as yet on the world of professional performance. If you have been booked to play Rachmaninoff's Second Concerto in a month's time, your priority is practicing the piece, not worrying about its ontological status in the way Goehr, Taruskin, or a volume such as Michael Talbot's *The Musical Work: Reality or Invention?* might prompt.[60] Yet questioning the eternal validity of the canon, and our performance practices surrounding it, can be profoundly liberating for the performer, even if one does not always agree with certain aesthetic arguments, or even if one simply thinks that the more abstruse philosophical issues belong to another domain.

Jim Samson too has eloquently pointed out the gradual shift in nineteenth-century performance from the player to the work as the chief center of interest, and broadly described the course of nineteenth- and twentieth-century pianism as going from the pre-recital, recital, and post-recital age, the last-named being the age of recording.[61] One can quarrel over the details of this shift, and indeed in subsequent chapters of this book I will argue, among other things, that some performer-centered practices such as preluding carried on far longer than is usually stressed, but Samson's general point is convincing and especially thought provoking for players, for it places the composition of familiar tranches of the standard repertoire squarely in an era where the performance often counted for as much as the work. It further emphasizes that the aesthetic environment of much romantic concert giving was vastly different from today's.

It is not surprising, in the light of such lively scholarly discussion, that Brown's and Gutknecht's assumption of a continuous handing down of stylistic awareness from the beginning of the nineteenth century to today is now seen in many quarters as largely discredited. It was openly rejected by Kern Holoman for the "Performing Practice" entry in the most recent edition (2000) of the *New Grove Dictionary*. In one of the most striking volte-faces from the 1980 *New Grove* to "the new *New Grove*" to occur in any article, Holoman treads sensibly and

---

[59] Richard Taruskin, Review titled "Speed Bumps," *Nineteenth-Century Music* 29, no. 2 (Fall 2005): 185–207.

[60] Michael Talbot, ed., *The Musical Work: Reality or Invention?* (Liverpool: Liverpool University Press, 2000).

[61] See Jim Samson, "The Practice of Early Nineteenth-Century Pianism," in Talbot, 110–27. Samson's arguments are expanded further in *Virtuosity and the Musical Work: The Transcendental Studies of Liszt* (Cambridge: Cambridge University Press, 2003).

warily: "It had become increasingly apparent by the end of the twentieth century that the idea of continuity of tradition even from the nineteenth century into the twentieth was problematic. In a period of such experimentation and change as the nineteenth century, exactly whose traditions were continued? And how are they related to what a composer might have heard or envisaged?"[62]

We should point out here that Brown's view was a little behind the musicological times even for 1980, although it certainly reflected the prevalent opinion in conservatories and probably among musicians in general. Robert Winter, in a 1977 article for the journal *Nineteenth Century Music*, had already raised many of the issues that were to become of increasing interest over the next few years,[63] and Jean-Jacques Eigeldinger, in the introduction to his indispensable *Chopin: Pianist and Teacher*,[64] had commented, "With Romantic piano music in particular, only recently have we begun to realise that they too present the performer with problems analogous to those encountered in the music of more remote periods."[65] In 1988 Sandra Rosenblum's thorough and thought-provoking *Performance Practices in Classic Piano Music: Their Principles and Applications* appeared,[66] dealing with the era circa 1770–1820. It should then have been obvious even to the most conservative scholar that the significant differences in instruments and performance practice between the classical and our modern period so tellingly documented by Rosenblum had ineluctable implications for the post-classical era. It was, to say the least, very unlikely that modern performance styles simply emerged, fully fledged, one bright morning in 1820. Just as significantly, the striking upsurge in the availability of, and interest in, hitherto almost forgotten early recordings added a long overdue aural component to philosophical discussions on the development of romantic performance practice.

Recordings from the 1890s onward, now easily accessible on CD, document undeniably profound changes in performance practice. They fashion the final nail in the coffin for the more extreme "continuous tradition" arguments, especially as far as playing after the establishment of editable recording technology is concerned. Even a cursory comparison of Moriz Rosenthal's recording of the

---

[62] Kern Holoman, "Performing Practice," in Stanley Sadie, ed., *The New Grove Dictionary of Music and Musicians*, 2nd ed., 29 vols. (London: Macmillan, 2000), 10:374.

[63] Robert Winter, "The Emperor's New Clothes: Nineteenth-Century Instruments Revisited," *Nineteenth Century Music* 7, no. 3 (April 1984): 251–65; and Winter, "Performing Nineteenth-Century Music on Nineteenth-Century Instruments," *Nineteenth-Century Music* 1, no. 2 (November 1977): 163–75.

[64] Eigeldinger, *Chopin: Pianist and Teacher*.

[65] Eigeldinger, *Chopin: Pianist and Teacher*, 1.

[66] Rosenblum.

Chopin-Liszt "Meine Freuden" with that of his pupil Charles Rosen is enough to show that whatever a continuous teaching tradition does, it does not necessarily cause performers to play in a stylistically similar way. Evolution is on display over the entire history of recording, affecting the performance styles of all instruments, with particularly drastic changes in the middle years of the twentieth century. A pioneer in the analysis of this material was Robert Philip, whose books *Early Recordings and Musical Style* and, more recently, *Performing Music in the Age of Recording* give a perceptive overview of significant trends.[67] Not only do recordings allow us (admittedly with severe limitations) to actually hear something of how the early players sounded, they also allow us to interpret writings on performance and performance style from the immediate pre-recording era more accurately.

This last point is sometimes overlooked, for there has been a tendency to treat the early recording era as mainly relevant, if at all, to performance practice from around 1900 onward, and of little importance to the preceding period. The fact that many of the first recording artists were well-established performers, and thus often relatively advanced in age (Paderewski was in his fifties and François Planté nearly seventy when they made their first recordings), has been used to argue that we hear them well past their best, in performances that are unrepresentative of what they may have produced thirty years before. This may be so in terms of technical facility, speed, bravura, and energy. We have already seen that in this respect the Liszt of the 1880s was hardly the man he was in the 1840s (who would be?). But we can nevertheless learn much from the general performance approaches evinced by these recordings. Early recordings allow us to hear much further back into the past than the bare recording date suggests, for many of the featured artists started their musical training in the middle years of the nineteenth century. Although Planté made his first discs in 1908, he was born in 1839, ten years before Chopin's death. As a young man he had even performed in a duo with Liszt. Pachmann was born in 1848, Paderewski in 1860. Paderewski's teacher, that pedagogue of pedagogues Theodor Leschetizky, was born as far back as 1830, only three years after Beethoven's death, and had been a pupil of Czerny himself. Even something of his playing can be heard nowadays, admittedly via the highly unsatisfactory medium of piano rolls. These are nonetheless vivid enough to tell us a lot about some important aspects of his performance style and how closely his most famous pupil followed it.

---

[67] Robert Philip, *Early Recordings and Musical Style* (Cambridge: Cambridge University Press, 1992); *Performing Music in the Age of Recordings* (New Haven, Conn.: Yale University Press, 2004).

What we can hear through the dark glass of the early recording process are musical styles that were initially formed decades before the recordings themselves were made—well before the age of recording itself. The vigor of the pianists' performances may well have been affected by old age and "recording fright," the nuances of their playing may have been inadequately captured or forced into caricature by primitive recording methods, and the pieces they played and the instruments they played them on may have been determined more by the demands of the recording process than by their own choice, but their fundamental approach to many elements of performance would not necessarily have changed dramatically from that of their earlier decades. At the very least, we can say for sure that pianists who played like this as old men were, as young men, highly unlikely to have played like modern performers.

If we compare their playing with printed sources for the nineteenth and early twentieth century—treatises, concert reviews, and reminiscences—there is a much greater correlation between nineteenth-century theory and the practice in early recordings than some scholars have been willing to admit. One can gather from a perusal of the writings that extensive use was made of chordal arpeggiation or asynchronization by many players, and that preluding was virtually universal up until the early decades of the twentieth century. Of course, theory and practice are often not the same thing, still less what one teaches and what one actually does, and certain elements of performance are especially difficult to describe in prose. We could reasonably remain surprised at how extreme rubato and tempo fluctuation could be on early recordings, for treatises could hardly give an accurate idea of this, but we should have been in no doubt about the frequency of arpeggiation and left-hand-before-right playing from a closer look at Corri's remarks in his *Original System of Preluding* (1813), Czerny's *Complete Theoretical and Practical Pianoforte School*, op. 500 (1838), and Thalberg's *L'art du chant appliqué au piano* (1853–64). Later, Malwine Brée's oft-ignored but superb *Die Grundlage der Methode Leschetizky* (1903),[68] treated more fully in chapter 5, advocates these techniques and describes them in unmistakable detail. That William Mason, in "Paderewski: A Critical Study" (1892),[69] could discuss Paderewski's playing extensively but never mention what seems to us the quite astonishing amount of arpeggiation and asynchronization of the hands heard in his recordings should show just how routine a part of performance practice this actually was, even if

---

[68] Malwine Brée, *Die Grundlage der Methode Leschetizky, mit Autorisation des Meisters herausgegeben von seiner Assistentin* (Mainz: Schott, 1903).

[69] *The Century Library of Music*, vol. 18, ed. Ignacy Jan Paderewski et al. (New York: Century, 1902), 577–84.

many of our present-day players would hardly have expected anyone—apart from maybe an eighteenth-century clavicenist—to sound quite like Paderewski.

Perhaps with hindsight we should have been less self-centered in our expectations. We tend to imagine earlier performance styles by working back from our own day, underestimating the chances that it is in fact we—with our recording-based music industry, standardized instruments, and standardized training—who may represent a radical break with the past. Nineteenth-century pianists inevitably inherited much from their eighteenth-century forebears. For the eighteenth-century player, the piano was only one of several keyboard instruments in common use, and by far the youngest of all of them. Among other things, it is hardly surprising that the techniques of arpeggiation and agogic dislocation used to lend expression, subtlety, and fullness to the tone of the harpsichord and clavichord should have been transferred, perhaps automatically, to the new piano. As the following chapters will illustrate, these practices (now tentatively being revived by a few players) did not entirely wither until the second half of the twentieth century. We, in fact, are the odd ones out.

## Romantic Pianism and Modern Pianism

My purpose in the subsequent pages is to examine some central characteristics of romantic pianism and concert conditions, of so-called Great Tradition playing, not in a musical equivalent of the quest for the Holy Grail, nor to reminisce wistfully about vanished and never-to-be-regained "good old days," but as a guide to performance practice for professional musicians, music students, interested amateurs, and—not least—critics of our own era. There were, evidently, many stylistic features and approaches to performance more common to the players of the romantic era than to those of the present day, but those features are mostly neither irreproducible nor irrecoverably lost. Whether one actually wishes to reproduce them nowadays is a separate question, but many of them, however frequently ignored, belong as firmly to the performance practice of romantic piano music as a historically informed interpretation of ornaments does to that of the eighteenth century. It is ironic that some players are happy to scour often dry and dusty early-classical treatises for advice on performing mordents but balk at the arguably much less onerous task of listening to a crackly disk by Arthur Friedheim for hints on how to play Liszt, let alone study the recordings—and even film—of the much-maligned Paderewski. His style is perhaps most at odds with contemporary taste. Yet for several decades from the 1890s onward Paderewski was regarded by many of his colleagues as the greatest all-round pianist in the world, and his pianism illuminates the priorities of musicians and audiences of his era as much as it sheds light on the different preoccupations of ours.

If my comparisons for convenience often refer to a broadly defined "average" concert practice of today, that is not to be taken to mean that I regard today's concert world as unvaried, or as some sort of "omega point" of idealized concert giving. It is evidently neither. We are especially fortunate that practices change and evolve, because many aspects of modern classical concerts can be glacial, tedious, and ridden with the historically unjustifiable snobbery commonly lauded as "serious listening." It was, as mentioned earlier, a deep unease with the sheer routine and funereal boredom of some piano recitals I have attended (and no doubt given) that partly prompted the writing of this book.[70] Of course, there have been several attempts at relaxation of concert etiquette over the last decades, but they seem to have had a limited effect in changing "standard" concert procedures, unless one counts the increasing fondness (at least with those male pianists whose figures can bear it) for wearing a sleek black shirt and trousers in place of tails. Whatever disadvantages early-romantic concerts had, they were often more informal and sound simply like a lot more fun, for both performers and audiences. A little less reverence and a bit more entertainment would do us no harm today.

The performers addressed here are not primarily those who play nineteenth-century repertoire on historical instruments. They have no doubt already discovered by personal acquaintance the differences between Pleyels and Érards, or how much easier and appropriate it really is to play the Chopin etudes at the marked metronome tempo on instruments of the 1830s. They might also acknowledge that there are very significant losses as well as gains in going back to original instruments, at least in the case of live performance. The older pianos are simply less stable, both in their tuning and in the reliability of their action. However, some modern players of nineteenth-century pianos seem to feel uncomfortable with certain performance practices associated with the era. It is surprising how many award themselves a gold star for using historical instruments on recordings (sometimes chronologically bizarre ones) but steadfastly ignore the improvisation, unmarked arpeggiation of chords, and tempo flexibility that was such an important feature of much romantic performance practice. Sitting in front of an 1830s Pleyel and playing it as much like a twenty-first-century

---

[70] One is reminded of a comment on a less than inspired early performance of Wagner's *Parsifal*: "Amfortas is the only sensible one here: he's at least brought his bed."

Steinway as possible is a not uncommon approach. We choose what we want to choose.

The picture presented in this book is a movie rather than a snapshot, for performance practice necessarily evolved over the period we are discussing and continues to do today. Every era is an era of transition, and we do not even have the option offered to Faust by Mephistopheles of saying to the moment, "So fair thou art, remain!" No overview can be complete, but the following chapters will attempt to delineate some of the most important aspects of pianism that characterized the nineteenth and early twentieth centuries. This will inevitably raise the question of whether we should strive to feature more of them in a modern pianism that seeks to be "historically informed," or even just a bit different from what is now the run of the mill (surely a worthy end in itself). Should we improvise preludes before pieces? Should we accept audience applause between movements? Should we treat seriously interpretative traditions not derived from the composer? Rediscovering practices of the past does not just satisfy curiosity, it offers opportunities.

# 2

# Creating the Solo Recital

Le Concert, c'est moi!
—Franz Liszt

## Paderewski, 1937: A Vignette

In 1937 filmgoers flocked, if not in droves, at least in very respectable numbers to
the film *Moonlight Sonata*.[1] A precariously flimsy love story displaying what now
seems—in our regrettably cynical postmodern times—to be a curious mixture of
charm and naiveté, its lasting value is not as a drama but as a showcase for the art
of the elderly Paderewski. Paderewski's playing is really the focus of the movie,
and his spoken scenes merely required him to play a charismatic elderly concert
pianist called Paderewski, which strained neither his thespian ability nor audience
credulity ("Paderewski plays himself without any apparent effort," enthused a
reviewer in the *New York Post*). Indeed the film's distinct success on its first
appearance can be attributed mainly to Paderewski's magisterial status as a grand
old man of music, for the girl-marries-true-love-after-heartbreak-with-dastardly-
seducer plot would hardly detain even the most unsophisticated audience for long
were it not galvanized by the powerful magnetism of Paderewski's presence. The
movie offers the only opportunity for subsequent generations to actually see him
playing the piano, as well as to hear him speak in a gracious, heavily accented
English. It also codifies a certain idea of what a piano recital "should" be like. This
turns out to be not that different from our present-day ideals, although the reality
on the ground in the 1930s was not quite what the film presents. The movie,
indeed, with its wide international exposure, helped to form these future ideals,

---

[1] *Moonlight Sonata*, dir. Lothar Mendes, first released 1937 (not 1938 or 1939, as some sources
indicate). A slightly misleading excerpt from the movie's opening recital is included in the DVD
*The Art of the Piano*. The context and background of the film footage is never made entirely clear in
the accompanying commentary.

both in the mind of the public and in the music profession. For the conductor Sir Henry Wood—of London Promenade concert fame—its pedagogical value was clear. He believed firmly it should be required viewing for all piano students.[2]

More than twenty minutes of *Moonlight Sonata's* opening is devoted—long before any distracting plot plods into view—to what are supposedly the last two numbers of a Paderewski piano recital, presented as if from real life. In case we are in any doubt about the identity of the event we are about to see, the camera initially shows us a swift glimpse of the advertising poster for the concert before cutting to an enormous art-deco hall, packed with a high-class audience dressed to the nines in tuxedos and tiaras. We know that the recital has been completely sold out, for even the standing room at the sides is full, thronged with eager (if poorer—no tiaras here) listeners in a manner that would appall a fire and safety inspector. Although the film was made a good many years before the Philharmonie (1956) in Berlin became one of the twentieth century's first concert halls to place the performance space in the center of the arena, at the center of this arena is Paderewski, with Chopin's Polonaise in A♭, op. 53, resounding resplendently on a Steinway concert grand.

The physical position of the performer is among the first of the hints we get that this recital belongs to the realm of mythology. The concert hall was actually a stage set constructed at a studio in London, and the members of the audience, however much they genuinely enjoyed hearing Paderewski play during filming, were extras paid to look moved, awed, and ultra-attentive.[3] The audience listens in admiring, respectful silence to the performance of Chopin's Polonaise, erupting in enthusiasm at the end. After a few curt bows, Paderewski begins the last item on his program, Liszt's Second Hungarian Rhapsody. At this point any pianists watching will begin to feel a little uneasy (and not only at Paderewski's rolled chords), for the synchronization between music and action begins to go more and more awry.

Although Paderewski is obviously giving a real performance of the piece in question (and this is very difficult to fake convincingly—despite Dirk Bogarde's conscientiously studied "playing" as Liszt to Jorge Bolet's soundtrack in the 1960 *Song without End*), we occasionally hear the music with almost a beat's delay compared with the image on screen. The reason is straightforward. It had been originally intended to use Paderewski's on-set performances for the soundtrack,

[2] Adam Zamoyski, *Paderewski* (London: Collins, 1982), 227.
[3] Paderewski was supposedly enormously popular with both cast and crew on the set. They had expected a moody "great artiste" but were pleasantly surprised by his patience and charm. The flood of goodwill apparent on screen was, accordingly, not completely artificial.

but technical difficulties in capturing an adequate piano sonority led to the music's being recorded separately in Abbey Road Studios, under the supervision of the veteran producer Fred Gaisberg.[4] Gaisberg was particularly pleased with the resultant "exceptionally fine" discs, which were also issued as stand-alone recordings by HMV, although he was convinced that nothing could equal the live impact of the master: "Of the greatness of Paderewski or Chaliapin neither gramophone or film can give anything but a faint suggestion. It is only when I hear a record of either that I realise the futility of trying to reflect their greatness by mechanical means."[5] The recordings included not just the Chopin and Liszt pieces already mentioned, but also the first movement of Beethoven's *Moonlight* Sonata (partially heard as an encore in the "recital" and then played complete at the close of the film) and Paderewski's own inevitable Minuet in G (performed by the maestro in a later scene as the accompaniment to a children's dance).

The pieces Paderewski played for the film were understandably biased toward the crowd pleasers at the end of his usual recitals (it is notable that we catch a glimpse in the movie of a printed program that includes such pieces as Bach's Chromatic Fantasy and Fugue but hear not a note of these rather more recondite works), which in turn had their popularity reinforced by their appearance in the movie. The *Moonlight* Sonata itself had been a favorite since Beethoven's day—the composer himself exclaimed to Czerny, "Everyone's constantly talking about this sonata!"[6]—and Mark Hambourg's 1909 disk of the opening movement had been one of the first piano best sellers of the recording era for HMV. Chopin's A♭ Polonaise, in the repertoire of many a virtuoso, got yet more celluloid exposure (this time performed woodenly on the soundtrack by José Iturbi, but, bizarrely, with the filmed hands of Ervin Nyíregyházi) in the beloved if ridiculously romanticized Chopin biopic *A Song to Remember* (1945). Artur Rubinstein just happened to choose to play the same piece for his cameo role in *Carnegie Hall* (1947), and it frequently ended Horowitz's recitals from the 1930s to the 1980s. It was, in fact, the closing item on the program of Horowitz's last-ever public performance, in the Hamburg Musikhalle on 21 June 1987 (followed by two encores—the Schubert *Moment musical* op. 94 no. 3, and Moritz Moszkowski's *Etincelles*). The trusty Polonaise even featured in the episode "Samantha on the Keyboard" of the television comedy series *Bewitched* in 1968, where the

---

[4] See Fred Gaisberg, *Music on Record* (London: Robert Hale, 1946), 175.

[5] Gaisberg, 177.

[6] Carl Czerny, *Über den richtigen Vortrag der saemmtlichen Werke für das Piano allein*, ed. Paul Badura-Skoda (Vienna, 1963), 13; my translation.

ability to perform it was treated as an instantly recognizable sign of a (magically enhanced) child prodigy—as indeed it probably would be.

Specially concocted piano and orchestra versions of the Liszt Second Rhapsody even more memorably turned up as fodder for Tom and Jerry and Bugs Bunny in the award-winning and hilarious cartoons "Cat Concerto" (1945) and "Rhapsody Rabbit" (1945).[7] For the former, the hand movements of Pachmann were apparently used as a general basis for the animation (although the piece in question was never in Pachmann's repertoire). It would be a mistake to underestimate the genuine influence—"just cartoons!"—of these enormously entertaining productions in fixing in the mind of the general public, and in the imaginations of children who will grow up to be the musicians of the next generation, the idea of what a concert pianist "does." The cartoons needed no recommendation from Sir Henry Wood to gain viewers, and their effect was sustained long after their initial release date, owing to frequent reappearance on television throughout the world. Even today there seems to be hardly a music student who is not familiar with at least one of them.

In both cartoons the coattail-flicking conventions of a piano recital à la *Moonlight Sonata*—the evening dress and white handkerchief, the supercilious demeanor of the performer, and the curt bow acknowledging applause—are mercilessly satirized in a way that only established conventions can be. (An equally amusing hatchet job was done by Bugs Bunny on the allegedly affected conducting style of Leopold Stokowski in "Long-Haired Hare" [1949] and on the pretentiousness of Wagnerian opera in "What's Opera, Doc?" [1957].) Yet some of these supposedly long-accepted piano-recital conventions were actually of relatively recent origin—some arising well within Paderewski's own lifetime— and a film such as *Moonlight Sonata* does not fully reflect even typical Paderewski concerts. They contained their fair share of the practices of an earlier period— hardly surprising for a man whose performing career started in the 1880s.

## From Variety Concert to Recital

So, in what respects might the film mislead us? We certainly get little idea of the sheer length of a Paderewski concert, or, understandably enough, of the relative

---

[7] I hesitate to use such a clichéd expression, beloved of mindless publicists everywhere. Nevertheless, they really were award-winning, and deservedly so. An interesting discussion of these and other "classical" music cartoons can be found in Daniel Goldmark, *Tunes for "Toons": Music and the Hollywood Cartoon* (Berkeley: University of California Press, 2005), 107–61.

novelty of the solo piano recital itself. This, in its rigidly stylized *Moonlight Sonata* form, was largely a product of the era of Paderewski's youth, when Anton Rubinstein, Hans von Bülow, and Clara Schumann, among others, established it as an accepted convention. Both Liszt and Moscheles had made experiments of this type (with much shorter programs) in the 1830s and 1840s, but a "variety" program would remain the norm for decades yet.[8]

Pianists during the first half of the nineteenth century performed in a variety of venues and circumstances, many of them quite unlike those familiar today.[9] Concert life developed at quite different rates in different countries, but if this important caveat is kept in mind it is possible to give a broad "European" summary that might be useful as a background. Genuinely public concerts would, unsurprisingly, often be given in a hall or theater. If in the latter, the concert sometimes took place in the intervals between the acts of a play, ballet, or opera—in other words, it formed entracte music. The advantage for players of the entracte concert was that they had a large and captive audience; the disadvantage was that the focus of the evening was not necessarily the music, and the public could be much noisier and more restless than usual during the performance. Salon concerts were exactly that—given in the (often fairly spacious) drawing-rooms or halls of the nobility or other "friends of art" such as music publishers or instrument manufacturers. (The Salles Pleyel and Érard in Paris, for example, could each seat several hundred people). Performers would sometimes be given a fee for salon concerts, but the audience generally comprised invited guests rather than paying auditors. It was understood that if a player gave his services gratis in an aristocratic salon, he was entitled to expect support for his own subsequent public concerts from the family concerned.

Princess Cristina di Belgiojoso's famous Parisian charity event (in aid of indigent Italian refugees) of March 1837 featuring Liszt and Thalberg was such a salon concert, although in this case members of the inevitably wealthy audience had paid a very large sum indeed for their tickets, and the performers played for

---

[8] A vast, if still necessarily incomplete listing of over a century of concert programs involving the piano can be found in George Kehler, *The Piano in Concert* (Metuchen, N.J.: Scarecrow Press, 1982). See also Janet Rittermann, "Piano Music and the Public Concert, 1800–1850," in Jim Samson, ed., *The Cambridge Companion to Chopin* (Cambridge: Cambridge University Press, 1992), 11–31. The latter work, though covering a shorter chronological span, offers a much more detailed analysis of certain trends than Kehler's relatively perfunctory introductory chapter.

[9] A splendid, thorough, and thought-provoking treatment of the broad development of nineteenth-century concert life can be found in William Weber, *Music and the Middle Class: The Social Structure of Concert Life in London, Paris and Vienna between 1830 and 1848*, 2nd ed. (Aldershot: Ashgate, 2003).

free—it was for a "good cause," after all. Some salon audiences simply treated the musicians as providers of background music to their gossiping. Charles Hallé was once bemused to be congratulated on playing more quietly than Alexander Dreyschock, who was "so loud that he made it difficult for the ladies to talk."[10] There is no reason, however, to believe that the audiences in aristocratic salon always consisted of a bunch of upper-class twits chatting vacuously and slurping Château Lafite as the piano tinkled pointlessly in the background (although the young Artur Rubinstein did once play at such an event in Paris as late as the early years of the twentieth century). Many members of the nobility—particularly the female ones—were well-educated musicians in their own right. A large proportion of both Chopin's and Charles-Valentin Alkan's pupils, for instance, were young ladies from wealthy or aristocratic families, some of whom had talents that could well have supported a professional career had this not been socially unthinkable. It would be a long time before Busoni could introduce Percy Grainger as "London's Society Pianist" and intend it merely as a mild insult.[11]

The most intimate performance circumstances were found in concerts given in the homes of musical connoisseurs (*Kenner*). A player might well be unpaid for this but would be compensated by the lively sympathy and engagement of the auditors, the opportunity of performing more "serious" music, and the possibility of increasing his own fame as a significant artist. Reports of these gatherings not infrequently appeared in the press, and good word-of-mouth publicity from the connoisseurs could increase interest in the artist among the public. It was quite common, therefore, for a player on arriving in a city to bolster his reputation by a few performances at such gatherings before essaying his own public "benefit" concert—that is, one organized with a view to making some money for the headlined performer.

Almost needless to say, the repertoire suitable for the three basic types of concert—private circle, salon, and public—was, theoretically at least, of a decreasing level of severity, although it is difficult to draw a completely clear distinction. Liszt was quite capable of playing some flimsy variations by Herz for private or salon events toward the end of the 1820s, yet offered up the occasional Beethoven sonata movement in public a few years later. Nevertheless, even if some connoisseurs might welcome hearing several long and complex multi-movement works in an avant-garde style, one had to think twice before playing

---

[10] Charles Hallé, *Autobiography, with Correspondence and Diaries*, ed. Michael Kennedy (1896; reprint, London: Elek, 1972), 100.

[11] John Bird, *Percy Grainger*, 2nd ed. (New York: Oxford University Press, 1999), 92.

many such things in front of a general audience. To ensure a good attendance, all tastes had to be catered for. What seems to us to be peculiar juxtapositions of serious and trivial pieces in a variety of genres was less an indicator of appalling insensitivity than an attempt to provide something for everyone.[12] Trying out a difficult piece by Beethoven might be off-putting for many listeners. If in doubt of applause, there was always Thalberg's *Moses* fantasy to fall back on.

But pianists usually shared the stage. They traditionally gave their own benefit concerts along with any number of so-called assisting artists (whose role was usually limited to providing accompaniments) or supporting artists (who would perform their own solo items). A pianist might thus give a concert with almost any combination of other performers, from a singer or chamber ensemble to a full orchestra. Although this provided for admirable aural and visual variety, it had the disadvantage for the pianist of considerably reducing his own fee and massively increasing the sheer hassle of the organization. The assisting artists had to be paid out of the ticket receipts, and if the supporting ones sometimes played for free it was in the expectation that the favor would be returned at their own benefits. All aspects of the arrangements, from hiring the hall, printing, and selling the tickets to booking the other artists, were undertaken by the "concert giver," and even a cursory reading of the memoirs of Berlioz or Ludwig Spohr, the letters of Clara Schumann, or the *Clavier und Gesang* of her father, Friedrich Wieck, shows what a time-consuming and frequently frustrating effort that was. Only very high-earning, top-flight performers such as Nicolò Paganini and Liszt could afford their own personal concert managers.[13] It was not until the 1870s that figures such as Albert Gutman in Vienna or Hermann Wolff in Berlin (intermittently manager to Eugen d'Albert and Busoni, among many others) emerged as general—and enormously powerful—concert agents to take over the

[12] Changing types of concert programming, and the increasing divide between "popular" and "serious" music are documented and discussed extensively in a forthcoming book by William Weber, *The Great Transformation of Musical Taste: European Concert Programs, 1750–1875* (Cambridge: Cambridge University Press). I am very grateful to Professor Weber for his generosity in allowing me a preview of this important and substantial work, and for subsequent correspondence on the topic. See also (for a slighter later period) Lawrence W. Levine, *Highbrow/Lowbrow: The Emergence of Cultural Hierarchy in America* (Cambridge, Mass.: Harvard University Press, 1988), and (for salon concerts and repertoire) David Tunley, *Salons, Singers and Songs: A Background to Romantic French Songs, 1830–70* (Aldershot: Ashgate, 2002).

[13] Although this could sometimes cause more trouble than it was worth: witness the debacle surrounding Liszt's Leipzig concerts in 1840, blamed by Mendelssohn and others largely on the inept handling of the arrangements by Liszt's young and inexperienced manager, Hermann Cohen.

role somewhat in the modern fashion.[14] That concert life somewhat in the modern fashion also began to establish itself at around the same time is no coincidence.

The types of program played by Clara Wieck in the first decades of her career were fairly typical for public concerts of the time—perhaps even on the straitlaced side, because she tended to play slightly fewer of the variations and fantasies favored by others and usually included one or two genuinely "severe" items, such as Bach fugues. In 1837, however, the even more ascetic Fanny Mendelssohn complained of the predominance of bravura solo items in the Berlin programs of Clara Wieck, Theodor Döhler, and Adolf Henselt ("Next they will give a piano lesson before an audience," she griped, unintentionally anticipating the advent of the "master class"). She even claimed that none of them had played "a proper concert" (*ein ordentliches Concert*) as a result,[15] although it is obvious from her own and other accounts that at least one major chamber piece was played on each occasion. The Hummel Trio in E♭, op. 83, for example, featured in Henselt's concert. Two years later, toward the end of 1839, Clara Wieck mulled over some new program ideas for a couple of "soirées" in Berlin, taking care to include a substantial chamber piece in each one and then some "serious" solo items before the obligatory virtuoso close. She wrote to Robert Schumann that for the first she might include Beethoven's *Archduke* Trio, solo pieces such as a Scarlatti sonata, Schubert's "Ave Maria" (in Liszt's transcription), a Schumann *Novellette*, and an etude by Henselt or Chopin, followed by a set of variations either by Henselt or of her own composition. For the second she suggested a trio by Schubert, a Bach fugue, a Chopin nocturne, a scherzo of her own, Liszt's transcription of Schubert's "Erlkönig" and his fantasy on "I tuoi frequenti palpiti" from Pacini's *Niobe*.[16]

Of course, if the variety recital had financial and logistical disadvantages for the solo pianist, it did have one major advantage—the amount of purely solo

---

[14] A more detailed discussion of this process can be found in Weber's essay "From the Self-Managing Musician to the Independent Concert Agent," in William Weber, ed., *The Musician as Entrepreneur* (Bloomington: Indiana University Press, 2005), 105–29.

[15] Eva Weissweiler, ed., *Fanny und Felix Mendelssohn. Briefwechsel 1821 bis 1846* (Berlin: Propyläen, 1997), 256.

[16] Eva Weissweiler with Susanna Ludwig, eds., *Clara Schumann und Robert Schumann: Briefwechsel* (Frankfurt: Stroemfeld/Roter Stern, 1984–2001), 802–3. Liszt was delighted and flattered that Wieck had chosen to learn the *Niobe* fantasy at a time when very few of his fellow virtuosi played his works, and still more that she played it with great success before the Empress in Vienna in 1838 ("an entirely new honour for me": Adrian Williams, trans. and ed., *Franz Liszt: Selected Letters* [Oxford: Clarendon Press], 85). Evidently the young Wieck's opinion of Liszt's compositional ability was less damning than it would later become.

repertoire one needed to master was much less. I am not slighting the skill and effort required to accompany a song well or to take a leading role in a chamber ensemble, but the collegiality of performing such music ensures that the spotlight is not constantly on the pianist. Understandably, it took several decades before both pianists and audiences got used to fairly long solo programs. In fact, Liszt's initial exclusively solo performances were only a little more ambitious than the piano solo items of his more lengthy "mixed" concerts would have been, and far from the marathons indulged in by the subsequent generation. They also concentrated as much, sometimes even more, on the performer as composer as on the performer as interpreter (an issue that I will discuss in more detail in the next chapters). The first of Liszt's entirely solo public piano concerts—or *monologues pianistiques*, as they were poetically called by the performer—were given in Rome in 1839, and made up entirely of his own original pieces and arrangements. Writing to his "beautiful and charming" friend Princess Belgiojoso, who had organized the Liszt-Thalberg "duel" two years previously, he wrote suavely about

> this invention of mine, which I have devised especially for the Romans, and which I am quite capable of importing to Paris, so boundlessly impudent do I become! Imagine that, failing to concoct a program that would have any kind of sense, I dared, for the sake of peace and quiet, to give a series of concerts entirely alone, affecting the style of Louis XIV and saying cavalierly to the public, "Le concert, c'est moi." For the curiosity of the thing, here is the program of one of these soliloquies.
>
> 1. Overture to William Tell, performed by M. L. [Monsieur Liszt]
> 2. Reminiscences des Puritains. Fantasy composed and performed by the above mentioned! [dedicated to the Princess Belgiojoso]
> 3. Etudes and fragments, by the same to the same!
> 4. Improvisations on given themes—still by the same.
>
> And that's all; neither more nor less, except for lively conversation during the intervals, and enthusiasm, if appropriate![17]

We of course do not know how long items 3 and 4 of this program were, but considering that the *William Tell* Overture in Liszt's transcription lasts around fourteen minutes and *Réminiscences des Puritains* around twenty in its very longest printed version (significant cuts are indicated in one version of the score), we

---

[17] Williams, *Liszt: Selected Letters*, 106–7.

might guess that the playing time of the concert as a whole was unlikely to have lasted much over an hour. Liszt obviously felt, from the mixture of ironically expressed pride and implied defensiveness in his comments to the princess, that solo public concerts were by their very nature open to the charge of both tedium and egotism, but were at least considerably less trouble to organize ("for the sake of peace and quiet"). In fact he had given two solo soirées in the Salle Érard in Paris in 1836, at one of which he famously played Beethoven's *Hammerklavier* Sonata—often described as the first "public" performance of the piece (although others claimed the honor went to Hummel's pupil Mortier de Fontaine)[18]—and in the other he had showcased his own latest compositions. But these were supposedly private occasions for a small invited audience of friends and fellow musicians (according to Berlioz, many more people turned up than were invited—"four to five hundred persons,"[19] if we can really believe that) and an initial salvo in the bourgeoning propaganda war against Thalberg. Liszt's repertoire here—the great Beethoven and his own latest compositions—reflected this.

So neither Liszt's private Paris soirées nor his public Rome "soliloquies" were exactly the established "recital" of future generations. Moscheles had been intending to give a few solo concerts in London in 1837, and thus would have predated Liszt by two years, but he was persuaded by friends to include some vocal numbers for the sake of variety.[20] The first use (in English) of the term "recital" itself—or rather "recitals," for the singular was used initially to refer to performances of individual pieces, and thus a concert comprised several "recitals"—appears to have been for a Liszt concert on 9 June 1840 in the Hanover Square Rooms, London. The connection of the term with music predictably caused the London public some bewilderment, since the word had hitherto been used only to refer to dramatic readings. Even now it did not necessarily imply an exclusively solo concert. Liszt's 9 June program was indeed entirely solo and consisted of his transcription of the Scherzo, "Storm," and Finale of Beethoven's *Pastoral* Symphony; two Schubert song transcriptions ("Ständchen" and "Ave Maria"); *Hexameron*; and his own *Neapolitan tarantella* and *Grand galop chromatique*.[21] His subsequent London recital on 29 June included

[18] Mason, 31.

[19] Hector Berlioz, *Revue et gazette musicale*, 12 June 1836; cited in Williams, *Portrait of Liszt*, 77–78.

[20] Charlotte Moscheles, *Life of Moscheles: With Selections from His Diaries and Correspondence by His Wife* (London: Hurst and Blackett, 1873), 2:22.

[21] An early version of the piece that was later to end *Venezia e Napoli*.

Beethoven's *Kreutzer* Sonata, performed with the violinist Ole Bull. The solo items here were Handel's Fugue in E Minor, the *William Tell* Overture transcription, two Schubert song transcriptions (one of which was a repetition of the "Ständchen" played at the earlier concert, the other "Erlkönig"), a few etudes and mazurkas by Chopin, and Liszt's own *Marche hongroise*. Again, both concerts were relatively short. (In the second, the etudes and mazurkas had been added at the request of Chopin's London publisher, Wessel, who hoped to encourage sales.) One can say here with greater confidence that the first recital must have had a programmed solo playing time for the pianist of a little over an hour, and the second—owing to the presence of the *Kreutzer* Sonata—significantly less.

For the rest of his career, Liszt alternated performing in variety and solo concerts. Indeed, the number of the former has likely been underestimated—and certainly underemphasized—probably because of his reputation as the "inventor" of the solo recital. On one occasion (Hamburg in 1840) when he had found it impossible to engage accompanying artists owing to a quarrel with the theater management, he even made a public (if perhaps tongue-in-cheek) apology for the resulting dullness of the program.[22] It is at times difficult to tell from the mere listing of pieces whether a particular concert was entirely solo or not. A popular work such as *Hexameron,* for example, was often performed in versions for piano and orchestra or for two pianos (a few other works also had now-lost concerted versions), and its presence on a program could imply that Liszt had assembled a small supporting orchestra for the event or had enlisted another player to play a second piano part. Sometimes otherwise detailed reviews are not specific on points like this, failing to mention an orchestral accompaniment when we know there must have been one. The soloist, obviously, was the chief interest, and the orchestra just a distracting noise in the background.[23]

---

[22] Michael Saffle, *Liszt in Germany, 1840– 45* (Stuyvesant, N.Y.: Pendragon Press, 1994), 106.

[23] Without being excessively cynical, we can easily see that assembling a "scratch" orchestra to perform the rudimentary accompaniment of a piece such as *Hexameron,* or asking a colleague to take on the fairly difficult second piano part, had significant advantages for Liszt beyond giving his concerts more variety. It must have frequently added to the impact of his playing. Scratch orchestras even today are not known for their precision, and a fellow pianist at the second piano—even one as accomplished as Clara Schumann, who played *Hexameron* twice with Liszt in December,1841, creating a "furore" (Eugenie Schumann, *Robert Schumann: Ein Lebensbild meines Vaters* [Leipzig: Koehler und Amelang, 1931], 313–15)—would have had difficulty matching the dexterity of the master in a taxing piece that he had not only arranged with his own playing in mind, but had performed many times before. The player of the second piano would not even have been able to get hold of a copy of the part before Liszt chose to give him or her one, for the two-piano version of the piece played in the 1840s has remained unpublished to this day. A much

## The Mood of the Moment

Liszt's post-1840 concerts were therefore not always given alone. Each required a relatively small number of solo pieces compared with modern recitals—hardly any by Anton Rubinstein's daunting standards—and often climaxed with a spontaneous display of improvisational fireworks. For variety concerts, the demands on Liszt were naturally even less, ranging during the British tours of 1840–41 from two to five solo items,[24] though he was customarily also called upon to accompany other pieces in the program. His partnering of the entrepreneur and singer John Orlando Parry in a rendition of Parry's own ballad "The Inchcape Bell" (a subject related to Robert Southey's popular poem "The Inchcape Rock") seems to have been a particular audience favorite, incorporating as it did an improvised storm and shipwreck at the keyboard at the climax of the narrative:

> As the waters dash
> 'Mid the thunder's crash,
> You hear that faithful bell.

There is so much storm music in Liszt's output for piano—"Orage," from the first *Année de pèlerinage*; "Un soir dans les montagnes," from the *Album d'un voyageur*; and the storms in the transcriptions of the *William Tell* Overture and Beethoven's *Pastoral* Symphony, to name just a few—that it is not too difficult to imagine what his thunderous improvisations in this style must have been like. "Storms," said Liszt proudly to Amy Fay, "are my *forte*."[25]

This was by no means the only extempore element. When asked for an encore, Liszt might, according to the mood of the moment, improvise on tunes he had

---

shorter version of *Hexameron* for two pianos was published in the 1870s. The very different one written for the same forces Liszt performed in the 1840s remains in manuscript in the Goethe- und Schiller-Archiv in Weimar, though it is obvious that he intended at one time to publish this also: there are two pages in Liszt's hand describing the origins of the work, designed as a preface to a printed edition. Both these versions are substantially altered from the original solo publication of 1839. Indeed from an examination of Liszt's concert programs, we can see that even when Liszt performed *Hexameron* as a solo, he often omitted certain variations (most frequently the Czerny) or changed their order. *Hexameron*, in other words, was more a protean concept than a fixed piece.

[24] Williams, *Liszt: Selected Letters*, 155.

[25] Amy Fay, *Music Study in Germany* (London: Macmillan, 1893), 221.

just played rather than offer a new piece—in Vienna in 1838, for example, a theme from Weber's *Invitation to the Dance* was varied extempore.[26] The celebrated climax of some of his solo recitals was a closing free improvisation on themes suggested by the audience, which also had the incidental but no doubt welcome effect that even less "repertoire" per concert hour was needed than one might otherwise assume. The practice of free improvisation, however, was hardly unique to Liszt. It carried on throughout the century, though to an ever lessening extent. Even as late as 1925 a two-volume manual for pianists by Gerhard Wehle, mostly dealing with the extempore treatment of folk songs and entitled *Die Kunst der Improvisation* (The Art of Improvisation), appeared in Germany to such acclaim that it was in its third edition by 1927 and was reprinted once again in 1940.[27] In his introduction Wehle lamented the decline of improvisation but hoped that the usefulness of the skill for pianists accompanying silent films might give it new life, a prospect soon blighted by the advent of the talkies.[28]

Today improvisation is mostly confined to the worlds of the jazz, ballet, or cocktail-lounge pianist, although it retains something of its former importance for organists. In the nineteenth century skill in that area was, if not entirely taken for granted, at least a widely acknowledged advantage. Herz, Moscheles, Ferdinand Hiller, and William Mason, among others, indulged in the practice in their own concerts, with greater or lesser enthusiasm. Busoni carried on the tradition in some of his earlier recitals, when he was asked to treat a stylistic mishmash of tunes ranging from Wagner and Rossini to Carinthian folk songs.[29] Hummel's lengthy extempore performances were particularly celebrated. According to Henry Chorley, "He would take the commonest tune, and so grace, and enhance and alter it, as to present it in the liveliest forms of new pleasure. I remember once to have heard Hummel thus treat the popular airs in Auber's Masaniello [*La muette di Portici*] for an hour and a half."[30] Even Mendelssohn was known to end an evening with an improvisation. On 2 December

---

[26] Legany, 46.

[27] Gerhard F. Wehle, *Die Kunst der Improvisation: Die technischen Grundlagen zum stilgerechten, künstlerischen Improvisieren nach den Prinzipien des Klaviersatzes unter besonderer Berücksichtigung des Volksliedes ausführlich erläutert*, 2 vols. (Köln: Musik Verlag Ernest Bisping, 1940), earlier editions 1925–27. There is certainly a possibility that the reprinting of Wehle's book in the middle of the Second World War may have had something to do with the perceived "national" significance of his chosen folk-song material.

[28] Wehle, 1:x, xxx.

[29] Edward Dent, *Ferrucio Busoni: A Biography* (London: Eulenberg, 1974), 30.

[30] Henry Chorley, *Modern German Music* (New York: Da Capo Press, 1973), 2:9.

1836, for example, at the first of the season's Leipzig Gewandhaus subscription concerts, he extemporized on themes from Beethoven's *Fidelio* just after one of the *Leonora* Overtures had been performed by the orchestra and excerpts from the opera sung. Mendelssohn's father mentioned one occasion on which, after Maria Malibran had sung five songs of different nations, his son was dragged to the piano, where he improvised upon them all.[31] At another event he took three themes from the Bach sonatas that had just been performed and impressed an audience of some of the finest musicians in Paris with his spontaneous inspiration.[32]

But having to drag the reticent Mendelssohn to the piano to play extempore was a predictable prelude. He tended to dislike improvising in public—less so before small groups of fellow musicians—and his letters are littered with remarks complaining about the unwelcome pressure he felt to conform to the practice. He wrote to his parents in 1831 telling them about the program for a forthcoming concert in Munich attended by the royal family at which "the first [half] closes with my new G-minor Piano Concerto, and at the end of the second [half] I unfortunately have to improvise. I'm not keen on doing this at all, believe me, but the people here are insisting upon it."[33] On the actual occasion he felt as awkward as he had anticipated: "The king had given me 'Non più andrai' [from Mozart's *Marriage of Figaro*] as a theme, and I had there and then to improvise on it. I've really hardened my opinion that it's madness to improvise in public. I rarely feel so stupid as when I sit down there to serve up my fantasy to the public. The people were very happy, would hardly stop clapping... but I was annoyed.... It is inappropriate [*ein Missbrauch*] and idiotic at the same time."[34] Despite his reluctant acquiescence—which surely had something to do with the element of distasteful "display" and the inevitable impossibility of exercising his usual careful quality control—Mendelssohn's extempore performances were apparently marked out by their lucidity, polyphony, and structure. "It was," said Macfarren, "as fluent and well planned as a written work, and the themes, whether borrowed or invented were not merely brought together but contrapuntally worked."[35] Mendelssohn was quick to notice a lack of contrapuntal

---

[31] S. Hensel, *Die Familie Mendelssohn* (Berlin, 1879), 377.

[32] Felix Mendelssohn Bartholdy, *Reisebriefe aus den Jahren 1830 bis 1832* (Leipzig: Hermann Mendelssohn, 1863), 305.

[33] Felix Mendelssohn Bartholdy, 289; my translation.

[34] Felix Mendelssohn Bartholdy, 299; my translation.

[35] George Grove, "Mendelssohn," in *Dictionary of Music and Musicians*, 1st ed. (London: Macmillan, 1882), 2:300.

imagination in the extempore playing of his fellow musicians. On first hearing the fourteen-year-old Liszt improvise in Paris, he described it as "wretched and dull, nothing but scale passages." But the dyspeptic young visitor had scarcely a good word to say about any musician he heard in Paris in the course of that trip, though he did grudgingly acknowledge that Liszt's pianistic skills were impressive.[36]

Mendelssohn was not the only player to resent the pressure to improvise. Even Liszt, as an old man, complained that it was "impossible to avoid commonplace passages" in large-scale concert improvisations, although he continued the practice both in public and in private until the end of his life.[37] Henri Herz positively recoiled in horror from the idea when it was suggested by his manager during his American tours, though eventually he caved in. In Herz's case, reticence seems to have been encouraged not so much by distaste à la Mendelssohn, but by a realistic anxiety about making a fool of himself—"one's imagination can suddenly fail, and it is painful to reveal oneself before the world in such pretentious impotence."[38] As luck would have it, the tunes suggested by the audience were often those already in his repertoire of variations and potpourris, such as that ubiquitous "Irish Air," "The Last Rose of Summer." An excerpt from his published setting of the theme is given in example 2.2. The ludicrously affected ornamentation soars stratospherically above the horizon of good taste after only a couple of bars, and the sheer triviality of the subsequent variations utterly destroys whatever delicate charm the tune originally had. Herz's worries about "pretentious impotence" were not unjustified.

We can perhaps get some hint of a Mendelssohn improvisation from his own fantasy on the very same melody, op. 15, a charming if rather uncharacteristic piece in his oeuvre. Mendelssohn once told Schumann that "he had never written occasional pieces, Fantasies on themes from, etc.—only once had he been in danger of this, in the presence of Malibran in London, who gave him the silly notion of writing such a piece."[39] The "Last Rose of Summer" Fantasy is, however, such a piece, though it is unlikely that it bears any relation to Malibran

---

[36] William Little, "Mendelssohn and Liszt," in R. Larry Todd, ed., *Mendelssohn Studies* (Cambridge: Cambridge University Press, 1992), 108. See also R. Larry Todd, *Mendelssohn: A Life in Music* (New York: Oxford University Press, 2003), 144.

[37] Stradal, 86. One of Liszt's last public improvisations was on themes from his oratorio *St. Elisabeth* during his London visit of 1886.

[38] Lott, 320 n. 14.

[39] Roger Nichols, *Mendelssohn Remembered* (London: Faber, 1997), 158.

and the occasion mentioned. It is a rather strange mixture of virtually unadorned statements of the tune (see ex. 2.1)—a stark contrast to Herz's version—interspersed with tempestuous episodes in the minor that, apart from a central, almost operatic recitative, appear to have little relation to the subject supposedly fantasized upon. Mendelssohn rounds his work off with a coda that makes a glancing, unexpected, and unexplained reference to Beethoven's "An die ferne Geliebte" (To the Distant Beloved).

EXAMPLE 2.1. Felix Mendelssohn, Fantasy on "The Last Rose of Summer," theme

EXAMPLE 2.2. Henri Herz, Variations on "The Last Rose of Summer," theme

EXAMPLE 2.2. (*continued*)

There is possibly a hidden programmatic intent here, for to some extent the work acts like a miniature drama—a fantasy against the melody rather than on it. Allusions to roses and separated lovers also suggest an intimate personal significance that, typically for Mendelssohn, remains discreetly unspecified (Liszt or Berlioz would have written a long confessional preface in purple prose). The general compositional approach sounds compellingly similar to an account of one of Mendelssohn's boyish improvisations before Goethe in Weimar, where an implicitly placid melody was also juxtaposed with more agitated passages. Zelter had offered an unknown tune as a basis:

> Felix played it through after him, and the next minute went off into the wildest allegro, transforming the simple melody into a passionate figure, which he took now in the bass, now in the upper part, weaving all manner of new and beautiful thoughts into it in the boldest style. Everyone was in astonishment, as the small childish fingers worked away at the great chords, mastering the most difficult combinations, and evolving the most surprising contrapuntal passages out of a stream of harmonies, though certainly without paying much regard to the melody.[40]

Nevertheless, the score may only give a hint of how Mendelssohn might have treated "The Last Rose of Summer" extempore. Even if the fantasy had its origins in an improvisation, the ultra-fastidious composer is quite likely to have made extensive revisions between its first conception in 1827 and its eventual publication around 1831.

Mendelssohn's prim character would doubtless have balked at the sheer theatricality of Liszt's and Herz's procedure in requesting themes from a general

[40] Clive Brown, *A Portrait of Mendelssohn* (New Haven, Conn.: Yale University Press, 2003), 223–24.

audience for a free improvisation, even if he was quite happy to accept one from the great Zelter. Herz would ask audience members to whistle any tune they were unable to notate while he desperately tried to scribble it down himself (one feels sorry for him when reflecting on the melodic exactitude of the average amateur whistler).[41] During Liszt's concerts, an urn was placed at the entrance to the hall in which interested members of the public would place scraps of paper containing tune suggestions. When the grand moment arrived, the maestro would empty it out and play over each suggestion in turn, requesting the audience to indicate by its applause which themes were to its taste. This process was carried out with debonair aplomb and was often accompanied by witty comments from the stage—also part of the act.[42] In some venues, the audience would play its full part in the entertainment. On turning out the urn in a concert on 15 March 1838 in Milan, Liszt found a piece of paper with the question "Is it better to marry or remain single?"—to which he slickly replied, "Whatever course one chooses, one is sure to regret it." Written on another scrap he found the words "the railroad"—which he illustrated on the keyboard with a swath of glissandi (Alkan's *Le chemin de fer* had, unfortunately, not yet been composed).[43] After finally settling on the favorite tunes, Liszt would launch into an improvisation "teeming with astonishing difficulties."[44] His skill at improvisations of this sort was obviously well out of the ordinary, but what came out of the urn was often hardly a surprise. The melodies—as Herz had also found—tended to be well-worn favorites from the world of opera or popular song, some of which Liszt had already treated in his published fantasies, and some of which he would use in his fantasies to come. At a concert in Como on 29 December 1837 the audience suggested the Huntsmen's Chorus from Weber's *Der Freischütz* and an (unidentified) theme from Bellini's *La sonnambula*. The same Weber theme would turn up again in Liszt's *Freischütz* Fantasy (written in 1840–41 but never published), and the one from *La sonnambula* could well feature in the oft-played *Sonnambula* Fantasy of the same period.

---

[41] Lott, 81.

[42] See, for example, a review by Heinrich Adami of a concert in Vienna given on 19 February 1840. In Legany, 82.

[43] Liszt's own published account of this incident can be found in J. Chantavoine, ed., *Franz Liszt: Pages romantiques* (Paris: Félix Alcan, 1912), 215–17. Because Liszt spoke little Italian, one does wonder just how many members of the audience understood Liszt's witticisms (presumably delivered in French).

[44] Hanslick's description. See Pleasants, *Hanslick's Music Criticisms*, 108.

The practice of requesting favorite themes from the audience also allowed Liszt to keep his finger on the pulse of public taste in each area of Europe that he visited. His programs were already specially tailored to this. The transcription of Schubert's "Erlkönig," for example, was played far more frequently in Germany, Austria, and England than in France; the transcription of the March from Glinka's *Ruslan and Lyudmilla* was naturally intended for Russia; and the Fantasia on English National Melodies and the transcription of Donizetti's *March for Sultan Abdul-Mecid* had absolutely specific countries in mind.[45] Italian opera was so popular everywhere in Europe that arrangements of its melodies could always be safely played, but it was wise to be careful with a less widely known opera such as Mercadante's *Il giuramento*. Liszt played his fantasy on this work only in Milan and Vienna, the two cities where the opera had enjoyed some success.[46] Not surprisingly, although a Meyerbeer fantasy was a straightforward choice for a concert in France, Liszt's elaborate arrangement of Beethoven's "Adelaide," let alone the Beethoven sonatas, were, on the whole, better suited to Germany and Austria. Liszt did indeed play a larger selection of Beethoven in German lands than elsewhere in the 1840s. *Hexameron*, on the other hand, went down well everywhere.

A particular hit in university towns was—predictably enough—"Gaudeamus Igitur," and the two versions (1843 and 1851) of Liszt's published paraphrase on this theme tally pretty closely with descriptions of his general approach to concert improvisation,[47] including extensive playing around with fragments of the tune in harmonic sequence, glittering glissandos, and even at one point a loose fugal exposition:

[45] The Fantasia on English National Melodies was unpublished and is extant only in a fragmentary manuscript. The themes treated are the overture to *Messiah* and "See, the Conquering Hero Comes" from *Judas Maccabeus* (by that celebrated English composer Georg Friedrich Händel), Arne's "Rule, Britannia!" and "God Save the Queen." That Liszt adapted his published Fantasia on "God Save the Queen" from this earlier piece seems especially likely considering that an otherwise inexplicable quote from "Rule, Britannia!" turns up in its coda. He is known to have played a separate fantasy on "Rule, Britannia!" that could well also have had its source in the Fantasia on English National Melodies.

[46] Liszt probably played an improvised version of his transcription of Giuseppi Donizetti's March for Sultan Abdul-Mecid during his stay in Constantinople in 1847. It was subsequently published in Vienna in both an original and simplified version. See Kenneth Hamilton, "Reminiscences de la Scala—Reminiscences of a Scandal: Liszt's Fantasy on Mercadante's 'Il Giuramento,'" *Cambridge Opera Journal* 5, no. 3 (1993): 187–98.

[47] Liszt also later composed a "Gaudeamus igitur" humoresque.

EXAMPLE 2.3. Franz Liszt, Concert Paraphrase on "Gaudeamus Igitur" (1843), fugue

Before one is tempted to go into panegyrics here about Liszt's astonishing contrapuntal facility (as some contemporary critics did), it should be pointed out that it is not enormously difficult to improvise an exposition of this sort, especially if little attention is paid to the rigor of the countersubjects and the polyphony doesn't last too long. Liszt usually breaks out of the fugal texture very quickly, to resume a more straightforward pattern of melody plus accompaniment. His treatment is therefore rather different from descriptions of Mendelssohn's (and J. S. Bach's) contrapuntal improvisations, which seem to have maintained (if we can rely on accounts by musicians present) a much stricter polyphonic texture for much longer. But Liszt's keyboard writing itself is, of course, never less than enormously inventive (significantly more so than Mendelssohn's), and his talents as one of the finest extempore players of the century were well attested. A final Lisztian signature is a swaggering transformation of the theme "alla ungarese" (see ex. 2.4), a musical counterpart to his notorious Hungarian "saber of honor" that likely brought the house down:

EXAMPLE 2.4. Franz Liszt, Concert Paraphrase on "Gaudeamus Igitur" (1843), "alla ungarese"

Another of the contrapuntal gambits featured in Liszt's concert improvisations was the climactic combination of themes, which have the slightly embarrassing side effect of pointing out just how many popular nineteenth-century opera melodies are based on identical, tired harmonic progressions.[48] These are naturally also found in his published fantasies, most spectacularly in *Réminiscences de Norma* and the Tarantella from *La muette de Portici* (where the combinations are borrowed from Thalberg's fantasies on the same operas); in the pieces on *Robert le diable*,[49] *La sonnambula*, and *Der Freischütz*; and in the waltz paraphrase on themes from Donizetti's *Lucia* and *Parisina*. Again, it is the pianistic setting that impresses

[48] One cannot say the same about the numerous contrapuntal combinations in Leopold Godowski's intricate and over-the-top Strauss waltz paraphrases. Here the tunes are forced, rather than fitted, together (unless, of course, one accepts with equanimity the regular harmonization of Strauss's melodies with piled-up chords of the major eleventh and thirteenth). The effect is of a chef seeking to impress by serving each dish of a three-course meal simultaneously on a single, unusually deep plate.

[49] Wagner may possibly have had one of the thematic combinations from Liszt's *Robert* Fantasy (the B-major mingling of "Sonnez clairons" and the lyrical *Valse infernale* melody) in the back of his mind when composing the famous three-fold thematic combination in the recapitulation of the overture to *Die Meistersinger*. It certainly sounds like it.

here rather than the all-too-easy polyphony. As Brahms once said to the young Richard Strauss, "There is no point in this piling up of themes that are only contrasted rhythmically on a single triad."[50] At a distance of nearly two centuries, it is impossible to trace in detail how Liszt's improvisations merged into his published output, but it is very likely that they were intimately related.

## The "Great Work"

Dazzling extempore treatment of catchy tunes was easier for audiences to digest than less deliberately populist fare, especially multi-movement works of serious intent that often had not even been composed with the possibility in mind of performance before a large public. Into this category undoubtedly fall the sonatas of Beethoven, which were regarded for the first decades of the nineteenth century as unlikely fare indeed for a public concert. According to Mary Sue Morrow's study of Viennese concerts in the eighteenth and early nineteenth centuries, there is no evidence of any solo piano sonata being publicly performed in Vienna between the years 1760 and 1810—"non-improvisational solo material occurred only rarely."[51] When sonatas were eventually programmed at all, it was often only single movements that were given, although Mendelssohn, after having regularly performed Beethoven's *Moonlight* Sonata at private soirées in Munich and elsewhere, performed it complete at a public concert at the Singakademie in Berlin toward the end of 1832.[52] Ignaz Moscheles a few years later included the *Tempest* and *Les adieux* Sonatas (and one by Weber) in his first (1837) "historical soirée" before a small audience in London. This, amazingly, included some pieces by Bach and Scarlatti played on the harpsichord as well as songs by Mendelssohn and Dussek to lighten the strain, but the program was still extremely severe for the era and not likely to fill a large hall.

Charles Hallé began to make something of a specialty of Beethoven sonatas during his time in Paris in the 1830s and 1840s. He had heard Liszt in 1836 play two Beethoven sonata movements at a concert in the city, but in this case they were from different works. Liszt had joined the first-movement set of variations from the Ab Sonata, op. 26, to the finale of the *Moonlight*, an approach

[50] See Michael Kennedy, *Richard Strauss* (New York: Oxford University Press, 1995), 10–11.

[51] Mary Sue Morrow, *Concert Life in Haydn's Vienna: Aspects of a Developing Musical and Social Institution* (Stuyvesant, N.Y.: Pendragon Press, 1989), 161.

[52] Todd, *Mendelssohn: A Life in Music*, 268.

that left Hallé rather nonplussed, despite his admiration for the playing itself.[53] It was just as well he had not been at Liszt's concert at the Paris Hôtel de Ville on 9 April the year before. This time the complete *Moonlight* Sonata was played, but only the last two movements on the piano. The first was given in an orchestral arrangement.

Such treatment became rarer in subsequent decades but did not disappear entirely. As late as 1890 Godowsky replaced the first movement of the *Appassionata* Sonata with Beethoven's Thirty-two Variations in C Minor. Nobody could quite work out why.[54] Hallé himself got through all the Beethoven sonatas in Parisian salon recitals in the 1840s, but he initially encountered resistance from impresarios in London when trying to program just one (op. 31 no. 3) in 1848.[55] He subsequently gave a complete cycle of the sonatas in London in 1861–62, although this was highly exceptional for the time. Some concerts in the cycle included the odd song, to lighten up the occasion. It was not until the twentieth century that such programming choices became routine, and other players were much more circumspect than Hallé. The *Appassionata* Sonata, for example, only slowly and hesitantly crept into the public repertoire of Clara Wieck during the 1830s. She at first played the finale alone. On receiving a positive reaction to it, she added the andante variations. Eventually she took the plunge and performed the whole piece in 1837 in Berlin (prompting an adulatory poem on her performance to appear in the press), but only "by popular demand."[56] Her daring programming of this same sonata in Vienna had caused "intense debate" in the newspapers about its wisdom, but so complete was her success that when Liszt played it in 1839 in the same city, he was openly said to have been building on the groundwork laid by Clara Wieck.[57]

Even multi-movement works that, unlike most sonatas, had been composed with a genuinely public audience in mind—symphonies and concertos, for example—could well have had single movements performed separately. This was, after all, an age in which an 1839 concert given by Marie Pleyel in Vienna

---

[53] Hallé, 58.

[54] George Bernard Shaw, *Music in London 1890–1894* (London: Constable, 1931), 1:20.

[55] Hallé, 116.

[56] David Ferris, "Public Performance and Private Understanding: Clara Wieck's Concerts in Berlin," *Journal of the American Musicological Society* 56, no. 2 (Summer 2003): 387. Ferris's article offers a particularly stimulating analysis of the tension between public and private piano repertoire in the early to mid–nineteenth century.

[57] Legany, 65.

was considered to have a "too severe" program when it consisted of a Hummel concerto, a fantasy by Döhler, and Weber's *Konzertstück*.[58] That not just the multi-movement Hummel concerto, but even the relatively short Weber piece, could be found a tough nut for audiences to crack is further illustrated by Liszt's comments on the public reaction to one of his concerts in Lyon in 1836: "The piece by Weber [the *Konzertstück*] was not understood. *La fiancée* [Liszt's fantasy on Auber's eponymous opera] accorded better with their retarded sensibilities."[59] When concerted, symphonic, or even chamber works were given complete, they might have had other pieces interspersed between movements—to give the audience a break, as it were. Liszt was in the habit of playing some lighter fare between movements of the Hummel Septet. But the most famously amusing example of this practice was the—rather unsuccessful—premiere of Beethoven's Violin Concerto in December 1806 at the Theater an der Wien. A novelty item of his own composition was offered by the soloist Franz Clement between the first and second movements, during which he held the violin upside down and played on only one string—no doubt much more fun than any dull first-movement sonata form. Chopin too performed his E-Minor Piano Concerto in Warsaw in 1830 with a very long intermezzo between the first and second movements, when various other pieces were sung and played, although this time apparently with the instruments the right way up. The practice of giving concerts between the acts of plays, operas, or ballets also promoted variety in entertainment and could feature isolated movements of larger works, although one can imagine that audiences on these occasions (those who had not already left in search of food, drink, or lavatory facilities) were more than usually restless. Liszt's concert on 31 January 1843 in the theater at Breslau was such an event. A four-act play called *Schwärmerei nach der Mode* (Fashionable Fads) was being staged. After the first act Liszt played the opening movement of Beethoven's *Emperor* Concerto accompanied by the theater orchestra, then his arrangement of Schubert's "Ave Maria" and his Fantasy on *Norma*. After the final act of the play he came back on stage to give not the other movements of the *Emperor*, but rather his arrangement of the Andante finale from *Lucia di Lammermoor*, some Hungarian melodies, and a Hungarian March.[60] No doubt Liszt's reputation and magnetic presence helped him get more attention than usual from the public on a fairly

[58] Williams, *Liszt: Selected Letters*, 121.

[59] Daniel Ollivier, ed., *Correspondance de Liszt et de la comtesse d'Agoult*, vol. 1 (Paris: Grasset, 1933), 157.

[60] Saffle, plate 5, reproduces the poster for this concert, to which I am indebted for the information.

lengthy evening like this. According to the playbill, the show was scheduled to start at six o'clock and not finish until around nine.[61]

It is not surprising, therefore, that Liszt's celebrated 1836 *Hammerklavier* Sonata performance was not officially a public concert at all. He would have been most unlikely to perform such a long and complex piece in Paris during those years at such an event. Its programming was as much a challenge to his rival Thalberg as anything else, and an attempt to position himself as a faithful inter-preter of the most difficult music by the greatest composers. These features—Liszt's interpretative fidelity and his musical bravery in offering a reputedly "un-playable" work—are among the points stressed by his very supportive friend Ber-lioz in a celebrated review. Liszt did perform other Beethoven piano sonatas—in whole or in part—later in his concerts of the 1840s (the *Tempest*, the *Appassionata*, and opp. 101, 106, 109, 110, and 111 among them), but they were certainly regarded as among the severe pieces in his repertoire and better suited to par-ticular venues (preferably in large cities, and preferably German or Austrian) with a high proportion of "connoisseurs" in the audience. When he played the *Hammerklavier* Sonata again, this time at a genuinely public concert—the Singakademie in Berlin on 6 February 1842—it was only as a two-movement excerpt.[62] The first movement of Beethoven's op. 26—given in isolation—began the program, which was made more palatable by Liszt's fantasies on *Lucrezia Borgia*, *Don Juan*, and themes of Paganini (*La campanella* and *Carnival of Venice*)[63] and his arrangement of Meyerbeer's *Der Mönch*. Liszt did, however, seize the op-portunity to play the complete *Hammerklavier* Sonata in Vienna in 1846, but this was for a specially invited audience at a "Beethoven-Feier" given in the salon of the publisher Karl Haslinger. According to one reviewer, those present formed a "select circle of musicians and poets, of connoisseurs and friends of art."[64] Not that different, then, from his own invited audience in the Salle Érard a decade before. For some audiences, even one movement of a Beethoven sonata remained tough going. Liszt's performance of the first movement of the *Pathétique* Sonata left Munich auditors in 1843 "rather cold," according to one review, yet they

---

[61] There were certainly earlier instances of events significantly longer than this mixed bill—"monster" variety concerts in London, for example, or Beethoven's notorious "Academy" concert of December 1808 in Vienna, which included premieres of the Fifth and Sixth Symphonies, the Fourth Piano Concerto, and the Choral Fantasy. The latter apparently lasted in excess of a grueling four hours.

[62] Beethoven himself had seemed relatively indifferent to whether or not movements should be omitted (or their order changed) for the London publication of op. 106.

[63] This little-known piece exists in an (unfinished) manuscript.

[64] Legany.

went crazy over the rest of the program, which included surefire winners like the *Sonnambula* Fantasy.[65]

With this background in mind, it is easy to understand why Robert Schumann initially believed that his larger solo keyboard works were not suited to public performance at all.[66] Toward the end of 1839 he changed his mind somewhat, largely prompted by personal circumstances that made it imperative that his music become better known. He then hesitantly suggested to Clara Wieck that she might play part of his Sonata no. 2 in G Minor—only the slow movement and finale, or else the finale alone and the fughetta from the *Clavierstücke*, op. 32.[67] In the end, she played the whole sonata at a concert on 1 February 1840 in Berlin as part of a mixed program of solo works, chamber music, songs, and an opera excerpt. The sonata ended the first half, after Schubert's E♭ Trio and a Spohr "Scene from *Faust*" (sung by Zschiesche). Following an interval the musicians offered two lieder by Lecerf (sung by Lehmann), three solo piano pieces (Wieck's own Scherzo, Liszt's transcription of Schubert's "Lob der Thränen," and a Chopin etude), Decker's "Goldschmidts Töchterlein" (sung by Zschiesche), and the Liszt *Niobe* Fantasy.[68] The sonata was fairly well received, although the critic for the *Neue Zeitschrift für Musik* openly doubted whether "a keyboard sonata without any accompaniment *of this school* belongs before a large mixed audience."[69]

Clara (Wieck) Schumann began to program Beethoven sonatas more regularly by the 1850s, but always as part of a variety program. Despite her celebrity, she hesitated regularly to give her own entirely solo concerts until the 1870s— remarkably late in her career. Many younger pianists had anticipated her. Von Bülow, Anton Rubinstein, and Tausig, among others, frequently played entirely solo in the 1860s. All played from memory, and all had a notable fondness for lengthy programs, including multi-movement works.[70] An 1870 Tausig solo

[65] Saffle, 159–60.

[66] For a discussion of the contemporary reception of Schumann's piano music, see Anthony Newcomb, "Schumann in the Marketplace," in R. Larry Todd, ed., *Nineteenth-Century Piano Music* (New York: Schirmer, 1994), 258–315.

[67] Weissweiler and Ludwig, 742.

[68] Ferris, 395.

[69] Ferris, 397.

[70] An extensive listing of Rubinstein's concert programs, including the famous "historical recitals," can be found in Larry Sitsky's pioneering study *Anton Rubinstein: An Annotated Catalogue of Piano Works and Biography* (Westport, Conn.: Greenwood Press, 1998), 140–63. For more detail on Von Bülow see Hans-Joachim Hinrichsen, *Musikalische Interpretation Hans von Bülow*, Beihefte zum Archiv für Musikwissenschaft, herausgegeben von Hans Heinrich Eggebrecht, Band XLVI

recital given in Berlin, for example, consisted of Beethoven's *Waldstein* Sonata; a bourrée by Bach; a Presto scherzando by Mendelssohn; Chopin's Barcarolle, Ballade op. 47, and two mazurkas; Weber's *Invitation to the Dance*; Schumann's *Kreisleriana*; the Schubert-Liszt "Ständchen" from Shakespeare "Hark, hark, the lark"; and a Liszt Hungarian Rhapsody. By the 1880s the practice of performing entirely solo was fairly well established, although it could still rate a mention from the critics and never entirely edged out more varied offerings. A *Musical Times* review of a Pachmann concert in June 1883 seemed happy enough with the tendency: "Emulous of von Bülow, Rubinstein, Sophie Menter, and other pianists of high rank, M. de Pachmann is now engaged in a short series of Recitals, in which he alone suffices to maintain interest and give pleasure. The performances, so far, have been highly successful."[71]

But not all were so welcoming. There were complaints at least up to the end of the nineteenth century about the monotony of concerts featuring only one performer, largely directed—and this is hardly surprising—against the perpetrators of the longer programs. Hanslick lamented the tendency in an 1884 article on Anton Rubinstein,[72] who, with Bülow, was setting a trend for solo recitals of "educational" value but gargantuan length. The didactic intent was especially obvious in Bülow's orchestral concerts—in one of which he conducted Beethoven's Ninth Symphony twice, in order to give the audience a better chance to appreciate its beauties—but also an undeniable feature of his programs as a keyboard soloist. In February 1881 Bülow gave a concert in Vienna consisting of the last five Beethoven piano sonatas, a program lasting over two hours of playing time that, according to Hanslick, severely tried the patience of his audience, whatever the fascination of the performance.[73] They were lucky on that occasion. Bülow sometimes threw in an encore at the end of this program—the *Appassionata* Sonata! The all-Beethoven concert in fact turned out only to be a preliminary warm-up for the indefatigable pianist, who proceeded to inflict on the already cowering Viennese an all-Liszt performance lasting three hours. It was not surprising that for his London recitals in 1865 Charles Hallé sought to reassure his prospective audience by advertising that no concert would last more than

---

(Stuttgart: Franz Steiner Verlag, 1999), 56–70. Hinrichsen's splendid work—which I was quite disgracefully unaware of until Gundula Kreutzer brought it to my attention—is a fascinating resource for all those interested in nineteenth-century pianism.

[71] Quoted in Mitchell, 35.

[72] Pleasants, *Hanslick's Music Criticisms*, 228. There were complaints also about the length of orchestral concerts. See, for example, Shaw, *Music in London*, 2:268, 2:279.

[73] Pleasants, *Hanslick's Music Criticisms*, 184–86.

two hours.[74] A grueling three hours indeed seemed to be the normal length of a Rubinstein concert. The second of his seventeen "historical" recital programs, for example (given in Moscow, St. Petersburg, London, Vienna, Paris, Berlin, and Leipzig in 1885–86), was also devoted to Beethoven and comprised eight sonatas, one after the other: the *Moonlight*, *Tempest*, *Waldstein*, *Appassionata*, op. 90, op. 101, op. 109, and op. 111. Liszt, who appears to have had a much more realistic idea of an audience's attention span, did not approve. When he heard Rubinstein give a program including four pieces in sonata form, he thought that even this was far too much.[75]

Programs such as these would have been quite unthinkable a few decades before, when the inclusion of even one solo sonata in a public concert could, as we have seen, elicit unfavorable comment. What had happened in the meantime? In the first place a standard repertoire of generally accepted masterworks had gradually solidified, and the pianist was increasingly taking on the role of an "interpreter" of these masterworks rather than a presenter of his own pieces. William Weber has persuasively argued that the revolutions of 1848–49, whether successful or abortive, formed a potent catalyst for this development. "The musical classics," he suggests, "came to offer morally uplifting, cosmopolitan leadership in a time that desperately needed strong new cultural traditions."[76]

To be sure, well into the twentieth century pianists would regularly include their own compositions in their programs—Paderewski's Sonata in E♭ Minor or Minuet, Hofmann's *Kaleidoscope*, Rosenthal's *Papillons*—but the balance had well and truly shifted from the heyday of Liszt and Thalberg, when an entire concert could regularly be formed from the pianist's own output. Anton Rubinstein would sometimes include groups of his own piano pieces in his programs or occasionally give whole recitals of his own music (such as his last American concert of 1873 in New York), but most of his programs were strongly biased toward the works of others, and in any case his compositional ambitions were hardly confined to works involving the piano, ranging widely through operatic and symphonic music. It was very much a throwback to the past when Busoni gave a recital of his own works as the final offering in a 1912 "historical survey" series of eight concerts in the Verdi Conservatory of Milan.

---

[74] Program listed on the Web site of the Royal College of Music Centre for Performance History. "Concert Programmes 1790–1914: Case Studies by William Weber," at http://www.cph.rcm.ac.uk/Programmes1/Pages/BtoR10.htm (accessed June 2006).

[75] Mitchell and Evans, 101.

[76] Weber, *Music and the Middle Class*, preface.

Clara Wieck—concertizing at the same time as Liszt and Thalberg in the 1830s and 1840s—was a pattern for the future. Her repertoire featured only a respectable handful of her own compositions (it would have been regarded as bizarre for a woman to present herself as a significant composer), and later not many even of her husband's during his lifetime. Indeed, owing to the general skepticism about women's creative faculty, female pianists such as Wieck and Marie Pleyel were among the first to confine their repertoire mostly to other people's music.[77]

As far as the audience was concerned, the more frequently "masterworks" were presented, the greater the expectation that they should sit through them silently—in however many movements they might be—and effectively should behave rather more like a contemplative gathering of connoisseurs than a lively assembly of socialites on pleasure bent. Just how quiet and attentive they actually became, however, has often been overestimated (see "Who Cares about Applause?" in the next chapter). Writing from Paris in 1832 to his teacher, Zelter, Mendelssohn had already attributed to snobbery the apparent willingness of the audiences at Habeneck's conservatory concerts patiently to endure entire symphonies by Beethoven: "Even the concert audience has an extraordinary love for Beethoven, because they believe that one would have to be a connoisseur [*Kenner*] to love him. In reality, they enjoy his works the least. . . . The Beethoven symphonies are like exotic plants to them."[78]

A small private gathering of supposedly genuine connoisseurs was fascinated to hear Clara Wieck play through Schumann's complete set of *Noveletten* in 1839 (which must have taken around forty-five minutes),[79] but she thought long and hard before she tried even a single one out on the public. Some decades later, the public were, if not completely happy with, then at least tolerant of sitting and listening to Rubinstein play "difficult" music for hours—they now wished to be seen as true connoisseurs and were willing to be appropriately educated. At the same time, recitals devoted entirely to the works of canonic or would-be canonic composers—Beethoven or Chopin, for example, latterly Liszt too—were becoming more frequent. The irony, of course, was that much of the "serious" music in the standard repertoire itself was written for more intimate performance circumstances and had certainly not been composed in an era when

[77] See Katharine Ellis, "Female Pianists and Their Male Critics in Nineteenth-Century Paris," *Journal of the American Musicological Society* 50, nos. 2–3 (Summer–Fall 1997): 353–85.

[78] Rudolph Elvers, ed., *Mendelssohn Bartholdy Briefe* (Frankfurt: Fischer Verlag, 1984), 155.

[79] Weissweiler and Ludwig, 795.

multi-movement works were played complete and uninterrupted before a rapt audience in a large hall. A public rite of silent reverence before these lengthy masterworks is profoundly unhistorical. Silent reverence before a Liszt Hungarian Rhapsody, in the manner of Paderewski's *Moonlight* Sonata recital, is not only unhistorical, but bordering on the ridiculous. Such an audience response in the era of the work's composition could have meant but one thing—the piece was a failure.

The gradual formation of a practically sacred standard repertoire had the inevitable side effects of concentrating programs more on the music of the past than of the present, of sidelining music that "hadn't made it"—from whatever era—and of increasing the expectation that the pianist play from memory (see "And All from Memory" in the next chapter). A pianist performing his own compositions was undoubtedly playing contemporary music, whatever one thought of its quality or durability, but one had to wait graciously for a work to be accepted as canonic. Once started, the process of canonization had its own momentum, and there was rarely a devil's advocate, as required for the analogous process in the Catholic church, to put a hiccup in the proceedings (despite George Bernard Shaw's well-publicized excoriations of Mendelssohn's "monstrous platitudes" or Busoni's open contempt for Wagner).[80] After a while, the fondness of audiences (and hence of impresarios) for certain standard works— the *Appassionata* Sonata, for example, or Chopin's ballades—imposed increasing pressure on players to keep these pieces in their repertoire, leaving less and less time for the study of new music. Pressure was more intense on pianists than on most other musicians, for they were granted the double-edged sword of a gloriously vast standard repertoire dwarfing that of any other instrument—thirty-two Beethoven sonatas, for starters. They could spend their entire lives trying to learn this body of music and still master only a fraction of it.[81]

The sheer stasis of the standard repertoire is quite remarkable. Typically in the concert world today, most players are pigeonholed as "standard-repertoire" performers and others ghettoized as advocates of contemporary music—even if a few hardy souls try to straddle the boundaries. The resilience of the basic repertoire itself has resulted in its stranglehold on much of concert programming

[80] Busoni did, nevertheless, put aside his contempt long enough to perform the Tausig transcription of "The Ride of the Valkyries" and his own arrangement of the funeral march from *Götterdämmerung* at some early concerts.

[81] Performing complete cycles of Beethoven sonatas is now common. Leslie Howard's complete recording of Liszt's piano music, on the other hand, is a unique and quite amazing achievement. Nevertheless, even this only scratches the surface of the repertoire.

since the 1860s. A program similar to Tausig's 1870 Berlin concert could easily be heard in many concert halls today. The roughly chronological, historical framework of the program—beginning with Beethoven and Bach, progressing through the romantics, and ending in a blaze of pyrotechnics with a Liszt rhapsody—is alive and well. But for Tausig, of course, Liszt and the romantics were contemporaries; the same can scarcely be said today. The programming legacy of Tausig's generation—becoming more ancient and ossified with every decade—was passed directly down via Bülow, Rubinstein, Paderewski, and others. It is today officiously kept alive by the traditional attitudes to recital construction frequently encouraged in conservatories and universities.

## Programming Post-Rubinstein

The now "traditional" piano recital, with its healthy opening of Bach or something else baroque,[82] followed by a "serious" classical sonata (Mozart, Haydn, or Beethoven, but definitely not J. C. Bach or Franz Benda), topped off with a second half of romantic music—first lyrical, then virtuosic—with maybe a tiny bit of modern music thrown in somewhere before the end (but not actually at the end) is a mini-version of Tausig's recitals or Rubinstein's "historical" programs. Rubinstein and Tausig were certainly not the first to have the idea of "historical survey" programs, though the concept is strongly linked with the former's name, owing to the success of his 1885–56 series. Fétis organized "Concerts Historiques" in Paris and Brussels as far back as the 1830s; Mendelssohn was conducting "Historische Konzerte" with the Leipzig Gewandhaus orchestra in the 1840s. Moscheles's experiments in this direction have already been mentioned, while Clara Wieck Schumann, followed by Bülow, often played short, self-assembled suites of pieces (linked by improvised preludes) that covered a wide chronological range from Scarlatti to Chopin. In the shadow of Rubinstein, both Rosenthal and Busoni would later give their own ambitious historical survey series. It is easy to see, however, why a slimmed-down survey became so beloved of finals recitals at conservatories and universities and even now underpin such widely promulgated examination schemes as those of the Associated Board of the Royal Schools of Music (a standard rite of passage for budding musicians

---

[82] On romantic attitudes to Bach, see John Michael Cooper, "Felix Mendelssohn-Bartholdy, Ferdinand David, und Johann Sebastian Bach. Mendelssohns Bach-Auffassung im Spiegel der Wiederentdeckung der 'Chaconne,'" in *Mendelssohn Studien: Beiträge zur neueren deutschen Kultur- und Wirtschaftsgeschichte* 10 (Berlin: Duncker und Humblot, 1997), 157–79.

in Britain and many Commonwealth countries). Programs like this supposedly allow students to demonstrate a healthily versatile stylistic understanding of wide swaths of the standard repertoire. The fact that Rubinstein himself apparently always sounded like Rubinstein no matter what he was playing or that scarcely any later professionals have successfully performed in such an extensive range of styles (Artur Schnabel was hardly admired for his Chopin playing, or Horowitz for his Beethoven) remains more a problem for the students than for the examiners.

Paderewski—easily the most popularly and financially successful pianist of the post-Rubinstein generation—duly adopted the programming approach of his young days, namely the marathon concert of Rubinstein and Bülow, as did contemporaries such as Liszt's pupils Frederic Lamond and Arthur Friedheim. Lamond, for example, gave a typically generous program from memory for his debut London recital in St. James's Hall in1886, which according to onlookers severely tested his aged master's ability to keep awake. In the hope of attracting a larger audience, Lamond had proclaimed "Dr. Liszt has consented to be present" on the concert posters. The stratagem worked rather too well. Liszt escorted his pupil toward the stage to a barrage of enthusiastic applause sustained for over ten minutes. Unfortunately, the ovation was for Liszt and not his student, for when Lamond rather than the master headed for the piano, a palpable sense of disappointment swept over the hall.[83] He nevertheless received complimentary reviews for a lengthy recital comprising the Bach-Tausig Toccata and Fugue in D Minor; Beethoven's *Appassionata* Sonata; Chopin's F-Minor Fantasy; two Brahms capriccios from op. 76; Liszt's *Harmonies du soir*, *Feuxfollets*, and *Mazeppa*; Raff's op. 91 Fantasy and Fugue; Lamond's own Impromptu; Rubinstein's Valse-Caprice; a Liszt *Liebestraum*; and the Ninth Hungarian Rhapsody; plus encores.

Arthur Friedheim, five years later, gave three huge concerts in the space of a week at Carnegie Hall as his American recital debut (a concerto had already been heard from him). He too had Rubinsteinian endurance, which was becoming by this time almost de rigeur for ambitious young performers. The astonishingly taxing program of the third, on 17 April, consisted of Wagner-Friedheim, "Wotan's Zorn" and "Abschied von Brünnhilde" from *Die Walküre*; Beethoven, Sonata in B♭ Major, op. 106 (*Hammerklavier*); Chopin, Nocturne in C Minor, op. 48 no. 1, Ballade in F Minor, op. 52, and Polonaise-Fantaisie in A♭, op. 61;

---

[83] Harold Bauer, *His Book* (New York: Norton, 1948), 22–23.

Balakirev, *Islamey*; Liszt, *Mephisto* Waltz no. 1; and Liszt, Fantasy on Bellini's *La sonnambula*.[84] These were not programs that would have been viable fifty years before, either in composition or in length. They must have made quite an impact—but an exhausting one.

The young Busoni had first heard Friedheim play in Vienna in 1883:

> Pose is the order of the day. There is a pianist here called Friedheim, a pupil of Liszt, with long hair and a face that looks half severe, half bored. When he plays he comes forward and bows in such a way that his hair covers up all his face; then he throws his head back to tidy his mane. Then he sits down with a great deal of fuss, and looks round waiting till the audience is quiet. . . . But the loveliest thing is to see him during the Tuttis of the orchestra. There he has room to show off all his tricks. He examines his nails, considers the audience, thrusts his hands into the air, and does other silly things.[85]

Busoni scarcely needed Friedheim's example, either in deportment or in program building, although he did later take some advice from him on Liszt performance style. By 1883—at the age of only seventeen—Busoni was already a proponent of the value-for-money event. A concert on November of that year had comprised Beethoven's op. 111 Sonata; Bach's *Italian* Concerto; Schumann's *Symphonic Studies*; Chopin's *Andante spianato* and *Grand polonaise*; two etudes of his own; and Liszt's "Hochzeitsmarsch und Elfenreigen" transcription from Mendelssohn's *Midsummer Night's Dream*. But these were only the solo items, for the audience also had to sit through more of Busoni as composer, in the shape of the Variations and Scherzo for Piano Trio and the Serenade for Cello and Piano. This concert was nevertheless of disarming modesty compared with Anton Rubinstein's first Viennese recital the following year, for which two sonatas by Beethoven and one by Schumann were merely the three longest of over twenty pieces played.[86]

---

[84] The other two concerts were as follows:

*10 April 1891.* Wagner-Friedheim: Vorspiel to *Die Meistersinger von Nürnberg*; Beethoven: Sonata in D Major, op. 10, no. 3; Beethoven: *Waldstein* Sonata in C Major, op. 53; Chopin: Selected preludes and etudes; Chopin: Sonata in B♭ Minor, op. 35; Liszt: Fantasy on Mozart's *Don Juan*.

*14 April 1891.* Liszt: Sonata in B Minor; *Harmonies poétiques et religieuses*, no. 3, "Bénédiction de Dieu dans la solitude"; Hungarian Rhapsody no. 9 (*Pester Karneval*); *Légendes*, no. 1, "St. François d'Assise: La prédication aux oiseaux"; *Légendes*, no. 2, "St. François de Paule marchant sur les flots"; *Après une lecture du Dante* (Fantasia quasi Sonata); *Études d'exécution transcendante d'après Paganini*.

[85] Dent, 47.

[86] Not thirty pieces, as Dent (*Ferruccio Busoni: A Biography*) and Couling (Della Couling, *Ferruccio Busoni: A Musical Ishmael* [Lanham, Md.: Scarecrow, 2005], 59) claim.

Busoni began to slightly moderate the generosity of his recitals, but they remained very much on the lengthy side. An 1888 concert in Graz, for example, was an interesting combination of the old Lisztian type of program—opera fantasy and free improvisation included—with the Rubinstein "historical concert" approach: Bach-Liszt, Organ Fantasy and Fugue in G Minor; Beethoven, Sonata op. 111; Busoni, *Variations and Fugue on a Theme of Chopin*; Schumann, Toccata; Mozart, Rondo in A Minor and Gigue in G Major; Weber, *Perpetuum mobile*; Strauss-Tausig, "Man lebt nur einmal"; a free improvisation on a theme suggested by the audience; and the Auber-Liszt Tarantella from *La muette de Portici*. In later years he extended the historical survey plan to the concerto, giving four concerts in Berlin composed entirely of works for piano and orchestra, with detailed explanatory program notes graciously provided by his fellow-virtuoso José Vianna da Motta.[87]

Such notes were still by no means routine. Charles Hallé had provided something similar for his London Beethoven series in the 1860s, but then he was known as a particularly serious and didactic performer. It is a sobering thought that to audiences of many of the massive concerts of Bülow or Rubinstein even the modest distraction of flicking through the program booklet was denied. Bülow did, however, include his own titles to most of Beethoven's *Diabelli Variations* on program leaflets to give the audience a helping hand. The captions he used were rather different in his concert series of 1866, 1867, and 1886, but included flights of fancy like "Widerhall" (Echo) for variation 13, "Geheimnis" (Secret) or "Vertrauliche Mittheilung" (Intimate Message) for no. 18. For variation 23 he oscillated between the titles "Humoreske," "Drunter und Drüber" (Topsy-Turvy), and "Explosion," presumably depending on his notoriously volatile temper.[88]

Busoni adopted his typically monumental approach in the concerts he devoted to Liszt's music in Berlin in 1904, which included the complete *Paganini Studies* (a

---

[87] Some of Busoni's and da Motta's correspondence on this can be found in Christine Weismann Beirao, *Ferruccio Busoni–Jose Vianna da Motta: Briefwechsel, 1898 bis 1921* (Wilhelmshaven: Florian Noetzel Verlag, 2004), 16–18. The first installment of Busoni's arduous piano-orchestra survey included the following concertos: Bach in D Minor, Mozart no. 23, Beethoven no. 4, and Hummel in B Minor; the second, Beethoven *Emperor*, Weber *Konzertstück*, Schubert-Liszt *Wanderer* Fantasy, and Chopin no. 2; the third, Mendelssohn in G Minor, Schumann in A Minor, and Henselt in F Minor; and the fourth, Rubinstein in E♭ Major, Brahms in D Minor, and Liszt in A Major.

[88] See Haas, *Hans von Bülow: Leben und Wirken; Wegbereiter für Wagner, Liszt und Brahms* (Wilhelmshaven: Florian Noetzel Verlag, 2002), 40, for a complete listing. Booklets with fuller program notes were usually provided for concerts during Paderewski's American tours.

speciality also of Arthur Friedheim) and *Transcendental Studies* in the first recital alone. He would later pursue this "completist" attitude to programming—so redolent of the current preferences of the recording industry—by programming all the *Paganini Studies* along with Chopin's complete op. 28 Preludes, to which he added Beethoven's *Hammerklavier* Sonata for good measure. Performing all twelve of Chopin's op. 25 Etudes (initially in Berlin in 1896) or the entire op. 10 set (Berlin, 1902) was also a Busoni speciality, although he did not always play them in the order set down in the score. At a 1904 performance in Chicago of the op. 25 set, for example, he ended with no. 11 in A Minor, extending the closing scale almost the entire length of the keyboard to make an even greater impact.[89]

We should emphasize how far from the imagination of the composers such cyclopean performances would have been. Neither Liszt nor Chopin ever played more than a short selection from their opuses of etudes and preludes, and the complete sets simply did not have any "unity" that was intended to be demonstrated by public performance, whatever some present-day analysts might find on paper. (This is not to say that the findings of modern analysis are irrelevant to our understanding of the music, but simply that they have little to do with the practical performance conditions prevalent at the time of composition, and for a good while afterward.) Later in his life, Liszt was astonished that Friedheim should perform all six of his *Paganini Studies* at a single concert, for he himself had given no more than two at a time. Chopin played four of his preludes, but no more, in a Paris concert on 26 April 1841. He subsequently suggested two similar groups of four preludes for study by his pupil Jane Stirling.[90] By the 1890s pianists such as Friedheim and Busoni were making complete performances of weighty groups of works a less uncommon experience, but it was at the cost of extending concerts to an almost purgatorial length. Even at this stage, Brahms, for example, was perfectly happy if a fine performer such as Rosenthal should choose to play conflated excerpts from his two books of *Variations on a Theme of Paganini* rather than both of them complete.

Of course, it was still quite possible to construct a mammoth recital program without complete sets of works, by the time-honored method of simply playing one unrelated piece after another until exhaustion was reached. Paderewski's famous "comeback" concert at Carnegie Hall on 22 November 1922 (after

---

[89] See the review in the *Chicago Journal*, 10 March 1904, quoted in Couling, 187.

[90] See Jean-Jacques Eigeldinger and Jean-Michel Nectoux, eds., *F. Chopin: Oeuvres pour Piano; Facsimile de l'exemplaire de Jane W. Stirling* (Paris, 1982), xxviii.

several years during which he was heavily involved with politics) was of a by now familiar three-hour length and included two of the filmed *Moonlight Sonata* selections—the Liszt Second Rhapsody and his own Minuet—among the seven encores. These encores were, astonishingly, played after an already Herculean offering consisting of Mendelssohn's *Variations serieuses*; Schumann's op. 17 Fantasy; Beethoven's *Appassionata* Sonata; Chopin's First Ballade, G-Major Nocturne, B♭-Minor Mazurka, and Third Scherzo; and Liszt's *Au bord d'une source*, *La leggierezza* Concert Study, and E-Major Polonaise. The other encores were Schubert's A♭ Impromptu, the Chopin-Liszt "Meine Freuden," Chopin's C♯-Minor Waltz, the Wagner-Liszt "Liebestod" from *Tristan und Isolde*, and the Chopin Etude in F Major (from op. 10). Audience and critical reaction was ecstatic, but it was a test of endurance as much as musicianship.

By the 1930s such monster programs were beginning to be jostled out by events that put fewer demands on both pianist and audience. Ignaz Friedman had already by the beginning of the century shown that he had a much more practical idea of the length of time an audience might genuinely be expected to concentrate on complex piano music. A typically concise, if strenuous, program from a 1905 recital in Berlin consisted of Beethoven's *Appassionata* Sonata, Brahms's *Variations on a Theme of Paganini*, Chopin's Third Sonata, and Liszt's *Réminiscences de Don Juan*. It is instructive to compare this with a Busoni recital from 1897, also given in Berlin, and also including the Liszt *Don Juan* Fantasy: the Bach-Busoni Chaconne; the Beethoven *Eroica Variations*; the Weber Sonata no. 1; the Meyerbeer-Liszt "Illustration" from *Le prophète*; the Liszt *Réminiscences de Don Juan*; and the Liszt-Busoni Fantasy and Fugue on the Chorale "Ad nos, ad salutarem undam" from Meyerbeer's *Le prophète*. The enormously long Busoni program has a logic of its own, with the second half centering around Liszt's reworkings of Meyerbeer and Mozart. But as a result the *Don Juan* Fantasy is slightly swamped among other works of comparable length and virtuosity, whereas in Friedman's structure it is treated as the bravura climax to the whole concert, the place it usually takes nowadays.

Liszt himself seems to have placed the *Don Juan* Fantasy at virtually any point in a program, even beginning with it in Vienna in 1846, before going on to play a couple of Schubert lieder transcriptions and then Beethoven's *Moonlight* Sonata—probably the reverse order from what many would now venture, for it is now thought difficult to tune into Beethoven's sublimity after a "tawdry" opera fantasy. Another Friedman recital, given in 1920, started like Busoni's with the Bach-Busoni Chaconne, but continued rather differently with the Chopin Third Sonata, Schumann's *Carnaval*, a Scriabin prelude, his own *Minuetto vecchio*, Liszt's Valse-

Impromptu, and the Wagner-Liszt *Tannhäuser* Overture.[91] Friedman's programs were not exactly short, but consistently of less overwhelming dimensions than Busoni's customary outings and likely easier for a general audience to handle.

But what of the concerts of "the last romantic"? Horowitz's recitals were always pretty skimpy for a romantic—around the present-day "average" of forty to forty-five minutes per half, which would have been little more than a preliminary warm-up for Anton Rubinstein or a group of encores for Paderewski. A Zurich program in December 1935, for example, found him playing the Bach-Busoni Toccata, Adagio and Fugue; Haydn's C Minor Sonata, Hob. XVI:20; Franck's Prelude, Aria, and Finale; Schumann's Toccata; and Chopin's Barcarolle, Etudes in C♯ Minor, op. 25 no. 7, and G♭ Major, op. 10 no. 5, Scherzo no. 4, Mazurka in C♯ Minor, and—yes—Polonaise in A♭, op. 53. This is well in line with programming advice given to piano students by Mark Hambourg in 1951. In *The Eighth Octave*, his supplementary volume of memoirs, he includes "specimen recital programs,"[92] most of which could easily be from concerts today.

The evolution of the "traditional" or "conservatory-model" piano recital into the length we are fairly familiar with today had been fully completed by the time Horowitz gave his own "comeback" recital in 1965 at Carnegie Hall (after a twelve-year absence from the concert platform). Over forty years had passed since Paderewski's memorable return to the same venue, and Horowitz's program also featured the Schumann op. 17 Fantasy. But in this case it was by far the longest item of a much less encyclopedic event. The Fantasy was preceded by the

---

[91] A fascinating listing by Allan Evans of over 800 Friedman programs can be found at http://www.arbiterrecords.com/musicresourcecenter/friedman.html, from which these specimens are taken (accessed April 2006).

[92] Mark Hambourg, *The Eighth Octave* (London: Williams and Norgate, 1951), 102. Hambourg suggests a "fantasia program" consisting of Bach's Chromatic Fantasy and Fugue, Schumann's op. 17, Chopin's Polonaise-Fantasy, and Schubert's *Wanderer* Fantasy. His own "Diamond Jubilee" program comprised Beethoven's Sonata op. 31 no. 3, Contretanz in C, Rondo op. 51 no.2, and *Waldstein* Sonata for the first half, followed by a second half exclusively devoted to Chopin: the Second Ballade, three etudes from op. 10 (E Major, F Minor, and F Major), three preludes from op. 28 (A♭ Major, C♯ Minor, and B♭ Minor), the Third Scherzo, and the Polonaises in B♭ Major, op. 71, and A♭ Major, op. 53. More redolent of the nineteenth century is a suggested "Sonatas and Etudes" program—Beethoven's Sonata op. 101, Thalberg's Tremolo Study, Leschetizky's etude "La source," Czerny's C-major Toccata, three Chopin etudes, 2 Liszt studies, Ravel's *Jeux d'eau*, Rubinstein's *Staccato* Etude, and Chopin's Second Sonata—owing to the modest presence of Thalberg, Czerny, and Hambourg's own teacher Leschetizky. Any pianist leafing through the Czerny Toccata will soon realize that it is in fact the unsung forebear of one of our most familiar double-note pieces: Schumann's Toccata in C.

trusty Bach-Busoni Toccata, Adagio and Fugue, followed by Scriabin's Ninth Sonata and Poem in F♯, and Chopin's Mazurka in C♯ Minor, Etude in F, op. 10, and Ballade in G Minor. Four relatively modest encores (Debussy's *Serenade for the Doll*, Scriabin's Etude in C♯ Minor, Moszkowski's Etude in A♭ Major, and Schumann's *Träumerei*), compared to Paderewski's seven, rounded off an evening of music similar in layout to but not much longer than half the length of his great predecessor's recital.

We are, Jim Samson tells us, in the "post-recital age."[93] In so far as the piano recital has now been supplanted by a host of other media as the most common way to experience professionally played piano music, this is undoubtedly true. Nevertheless, the recital has retained its iconic importance in the training of pianists and in the way the classical concert world is organized. Piano students still work toward building repertoire for recital programs, the examinations at the end of their course of study usually put the greatest emphasis upon them, and woe betide any would-be professional concert pianist who does not have several programs that he can trot out at short notice in response to a call from an agent or impresario. Although the historical survey, "single-great-composer," and "complete this and that" models of recital construction are not the only ones to be heard today (programs of transcriptions are certainly making a come-back), they have been strikingly tenacious and pervasive—in outline if not in duration—for the last century or so. That they have become significantly shorter than the Herculean offerings of Anton Rubinstein and his contemporaries is indeed a "post-recital age" phenomenon.

If our only chance to hear the canon of piano masterworks played professionally is at a live concert, then naturally a comprehensive program of enormous length may seem to offer satisfying value for money, even if the pianist doesn't get through the entire event without the odd memory slip or three. If we can hear a Beethoven sonata any time we choose to put on a CD, then the quantity-versus-quality argument takes on another perspective. I am not slighting the reputation of Anton Rubinstein's playing here, or indeed that of any of the masters of the past who programmed generously. Rather, I am simply suggesting that the recording age gave pianists another good reason to pay attention to their audiences' ability to concentrate on longer programs, and on their own ability to play them. The much higher demands for accuracy in performance fostered (perhaps regrettably) by recordings has also meant likely career suicide for those who too often take the risk of playing like Rubinstein at his most inaccurate or

---

[93] Samson, "The Practice of Early Nineteenth-Century Pianism," 23.

d'Albert at his most slapdash. Rosenthal reckoned that Rubinstein had around 180 works in his active repertoire, but some of them had been imperfectly mastered, and "if there was a large number of such 'dangerous' pieces on the programme, the result was a bad evening."[94] Most of us have to be more circumspect now, but there have certainly been huge losses in spontaneity along with the gains in right notes.[95]

A knowledge of the historically contingent nature of recital programming should be liberating for the pianist interested in trying out new patterns. There is no reason to worship the standard outline as a divinely ordained design, brought down from the mountain by Moses on a supplementary tablet along with the Ten Commandments, even if we are sometimes forced to conform to it to get a degree or diploma or to satisfy the marketing departments of recording companies. As we have seen, much of the music that makes up our standard recitals was composed long before such programs were a practical possibility for a public concert, and when they did become so, many composers, critics, and audiences reacted to them with less than unalloyed enthusiasm. Such things as Beethoven sonata cycles or series of concerts comprising Bach's complete *Well-Tempered Clavier* are programs designed as much for a box set of CDs as for a live audience. Financial considerations, if nothing else, would put significant obstacles in the way of a general return to the "variety" program involving a host of artists.[96] But rethinking the organization of our solo recitals, including the placing of the mid-concert break, if there is to be one, might allow us more regularly to fit in pieces of awkward length or gargantuan demands, like the Alkan op. 39 Solo Concerto. And what of the once common practice of playing isolated movements from sonatas or other such works? Would a return to this really be so dreadful, or would it encourage us to present more frequently attractive single movements of pieces that are rarely given as a whole anyway? Nothing is set in stone.

[94] Mitchell and Evans, 102.

[95] See chapter 3, pp. 97–100.

[96] Such "throwback" mixed programs, each showcasing many different performers, are an interesting feature of the music festivals held in Bard College, New York, in recent years.

# 3

# With Due Respect

Ehrt eure deutschen Meister, dann bannt ihr gute Geister [Honor your German masters; you'll conjure up benevolent spirits].

—Richard Wagner, *Die Meistersinger von Nürnberg*

## And All from Memory

The strain on the performer of the late-nineteenth-century marathon concert was even more severe than on the audience, especially considering the increasing tendency to play entire recitals from memory, with due respect to the great (usually German) musical masterpieces of the past. We might, nevertheless, express some skepticism over Amy Fay's belief that Tausig "died . . . of typhus fever, brought on by overtaxing his musical memory."[1] Rubinstein, at least, did not suffer from "death owing to memorization," despite the length of his programs. But it is not surprising that his legendary memory suffered equally legendary lapses, which grew more and more severe as he got older. He himself perhaps even understated the case when he admitted:

My musical memory . . . until my fiftieth year was prodigious, but since then I have been conscious of a growing weakness. I begin to feel an uncertainty; something like a nervous dread often takes possession of me while I am on stage in the presence of a large audience. . . . One can hardly imagine how painful this sensation may be. I often fear lest memory betray me into forgetfulness of a passage, and that I may unconsciously change it. The public has always been accustomed to see me play without notes, for I have never used them; and I will not allow myself to rely upon my own resources to supply the place of some forgotten passage, because I know that there will always be many among my audiences who, being familiar with the piece I am performing, will readily detect

[1] Fay, 127.

73

any alteration. This sense of uncertainty has often inflicted upon me torture only to be compared with those of the Inquisition, while the public listening to me imagine that I am perfectly calm.[2]

Stories of Rubinstein's memory difficulties in performance are legion and include forgetting parts of his own D-Minor Concerto.[3] Leschetizky, once the conductor of a performance of the Schumann concerto with Rubinstein as soloist, was forced to stop the orchestra when he took a disastrous wrong turn in the first movement. He blustered away for several minutes playing anything that randomly came to mind, until he luckily arrived at a passage from the cadenza that Leschetizky recognized, enabling him desperately to cue the bewildered orchestra back in.[4] Similar disasters happened not infrequently to Alfred Cortot, whose conductor on one memorable (or not) occasion, Sir Thomas Beecham, suavely quipped: "We started with the Beethoven, and I kept up with Cortot through the Grieg, Schumann, Bach and Tchaikovsky, and then he hit on one I didn't know, so I stopped dead." Ironically, Cortot was a staunch supporter of the idea that pianists should play their solo repertoire from memory. There was "certainly no harm" in playing things through from the music, he conceded, but serious study of a piece required memorization.[5] Josef Hofmann agreed that playing by heart was "indispensable to the freedom of rendition."[6] Leschetizky, despite the warning of his experiences with Rubinstein, advised his pupils to fix pieces in their memory before beginning to practice them in detail; they were subsequently discouraged from consulting the score except when their recall was found to be wanting.[7] Leschetizky did, however, also expound some slick stratagems about what to do when the memory failed, which included turning angrily to the audience, complaining a note was disgracefully out of tune, and then leaving the stage demanding a tuner be called. The pianist could then surreptitiously consult his score in the artist's room while the tuner dealt with the allegedly offending note.[8] Bülow, with his usual dogmatism, declared flatly that

[2] Rubinstein, *Autobiography*, 17–18.

[3] Lott, 183.

[4] Annette Hullah, *Theodore Leschetizky* (London: John Lane, 1906), 14–15.

[5] Jeffrey Johnson, ed., *Piano Mastery: The Harriet Brower Interviews, 1915–1926* (Mineola, N.Y.: Dover, 2003), 162–63.

[6] Joseph Hofmann, *Piano Playing with Piano Questions Answered* (Mineola, N.Y.: Dover, 1976), 112 in "Piano Questions Answered."

[7] Brée, 75–77.

[8] A. Newcomb, 136–37.

no one could call himself an artist who did not have at least 200 pieces firmly fixed in the memory.[9] How he arrived at the magic figure is nowhere recorded.

Yet it is obvious from the passage in Rubinstein's memoirs just quoted that the "requirement" for pianists of playing from memory, which, once encouraged, gained ineluctable force as the century drew to its close, was self-inflicted—"the public has always been accustomed to see me play without notes." Rubinstein's fear of "unconsciously changing a passage," moreover, seems amusingly ironic in the light of his notoriously extensive conscious changes. What we have here is not the modern preoccupation with respect for the score, but simply a worry about losing control. In the first decades of the century there was no such worry. Performing without the music was certainly not a requirement, and so doing would often be specially remarked upon by reviewers. Czerny, whose own powers of recall were developed to an unusually high degree, recommended memorizing pieces for performance in larger venues, but it is clear that his advice was only partially followed by his contemporaries. The young Clara Wieck was encouraged to memorize by her father—Robert Schumann mentions this specifically in his biographical note on Clara—but her "pretentiousness" in so doing was not looked upon with favor by some.[10] Mendelssohn's prodigious musical memory drew particular attention to itself. His masterly performances of Beethoven's *Emperor* Concerto and Weber's *Konzertstück* excited bewildered admiration, although playing such concerted works by heart is routine now. This is not to imply that evolution has miraculously provided us with more retentive memories in the space of not much more than a century and a half, but simply that custom forces us to memorize. That Mendelssohn's musical memory was extraordinary even by present-day standards is demonstrated by several accounts of his memorization—seemingly more or less by accident—of long piano accompaniments and even of individual parts in orchestral scores. This outstanding ability obviously aided him in his concert improvisations, as no doubt was also the case with Liszt.

Some contemporary drawings of Liszt in concert clearly show a score before him—even if he did play many things in his central repertoire without the music. An article in the *Wiener Zeitschrift für Kunst* of 5 May 1838 was in awe of his

---

[9] Jeffrey Johnson, *Piano Mastery*, 200.

[10] Nancy Reich, *Clara Schumann: The Artist and the Woman* (Ithaca, N.Y.: Cornell University Press, 1985), 280. Kehler's blanket statements that Clara Schumann was the first pianist to play in public from memory and that "up to 1840, no pianist played the works of a master-pianist without the notes in front of him" (Kehler, 1:xxxiii) are demonstrably—and unsurprisingly—incorrect.

"astonishing memory, that allows him to play several hundred pieces by heart,"[11] but since this was written (under a pseudonym) by one of Liszt's very own Viennese publishers, Pietro Mechetti, and since he had played nowhere near hundreds of pieces (around twenty, in fact) during the four Viennese concerts he had given just before Mechetti's encomium, one might reasonably suspect more than a little exaggeration here. It was all part of the bourgeoning Liszt legend. Liszt had indeed played Beethoven's *Emperor* Concerto (one of only a handful of concertos in his active repertoire) so frequently from memory that the critic J. W. Davison remarked on how unusual it was that he had the score in front of him for a performance during the 1845 Beethoven monument celebrations in Bonn. But when Davison reflected on all the difficulties Liszt had to endure while organizing the event, he considered it remarkable that he had managed to play at all.[12] For Liszt's Berlin public recitals of 1841–42, somewhat more than half of the (few dozen) items appear to have been performed without the score, a far cry from the level usually expected today and hardly deserving of the stunned astonishment of some of his biographers, but enough to amaze his audiences. Liszt's playing from memory of Beethoven's *Moonlight* Sonata as an encore by public request at an 1840 concert in Hamburg was acclaimed in the press as an exceptional feat.[13]

In 1874, long after his official "retirement" from the concert platform, Liszt took part in a charity concert in Vienna, performing his Hungarian Fantasy for Piano and Orchestra and his own arrangement of Schubert's *Wanderer* Fantasy for the same forces. Characteristically for Liszt, when he looked at the music and when he didn't, and even his mild myopia, became part of the act. As Hanslick noticed:

> Not only does one listen with breathless attention to his playing; one also observes its reflection in the fine lines of his face. His head, thrown back, still suggests something of Jupiter. Sometimes the eyes flash beneath the prominent brows; sometimes the characteristically upturned corners of the mouth are raised even higher in a gentle smile. Head, eyes, and sometimes even a helping hand, maintain constant communication with orchestra and audience. Sometimes he plays from notes, at other times from memory, putting on and taking off his spectacles accordingly. Sometimes his head is bent forward attentively, sometimes thrown back boldly. All this has the utmost fascination for his listeners—particularly feminine listeners.[14]

---

[11] Quoted from Legany, 40.
[12] Saffle, 177.
[13] Saffle, 107.
[14] Pleasants, *Hanslick's Music Criticisms*, 110.

But Liszt was Liszt and was not expected to conform to the increasing pressure for routine memorization that by 1874 was gradually taking hold. In 1878 the *Musical Times* could still describe a performance by heart of Brahms's *Variations on a Theme by Handel* as an "extraordinary feat," adding that "such mental efforts are, indeed, not now altogether uncommon among executive artists, but they never fail, as yet, to act as a surprise when exhibited."[15] By 1892 the surprise was over, and Pachmann was granted little indulgence for his lack of confidence in his powers of recall. When he performed Beethoven's Third Concerto in London with the score in front of him, a reviewer remarked—with negative implication—upon it.[16] One experience of a bad memory lapse made Pachmann understandably reluctant to play concertos without the notes, but he could do little against the fact that by the turn of the century playing from memory had become virtually a sine qua non for pianists in the solo and concerto repertoire. Busoni's pupil Leo Sirota once recalled working feverishly to master Brahms's *Paganini Variations* in the space of only a week for a lesson with his teacher. Despite Sirota's accomplished performance, Busoni's reaction had been one of enormous disappointment—because he hadn't played from memory. Busoni had indeed committed himself publicly on the issue, writing that playing by heart was "necessary for freedom and precision."[17] The argument that it also increased a player's nervousness was met with scant sympathy. If the score was on the music stand, then anxiety would just focus itself on some other area of performance. Busoni's message was a bleak one: stage fright, like the poor, will always be with us.

Whence came this pressure to memorize? In the early part of the nineteenth century, it was not only unusual, but sometimes unwelcome. When Beethoven discovered that his pupil Czerny was giving private performances of his music from memory to Prince Lichnowsky in the years 1804–5, he was not pleased at all. He complained that Czerny would begin to lose the skill to play at sight, the ability to get a quick overall impression of a piece, and even sometimes the habit of giving the correct emphasis (*richtige Betonung*) in performance.[18] The last point is rather ambiguous, but perhaps Beethoven was convinced that an obsession with remembering the notes would be to the detriment of attention to dynamics, articulation, and expression. George Barth has intriguingly argued that it was

[15] Percy Scholes, *The Mirror of Music, 1844–1944: A Century of Musical Life in Britain as Reflected in the Pages of "The Musical Times"* (London: Novello and Oxford University Press, 1947), 1:321.

[16] Mitchell, 26.

[17] Ferrucio Busoni, *Wesen und Einheit der Musik*, ed. Joachim Hermann (Berlin: Max Hesses Verlag, 1956), 118.

[18] Czerny, *Über den richtigen Vortrag*, 14.

Czerny's imperfect memory for phrasing that concerned Beethoven, and that the frequent discrepancies between the music examples in Czerny's treatise *Über den richtigen Vortrag* (On the Correct Performance [of Beethoven's piano music]) and the relevant passages in contemporary editions can be partly accounted for by Czerny having written out some of the examples from memory.[19] At any rate, Beethoven seems to have held entirely the opposite view from those who later claimed that memorization was essential for unfettered attention to musical detail.

And he had many who agreed with him. Chopin was angry when he discovered that one of his students was intending to play the Nocturne op. 9 no. 2 for him from memory, and what is more had failed to bring the score along at all. "I don't want any of this: are you reciting a lesson?" he complained.[20] Charles Hallé encountered a similar reaction from audiences. He had started his Beethoven 1861–62 sonata cycle in London without the music on the stand, but by the third concert he responded to public disapproval and put the score in front of him. He still felt that looking at the music was unnecessary, but for his auditors the memorized performances had seemed more arrogant than astonishing. Even as late as the 1870s in London, according to Harold Bauer, "artists who played solos 'by heart' . . . were criticized openly for lacking in respect both for the audience and for the composer by indulging in such theatrical display."[21]

As far as Beethoven had been concerned, knowing the music well enough to play without the score was not just a matter of respect or accuracy, but the unnecessary mixing up of two areas that should be kept distinct: the performance of previously worked out music, and improvisation. In his day, the performer was normally without a score only when improvising. There would thus be an explicit visual contrast between the performance of composed pieces (from the notes) and a free fantasy. In the first (1828) publication of his treatise on piano playing, the famed improviser Hummel devoted a slender page to explaining how he trained himself in the art, but in response to insistent requests he extended this section considerably in later editions.[22] At the end of his learning process, he

---

[19] George Barth, *The Pianist as Orator: Beethoven and the Transformation of Keyboard Style* (Ithaca, N.Y.: Cornell University Press, 1992), 96–97.

[20] Eigeldinger, *Chopin: Pianist and Teacher*, 28.

[21] Bauer, 16–17. According to Constance Bache (*Brother Musicians: Reminiscences of Edward and Walter Bache* [London: Methuen, 1901], 26–27), Arabella Goddard elicited astonishment by playing Beethoven's *Hammerklavier* Sonata from memory in London in 1853, "a procedure which in the case of other pianists later and greater was severely reprehended!"

[22] A subsequent edition of Hummel's treatise, probably from 1829, treats improvisation much more extensively.

claimed, it was less trouble for him to improvise before an audience of 2,000–3,000 listeners than to play a composition from a score "to which I would be slavishly tied."[23] In the same decade, the young Liszt, according to a review of an 1824 Paris concert, played a set of variations for piano and orchestra by Czerny during which he "scarcely looked at his notes, and then only at long intervals. His eyes wandered continually around the hall, and he greeted the persons he recognized in the boxes with friendly smiles and nods." After this he cast "stand and notes aside, and gave himself up to his genius in a free fantasy."[24] It is evident that even at the age of twelve, Liszt was not insensible to the interest an audience would take in his engagement (or lack of it) with the printed score. It was there in front of him, but he made sure everyone saw he didn't really need it. The difference to be demonstrated, however, was still that between the performance of printed music and the spontaneity of improvisation.

In 1850s Weimar, when Liszt was trying to make a name for himself as a composer rather than a performer, playing from the score served a related purpose—to demonstrate that his compositions were seriously thought out, and more than just offshoots of his concert improvisations. His intent was to claim for them a place in the developing canon. Critics had constantly carped that he was a superb pianist, a gifted improviser, and a wonderful arranger, but had next to no talent for original composition. Even an enthusiastic supporter like the journalist Heinrich Adami, for whom Liszt could almost do no wrong, had thought that the first version of the *Dante* Sonata, when performed in 1839 in Vienna under the title "Fragment nach Dante," sounded like an improvisation.[25] In determining to prove that he was a "real" composer, he always ostentatiously—and no doubt unnecessarily—used a score when playing to visitors pieces such as the Sonata in B Minor or the *Bénédiction de Dieu dans la solitude*, works he rightly believed to be his compositional proofs of mastery.[26] Of course, there was a big difference between playing from notes a piece that had been thoroughly studied and giving a stiff, nervous performance of a work one hardly knew with the eyes glued to the page, as Clara Schumann remarked of one of Liszt's Leipzig concerts (see pp. 230–31). But the deciding factor, sensibly enough, seemed to be mastery of the music, not memory of the score.

---

[23] J. N. Hummel, *Ausführliche theoretisch-practische Anweisung zum Piano-Forte-Spiel* (Vienna: Haslinger, 1828), 444.

[24] Review from *Le drapeau blanc* (9 March 1824). Quoted in Walker, *Franz Liszt: The Virtuoso Years*, 100.

[25] Legany, 70.

[26] Mason, 118–19.

As the practice of concert improvisation slowly declined, so the practice of playing from memory increasingly flourished. Performing a composition by heart fostered the impression that interpretation could have the freedom and spontaneity of an improvisation, but linked to music of greater complexity and— implicitly—quality.[27] For Czerny this was the main reason to learn things from memory, as he later pointed out in his op. 500 *Pianoforte School*. The illusion of improvisation, of course, worked best when there was no genuine full-scale improvisation on the program to spoil the effect, and it is hardly a coincidence that Tausig and Rubinstein, who were famous for always playing their entire solo programs from memory, confined their improvisation to the standard preludes and transitions between pieces. In their wake, it became a sign of seriousness to have memorized the program: it showed due reverence to the masterworks presumably contained therein. There was also, doubtless, the attraction for the audience of what Bauer called "the element of danger"—the exciting risk that the player might fall off the tightrope of memory and sprawl briefly on the ground, revealed as a fallible human being.[28] When Bülow played in London in 1873, the *Musical Times* superciliously commented that he "created an excitement which must be partially credited to the fact of his performing entirely from memory, a feat which, from a purely artistic point of view, claims but small acknowledgement."[29]

Whatever the attractions of the gamble with memory, the establishment of the practice as virtually a sine qua non for a professional solo performer has had the unfortunate consequence that "no pianist can play the whole piano repertoire," as Schnabel once baldly told a student.[30] Horowitz, for example, reputedly played privately a vast number of pieces, but the number he essayed in public was relatively small. There can scarcely be a player who has not felt restricted in the same way. Memorization is additionally, like so many other aspects of modern performance style, a profoundly unhistorical way of playing much of our concert music, which was composed before it became customary or even welcome.

What is more, routinely forsaking the score isolates contemporary music. Players are silently excused memorizing it, not only because its complexity often renders it phenomenally difficult to remember accurately (Pollini's memorization of Pierre Boulez's Second Sonata was rightly regarded as a stupendous

---

[27] Some modern research claims to demonstrate that audiences often do indeed perceive memorized performances this way. See Aaron Williamon, "Memorising Music," in Rink, 113–26.

[28] Bauer, 17.

[29] Scholes, 1:315.

[30] Artur Schnabel, *Aus dir wird nie ein Pianist* (Hofheim: Wolke Verlag, 1991), 157.

achievement), but also because it is felt frequently to be a waste of time. After all, who wants to spend enormous effort learning by heart a complicated piece that one may get the chance to perform only once or twice? It is no coincidence that the growth of the custom of playing from memory went hand in hand with the establishment of a canonic repertoire. Until we know for sure that a piece is going to be a permanent fixture, it's sensible to have the score on the stand.

There are certainly some who have tried to resist the expectation of memorizing solo repertoire. Sviatoslav Richter notably performed with the music during his later years. "Following an absolutely frightful concert," he recalled, "that I gave at the Fêtes Musicales de Touraine, when I played eight of Liszt's *Transcendental Studies*, and a recital in Japan, where I took fright even before launching into Beethoven's op. 106 Sonata, I made up my mind never again to play without a score."[31] Since he did not seem to need or want the score in front of him in his younger days, it was easy to discount this decision as a forced concession to failing powers of recall, rather than a free artistic choice. (Clara Schumann too became increasingly worried about forgetting the music in her later years.) Richter even managed to make something of a theatrical virtue out of his new need for the score, reading the music by the light of a standard lamp while insisting that the rest of the hall be enshrouded in Bayreuth-like darkness. The audience now had no option but to concentrate on the performer—they couldn't see well enough even to leaf through their program notes.

Long before Richter, Percy Grainger had railed against the memorization requirement while still mostly conforming to it, quite in contrast to Cortot and others who argued that memorization was a prerequisite for interpretative seriousness. "It is to be regretted," Grainger said in an interview, "that the custom prevails of playing everything without notes. I think many a fine pianist is greatly worried over a fear of failure of memory. This may affect his playing; it may prevent the freedom of utterance he might have, were he relieved of the fear of forgetting. . . . It is no wonder that even the greatest artists occasionally forget. Most artists would play more naturally with notes before them—if accustomed to use them."[32] And Grainger's perfect compromise? "The comfortable, the ideal way, I suppose, would be to really know the piece from memory, yet play from the notes." In other words, the custom of the early nineteenth century. Back to the future, indeed.

[31] Bruno Monsaingeon, *Sviatoslav Richter: Notebooks and Conversations*, trans. Stewart Spencer (London: Faber and Faber, 2001), 142.

[32] Jeffrey Johnson, *Piano Mastery*, 101–2.

## Who Cares about Applause?

If the pianist should take the trouble to learn by heart a great masterwork, how should an audience behave while listening to it? The modern answer—with great respect in hushed silence—is a relatively recent expectation, and one that was certainly not welcomed by all pianists. For the nineteenth century, silent, contemplative listening—as in Paderewski's film—was more characteristic of renditions of serious music at the homes of connoisseurs than of any truly public event, let alone a performance of piece such as a Liszt Hungarian Rhapsody in a large hall.[33] It was an idealized type of listening, particularly revered in the German-speaking world, and one that was really only expected to be found in private, cultured circles. Josef Danhauser's iconic portrait of 1840, *Franz Liszt Fantasizing at the Piano* (*Franz Liszt, am Flügel phantasierend*, also sometimes known as *Eine Matinee bei Liszt*) is a well-known image of such an ideal occasion, created in the wake of Liszt's staggering Viennese successes in the previous two years.[34]

There is some disagreement as to who exactly is portrayed in this enormously well-known picture, which should give us an initial hint that the image may belong as much to myth as to reality. All present are certainly artists of some sort—musicians or writers—and the setting seems to be an unspecified music room of Liszt's (or perhaps of his then partner, Marie d'Agoult's). It must at least be somewhere in Paris, because it is inconceivable that all the figures portrayed—doyens of French romanticism—should just happen to find themselves together anywhere else. Danhauser knew Liszt personally and even made him a treasured present of Beethoven's death mask, taken by him on the composer's demise in 1827, but he rarely traveled from Vienna and is unlikely to have made the acquaintance of most of the other persons in the picture, or indeed to have seen Liszt's Parisian accommodation, whatever that would have been. By 1840 Liszt had not been permanently resident in Paris for a number of years, and when he did visit he often rented an apartment in a hotel (the alternative to be avoided was staying at his mother's). Bizarrely, considering the presumably Parisian setting, the piano is a Viennese Graf—a decision that may seem less

---

[33] For a related discussion on the changing behavior of Parisian audiences, see James H. Johnson's perceptive and entertaining *Listening in Paris: A Cultural History* (Berkeley: University of California Press, 1995), especially 228–36, "The Social Roots of Silence."

[34] See Richard Leppert, "Cultural Contradiction, Idolatry and the Piano Virtuoso, Franz Liszt," in Parakilas, 256–57; also Katharine Ellis, "Liszt: The Romantic Artist," in Hamilton, *Cambridge Companion to Liszt*, 8–10.

FIGURE 3.1. Josef Danhauser, *Liszt am Flügel phantasierend* (by permission of the Bildarchiv Preussischer Kulturbesitz)

peculiar if we remember that the picture had been commissioned by none other than Conrad Graf himself.

Of the identity of the female listeners there can be no doubt. The Countess d'Agoult, with her back to the viewer, and George Sand are swooning in artistic ecstasy. The male figures—including Victor Hugo, Rossini, and Berlioz (or Paganini) standing, and Alexandre Dumas (or Alfred de Musset) seated[35]—are

---

[35] According to the Berlin National Gallery, which owns the painting, the male figure standing on the far left is Berlioz. Most commentators, however, seem to think this is a representation of Victor Hugo (there is a copy of one of his writings in his hand). According to Leppert (see n. 34), with Rossini is an "improbably fit" Paganini; according to Ellis (see n. 34), the figure is Berlioz (presumably, then, an improbably ill Berlioz). I suspect the latter is correct, though either is possible. With George Sand is Alexandre Dumas, père, according to Leppert. It certainly looks more like pictures of the young, slim Dumas than the (full-bearded) portraits of Alfred de Musset, but considering the carefree position of George Sand's right hand, it might be that the latter, with whom she was in a relationship from 1833 to 1835, was intended. On the other hand, you never know what went on with these artistic types . . .

respectfully fixated on the performance, giving it their undivided, silent, more intellectual attention. Liszt, for his part, has a score open in front of him. Yet he seems nevertheless to be playing from memory, in Percy Grainger's ideal fashion, for his visionary gaze is directed not at the music, but at the bust of Beethoven that seems to hover in a gravity-defying manner between the piano and the window. Just in case the viewer is in any doubt of the allegorical, echt-romantic nature of the occasion, a portrait of Lord Byron hangs on the wall. We do not know exactly what theme Liszt is fantasizing upon—but the eyes fixed on Beethoven's stern countenance (a depiction of a bust by Anton Dietrich) gives us a hint that it is not the *Grand galop chromatique*.

In fact the whole image seems like a fantastically intensified version of a genuine incident of 1831, which Danhauser may have heard about from Liszt or read something of in newspapers (Berlioz had written up slightly differing accounts of it in the *Journal des débats* and elsewhere)[36] although it did not appear in the form quoted here until Ernest Legouvé's *Memoirs* of 1886. Liszt played the first movement of Beethoven's *Moonlight* Sonata to a similarly enraptured private group, Berlioz among them. According to Legouvé,

> I had invited a few friends around one evening: Liszt, Goubaux, Schoelcher, Sue, and half a dozen others. Berlioz was one of us. "Liszt," he said, "why not play us a Beethoven Sonata." From my study we passed into the salon.... There were no lights, and the fire in the grate had burned very low. Goubaux brought the lamp from my study, while Liszt went to the piano and the rest of us sought seats. "Turn up the wick," I told Goubaux....But instead he turned it down, plunging us into blackness, or, rather, into full shadow; and this sudden transition from light to dark, coming together with the first notes of the piano, had a moving effect on every one of us.... Whether by chance or by some unconscious influence, Liszt began the funereal and heart-rending adagio of the Sonata in C♯ Minor. The rest of us remained rooted to the spot where we happened to be, no one attempting to move....I had dropped into an armchair, and above my head heard stifled sobs and moans. It was Berlioz.[37]

This reminiscence too is presented as idealized listening—complete concentration on the music from auditors who are themselves artists, and who can

---

[36] *Journal des débats*, 12 March 1837. Also in *À travers chants*, 83–85.

[37] Ernest Legouvé, *Soixante ans de souvenirs*, vol.1 (Paris, 1886), 297–98. Quoted in translation in Williams, *Portrait of Liszt*, 42–43.

understand—or at least feel vividly—what they hear. There is no suggestion of any overt acknowledgement of the performer—no bravos, no applause at the end. The performance, in fact, is quite literally invisible—Beethoven's music emerging from the dark as if from a recording. Only Berlioz's involuntary sobbing disturbs the contemplation, itself a sign of the intensity of the moment. If the incident itself had a basis in reality, with Danhauser it is further idealized and turned into propaganda for Liszt and his artistic mission. A very similar picture (yet again from Vienna and also entitled *Eine Matinee bei Liszt*) came in 1846, after Liszt's next main round of Viennese concerts, from the hand of Josef Kriehuber. (Danhauser was unavailable—he had died the year before.) Liszt's adoring listeners here were Berlioz, Czerny, the violinist Heinrich Wilhelm Ernst, and (a nice touch this) Kriehuber himself. The many points of resemblance between this and the Danhauser portrait, including Liszt's ethereal demeanor at the keyboard, confirm that it was modeled on the earlier work and also propagandistic in intent (copies were to be had at the music shop of Carl Haslinger, one of Liszt's Viennese publishers). Yet again the auditors are an imaginary assembly. A hitherto unrecognized artistic affinity between Berlioz and Czerny should not be inferred—they are merely here as components of Liszt's biography. The presence of the Countess d'Agoult in the 1840 grouping and her Stalinesque disappearance in 1846 do, nevertheless, pretty accurately reflect recent developments in his personal life.

Concerts today often attempt to replicate this supposedly ideal, intimate listening, but there is usually an unavoidable tension between this and the public nature of the event. The portraits, of course, were as much a fantasy as Paderewski's recital in *Moonlight Sonata*. Can anybody ever have believed that six of Paris's most famous figures took time out to pose for a few hours one day at Liszt's place for a group portrait? Liszt's own public concerts in Vienna were packed, noisy, at times almost riotous affairs, far from Danhauser's or Kriehuber's *Matinee*. Many hundreds or even thousands of people in a large hall transparently does not make for an intimate, contemplative atmosphere. Indeed, such an internalized audience response in a public concert would have been thought inappropriate, even downright peculiar, for much of the nineteenth century, when the yardstick of success for a pianist was not the silence of the audience, but exactly the opposite. Accordingly, George Bernard Shaw in 1885 felt sure that he was not alone in his opinion of the demerits of Liszt's *Dante* Symphony at a London concert when, after the first movement, "the majority of the audience...showed by their silence that the composer had gone too far in offering them this obscene instrumental orgy as a serious comment on a great poem."[38] Obviously a few tolerant souls had still applauded.

Nineteenth-century concert practice accepted, sometimes reluctantly, that the audience would give what amounted to a running commentary on the performance—if, that is, the performer was lucky enough to engage their attention at all. Particularly effective passages at any point in a work could be applauded or rewarded with bravos, even encored on some occasions. "I have always had applause after the cadenza," Bülow told his students with some satisfaction in the late 1880s.[39] He was not referring to the end of a work, but to the opening cadenza of Beethoven's *Emperor* Concerto. Beethoven himself would have shared Bülow's pleasure. Silence, he declared, "is not what we artists wish—we want applause."[40] Applause could well have drowned out a fair amount of the orchestral tutti of any concerted piece, as in fact it did once when Chopin performed his *Variations on "Là ci darem"* for Piano and Orchestra. The audience showed its loud appreciation after each one.[41] Indeed, many of the variation sets of the time for piano and orchestra (such as those of Herz, or even the first version of *Hexameron* by Liszt et al.) have the odd, especially dull orchestra ritornello interpolated between variations, presumably envisaged as a background to the audience's applause. (In the score of *Hexameron*, Liszt instructs the pianist simply to omit some of these passages when the work is played without orchestra.)

In his edition of Beethoven's op. 26 Sonata, the first movement of which is also a set of variations, Bülow showed himself alive to the problems of continuity frequent bursts of clapping between sections might bring. He advises the player to make the transitions between the variations of the first movement "as imperceptible as possible," in order to avoid applause that might interrupt the flow from one to another. Nevertheless, he acknowledged that applause is quite in order for bravura variation sets. Harold Bauer even claimed that in late-nineteenth-century London, applause after the second variation of the slow movement of Beethoven's *Kreutzer* Sonata was so routine that performers were

[38] George Bernard Shaw, *The Great Composers: Reviews and Bombardments*, ed. Louis Crompton (Berkeley: University of California Press, 1978), 133.

[39] Richard Zimdars, trans. and ed., *The Piano Masterclasses of Hans von Bülow* (Bloomington: Indiana University Press, 1993), 44.

[40] Eliot Forbes, *Thayer's Life of Beethoven* (Princeton, N.J.: Princeton University Press, 1964), 1:187.

[41] B. E. Sydow, ed., *Korespondencja Fryderyka Chopina* (Warsaw: Panstwowy Instytut Wydawniczy, 1955), 1:37.

"intensely mortified" should it fail to arise.[42] Leschetizky would advise his students to avoid pausing after certain first movements—"you will have applause if you do, and it may spoil your quiet mood for the second movement—it might break the thread; hold the pedal a little longer then go straight on."[43] Bülow even had to interrupt the Fugue of Beethoven's op. 106 at a Paris concert in 1860 because the audience was determined to show its appreciation.[44]

Applause, however, was usually welcome. Busoni was easily able to judge the success of his London performance of *Hexameron* in 1897 directly from the ardor and timing of the clapping. He reported delightedly to his wife that there was enormous applause after the theme itself, and then after every variation.[45] A triumph, certainly, but in fact the London audience was relatively restrained—at least they waited till the end of each section. In Berlin in 1920 the audience started clapping in the middle of Busoni's performance of Liszt's *La campanella*,[46] and an audience in Chicago interrupted his performance of the complete Chopin op. 25 Etudes with demands for an encore after no. 9.[47]

Such incidents were certainly becoming rarer by 1920. In 1931 Rachmaninoff would gauge public reaction to his *Corelli Variations* not by applause, but by the amount of discreet coughing during each variation—too much meant the audience was bored, and he would cut the subsequent variations accordingly.[48] A both visible and loudly audible audience was absolutely commonplace a century before. Liszt was fond of telling his students how the public would go wild at performances of his fantasies on Bellini's *La sonnambula* or Meyerbeer's *Robert le diable*, especially at the climactic combinations of themes. During a Paris concert in the 1840s when he played the latter piece, the applause supposedly lasted a good ten minutes before he was able to carry on to the final pages (but maybe it just seemed like ten minutes).[49] Charles Hallé recalled a related incident in 1841:

---

[42] Bauer, 13–14.

[43] A. Newcomb, 139.

[44] Haas, 50.

[45] Friedrich Schnapp, ed., *Ferruccio Busoni: Briefe an seine Frau, 1895–1907* (Zurich: Rotapfel Verlag, 1934), 17.

[46] Dent, 253.

[47] Couling, 187.

[48] Barry Martyn, *Rachmaninoff: Composer, Pianist, Conductor* (Aldershot: Scholar Press, 1990), 320.

[49] According to Liszt's own account in August Göllerich, *Franz Liszt* (Berlin: Marquardt Verlag, 1908), 109. There are two slightly different versions of this story in the Göllerich diaries and in Lachmund's *Living with Liszt*, but the general point remains the same.

The programme given in the Salle du Conservatoire contained the *Kreutzer* Sonata, to be played by Liszt and [Lambert] Massart, a celebrated and much esteemed violinist. Massart was just commencing the first bar of the introduction when a voice cried out "Robert le Diable!!" At that time Liszt had composed a very brilliant fantasy on themes from that opera, and played it always with immense success. The call was taken up by other voices, and in a moment the cries of "Robert le Diable! Robert le Diable!" drowned the tones of the violin. Liszt rose, bowed, and said, "Je suis toujours l'humble serviteur du public, mais est-ce qu'on desire la fantaisie avant ou après la Sonate?" [I am always the humble servant of the public, but do you want the fantasy before or after the Sonata?] Renewed cries of "Robert, Robert!" were the answer, upon which Liszt turned half round to poor Massart and dismissed him with a wave of the hand, without a syllable of excuse or regret. He did play the fantasy magnificently, rousing the public to a frenzy of enthusiasm, then called Massart out of his retreat, and we had the *Kreutzer*, which somehow no longer seemed in its right place.[50]

This was not an isolated demonstration. A little later Liszt was again encouraged to play the *Robert le diable* Fantasy by a persistent audience before he commenced a performance of Beethoven's *Emperor* Concerto, conducted by Berlioz. Richard Wagner, who was then in Paris as a correspondent for a German newspaper, wrote that one day Liszt would no doubt be expected to play his fantasy on the Devil before St. Peter and the assembled company of angels—as his very last performance.[51] And such audience enthusiasm was not just confined to Liszt's fantasies. Thalberg was insistently called upon to play his greatest hit, the Fantasy on Rossini's *Moses in Egypt*, by a clamorous audience at a Paris concert in 1838. This he duly did, the only problem being that it was not actually his concert. The performer was supposed to be Döhler, and Thalberg had simply been sitting in the hall waiting to hear him.[52]

These examples of spirited audience outbursts are more comprehensible when seen in the context of the much more relaxed nineteenth-century concert etiquette—radically different from the extreme formality that is lamentably the accepted practice today. Writing in the 1940s, Percy Scholes deplored the scene depicted in two drawings of London concerts from a century before, in which

[50] Hallé, 88–89.

[51] Robert L. Jacobs and Geoffrey Skelton, trans., *Wagner Writes from Paris* (London: Allen and Unwin, 1973), 133–34.

[52] Henri Blanchard, *Revue et gazette musicale de Paris*, 5/16 (22 April 1838), 168.

some "auditors" were shown standing, some sitting, and many talking. "The behaviour of the audience," he grandly declared, "is, by our modern standards, unsatisfactory."[53] Some modern critics, in fact, seem to find it emotionally impossible to believe that nineteenth-century concert audiences could be as "disrespectful" as they apparently often were. As James H. Johnson remarked about audiences in Paris during the previous century,

> The portrait of a bustling, rambunctious, minimally attentive audience that emerges from eighteenth-century memoirs, police records and pamphlets stands in sharp contrast to traditional scholarly depictions of the Old Regime French musical public. For altogether laudable reasons—though with very little evidence—scholars have assumed that the seriousness of the music must have brought an appropriately respectful silence from the public.[54]

A nineteenth-century audience could be somewhat more sober than an eighteenth, but their conduct was often far from today's worshipful behavior. A concert then was indeed much more like a modern jazz or pop gig than the sometimes quite astonishingly frigid trotting out of the standard repertoire we call a recital. Now the formally attired performer bows unsmilingly before a respectful audience, sits down at the piano, waits for silence and for the muse to descend (sometimes it can be a long wait), plays his program, bows, and leaves the stage. (All, therefore, as in "Cat Concerto," apart from the mouse.) Often the only thing one hears the pianist say during the entire event is the title of the encore—sometimes not even that.

When Liszt described his *monologues pianistiques* as having "lively conversation" in the intervals between pieces, he was describing a musical and social event in which he himself took an active, even enthusiastic part. His concerts were even more informal than the reasonably relaxed norm for the time. Seated in a semicircle around his grand piano would often be a bevy of the more distinguished audience members, usually aristocratic and frequently female. It was Liszt's custom not only to announce loudly the pieces he was about to perform, but to chat to the closest members of the audience before and after playing each work on his program. Admittedly, he did not give a running commentary on his own playing as Pachmann was later to do (and listeners loved this), or sit among the audience knitting until it was time to play again as Clara Schumann

[53] Scholes, 1:frontispiece.
[54] James H. Johnson, *Listening in Paris*, 290 n. 36.

allegedly did in her later years,[55] but he would often mill around the body of the hall itself (if its design allowed this) between pieces, especially if he recognized friends there. In 1838 he had delighted the Viennese by welcoming the listeners as they entered the hall itself: "Liszt also always appears long before the beginning of the concert in the middle of his public, speaks and chats to everyone, leads the ladies to their seats, sorts everything out, is now here, now there, and absolutely does the honors of the house. This sort of thing is completely new in Vienna. You observe this, it awakens the interest, and you spend a pleasant hour despite the most uncomfortable crush."[56] Liszt made the audience feel genuinely welcome, rather than an irritating nuisance disturbing his communion with the muse, and they welcomed him in turn. It was not surprising that his Viennese recitals were so full that there was no room for him to get off the stage between pieces, even had he wanted to. Liszt—like Pachmann—knew how to give an act.

There was also the exciting prospect of at least one broken piano at a Liszt concert to entertain the audience, as there would be later at Rubinstein's.[57] Many reviews not only mention the make of the instruments he played on, but also whether they coped without mishap. The event was therefore a test for a piano and its manufacturer as much as for the player. Friedrich Wieck described a particularly theatrical incident at the first concert of the 1838 Viennese season: "He played the fantasy [Réminiscences des Puritains] on a C. Graf, burst two bass strings, personally fetched a second C. Graf in walnut wood from the corner and played his Etude. After breaking yet another two strings he loudly informed the public that since it didn't satisfy him he would play it again. As he began he vehemently threw his gloves and handkerchief on the floor."[58] As a reviewer sagely remarked, the fact that Liszt had three pianos on the stage (including an Érard borrowed from Thalberg) in the first place suggested that the broken strings were not exactly unforeseen.

[55] Ethel Newcomb, Leschetizky as I Knew Him (1921; reprint, New York: Da Capo Press, 1967), 259.

[56] Legany, 41.

[57] For Rubinstein see Bauer, 18–19: "There were two grand pianos on the stage. They had come from Russia, made by Becker. I wondered why one piano was not enough, even for the greatest of pianists. But I found out soon enough. Something broke—string, hammer or key?— under the master's mighty blows, and he transferred to the other. During the intermission a mechanic repaired the first piano, to which Rubinstein returned later, when the second went out of tune."

[58] Derek Watson, Liszt (London: Dent, 1989), 45.

The business with the gloves and handkerchief, peculiar to us, was only a more melodramatic version of the procedure recommended by Czerny at the start of a concerto, when even the color of the required piece of cloth was specified: "After making the usual obeisances, first toward the principal boxes, then toward the sides, and lastly toward the middle of the theatre, he [the performer] must then take his seat. Depositing his dress hat, and drawing out his white handkerchief, he must then give the signal to the orchestra."[59] Liszt played excerpts from a Czerny sonata in his third Viennese concert that season as a tribute to his master's teaching. He was obviously grateful for more than just the advice about the handkerchief. Later his own student Bülow would cut a similarly dapper figure, coming on to the stage with silk hat and cane in his gloved hands. The gloves were discarded elegantly before he sat down to play.[60]

Liszt recalled the frequent piano smashing with wry amusement in later life: "In those times pianos were built too lightly. I usually had two grands placed on the platform, so that if one gave out it could be replaced without delaying the recital. Once—I think it was in Vienna—I crippled both grands, and two others had to be brought in during the intermission."[61] He had a point—a large part of the problem was with early pianos rather than pianists. According to Spohr, Beethoven had "broken half a dozen strings" during the first solo entry after the tutti when playing his Fourth Concerto in 1808.[62] What the rest of the performance must have sounded like after this hardly bears thinking about.

No doubt the chance of witnessing the smashing up of expensive grand pianos helped to sell tickets for Liszt's recitals (and many reviews are quite explicit about the sheer violence of some of his playing as a young man), as did the possibility of observing an unfortunate piano tuner trying to repair a piano while Liszt continued to play on it—a Laurel-and-Hardy-like scene that actually occurred in Trieste in 1839. According to Liszt himself in a letter to the Countess d'Agoult:

> Shortly before the entry of the theme from *I Puritani* a string broke. The tuner immediately came on to extract it, but without managing to do so. As the string was not getting in the way of anything else on the piano, I went on playing; and as the tuner likewise went on fiddling about unsuccessfully with the string, I told him two or three times to go away and leave it. This worthy tuner didn't hear me.

[59] Carl Czerny, *Complete Theoretical and Practical Pianoforte School, Op. 500* (London, 1838), 3:87.
[60] Bauer, 21.
[61] Walker, *Living with Liszt*, 35.
[62] Czerny, *Über den richtigen Vortrag* commentary by Badura-Skoda, 11.

In the end, growing impatient, I gave him a violent slap on the hand, while continuing with my piece. It, the slap, could be heard all over the hall. A few malicious people tried to stop the applause which broke out at the end of the theme. The audience were in two minds; the tuner had returned to the wings. Aware of that, I stood up and, facing the audience, told the tuner to remove the piano I was using and to bring on another which was waiting there in reserve; and this was done in less than two minutes. This was time enough to erase the bad impression made by the slap . . . and in the following variation I was greeted by a storm of applause.[63]

As the century progressed, the new cast-iron frame made sadly ruined pianos a less common sight (Rubinstein must really have been impressively powerful to have made such a profound impact on the later instruments), and disruptive displays of audience enthusiasm during the music itself began to be regarded as unsophisticated. Performers customarily interacted less directly with their public (the eccentrics Pachmann and Planté excepted, who loved to give the audience a running commentary on their own playing). Rubinstein, unlike Liszt, was rarely in the mood to chat to the auditors, yet he also disliked going backstage during his marathon concerts. Bizarrely, his custom was to wander around the stage between pieces and stare silently at the decoration of the hall as the bemused public waited for him to be in the mood to play again. But Rubinstein certainly expected his audience to applaud after each movement of a multi-movement work (even a sonata or concerto) and after particularly attractive individual variations in a variation set. The public were still active participants in the concert experience, rather than simply passive receptacles of artistic benediction from the stage.

A closer audience contact with the entire performance process was also maintained by the practice of open rehearsals for concertos—in other words, rehearsals (usually on the day of the concert) attended by critics and members of the public. Some of the former, allegedly, often wrote their reviews based on the rehearsal because they couldn't be bothered to attend the subsequent concert.[64] The custom was naturally hated by most soloists, who were thus unable even to make their mistakes in private, but because it provided an extra source of income for concert hall managers, they were often forced to accede to it. There were, for

---

[63] Williams, *Liszt: Letters*, 113.

[64] An analogous practice to that of those critics today who attend only the first half of a recital and then seek to disguise the fact by the ambiguity of the latter part of their review. They are usually exposed only by a last-minute program change, of which they are of course completely unaware, or by a surprising reluctance to comment on the encores.

example, open rehearsals (with orchestra) for Liszt's charity concert in the Musikvereinsaal in Vienna of 16 March 1877 on both the previous days. The hall was a sellout on every occasion, so Liszt effectively played the *Emperor* Concerto in public three times that week on consecutive days, although the event was officially only one single concert. It is a measure of Liszt's generosity that he was willing to go through with all this at his age and provides perhaps another explanation for the rather lackluster playing on the evening of the concert itself that so disappointed the young Busoni.[65] Busoni later on had more understanding of the strain placed on the player by open rehearsals and wittily satirized the depressing awfulness of the tradition in some doggerel verses, written around 1895, which he entitled "Virtuosenlaufbahn" (A Virtuoso's Career). Part of this reads:

Verschlafen, fröstelnd, komm ich elf Uhr an.
Da steht ein Mann: "Die Probe wartet schon!"
—"Ich hab' noch nicht gefrühstückt." Sagt der Mann:
"Mir leid, doch öffentlich ist die Repetition."

Nun hin denn! Das Hôtel wird übersprungen,
Der Stadtrath, der empfängt mich sauer-süss:
"Sie sind ein bischen spät! Schon längst gesungen
Hat ihre Nummern die betreffende Miss."

Ich stürze an's Clavier. Die Reisekleider
Sind nicht gewechselt. Und die Hände kalt.—
Nun ist's vorbei. Der Kritiker war leider
Schon da. Zum Spät—Ausgeh'n ist er zu alt.

Was hilft es, dass es Abends glänzend geht?
Die Recension bespricht das Probespiel.
Nur keine Zugabe, sonst wird's zu spät,
Und bis zum Banhof ist's ein weites Ziel.

Noch nass erreich'ich richtig mein Coupé,
"Abfahren!" und der Zug ist schon im Gehn
Und wieder musst' ich fort ohne Souper,
Und morgen früh die Probe ist um Zehn.

[I arrive exhausted and chilly at eleven. A man is standing there: "The rehearsal's waiting for you!"—"I haven't had breakfast yet." The man says, "Sorry, but it's

[65] See chapter 1, n. 21.

an open rehearsal." Well, to it then! I'll give the hotel a miss. The town councilor receives me somewhat ambivalently: "You're a bit late! The relevant Miss So-and-so has long ago finished singing her numbers." I stumble to the piano. My traveling clothes haven't been changed. My hands are cold. Now it's over. The critic, unfortunately, was already there. He's too old to go out late. What does it matter that it goes splendidly in the evening? It's my playing at the rehearsal that's reviewed. No encore—otherwise it'll get too late, and the train station's quite a distance. I get to the railway carriage on time, still in damp clothes. "Ready to leave!" and the train is already moving. And once more I have had to depart without supper, and tomorrow morning the rehearsal's at ten.][66]

However abhorred open rehearsals were by players, they at least served to reduce the sense of distance between performers and public. This was further emphasized during the era of Liszt and Thalberg by the verbal audience comment common during the performance. When the aged Liszt attended Anton Rubinstein's concert in Pressburg in 1885, he was so pleased with Rubinstein's playing of Mozart's melancholy and intimate Rondo in A Minor that he shouted out "a series of loud bravos" during the piece. This was rather embarrassing, old-fashioned behavior by the 1880s, and Moriz Rosenthal, who also attended the concert and much later wrote about it, excused his master by pointing out that he "came from the virtuoso epoch when no consideration for the composition itself restrained any applause during the performance."[67]

Yet Rosenthal was no advocate of a silent audience in the modern fashion. In particular he abhorred the increasing tendency in the twentieth century to save the applause until the end of a multi-movement work. Writing in 1940 "on the question of applause" he complained, "If there is no applause the artist infers unconsciously that the audience is cold and uninterested. . . . Moreover, he cannot know which of the movements were best or least liked." He took as an example Schumann's Fantasy op. 17, with its stirring central march, followed by a contemplative final movement: "Obviously, without the Dionysian applause that crowns the second movement ('Triumphbogen'), the work would seem to create no impression, because the closing movement of this powerful and noble song of a lofty soul is not directed to the brain centres that control the motor nerves of applause."[68]

[66] Poem from Dent, 106–7; my translation.

[67] Moriz Rosenthal, "Anton Rubinstein's Concert in Pressburg," in Mitchell and Evans, 99.

[68] Moriz Rosenthal, "On the Question of Applause," in Mitchell and Evans, 127.

Rosenthal was not the only performer to object to what he called this "concert-hall snobbery." Mark Hambourg also hated it, and he knew exactly who to blame—the Dutch. They were "the coolest audience I have met with . . . the first people to initiate the fashion of no applause between the movements of a sonata or other sectional composition." Bauer also remarked on the chilly atmosphere in the Netherlands, remarking that there "faint applause" constituted a great success.[69] Hambourg's reasons for disliking the new etiquette were similar to Rosenthal's:

> Personally I have always found it damping to come down to earth in chilly silence at the end of a movement after moments of great musical exaltation, and then have to conjure up the "raptus" again in cold blood in the succeeding movement, without being able to sense that the audience is throbbing with you, as you feel if they break into applause between the various parts of a work played. It is a modern innovation to sit in "solemn silence" right through a long work of many movements, it was never done in the old days.[70]

Exactly how modern was this deplorable innovation? Rosenthal was writing in 1940, Hambourg in 1951, and the practice had obviously been growing more prevalent in the previous decades. Nevertheless, it was not fully established even by 1937, when Josef Hofmann's golden jubilee concert was given in the Metropolitan Opera House in New York. The performance was one of the relatively few recorded live before the advent of the long-playing record, and here the whole audience applauds quite unselfconsciously after each movement of Rubinstein's D-Minor Concerto. There is none of the shocked "hushing" one sometimes hears nowadays when a naive member of the public commits the appalling solecism of enjoying a movement enough to do likewise. Hofmann's golden jubilee was undoubtedly a special occasion, but it seems to reflect an etiquette of applause that was still active in some countries, if declining, up until at least the Second World War. Only the decade before, Ernest Newman had written that "the day will come when the audience will not want to applaud after each movement. Later the day will come when they will not want to applaud at all, but will go out in rapt silence after the performance of a great work."[71] He

[69] Bauer, 75. Bauer, in contrast to Hambourg, claimed that as far as he was concerned, the Dutch began to warm up a little toward the middle of the twentieth century.
[70] Hambourg, *Eighth Octave*, 126–27.
[71] Scholes, 1:219.

obviously felt that these glorious days were far off, but the first at least came sooner than he expected.

What put an end to the custom of applause between movements, assuming we do not grant a massive, and hitherto unacknowledged, international influence to the habits of Hambourg's frighteningly glacial Dutch? There are no doubt many factors, but one obvious culprit is recordings, which have changed so much about the way we listen to music, and further ossified the classical concert experience. They, rather than live performances, are now the largest source of our exposure to music. We now tend to listen to live music in the same way as we do to recordings. It is the way the auditors in Danhauser's Liszt portrait listened—passively. We do not shout "Bravo!" to the CD player when we hear a particularly wonderful turn of phrase, nor do we applaud between movements, or even after the final one. Concert behavior has long reflected this. Applause given only at the end of the piece is probably the absolute minimum that natural good manners will allow—although applause only at the end of each concert half is a possible further development, or even a *Parsifal*-like departure in solemn silence.[72] It is also the final triumph of the ideal of contemplative listening so extolled by some eighteenth- and nineteenth-century critics, but applied to all venues, and to all music no matter how inappropriate, to an opera fantasy as much as *The Art of Fugue*.

If Hambourg's and Rosenthal's views are anything to go by, or Busoni's delight at the applause after each of his *Hexameron* variations, modern concert etiquette can be profoundly dispiriting for many performers. Ironically, if our concert etiquette is modern, then the music played at them is often anything but. We seem very keen to revive certain customs of historical performance practice but anxious to keep others buried—often the ones regarded as less reverential. It is quite conceivable that we could give a period-instrument performance of Tchaikovsky's Sixth Symphony paying enormous attention to "historically informed" playing styles, yet condemn a member of the audience galvanized enough to applaud after the stirring penultimate movement. An audible audience reaction, however, is certainly what Tchaikovsky would have hoped for and expected here. Emotionally—as Rosenthal would argue—enthusiasm is quite fitting. This is not to say that we cannot admire some of the practices of the past while deprecating others, adopt some while rejecting others, but we should be aware that the modern choices we make are, inevitably, exactly that. Applause can be historically informed, too.

---

[72] Wagner initially forbade applause after each act of *Parsifal*, but then changed his mind: he missed the adulation.

## Uninvited Guests

Our modern obsession with accuracy, our fear of striking a false note, has also been encouraged by editable recording technology. Audiences increasingly began to expect in concert the note-perfect renditions modern editing allows, and artists necessarily went with the flow. That is not to deny that there are more and less accurate performers now, just as there always have been. Josef Hoffman was famously precise and reliable in his playing; there are a few pianists today who need every conjuring trick that digital editing can bestow to make it through a CD unscathed. It might, however, seriously be doubted whether an Anton Rubinstein (for whom wrong notes were all too common "uninvited guests") or a d'Albert could maintain a career today without more attention to getting the notes right than they paid in their last few decades before the public.

Rubinstein seems simply to have taken on too much—too many recitals, too many pieces imperfectly mastered. Considering the length, arduousness, and sheer frequency of his concerts, it would have been a miracle if he had also managed to maintain a consistent standard. According to Paderewski, "His playing revealed a remarkable command of the instrument, and at the same time shortcomings in memory and technique as well . . . it could be dreadful—dreadful!"[73] With d'Albert things were slightly different. He deliberately neglected piano practice in favor of composition, yet felt that this did not require retirement from the concert stage as a pianist. The ensuing gales of wrong notes seemed only to enhance the effect of his cavalier enthusiasm. When Percy Grainger heard him in 1896, he was

> enthralled by his slapdash English style. . . . He played his piano sonata with his feet and hands flying all over the place and wrong notes one or two to the dozen. Of course, d'Albert was full of un-English blood and un-English backgrounds, yet his overweeningness, his Cockney patter, his flirtatiousness, his overpowering energy were all as truly English as his early influences and his early pianistic training. When I saw d'Albert swash around the piano with the wrong notes flying to the left and right and the whole thing a welter of recklessness, I said to myself "that's the way I must play." I'm afraid I learnt his propensity for wrong notes all too thoroughly.[74]

[73] Paderewski, 112–13.

[74] John Bird, *Percy Grainger*, 1st ed. (London: Paul Elek, 1976), 29–30. Grainger seems to have been the only one to consider d'Albert's devil-may-care quality an "English" feature: his racial theories were notoriously peculiar.

Claudio Arrau—certainly about as different in temperament from Grainger as it was possible to be—took away a similar impression of d'Albert:

> He never practised. He used to have a big technique. Then he started losing interest in piano playing in order to compose. And yet his performance of the Liszt Sonata was still marvelous. Full of wrong notes, and missed passages. But the feeling was wonderful—coordinating the whole thing, with each idea coming out of the one before.[75]

Arrau went on to say that not only did audiences in d'Albert's day not mind the wrong notes, they considered it a sign of genius.[76] After all, if one gives oneself entirely up to the muses, a certain loss of control is inevitable.

Wrong notes are more or less unavoidable in some virtuoso compositions—after all, it is a rare live performance of Mily Balakirev's *Islamey* that gets through the piece with both flair and total accuracy.[77] For Bülow, the occasional mishap might even be courted. He told his students, seemingly in all seriousness: "In large leaps, now and then you must claw a wrong note; otherwise no-one will notice that it is difficult."[78] It was not for nothing that the English version of Moriz Rosenthal's *Schule des höheren Klavierspiels* translated *Sprünge* as "Jumps—Chance Movements."[79] Handling the odd chance note with unruffled aplomb elicited admiration, as Amy Fay described in the case of Liszt:

> It always amuses him instead of disconcerting him when he comes down squarely *wrong*, as it affords him an opportunity of displaying his ingenuity, and giving things such a turn that the false note will appear simply a key leading to new and unexpected beauties. An accident of this kind happened to him in one of the Sunday matinees, when the room was full of distinguished people and his pupils. He was rolling up the piano in arpeggios in a very grand manner indeed, when he struck a semitone short of the high note upon which he had intended to end. I caught my breath and wondered whether he was going to leave us like that, in

---

[75] Horowitz, 91.

[76] Horowitz, 91.

[77] From the initially unissued alternate take of Simon Barere's famous studio account of *Islamey* (on Appian CD), we can hear just how much "on the edge" of even his prodigious technique the piece was when taken that fast. There is also an exciting performance by the same artist (released on the same label) recorded live at a Carnegie Hall concert.

[78] Zimdars, *Masterclasses of von Bülow*, 67. The piece under discussion was Liszt's *Au bord d'un source*.

[79] Moriz Rosenthal and Ludwig Schytte, *Schule des höheren Klavierspiels: Technische Studien bis zur höchsten Ausbildung* (Berlin: Fürstner, 1892), 61.

mid-air, as it were, and the harmony unresolved, or whether he would be reduced to the humiliation of correcting himself, like ordinary mortals, and taking the right chord. A half-smile came over his face, as much as to say, "Don't think that *this* little thing disturbs me,"—and he instantly went meandering down the piano in harmony with the false note he had struck, and then rolled deliberately up in a second grand sweep, *this* time striking true. . . . It was so quick witted, and so exactly characteristic of Liszt. Instead of giving you a chance to say "he has made a mistake," he forced you to say, "he has shown how to get out of a mistake."[80]

Of course, this sounds very much as if Liszt were preluding or improvising rather than performing a written composition, but his attitude to inaccuracy is likely to have been similar whatever the situation. Wrong notes were simply a part of life when performance was always live. When Charles Stanford heard Brahms smash his way through his own Second Piano Concerto, he remarked that Brahms "took it for granted that the public knew he had written the right notes, and did not worry himself over such little trifles as hitting the wrong ones." "The wrong notes did not really matter," claimed Stanford, "they did not disturb his hearers any more than himself."[81] Bülow even insisted that he enjoyed Rubinstein's wrong notes more than his own right ones,[82] while Busoni, in recording his version of *La campanella*, argued that any inaccuracies that cropped up were integral to the bravura character of the piece. (Perhaps not everyone agreed—the disc was never issued.) Faced with grumbling from the young Egon Petri about d'Albert's unacceptable splashiness, Busoni retorted, "If you put as much conviction into your right notes as d'Albert does into his wrong ones, then you'd have cause to criticize."[83]

But by the second half of the twentieth century things were very different. Nowadays even CDs announced with great fanfare as records of a live performance are often silently edited to remove mistakes. Sometimes the "live performance" is in fact several live performances, with the best bits of each spliced together to secure a flawless rendition. Orchestras (and occasionally even audiences, to retain an identical acoustic) might be asked to stay behind after a concert to retake certain passages. Pianists regularly return to the recital hall (in

[80] Fay, 222–23.
[81] Charles Villiers Stanford, *Pages from an Unwritten Diary* (London: Edward Arnold, 1914), 200.
[82] Haas, 55–56.
[83] This story has been passed down by pupils of Busoni and was told to me by Ronald Stevenson.

their case without the audience—it would be just too embarrassing) to correct the passage or two that got out of control. Needless to say, none of this is necessarily inadvisable, or even unethical—except when the listener (especially if it is a consequently dispirited music student) is given the impression that such a recording is indeed an unedited souvenir of a single, inhumanly note-perfect recital. Such, notoriously, was the case with Horowitz's 1965 Carnegie Hall comeback concert. Horowitz, understandably a bundle of nerves after many years of voluntary retirement, struck a prominent wrong note in the first bar of the first piece (the Bach-Busoni Toccata, Adagio and Fugue), and carried on in a potentially hazardous manner. The dreaded leaps at the close of the March from Schumann's Fantasy op. 17 were far from perfect. Yet when the recording of the historic event was issued, many of these flaws had miraculously disappeared. For those who had attended the concert, sanitization was especially obvious in the Schumann—it was simply not what they had heard in the hall.[84] Not for Horowitz the von Bülow view that getting a few notes wrong just helped to show how difficult it all was. That he had in every other respect played superbly was not enough; the pressure to be accurate was now overwhelming, and—likely enough—inhibiting.

---

[84] For a more detailed discussion, see Harold Schonberg, *Horowitz: His Life and Music* (New York: Simon and Schuster, 1992), 218–20. Horowitz on several occasions even denied that any significant edits to the recording had been made—despite more than 2,000 witnesses to the contrary.

# 4

# A Suitable Prelude

Begin, and somewhat loudly sweep the string.
—John Milton, *Lycidas*

How do we begin a piece of music? The self-evident modern answer—with the first notes of the score—is not the only possibility, and not even the most common one before the twentieth century. An improvised introduction was, for hundreds of years, a sign of musical good manners and a chance for the player to frame appropriately the pieces in his program. It was also an opportunity to give the audience a gentle reminder that the player too was a creative artist. Indeed, fundamental to the pianism of the romantic era was the fact that most performers were also composers and projected themselves as such. Some were much better composers than others, it is true, but almost all asserted their individuality in concert by performing their own music, by improvisation, and by rearranging—to a greater or lesser extent—the works of other composers in their programs. We have seen in the previous chapters how the piano recital evolved from an event that regularly might include nothing but the pianist's own arrangements, improvisations, and compositions to something approaching the set-up of our own day. But the pieces officially listed on the program were far from all that the pianists played. The rest was improvisation—of preludes to and transitions between pieces.

In our modern concert repertoire, Chopin's *Twenty-four Preludes* in all the major and minor keys, op. 28, occupy a somewhat lonely, if splendid position. They are often performed complete, Busoni style. Occasionally a selection is given, and sometimes the more substantial numbers (the A♭-Major, or the D♭ *Raindrop*) are played on their own. What we rarely find, however, is a prelude being used simply as that—a prelude—because the custom of preluding has almost entirely been abandoned. Yet this was virtually universal performance practice during the romantic era, and indeed it was not uncommon up to the Second World War. Busoni himself, for all his fondness for playing the preludes as a complete set, was well aware of their ability to function as what they claim to be. When he made his second recording of Chopin's *Black Key* Etude in G♭ Major, op. 10 no. 5, in 1922,[1] he included a piece before it—Chopin's Prelude in A Major, op. 28 no. 7. In Busoni discographies, these tend to be listed as separate recordings. They are not. The prelude here hardly has the status of a miniature independent work but is treated instead as a short introduction to the *Black Key* Etude. This even involves a little recomposition. Busoni inserts a transitional bar of his own between the pieces, modulating to the dominant of F♯ minor (enharmonic G♭ minor) the relative minor of the prelude's A major, to facilitate the A-major–G♭-major change of key, before launching straight into the etude.

This neglected recording shows us that as late as the 1920s some of the shorter of these works were not only genuinely used as preludes to other pieces, but could even function as preludes to works in a fairly distant key, admittedly with the addition of a suitable link. More frequently, however, a prelude in the tonic or dominant of the following piece would naturally be chosen. Owing to their similarity in thematic contour, use of the C-Minor Prelude as an introduction to the C-Minor Nocturne, op. 48, seems to have been particularly frequent (it was so played by a pupil at one of Liszt's master classes in 1885).[2] Busoni's approach, with its unexpected modulation, is certainly more unusual and seems surprising, even bizarre, when we hear it now. But this is a question of perspective. As in so many other things, we—not Busoni—are the ones who have broken with a tradition of preluding that lasted for centuries.[3]

Chopin's preludes (composed 1836–39) are the only substantial set of that vintage to survive in the standard concert repertoire. They are nevertheless the tip of a very large iceberg, which includes collections by Clementi, P. A. Corri, Hummel, J. B. Cramer, Czerny, Kalkbrenner, and J. C. Kessler, whose *Twenty-four Preludes*, op. 31 (1834), were dedicated to Chopin.[4] The German edition of

---

[1] London, 27 February 1922. His first recording of this piece was made in November 1919.

[2] Richard Zimdars, trans. and ed., *The Piano Masterclasses of Franz Liszt: Diary Notes of August Göllerich* (Bloomington: Indiana University Press, 1996), 115. In modern times, Ronald Stevenson has made a fine recording of the C-minor Prelude and Nocturne as a pair (on Altarus Records).

[3] Jeffrey Kallberg's chapter, "Small 'Forms': In Defence of the Prelude," in Jim Samson, ed., *The Cambridge Companion to Chopin* (Cambridge: Cambridge University Press, 1992), 124–44, discusses in detail Chopin's preludes and their practical uses in the concert world of the time (a version of this chapter also appears in Kallberg, *Chopin at the Boundaries* [Cambridge, Mass.: Harvard University Press, 1996], 135–60). For a rather more abstract view of the collection, see Jean-Jacques Eigeldinger, "Twenty-four Preludes, Op. 28: Genre, Structure, Significance," in Jim Samson, ed., *Chopin Studies* (Cambridge: Cambridge University Press, 1988), especially 177.

[4] Muzio Clementi, *Appendix to the Fifth Edition of Clementi's Introduction to the Art of Playing on the Pianoforte, containing Preludes, Exercises, National Airs and Variations, with other pleasing and Instructive Pieces*

Chopin's own set of preludes was inscribed to Kessler in return. We can gauge the popularity of all these works by their frequent reprinting throughout the century, even if they remain mostly undisturbed on library shelves now. Chopin is likely to have known every one of them (he used the Clementi *Preludes and Exercises* as teaching material), with the possible exception of the Corri. The flow of preludes continued later in the nineteenth century, including Alkan's op. 31 collection of 1847, which contains twenty-five numbers rather than twenty-four, owing to the double appearance of the key of C major at the beginning and the end.[5]

But the prelude was primarily an improvised genre, and preluding before the performance of a piece had been an established practice from time immemorial. It was a normal part of the custom of concert improvisation that ranged from the performance of entire fantasies extempore to the improvisation of cadenzas, lead-ins, and additional ornaments.[6] A piano pupil might be taught such things at a relatively early stage of study. Friedrich Wieck advised the student playing simple rondo or variation themes:

> If at the fermata in the second half, another passage occurs to you, leading neatly to the dominant, try it out, and perhaps combine it with what is already there. . . . That's the way the singer does it. With such gracious variations one can always introduce a number of embellishments, just so long as they are tastefully chosen and prettily executed. It's another matter with pieces by Beethoven, Mozart, Weber, etc., where piety requires a more severe approach, although this too can be carried too far, and lead to pedantry.[7]

---

(1811 and 1821); Phillip Corri, *Original System of Preluding comprehending instructions in that branch of pianoforte playing with upwards of two hundred progressive Preludes in every key and mode, and in different styles, so calculated that variety may be formed at pleasure* (1813); Hummel, *Vorspiele vor Anfang eines Stückes aus allen 24 dur und moll Tonarten zum nützlichem Gebrauch für Schüler* (1814); Cramer (*Twenty-six Preludes or Short Introductions in the Principal Major and Minor Keys for the Pianoforte* (1818); Czerny, *48 exercises en forme de préludes ou cadences*, op. 161 (c. 1820); Moscheles, *50 Preludes in the Major and Minor Keys, intended as short introductions to any movement, and as preparatory exercises to the author's studies, for the pianoforte*, op.73 (1827); Kalkbrenner, *24 Preludes for the Pianoforte, in all the major and minor keys, being an introduction to the Art of Preluding* (1827); and J. C. Kessler, *24 Preludes*, op. 31 (1834). These works are also listed in Valerie Woodring Goertzen's superb article, "By Way of Introduction: Preluding by Eighteenth- and Early Nineteenth-Century Pianists," *Journal of Musicology* 14, no. 3 (Summer 1996): 301. A substantially different bibliography—concentrating especially on the German literature—can be found in Wehle, 1:xxiv–xxix.

[5] Alkan's set was published "for piano or organ," but most of the pieces would be rather unsuitable for the latter instrument.

[6] See chapter 2, pp. 44–54.

[7] Wieck, 134.

The collections of preludes listed earlier had a similar didactic purpose—they were designed just as much to give other pianists models for their own improvisations as to be performed themselves. More detailed information on exactly how to improvise and to go about constructing an extempore prelude is found in the second edition of Hummel's *Ausführliche theoretisch-practische Anweisung zum Piano-Forte-Spiel* (1829); Czerny's *Systematische Anleitung zum Fantasieren auf dem Pianoforte*, op. 200 (1829), and *Complete Theoretical and Practical Pianoforte School*, op. 500 (1839);[8] and Kalkbrenner's *Traité d'harmonie du pianiste: Principes rationnels de la modulation pour apprendre à préluder et à improviser*, op. 185 (1849). All these treatises considered improvisational ability to be an essential part of the trained musician's education. Czerny enthused: "It is akin to a crown of distinction for a keyboardist, particularly in private circles at the performance of solo works, if he does not begin directly with the composition itself, but is capable by means of a suitable prelude of preparing the listeners, setting the mood, and also hereby ascertaining the qualities of the pianoforte, perhaps unfamiliar to him, in an appropriate fashion."[9] Friedrich Wieck advised more trenchantly: "Before beginning a piece, play a few fluent arpeggios and some decent passages or scales, piano and forte, up and down the keyboard—but none of the stupid stunts I have heard from many a virtuoso."[10] Such a deplorable display of stupidity might, according to Wieck, consist of "a few hazardous flights up and down the keyboard, along with many octave passages, fortissimo, with depressed sustaining pedal."[11]

Rondos and variations beginning directly with the theme were considered by Czerny especially suitable for a more extensive extempore introduction, though whether this also might have been considered a stunt by the querulous and grumpy Wieck is difficult to tell. Here, for Czerny, it was "not inappropriate if the improvised prelude is proportionately longer and more elaborate, and if materials from the following theme are included."[12] One may assume that such a prelude from the pianist would also have been expected when accompanying Lieder that begin, in the score, directly with the voice.[13] The longer introduction,

---

[8] 3:116–23.

[9] Czerny, *Systematic Introduction*, 6.

[10] Wieck, 113.

[11] Wieck, 139.

[12] Czerny, *Systematic Introduction*, 17.

[13] A short discussion of this practice in relation to Schubert can be found in Walther Dürr, "Schubert and Johann Michael Vogl: A Reappraisal," *Nineteenth-Century Music* 3, no. 2 (November 1979): 126–40.

possibly with thematic anticipations of the coming piece, is one of Czerny's three basic categories of prelude, the other two being the brief prelude, which at its scantiest might be only a chord or two long; and the free-fantasy-like prelude, especially associated with C. P. E. Bach, which might contain passages of instrumental recitative and unusually bold modulations.

Although in the passage just quoted Czerny implies that preluding is better confined to salon recitals or other more intimate settings, it is obvious that the custom was of virtually universal application. In practice, it was a quite normal feature of public concerts, and almost any piece could have an improvised prelude, unless the composer had already included a prelude-style introduction in the score, and, perhaps surprisingly, even then. Czerny is not always quite consistent in his advice from volume to volume (and he did write so much that a certain incoherence is forgivable). In op. 200 he stakes out a position against preluding when performing the solo part in a concerto, but he elsewhere supplied a specimen prelude of his own to the last movement of Ries's E♭-Major Piano Concerto.[14] But "do as I say, not as I do" is a common attitude in all walks of life, and it is evident from other sources that it was indeed quite normal to improvise even in such situations, whatever Czerny said in his more judicious moments. Liszt, astonishingly to us, seems always to have preluded energetically and extensively on the initial piano entry in Weber's *Konzertstück*, even introducing a foretaste of one of the themes from the work's finale. On several occasions his dramatic effusions attracted more attention than anything in Weber's original.[15]

A sonata could also well have an improvised introduction, though Czerny took it as self-evident that a magisterial work such as Beethoven's *Appassionata* was unsuited to a more extended prelude. His assumption was that a short one would be quite normal, and we know that even in the late nineteenth century Paderewski—to name but one player—apparently played a few chords extempore before beginning this piece. As usual there is a certain disjunction between the tasteful exhortations in the treatises and actual practice. Liszt, at least before a small private audience, seems to have played a fairly elaborate prelude, complete with thematic anticipations, to that grandest of grand sonatas, Beethoven's *Hammerklavier*. The composer Wendelin Weissheimer heard him in 1858 "prelude, as the fancy took him to begin with, and then more and more in the manner

[14] In *Präludien, Cadenzen und kleine Fantasien*, op. 61 (1824), discussed in Czerny, *Systematic Introduction*, 25.

[15] For a detailed and perceptive account of Liszt's performances of the *Konzertstück*, including discussion of his preluding, see Dana Gooley, *The Virtuoso Liszt* (Cambridge: Cambridge University Press, 2004), 78–116.

of Beethoven—until at last the principal theme of the opening movement boomed forth in all its splendour."[16] Bülow seemed to be particularly fond of weaving thematic references into his preludes to Beethoven Sonatas—and often not even themes from the piece he was about to play. During his American tours of the 1870s he used "a kindred passage of a few measures of the slow movement of the Ninth Symphony" as an introduction to the *Moonlight* Sonata and even utilized a quote from the Sonata op. 31 no. 3 as a prelude to the *Tempest* Sonata, op. 31 no. 2.[17] The latter case is especially illustrative of just how imbedded and automatic the practice of improvised preluding had become, for the *Tempest* Sonata arguably begins in the style of an extempore prelude with thematic anticipations. Bülow was, effectively, improvising a prelude to a prelude.

Few sonata preludes have survived in concrete form, but some eighteenth-century composers, such as Dussek and G. M. Rutini, did supply fairly long written-out ones in improvisatory style to their own sonatas.[18] Mozart's magnificent Fantasy in C Minor, K. 475, published together with his Sonata in C Minor, K. 457, is even longer than any of Dussek's, and, unlike these, easily performable independently. It is perhaps not the only one of Mozart's more ambitious sonata prefaces to remain in the standard repertoire. His popular Fantasy in D, K. 397, written in the 1780s, may well have been originally intended as an introduction to some larger work. The first edition (printed in 1804, long after Mozart's death) ends inconclusively on the dominant seventh of D, and the piece was accordingly described by the publisher as a *fantaisie d'introduction*. The familiar closing ten bars were added only in later editions (their authorship is unknown, though some candidates have been suggested). It only these that allow the work to be performed independently in the fashion heard now. The assumption that the piece was left unfinished by Mozart is, however, an unnecessary conjecture, if one takes into account the possibility that it was intended all along to be an extended prelude. It was at any rate not regarded as unviable to publish it as such in 1804.

We have a few manuscript examples of shorter sonata preludes from the nineteenth century. Clara Wieck Schumann wrote one down for the slow movement of her husband's F-Minor Sonata (slyly slipping in a cryptic allusion

---

[16] Williams, *Portrait of Liszt*, 342.

[17] Lott, 338 n. 12. See also Hinrichsen, 100.

[18] For example, Dussek's *Three Sonatas with Scotch or German Airs* and *Three Preludes*, op. 31 (London, c. 1795). An excerpt from one of those is published in Goertzen, "By Way of Introduction," 324–25. Rutini's op. 7 sonatas (1770) all have preludes supplied by the composer.

to *Bunte Blätter*, op. 99). When Bülow performed his famous program of the last five Beethoven sonatas in the 1880s, he improvised short transitional preludes that molded a fragment from a previous sonata to serve as a modulating introduction to the next one.[19] His link between op. 101, in A major, and op. 106, in B♭ major, consisted of a version of the chordal flourish from the last three bars of op. 101, but this time on a dominant seventh of B♭ rather than a tonic chord of A. Before beginning op. 111, he would play the first bar of Beethoven's most famous sonata in that key—the *Pathétique*—for the harmony on which that bar ends is the harmony that begins op. 111.

I have played Bülow's transitional preludes many times as examples in master classes and lecture-recitals. Audiences almost always laugh uproariously at his cheek in daring to improvise something of his own between works of the great Beethoven. But it is worth remembering that Bülow was widely regarded in his day as an objective and cerebral player, if anything too cold and unbending rather than disrespectful. These preludes and transitions were a quite unexceptional part of concert giving. Bülow's were considered "ingenious" by at least one of his pupils,[20] and rarely mentioned in reviews at all, except when it was felt they went on a bit too long. Beethoven himself, if we can hazard a guess, would also have found the preluding unremarkable, though he would probably have been surprised to hear op. 106 played in public at all.

In at least one Beethoven sonata, the custom of improvising a prelude seems to form an important part of the context of the opening—ironically, not either of the op. 27 "Quasi una fantasia" sonatas, but the *Tempest* Sonata, op. 31 no. 2, which toys subtly with contemporary listeners' expectations. All three op. 31 sonatas were commissioned by the Swiss publisher Nägeli, who was interested in "piano solos in the grand style, large in size, and with many departures from the usual form of the sonata."[21] As far as the *Tempest* piece is concerned, one of the "departures from the usual form" seems to be that the first movement starts with its own pseudo-improvised prelude:

[19] Zimdars, *Masterclasses of von Bülow*, 135. One does not have to look far for a compelling explanation of the aforementioned *Bunte Blätter* allusion in Clara Schumann's prelude to the slow movement of Robert's F-minor Sonata. The sonata movement is a set of variations on a theme by Clara, while Robert's own *Bunte Blätter* theme was used by Clara herself for a set of variations. To add to the web of intimate references, Robert's theme was utilized allusively yet again in Brahms's Variations op. 9.

[20] Theodore Pfeiffer. See Zimdars, *Masterclasses of von Bülow*, 135.

[21] *Allgemeine musikalische Zeitung* 5, no. 35 (25 May 1803). Quoted from Timothy Jones, *Beethoven: The "Moonlight" and Other Sonatas, Op. 27 and Op. 31* (Cambridge: Cambridge University Press, 1999), 9.

EXAMPLE 4.1. Ludwig van Beethoven, *Tempest* Sonata, op. 31, no. 2, opening of the first movement

We initially hear a dreamily arpeggiated chord, abruptly followed by a few more agitated thematic fragments. The immediate repetition of this opening arpeggiation a minor third higher dislocates the listener's sense of key and heightens the improvisatory impression. It is only when the agitated figuration returns to cadence fully in D minor that we get a sense of the piece really "starting," and—if we are as accustomed to pianists' preluding as Beethoven's audiences certainly were—it is perhaps not actually until the exposition repeat that we might realize that the extempore-style opening was "officially" part of the work itself. The similarity of this opening gambit to that of Beethoven's much later published Fantasy op. 77, is striking. According to Czerny and Moscheles, this work gives a very good idea of the style and form of Beethoven's genuine extempore playing, and may well be a version of an improvisation he gave during a lengthy evening on 22 December 1808 at the Theater an der Wien, at which the Fourth Concerto also received its premiere.[22]

---

[22] Czerny, *Über den richtigen Vortrag*, 62. C. Moscheles, *Life of Moscheles*, 2:229–30. Moscheles, no mean improviser himself, described this style of Beethoven improvisation as "rhapsodical and eccentric."

EXAMPLE 4.2. Ludwig van Beethoven, Fantasy op. 77, opening

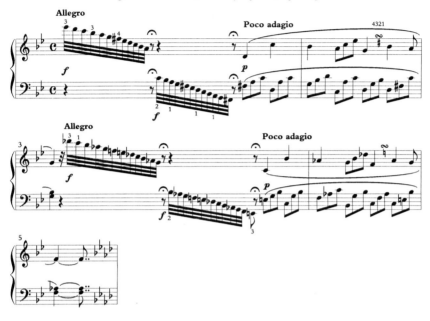

Here we have the same jarring oscillation between lyrical material and agitated passagework (in this case in reverse order), immediately repeated in transposition. Of course, the fantasy predictably takes much longer than the sonata to settle down into a more extended and coherent structure. Stability is eventually established toward the end of the piece in the shape of a theme and variations, but I am not arguing here that the first movement of the sonata really is a fantasy, only that the sonata's opening bars effectively form its own quasi-improvised prelude and have to be heard in the context of this custom for their full effect. Interestingly, the second movement also alludes to this idea, beginning as it does with another leisurely arpeggiated chord, but here the strategy is carried no further, and in the final movement it is abandoned entirely.

The approach in the *Tempest* Sonata is, however, not an entirely isolated phenomenon in Beethoven. The Sonata in F♯ Major, op. 78, also begins with a strangely short introduction that has a preludial function to the rather different main material introduced a few bars later. The melody of this brief introduction does not recur anywhere else in the movement. Despite the desperation of analysts to show how it is unmistakably "related" to what follows, it sounds quite intentionally unrelated, is deliberately set off from the rest of the piece, and never returns. It is, in fact, a lyrical "prelude in the tonality" before the start of the piece proper (according to Bülow's edition, a "fervent and melodious prelude"), and an example of Beethoven's increasing—if sporadic—tendency to set down some of these usually extempore elements in his scores. Bülow himself was particularly fond of this opening. He often detached it from its relevant sonata, transposed it into A♭, and used it as a prelude to the Sonata op. 110.[23] His students were told, as a waspish aside, "If Ferdinand Hiller had composed these first four bars in a ladies' album he would be immortal; unfortunately he failed to do it."[24]

Another allusion to a "written-in" improvised prelude is the famous solo opening of the Beethoven Fourth Concerto. The extempore effect is considerably enhanced here if the opening G-major chord is arpeggiated broadly, rather than played together as a block. It was not marked with an arpeggio in the original edition but is so printed in the excerpt reproduced by Czerny in *Über den richtigen Vortrag*. Czerny heard Beethoven perform this piece at its premiere and may be reflecting the composer's practice here.[25] We rarely come across this chord arpeggiated nowadays, partly because it is not indicated in the score—modern performers are of course not in the habit of playing "unauthorized" arpeggiations—and partly because present-day players are largely unaware of the custom of improvising preludes.[26] They are naturally more concerned with pointing out the connection of their opening G-major chord with the orchestra's (distinctly non-arpeggiated, when played with modern discipline) B-major chord a few bars later. But the omission of an arpeggiando marking would certainly never have stopped any nineteenth- or early-twentieth-century player spreading a chord, and it was especially customary to do so in extempore introductions.[27] It is possible, then, that we hear this concerto opening in a contrasting way to Beethoven and his contemporaries—we certainly respond to it in the context of very different performance practices. Perhaps we also miss a little of the radicalism of the succeeding *Emperor* Concerto, where the piano and orchestra amazingly

---

[23] Zimdars, *Masterclasses of von Bülow*, 135.

[24] Zimdars, *Masterclasses of von Bülow*, 36.

[25] Czerny, *Über den richtigen Vortrag*, commentary by Badura-Skoda, 111. Badura-Skoda notices Czerny's arpeggiation of this opening chord and comments that it "seems strange" [*wirkt befremdend*] (commentary, 11). It is true that the musical examples in Czerny's Beethoven treatise often differ in details from any contemporary score. Whether this originates from Czerny's memories of Beethoven's own playing, from deliberate "improvement," or simply from carelessness is unlikely ever to be completely settled. For Barth's view, see chapter 6, p. 183.

[26] Some performers, of course, may well simply not like the effect.

[27] See chapter 5.

give the "improvised" prelude together in the first movement, then collaborate in a quasi-extempore (cf. Czerny's prelude to the last movement of Ries's concerto) transition between the second and third.

Improvising yet another prelude on top of the "written-in" version might seem inappropriate for the *Tempest* Sonata or the concertos, but we know that Bülow would have disagreed, at least in the former case. It was certainly quite normal in virtuoso works to modify any printed prelude or introduction according to taste, and even to replace it entirely with one of the performer's own devising. This seems to have been the purpose of a puzzling Liszt manuscript usually described as an *Introduction to Variations on a Theme from Rossini's Siège de Corinthe*. No such variations by Liszt are extant, and it has accordingly often been surmised that we are here dealing with the opening of an otherwise lost work. Yet Liszt in 1828 did play at a public concert in Paris a set of variations on the popular *Siège de Corinthe* march, one not of his own composition but by Henri Herz. It has been convincingly proposed by William Wright that Liszt's manuscript, which features some material not found originally in Rossini's opera but certainly occurring in the Herz piece, is his replacement for Herz's own introduction.[28] Such an extensive new prelude was a quite acceptable means of personalizing a virtuoso work.

That is not to say that there were not occasions when certain styles of preluding were discouraged. At a Weimar master class in 1885, Liszt complained when a student extemporized an introduction—"a couple of runs in A-major"—to the dreamily lyrical opening movement of Beethoven's A-Major Sonata, op. 101. His objections were not to the idea of having a prelude here at all, but rather to the crassness of announcing the tonic key in a prelude when Beethoven takes pains to avoid a firm tonic confirmation until later on in the movement: "That is of little consequence—Beethoven does not touch upon the key of A-major for long at all—only on the third page—here you may not prelude in A-major."[29] On another occasion, Liszt parodied what had become the boringly clichéd style of tonic-confirmation preluding while simultaneously expressing his approval of more imaginative examples: "The lady [Adele aus der Ohe] played a very interesting prelude [to a polonaise by Zarebski] that pleased

[28] William Wright, ed., *Herold-Herz-Liszt Cavatine de "Zampa"* (Glasgow: William Wright, 2005), preface n. 5.

[29] Zimdars, *Masterclasses of Liszt*, 64. Zimdars (working from a German edition of the Göllerich diaries by Wilhelm Jerger) lists the sonata in question as the early A Major, op. 2 no. 2. Liszt's comments, in my view, make no sense in relation to this work, but a lot of sense in relation to op. 101.

the master very much. He gave a humorous imitation of the usual Prelude in the Tonality."[30] It's not what you do, as the song said, but the way that you do it.

## Why and How

But let us look in a little more detail at Czerny's justification of preluding in general, for there were good practical reasons underpinning the practice. "Preparing the listeners and setting the mood"—indeed actually attracting their attention in the first place to let them know that the performance was about to start—was absolutely essential, whether in a cosmopolitan salon or in the noisy crush of a public event. The potential audience might well be milling around and talking rather than sitting in silence waiting for the player to begin. They needed a signal that the music was now on offer. This would have been even more essential for concerts given during entractes in theatres, or in large salons where social pleasures offered the music loud competition. Liszt joked that the opening page of his Fantasy on Bellini's *La sonnambula* was included only to allow the audience "to assemble and blow their noses." When he got to the second page he said, "So, now everyone sits!"[31]

An attention-getting prelude would likely be needed for each new piece in a concert, if the "lively conversation" between numbers at Liszt's recitals is anything to go by. Even Anton Rubinstein, wandering around the stage distractedly between items, could hardly have expected the audience to remain in solemn silence until such times as he happened to be ready to play again. Bülow, despite the ingenuity of his preluding, sometimes regretted the need for it at all. He remarked ruefully, "Properly speaking, one should not prelude before a piece. But sometimes one must do it; if, for example, the listener wants to hear the whole piece and will be prevented from doing so by his neighbor's need and its satisfaction [presumably the desire to chatter]. Then it had best be done in the spirit of the composer."[32] A suitable improvised prelude was one that would not only alert listeners, and put them in the mood, but hopefully shut them up as well.

That Czerny mentions "ascertaining the qualities of the pianoforte"—advice seconded by Friedrich Wieck—will be of no surprise to anyone who has experience of playing early pianos. Although there are even nowadays—in our machine-manufactured age—large differences between individual instruments,

---

[30] Zimdars, *Masterclasses of Liszt*, 62.
[31] Zimdars, *Masterclasses of Liszt*, 59.
[32] Zimdars, *Masterclasses of von Bülow*, 114.

the differences between pianos in Czerny's day, when they were made almost entirely by hand and each manufacturer had his own specific methods of construction, were vast indeed. The early pianos have always been far less stable than the modern—keys stick, hammers break, and strings go drastically out of tune with depressing regularity (defects naturally less obvious when these instruments are recorded and can enjoy the loving ministrations of a technician as often as necessary between takes). On being confronted with an unfamiliar early instrument, it would quite simply be imperative to find out what was functioning and what was not, how clean the damping was, what differences in tone color there were between registers, and a host of other things before trusting oneself to be able to make a good effect on it. Even after 1865, by which time the piano was more similar to its modern incarnation, it was merely good sense to test both the instrument and one's ability to play on it before launching into the piece proper. On demonstrating his talents to Anton Rubinstein in the late 1870s, a nervous Emil von Sauer first improvised a prelude, "to make sure that my fingers, even in his presence, would do their duty," before essaying the first movement of Bach's *Italian* Concerto.[33]

But what would a typical improvised prelude sound like—of the sort that was familiar enough to be parodied by Liszt in 1885? As we might expect from the numerous collections of "specimen" examples, this is hardly difficult to ascertain. According to Philip Anthony Corri (1784–1832), who as well as his own accomplishments as a musician happened to be Dussek's brother-in-law:[34]

> Every performance should be introduced by a prelude, not only to prepare the ear for the key in which the air or piece is to be played, but to prepare the fingers, and therefore should in general consist of some rapid movement intermixt with chords, arpeggios and other passages. A prelude is supposed to be played extempore, and to lay down rules would be as impossible as wrong, for the fancy should be unconfined; but for those who are not acquainted with the rules of counterpoint or composition I shall submit several specimens or styles of prelude, adapted to every capacity.[35]

---

[33] Von Sauer, 58.

[34] Corri was a fascinating figure in his own right. A singer, pianist, and composer from a family of musicians, he was involved with the setting up of the Philharmonic Society and the Royal Academy of Music in London in 1813. Fleeing domestic difficulties of the sort not uncommon with musicians, he immigrated to Baltimore, Maryland, where he adopted the cunning disguise of the name "Arthur Clifton." It was under this pseudonym that he composed one of the earliest American operas, *The Enterprise, or Love and Pleasure*, in 1822. He did, however, return to London sporadically in the 1820s, presumably when the coast was a little clearer.

[35] P. A. Corri, *Original System of Preluding* (London: Chappell, [1813?]), 1.

The examples that follow proceed through six "styles," the first being nothing but three cadential chords, tonic–dominant–tonic (approximating to Czerny's "simplest type of prelude"). The second style is a slight expansion that adds the subdominant chord in a moderately more discursive manner. By the time we reach the heady heights of style number 6, we should be producing something like the following:

EXAMPLE 4.3. P. A. Corri, *Complete System of Preluding*, p. 22, Preludes 1–3

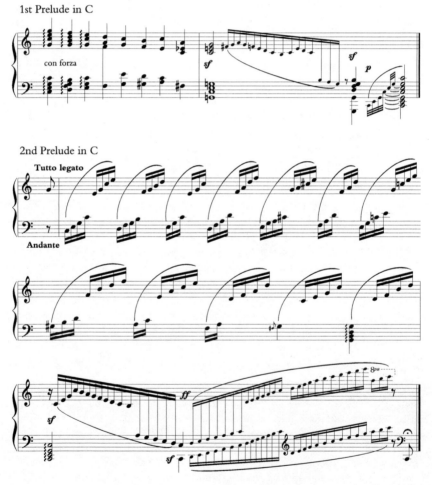

EXAMPLE 4.3. (*continued*)

3rd Prelude in C

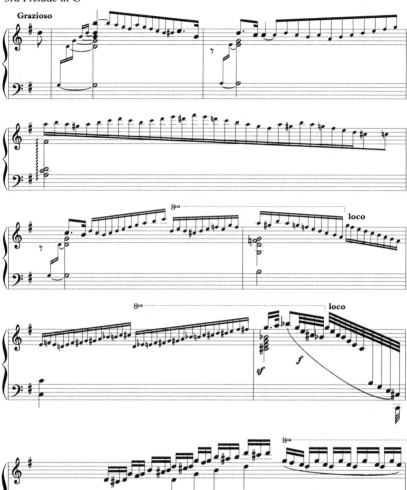

EXAMPLE 4.3. (*continued*)

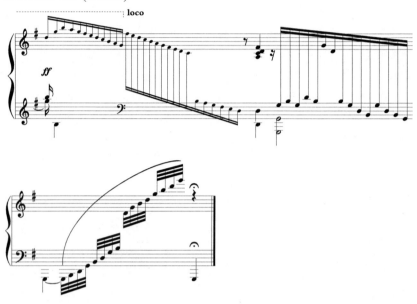

As for general manner of performance, Corri advises us that "all formality or precision of time must be avoided; [preludes] must appear to be the birth of the moment, the effusion of fancy, for which reason it may be observed that the measure or time is not always marked at Preludes."[36] In other words, even if you're playing a previously composed prelude, it should sound as if made up on the spot. This was a particularly important point in an age when skill in improvisation was prized as a sign of true musicality. According to Ferdinand Hiller, Mendelssohn's opinion of Kalkbrenner sank drastically—never to resurface—when he discovered that a supposedly improvised "effusion of fancy" played by him to the Mendelssohn family in Berlin was virtually identical with a published piece called "Effusio Musica."[37] The moral of the story was, as ever, "Don't get caught."

But we do not have to ransack the now relatively obscure collections of Corri, Cramer, or Kalkbrenner to come up with examples of preludes or transitions in

[36] Corri, 4.
[37] Nichols, 176.

an extempore style, for quite a few of a similar nature have survived in the standard repertoire, sometimes unrecognized for what they are. Liszt's *Transcendental Studies* (1851) supply convenient examples. The first study, suggestively entitled Preludio—in one manuscript from the 1830s *Préludes*[38]—is nothing less than a written-down version of an improvised prelude, or perhaps several short preludes strung together, if one stresses the plural version of the title and the three distinct sections the work falls into. The piece tests each register of the piano, as Czerny recommends, with a variety of characteristic figurations:

EXAMPLE 4.4. Franz Liszt, Preludio, from *Transcendental Studies*

[38] National Szechenyi Library, Budapest, Ms. mus. 24. Jim Samson points out evidence (*Virtuosity and the Musical Work*, 10) that at one time Liszt may have intended to call the entire set "preludes" rather than "etudes," so it is quite possible that the title of this manuscript could refer to the set as a whole. There are nevertheless also good reasons for thinking that the C-major study could represent a string of short "preludes."

EXAMPLE 4.4. (*continued*)

EXAMPLE 4.4. (*continued*)

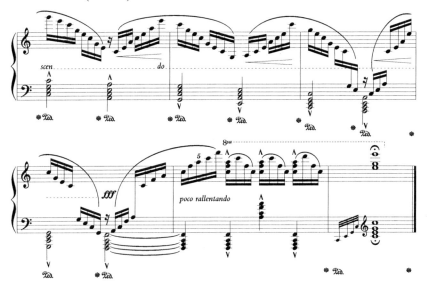

After the initial peremptory octaves and arpeggio sweep from the top to the bottom of the keyboard (bar 1)—drawing the attention of the audience in no uncertain manner—Liszt tries out a sixteenth-note figure in the bass (bars 1–3). This presumably proving successful, he repeats the entire procedure, now extending the figure through the entire range of the piano up to the high treble (bars 3–9). He then tests the instrument's ability to play staccato chords (bars 9–11) and trills in the bass (bars 12–13), closing with a slightly more lyrical passage that climaxes majestically (bars 14–23). The whole piece is only two pages long, much shorter than any other of the *Transcendental Studies*. We can be certain that it was only notionally intended to be a prelude to a rendition of the whole set—a complete public performance of which, as we have seen, was simply not in the cards during Liszt's day. It does, however, function superbly as a warm-up prelude before a performance of one or a selection of the studies and gives us a very good idea of the sort of improvisation we might in general have heard from Liszt when he first stepped up to the concert platform.

The very earliest version of the *Transcendental Studies* dates from 1826, the second from 1837–38, and the final from 1851. Liszt had at one time intended to write a set of twenty-four studies, going through all the major and minor keys, rather than the twelve he eventually contented himself with.[39] Two separate incomplete manuscripts of a piece in F♯ major, sold at auction some years ago, probably relate to a potential continuation of the set.[40] This piece too is in the style of an improvised prelude, and in the second manuscript—written down on 13 September 1838 in Milan—it is actually entitled Preludio. All of the published studies underwent a massive increase in length between the 1820s version and the 1830s, with one exception—the C-major Preludio. However imposingly this is expanded in keyboard texture and range, it is only approximately one-third as long as the first version. Liszt undertook, in effect, a recomposition mainly of the exposition of the 1826 study. The new version, therefore, seems like an exposition without a recapitulation. Structurally, the closed form of the early version now becomes open-ended and fragmentary—preludial, in other words, both in terms of organization and material.

But the *Transcendental Studies* contain other examples of preludes, some more carefully hidden. The introductions to the A♭-major study, and to the B♭-minor (in its 1837–38) version, are certainly worked-out examples of the more extended "adumbratory" preludes described by Czerny. In its later 1851 format, the B♭-minor study was shorn of this printed introduction, but since the piece now begins immediately with the theme, the performance practice of the time would ironically have demanded the addition of some sort of extempore opening, even if shorter than the one Liszt had excised. The opening gesture of the E♭ study too is transparently preludial. It is reworked from the early *Impromptu on Themes of Rossini and Spontini*, a remarkably honest piece that wears its improvisatory origins on its sleeve, especially in the weakly waffling transitions,[41] where we can almost see the young artist on the spot repeating chords aimlessly until he thinks of something else to do.

In the F-minor study, on the other hand, we find something much more remarkable. Toward the end of the piece, at bar 159, a dramatic string of diminished-seventh chords over a descending whole-tone bass leads into the coda. We can now say for sure that this passage is virtually identical with the mysterious *Prélude omnitonique* (1844) long listed as lost in catalogs of Liszt's works.

---

[39] In fact, originally forty-eight were planned. For a detailed discussion of the genesis of the *Transcendental Studies*, see Samson, *Virtuosity and the Musical Work*, and Christian Ubber, *Liszt's Zwölf Etuden und ihre Fassungen*, Weimarer Liszt Studien 4 (Regensburg: Laaber Verlag, 2002).

[40] Sotheby's, London, auction catalog of 17 May 1991, lot. no. 302; and Stargardt's, Berlin, auction catalog of 25–26 November 1997, lot no. 837.

[41] Mm. 48–56, 136–48, 192–96, and 277–85.

EXAMPLE 4.5. Franz Liszt, *Transcendental Study* in F Minor, bar 159

In recent years several manuscript leaves have emerged containing short preludes jotted down by Liszt during his concert tours, including the *Prélude omnitonique* and preludes written out in Exeter (1840), Berlin (1842), Braunschweig (1844), and Lyon (1844). Speculation that the *Prélude omnitonique* was some sort of complex extended piece in a futuristic, atonal style was quashed when it was discovered not to be an independent work at all, but rather a short, quasi-improvised flourish of indeterminate tonality like example 4.5, which has the resulting advantage that it can be used as a prelude or transition to a piece in any key. In fact the Berlin and Braunschweig preludes use the same flourish, but the former cadences in C major, the latter in F♯ major. It might now come as no surprise that the Lyon prelude, though not identical to the others, is also chromatic, tonally indeterminate, and hence of universal utility.[42] The Exeter prelude is slightly different but also features figuration based on diminished-seventh chords; it is obviously a version of the introduction to the *Petite valse favourite*, later to be reworked as the Valse-Impromptu.[43] This might lead us to wonder how many other introductions are effectively worked-out improvised preludes, and indeed how many of Liszt's chromatic linking passages arose from his extempore transitions.

The introduction to the *Transcendental Study* "Mazeppa" (1851) is certainly another prelude. Neither of the early versions of the study (1826 and 1838) have any introduction at all. Alone of the *Transcendental Studies*, however, "Mazeppa" appeared in an intermediate version, probably conceived around 1840 and published in 1847. By this time it had acquired its title, a new—evidently

---

[42] Recordings of all these preludes will be found in vol. 56 of Leslie's Howard's *Complete Liszt Series* (Hyperion Records). It was the tonal waywardness of some styles of preluding that led the conservative Moscheles to complain of Chopin's Cello Sonata, "I often find passages which sound to me like someone preluding on the piano, the player knocking at the door of every key and clef to find if any melodious sounds are at home." C. Moscheles, *Life of Moscheles*, 2:172.

[43] See chapter 7, p. 252.

programmatic—coda, and a Preludio (so called by Liszt),[44] consisting of a few diminished-seventh chords cadencing into the D-minor main theme (example 4.6). It is very likely that Liszt had always played the work in concert with such an introduction (the score of the 1837–38 version starts directly with the theme), and was here simply acknowledging this. In the Schlesinger edition of the intermediate *Mazeppa*, this added introduction is even printed in manuscript facsimile, setting it apart from the main body of the work and further emphasizing its preludial status. The prelude was retained for the 1851 version and expanded by the addition of an excitingly dramatic run starting on the dominant in the bass. It then rushes headlong toward the principal melody (example 4.7):

EXAMPLE 4.6. Franz Liszt, *Mazeppa* preludio, 1846 version

EXAMPLE 4.7. Franz Liszt, *Mazeppa* preludio, 1851 version

[44] See Samson, *Virtuosity and the Musical Work,* 199.

EXAMPLE 4.7. (*continued*)

From the evidence of the *Transcendental Studies* and the various surviving prelude manuscripts, we would probably be on safe ground in claiming that Liszt's improvised introductions to and transitions between pieces tended to be short and frequently made use of diminished-seventh and other chromatic passages that have a protean ability to function in any key. We can also see more clearly why Liszt at one time may have considered calling the first *Transcendental Study Préludes*, because, though hardly lengthy, it is considerably longer than his other sketched-out preludes and contains individual passages—especially the chromatic chordal flourish in bars 9–13—that could well have made separate preludes themselves in his favorite tonally ambiguous style. Amusingly, and perhaps not entirely by coincidence, preludes thundering through "a sequence of exotic chords at top speed" and featuring "a few disconcerting diminished-7th chords" are specifically singled out for parody by Friedrich Wieck in *Klavier und Gesang*, accompanied by sarcastic remarks about "inspired pianistic genius."[45] One wonders whom he could have meant. But of course, the "disconcerting" nature of all this was part of the point—a disconcerted audience is, for a few moments at least, not likely to be a chattering one. According to Leschetizky, Liszt habitually played the first few chords of these dramatic preludes simultaneously with sitting down at the keyboard—another surprise tactic no doubt intended to ensure

[45] Wieck, 140.

silence. He would, however, make a slight pause between the end of the prelude and the piece proper.[46]

Evasive tonal ambiguity is a feature of some much earlier printed preludes that wander from one key to another, for example Mozart's *Modulierendes Präludium*.[47] This appears also to have been intended as a multipurpose transition between pieces. Starting from an ornamented seventh chord on F, it ends up in E minor after a profusion of chromatic figuration. Mozart indicated in a 1778 letter to his sister, Nannerl, that in similar but probably more ambitiously modulating pieces, "the performer can stop when he likes," namely when the correct key for the next piece has been reached.[48] The likelihood is that two Beethoven pieces of a kindred type—the *Zwei Präludien durch alle Dur-Tonarten für das Pianoforte oder die Orgel*, op. 39—were intended to perform the same function, as was Clementi's *Étude journalière des gammes dans tous les tons majeurs et mineurs* and Field's *Exercice modulé dans tous les tons majeurs et mineurs*. It has been suggested that works such as Beethoven's op. 39 are simply "student exercises in modulation,"[49] but if this is so there seem to have been a surprising number of student exercises published in the early nineteenth century. Moreover, Bülow recommended Beethoven's preludes to his pupils as practical models for their own.[50] Jean-Jacques Eigeldinger has intriguingly argued that even Chopin's sinuously beautiful Prelude op. 45, which does indeed modulate swiftly and extensively, is a transfiguration of this style of prelude, though there is no suggestion here that one should stop dead when the key of the next piece in the program turns up.[51]

But it was, of course, possible to prelude more simply than even the shortest examples from Liszt, Czerny, or Corri. At its most basic, an improvised introduction could consist of a single chord or an elaboration of it. An isolated chord from the accompanist was especially welcome as a preface to any lied that in the printed music began immediately with the voice, for it fulfilled the valuable function of helping the singer to pitch the first note. We find a written-out imitation of this—for piano solo—in the opening arpeggiated chord of Men-

---

[46] E. Newcomb, 144.

[47] No Köchel number. Contained in the *Neue Mozart Ausgabe* (Kassel: Bärenreiter, 1982), Ser. 9, Werkgruppe 27, Bd. 2, 4–5.

[48] Emily Anderson, trans. and ed., *The Letters of Mozart and His Family* (London: Macmillan, 1938), 2:874.

[49] Howard Ferguson, "Prelude," in Stanley Sadie, ed., *The New Grove Dictionary of Music and Musicians* (London: Macmillan, 1980), 15:211.

[50] Zimdars, *Masterclasses of von Bülow*, 114. He also recommended the preludes of Moscheles.

[51] See Jean-Jacques Eigeldinger, "Chopin and 'La note bleue': An Interpretation of the Prelude, Op. 45," *Music and Letters* 78, issue 2 (May 1997): 233–53.

delssohn's *Fantasy on the "The Last Rose of Summer"* (see chapter 2, ex. 2.1), where the contrast between the somber D♯-embellished opening chord of E minor and the melody's entry in the major makes a particularly piquant effect.[52] Slightly more extended versions of this type of simple prelude can be found in Mendelssohn's *Lieder ohne Worte* op. 30 no. 3 and op. 38 no. 4, which of course are instrumental imitations of vocal models:

EXAMPLE 4.8. Felix Mendelssohn, *Song without Words* op. 30 no. 3, opening

EXAMPLE 4.9. Felix Mendelssohn, *Song without Words* op. 38 no. 4, opening

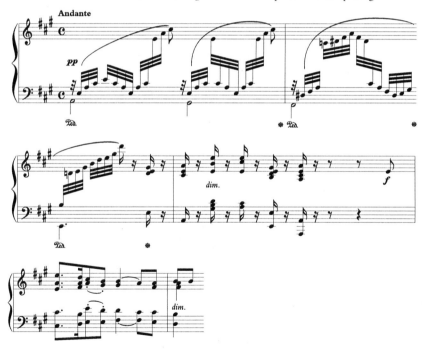

[52] Larry Todd has made the intriguing suggestion to me that the opening G–D♯ here is a reminiscence of the initial piano entry of Weber's *Konzertstück*.

These arpeggiated preludes and postludes also allude to a "Bardic harp" (with shades of Ossian idolatry). The strings are swept with practiced panache to frame the song itself, as Milton exhortes the muses in *Lycidas*, who are requested to "Begin, and somewhat loudly sweep the string." Doubtless in all these cases, no further prelude would normally be improvised (unless Bülow was at the keyboard). In the two *Lieder ohne Worte* Mendelssohn neatly brings back the prelude at the end of the piece as a slick closing gesture. A realization that these passages are imitative of independent extempore preludes helps us to understand their otherwise rather peculiar isolation from the main body of the piece. The harp figuration employed has little relation to that found in the rest of the work, and the introductions cadence firmly on the tonic (rather than remaining poised on the dominant) in a manner that seems premature and rather too decisive. A similar effect is produced, no doubt for the same reason, by the opening of John Field's Nocturne in A Major (no. 7 in Liszt's edition):

EXAMPLE 4.10. John Field, Nocturne in A Major, opening

EXAMPLE 4.10. (*continued*)

This is slightly longer than the Mendelssohn examples, but of exactly the same preludial character. To a modern pianist the impression of openings like these—independent and closing with a full cadence—can be slightly puzzling. We think of introductions as generating a feeling of expectation (by, for example, ending on the dominant or a substitute), rather than confining themselves to a few bars of self-contained strumming before the "real" start of the piece. But a little historical awareness makes the scales fall from our eyes.

Written-out extended versions of the introduction in improvised style are not uncommon. As Czerny advises, they tend to appear most frequently before rondos and variations. Chopin's *Variations on Hérold's "Je vends les scapulaires,"* op. 12, has a typical example, with its initial loud appeal to the audience's attention, followed by a more lyrical passage, and finishing with a dominant preparation for the theme itself. Less judicious attempts at this sometimes resulted in comically overblown introductions to miserably trivial melodies—a particular specialty of Henri Herz, whose *Variations in F Major on a Theme from Hérold's "Le pré aux clercs"* has a prelude of such portentous grandiloquence that one is forced to laugh when the childish little tune finally comes along.[53] The suspicion that Herz is deadly serious throughout only makes it funnier, and the whole preposterous procedure was wittily parodied by Ernő Dohnányi in his *Variations on a Nursery Tune.* Liszt

---

[53] I have played the introduction and theme of this piece several times before an audience; and yes, they do laugh.

himself was hardly free from similar misjudgments, for the introduction to his early *Fantasy on a Theme from Auber's La fiancée* also hurtles headlong over the brink of self-parody, at least from a modern point of view. His later attempt to reposition this piece as an exercise in satire smacks a little too much of damage limitation.[54]

We have, naturally enough, no trace left of most improvised preludes and transitions, but we can infer some detail about them from similar introductions in published pieces. The Andante spianato preface to Chopin's *Grand polonaise* for piano and orchestra (now almost always performed purely as a piano solo) seems very like the sort of slow introduction often improvised before such works, in an extempore style with no thematic connection whatsoever to the following polonaise. Bülow advised his students to play the opening of Mendelssohn's *Capriccio brillante*, op. 22, like the prelude of an impatient performer "abruptly, as if you wanted to try out the piano."[55] For a concert in 1846 Mendelssohn reportedly improvised an entire slow introduction to the same sort of piece, the *Rondo brillant* for piano and orchestra, op. 29. We can perhaps get a broad idea of what this might have involved in his case by glancing at the andante introduction to the very familiar *Rondo capriccioso*, op. 14. This was written later than the rondo itself and likely represents Mendelssohn's idea of an extended prelude or improvised slow introduction. Virtuoso bombast is predictably absent here. Mendelssohn ends on the time-honored dominant preparation familiar from countless such introductions and uses a simple, slow melody that follows the rough outline of the opening theme of the rondo to come.

We are lucky enough to have an unusually detailed account of other Mendelssohn improvisations, namely extempore additions during a performance of two of his *Songs without Words*. For an 1845 charity concert in the Leipzig Gewandhaus featuring Jenny Lind among the performers, he both improvised a prelude before and an extensive modulating link between the pieces. William Rockstro left a very detailed account:

> Mendelssohn's own contribution to this performance were his First Concerto in
> G Minor, and a solo für pianoforte, which consisted of two *Lieder ohne Worte*—no.
> 1 Book VI, and no. 6 Book V—both evidently chosen on the spur of the
> moment, and rendered intensely interesting by a prelude and interlude such as
> he alone could have improvised. (Beginning with a characteristic prelude in
> E♭, Mendelssohn played, as only he could play it, his own *Lied ohne Worte*, no. 1

---

[54] See Kenneth Hamilton, "Liszt's Early and Weimar Piano Works," in Hamilton, *Cambridge Companion to Liszt*, 60–61.

[55] Zimdars, *Masterclasses of von Bülow*, 62.

book VI.) Then . . . during the course of a long and masterly modulation from
the key of E♭ to that of A major he carried on the quiet semiquaver accompaniment of the first Lied for some considerable time, without interruption,
treating it with new and unexpected harmonies, so contrived as to permit the
continuance of the bell-like B flat in the form of an inverted pedal-point, and
always presenting the re-iterated note in some novel and captivating position. As
the modulation proceeded, the B flat gave place to other notes, treated in like
manner; and presently these were relieved by a new figure, which rapidly developed into the well-known feathery arpeggio of the famous *Frühlingslied*. Every
one thus knew what was coming: but no-one was prepared for the fiery treatment
which first worked up this arpeggio-form into a stormy climax carrying all before
it, and then as it gradually approached the long-expected chord of A-major, died
gently away, in a long-drawn diminuendo, so artfully managed that, when the
delicious melody was at last fairly introduced, it sent an electric thrill through
every heart in the room. This was indeed a "gentlemanlike modulation," never to
be forgotten by anyone who heard it.[56]

The practice of improvising a transition between pieces remained common
throughout the nineteenth century and was heard well into the twentieth. When
Ethel Newcomb played to Leschetizky's class at the turn of the century, she was
reprimanded by the master for not having made "a little modulation from the first
piece to the second."[57] Leschetizky summoned another of his pupils to provide
the missing modulation—his name, Artur Schnabel. As we have already seen,
most of Liszt's short preludes could have functioned just as slickly as transitions,
owing to their tonal instability, and published specimens of more extended
transitions similar to the Mendelssohn example just described can be found in the
larger-scale opera fantasies of Liszt, Thalberg, and others. Amy Fay once heard
Liszt "pass from one piece into another by making the finale of the first one play
the part of the prelude to the second. So exquisitely were the two woven together
that you could hardly tell where the one left off and the other began."[58]

Printed versions of such transitions between independent pieces are very rare,
but at least one does exist: the fascinatingly elaborate link between the last two
pieces in Alkan's *Fifth Book of Chants*, op. 70 (1872). All five of Alkan's books of
*Chants* are closely modeled on the first book of Mendelssohn's *Songs without Words*,

[56] C. Brown, 228–29. Brown here usefully conflates two separate Rockstro accounts from his
respective biographies of Mendelssohn and Jenny Lind. I have added the last sentence (with the
"gentlemanlike modulation"), which was omitted by Brown, from William Rockstro, *Felix
Mendelssohn-Bartholdy* (London: Sampson, Lowe, Marston, 1884), 117.

[57] E. Newcomb, 16.

[58] Fay, 223.

even following its key scheme exactly. The fifth book consists of a lyrical Duettino in E Major (with more than a hint of Mendelssohn's Duetto in A♭ Major), an Andantinetto in A Minor featuring constant cross-rhythms, a vigorous Allegro vivace in A major, an imitation of the cello "La voix de l'instrument" in A major, an aggressive Scherzoso-Coro in F♯ minor, and finally a barcarolle in G minor. Between the Scherzoso-Coro and the barcarolle, Alkan inserts two pages he describes as "Récapitulation, en guise de Transition, ou Introduction, pour le Numéro suivant" (Recapitulation, in form of a Transition, or Introduction, to the following Number):

EXAMPLE 4.11.  Charles Valentin Alkan, *Fifth Book of Chants*, op. 70, "Recapitulation"

EXAMPLE **4.11.** (*continued*)

EXAMPLE 4.11. (*continued*)

This begins in the same key as the Scherzoso-Coro, but with the theme from the Duettino. Next appears a reminiscence of the Andantinetto, followed by another fragment of the Duettino. Excerpts from "La voix de l'instrument" and the Allegro vivace now ensue, before a final even more fragmentary memory of the Duettino leads the music to the dominant of G minor, ready for the concluding barcarolle. Such a complex and elaborate transition is quite remarkable in an otherwise independent set of lyrical pieces. Uncannily similar in several respects to Rockstro's description of Mendelssohn's performance, it gives us a rare insight into how nineteenth-century audiences might actually have heard strings of separate pieces played.

Clara Wieck Schumann, too, was noted for the improvised transitions between the works of various vintages that she would present as suites. Though none of these transitions seem to have been written down (or at any rate to have survived), there are extant manuscripts of her improvised preludes, some of a general type and others for a few of her husband's pieces. Examples of her preludes for Robert Schumann's Sonata in F Minor (discussed earlier), "Des Abends" and "Aufschwung" (from the *Fantasiestücke*, op. 12), and the "Schlummerlied" from op. 128 have been published in articles by Valerie

Woodring Goertzen.[59] Wieck Schumann had no doubt been accustomed to prelude from her earliest piano lessons, and Czerny makes it clear that piano students should practice making a prelude to every piece they learn.[60] While studying music in Germany in the 1870s, Amy Fay both heard her fellow students at Tausig's conservatory play preludes before performing pieces to their teachers and eventually learned how to do so herself during her studies with Theodore Kullak. It is clear that what the latest edition of the *Grove Dictionary* describes as "the demise of preluding mid-century" was, like the famous rumors of Mark Twain's death, greatly exaggerated. In fact, it was hardly underway even by the 1870s and 1880s. The early decades of the twentieth—rather than the nineteenth—century mark the point where we could begin to whisper a rueful *requiescat in pace* over the practice.[61]

For nineteenth-century musicians, despite occasional jaundiced comments from Bülow, preluding was more of a requirement than an option. It was a sign of civilized training in harmony and a gesture of musical good manners that put the work that followed in an appropriate context. Schumann wrote that for public performance, his *Concert Studies*, op. 10, might be provided with improvised preludes—"free, short, appropriate introductions."[62] When Ludwig Deppe reminisced to Fay that Tausig used to come to play to him at home "beginning at once, without prelude," it was presented as an unusual procedure, not to be recommended even in private surroundings, and an indication of Tausig's

[59] Goertzen, 320–22, reproduces the prelude to *Des Abends*. Others appear in Valerie Woodring Goertzen, "Setting the Stage: Clara Schumann's Preludes," in Bruno Nettl, ed., *In the Course of Performance: Studies in the World of Musical Improvisation* (Chicago: University of Chicago Press, 1998), 237–60. The entire collection of Clara Schumann preludes can be found in Valerie Woodring Goertzen, *Clara Schumann: Exercises, Preludes, and Fugues* (Bryn Mawr, Pa.: Hildegard, 2001).

[60] A. Mitchell, 15.

[61] John Rink, "Improvisation," in Stanley Sadie, ed., *New Grove Dictionary of Music and Musicians*, 2nd ed. (London: Macmillan, 2000), 2:5, "Instrumental Music." Rink—an acknowledged expert on romantic improvisation—nevertheless does mention that transitions between pieces continued to be extemporized in later decades. For Amy Fay's preluding, see Margaret William McCarthy, *Amy Fay: America's Notable Woman of Music* (Warren, Mich.: Harmonie Park Press, 1995), 37. Fay also commented in 1894 on the skill of Teresa Carreño's preluding: "And then, her extemporization before every piece; there has never been anyone to compare with her in that, always striking into the key of the artist who preceded her on the programme, and modulating into the one in which her solo was written. I have never known her to fail, so absolute is her sense of pitch" (McCarthy, p. 161).

[62] A. Newcomb, 278.

impetuous nature.[63] Deppe had also claimed that the opening of a certain (un-identified) piece would only sound correct with a preludial chord played before it, which would "fix the key."[64] Liszt too had demanded in the 1880s that a student play "a little prelude" when beginning a performance of his third *Liebestraum*. He had then shown exactly what he meant by playing one that was three chords long.[65] His advice to a pupil playing Henselt's Concert Etude "Danklied nach Sturm," op. 2 no. 1, was to "first play the theme without the rustling left hand" as an introduction before starting the piece itself.[66] It was evidently not only Leschetizky for whom preluding was an essential part of performance.

Of course there were voices raised against the abuse of the practice, for every practice has its abuses, although what exactly they are thought to be varies with changing tastes and times. By 1892 the London *Musical Times* was mightily offended when Pachmann inserted a transitional prelude into Beethoven's Third Concerto during a concert:

> The cadenza played at the close of the [first] movement was by Liszt, and was played with extraordinary fluency. But M. de Pachmann spoilt everything by what followed. The opening movement of the concerto is in C minor. The Largo is in E-major, and the sequence of keys apparently jarred on the nerves of the susceptible virtuoso, for he must needs preface the slow movement with a modulatory improvisation of his own, and act of artistic impertinence for which he deserved to be hissed. What was good enough for Beethoven should be good enough for M. de Pachmann . . . as a whole, the performance was artificial, affected and irreverent.[67]

It is genuinely difficult to say whether such additions might have been re-garded as "irreverent" by Beethoven, or simply quite normal. Pachmann could well have made an arguable case that his approach was appropriate on historical grounds, whatever one thought of the result in practice. Beethoven must have intended his own modulatory preludes, op. 39, for some purpose or other, and the most obvious is indeed as transitions between pieces or movements in different keys. Moreover, his well-known objections to Czerny's spontaneous modifications in one particular chamber-music performance concerned extrav-agant alterations to the body of the piece, rather than the inclusion of a prelude

---

[63] Fay, 279.
[64] Fay, 203.
[65] Zimdars, *Masterclasses of Liszt*, 87.
[66] Zimdars, *Masterclasses of Liszt*, 149.
[67] Mitchell, 26.

between movements.[68] The one thing we can say for sure is that pianists—even "the great Pachmann," as he so often described himself—had to proceed rather more cautiously with "the great Beethoven" by the 1890s.

By the end of the nineteenth century, Beethoven had been deified for decades, and the sheer intensity of the critic's abhorrence of the "impertinence" and "irreverence" that "deserved to be hissed" suggests that Pachmann had a committed a sacrilege akin to sleeping with a vestal virgin rather than having simply taken a questionable artistic decision in a concert. (It also, incidentally, tells us that Pachmann was not, in fact, hissed.) Such blasphemy might not have been so readily noted with composers whose place in the pantheon was slightly more tenuous (in other words, almost everyone else). Only a few years before, in 1885, Anton Rubinstein in Pressburg seems to have been able to get away with playing "four crashing B-flat-minor chords in the deepest bass range of the piano" between more than one movement of Chopin's Second Sonata, to increase the dramatic effect.[69] The audience included Liszt, Leschetizky, Rosenthal, and Ludwig von Bösendorfer. Liszt later told Rosenthal that the Chopin Sonata was the high point of the program for him, though he had reservations about certain aspects of Rubinstein's programmatic approach.[70] Once more no one hissed.

## A Delayed Demise

Preluding continued through the late nineteenth and well into the twentieth century despite the fact that audiences were becoming increasingly quiet and respectful and pianos increasingly standardized, which would supposedly have eliminated two of the original reasons for the practice. Paderewski was accustomed to improvising a short prelude at the beginning of a concert, perhaps largely to put an end to the enthusiastic applause as he stepped on to the stage rather than to silence chattering. An audience member at a recital in 1914 commented: "Two or three imperative chords commanded absolute silence, which was maintained unbroken throughout the three hours over these thousands of people by the wonderful spell of his magnetic presence."[71] At an 1892 concert in Rochester, New York, the piano had retaliated with a vengeance

---

[68] See chapter 6, pp. 182–83.

[69] Mitchell and Evans, 99–100.

[70] Mitchell and Evans, 101. See also Stradal, 84–87.

[71] Nellie R. Cameron Bates, "A Country Girl at a Paderewski Concert," *Musician* 19 (February 1914): 125–26.

during these opening chords. According to Paderewski's *Memoirs*, he felt something tear in his arm as he played his prelude before the first piece, Beethoven's *Appassionata* Sonata. It turned out that the Steinway piano had inadvertently not been regulated to his specifications—he normally demanded a specially lightened action, more comparable with the feel of the Érards he preferred to play in Europe—and he had reached the hall late, without the opportunity to try out the instrument.[72] So ignored now is the custom of preluding that Paderewski is sometimes thought to have injured himself on the opening bars of the *Appassionata* Sonata itself—not likely from a glance at the score of the piece, and obviously incorrect from his subsequent comment: "But somehow I held myself together and began the playing of Beethoven's *Appassionata*."[73]

Percy Grainger provides us with a fairly late (1916) specimen of a short preludial piece in his version of the sea shanty "One More Day, My John" (example 4.12). With characteristic verbal novelty, he described this on the title page as "set for Piano in the form of a Preliminary Canter." Accordingly, "this piece may be key-shifted (transposed) into any key." Unsurprisingly, the work is suffused with languorously arpeggiated chords, the whole to be "lazy and dreamy, with a somewhat far-away lilt." Grainger prescribes the voicing of these chords with enormous attention to detail, each register using a subtly different dynamic, though the eventual effect is obviously intended to be one of spontaneity rather than studiousness.

Even without other evidence, a piece such as this shows us that the custom of preluding was far from forgotten by the time of the First World War. Studio recordings, however, rarely document the practice, with the notable exception of the Busoni example discussed toward the beginning of this chapter. Live recordings are another matter, though these are themselves rare, owing to the technological limitations of the era. It is not surprising that we do not hear many studio recordings with an improvised prelude or transition. In the first place, such an introduction was by definition ephemeral, would vary according to the mood of the moment, and was not intended to be immortalized on shellac. In the second place, the amount of music that could be fitted on the side of a disk (roughly four and a half minutes) was scanty enough as it was, without the performer's taking up space to play an extempore introduction that was not part of the piece "proper." Even pianists that we know played preludes in concert—such as Paderewski, Rachmaninoff (who would repeat the same chord again and

---

[72] Paderewski, 227–28.

[73] See, for example, David Taylor, "Paderewski's Piano," *Smithsonian* (March 1999), 1–3.

EXAMPLE 4.12. Percy Grainger, Preliminary Canter, "One More Day, My John," opening

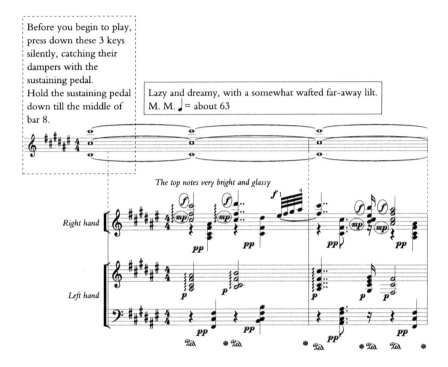

> N. B. This piece may be key-shifted (transposed) into any key so as to serve as a "preliminary canter" before any piece in any key. All big stretches may be harped (played *arpeggio*) at will.

> Before you begin to play, press down these 3 keys silently, catching their dampers with the sustaining pedal. Hold the sustaining pedal down till the middle of bar 8.

> Lazy and dreamy, with a somewhat wafted far-away lilt. M. M. ♩ = about 63

*The top notes very bright and glassy*

again until the audience was quiet),[74] Sauer, and Percy Grainger—did not feature them on recordings, although there are some obscure tapes of Grainger in concert on which he is heard strumming modestly before beginning each piece. With Josef Hofmann, the situation is intriguingly different. His studio recordings are notably prelude free, but we are lucky enough to have several discs of him playing live on special occasions in the late 1930s. These include his Golden Jubilee concert in the Metropolitan Opera House in 1937, a recital from Casimir Hall at the Curtis Institute, Philadelphia, and part of his penultimate Carnegie Hall recital of 1945. In all these recordings, Hofmann sometimes preludes between pieces.

[74] Martyn, 397.

It was, once again, recordings themselves that probably sounded the final death knell for the practice of preluding, despite its usefulness for pianists. Many performers today would be glad of the opportunity of trying out a few chords or runs to warm up on the keyboard at the start of a solo recital and perhaps get a chance to steady their nerves somewhat. Yet audiences are now used to the idea that what they should hear at a recital is what they would hear on a recording. The pianists' own effusions, be they Josef Hofmann's doodlings, Grainger's "preliminary canters," or Paderewski's peremptory chords, are not regarded as part of "the piece" to be performed, even if some composers would have expected their works to be introduced by a prelude. As we have seen, in several cases it was regarded not as an option, but as a necessity.

Modern players, with a few notable exceptions, have been extremely reluctant to reintroduce the spontaneous improvised elements that were a normal feature of the concerts of the past. Preluding is unthinkable, ornaments are rarely varied in repeats or reprises, and cadenzas are memorized as if they were simply a part of the printed score. Like Henri Herz, performers are partly worried about inspiration failing and disaster ensuing should they rely spontaneously on their own powers of invention. Such diffidence, to be sure, is not merely to do with changing tastes, the standardization of audience expectations after over 100 years of recordings, or the critical concerns for "unity of style" that seem rarely to have troubled musicians of previous eras. Many players in the classical performance world quite simply lack the training in improvisation that Liszt, Chopin, and their contemporaries received as a matter of course. After a few years of practice, earlier pianists would have built up a large store of typical figuration patterns, adaptable harmonic progressions, and standard styles of thematic variation. They would also have been looking out for opportunities to use them. This manner of thinking is as foreign to most classical pianists today as it is second nature to jazz players. When fledgling concert pianists begin a piece of music, they begin with the first notes of the score. When they are subsequently faced with 6/4 chords and glaring gaps at the end of a movement, their first reaction is to search around to find stylistically appropriate cadenzas printed elsewhere.[75] Yet there is a wealth of material available for those who wish to learn the skills of preluding and improvisation. This is not a lost art—it is simply one that has been deliberately neglected.

---

[75] A few modern players are taking improvisation seriously. Robert Levin, for example, has introduced imaginative extempore ornaments and cadenzas into his performances of Mozart and other classical composers with striking success.

# 5

# A Singing Tone

Kein Leben ohne Kunst,
Keine Kunst ohne Leben.

Man gewinnt nicht der Menschen Herzen
Nur mit Skalenläufen und schnellen Terzen,
Wohl aber mit edler Gesangsweise,
Hell und kräftig, und sanft und leise.

Nicht mit Skalen und Terzen
Gewinnt man der Menschen Herzen,
Wohl aber mit schönem Sang,
Tiefem Sinn und edlem Klang.
                    —Theodor Leschetizky

On 17 January 1907, in Vienna, the venerable and vastly influential piano pedagogue Theodor Leschetizky was asked to record a few words on an Edison cylinder. He accordingly declaimed with touching conviction the little poem in the epigraph.[1] Whatever its literary merits, it certainly enshrined his pianistic priorities. According to Paderewski, "All his pupils could get some beauty of

[1] "No life without art, no art without life. One does not win people's hearts only with runs of scales and fast thirds, but rather with a noble singing style, clear and powerful, gentle and soft. Not with scales and thirds does one win people's hearts, but rather with beautiful song, profundity, and noble tone." Leschetizky often inscribed this on presentation photographs of himself and can be heard intoning it on Arbiter Records CD 116 (Ignace Tiegerman, *The Lost Legend of Cairo*). Tiegerman was a pupil of Ignaz Friedman, one of Leschetizky's finest students. The poem is also reproduced (with a translation) in the extensive sleeve notes by Alan Evans (which, unlike most routine productions of this sort, constitute a significant piece of original research in themselves). My translation differs slightly from that of Evans. See also E. Newcomb, vii of the introduction by Edwine Behr.

tone. That applies to every one. . . . They all had a singing tone. That was very, very important."[2]

A preoccupation with a "noble singing melody" was shared by many pianists, John Field and Chopin among them, long before Leschetizky was born. "Cantabile" playing was a goal of J. S. Bach and an important part of Mozart's arsenal of effects.[3] By the early nineteenth century it was increasingly identified with the imitation of celebrated singers of Italian opera. Chopin, openly delighted when Kalkbrenner said his limpid cantabile made him sound like a pupil of Field, encouraged his students to take the opera stars of the day—Giuditta Pasta, Giovanni Battista Rubini, Maria Malibran—as models for "singing" on the keyboard. He accordingly put enormous emphasis on the requisite requirements in tone production and rubato.[4] Vocal phrasing and vocal ornamentation are found throughout his piano music, "pauses for breath" were added to his pupils' scores, and profuse operatic embellishments to the Nocturne op. 9 no. 2.[5] He also apparently improvised *fioratura* in his performances of Field's nocturnes. Although Liszt's cultivation of an "orchestral" style at the keyboard is well known, he undoubtedly did not intend this to be to the detriment of his ability to make the piano sing, and some critics could find no better compliment than to say that the piano under his fingers resounded out like the voice of Luigi Lablache. Bülow summed things up in a typically doctrinaire fashion: "Anyone who cannot sing—with a lovely or unlovely voice—should not play the piano."[6] All of this represents a different emphasis from modern pianism, the standard metallic crash of which is extensively documented on CD. Of course, one should not exaggerate; there are some contemporary performers with a fine cantabile and a remarkable variety of tone color. But it would nevertheless be true to say that much modern piano playing and criticism have different priorities, even if au-

[2] Paderewski, 111.

[3] Though in the cases of Bach and Mozart, probably more connected with a singer's style of rhetorical delivery than with a pianistic imitation of the singing cantabile.

[4] See Eigeldinger, *Chopin: Pianist and Teacher*, 44–45, 110–15; Richard Hudson, *Stolen Time: A History of Tempo Rubato* (New York: Oxford University Press, 1995), 208–9.

[5] For ornaments to op. 9.no. 2 see Jan Ekier's Wiener Urtext edition; also Eigeldinger, *Chopin: Pianist and Teacher*, 77–79. Especially interesting in this context are three articles by Jonathan Bellman, "Improvised Ornamentation in Chopin's Paris," *Early Keyboard Studies Newsletter* 8, no. 2 (April 1994): 1–7; "Chopin and the Cantabile Style in Historical Performance," *Historical Performance* no. 2 (Winter 1989): 63–71; and "Chopin and His Imitators: Notated Emulations of the 'True Style' of Performance," *Nineteenth-Century Music* 24, no. 2 (Fall 2000): 149–60.

[6] Haas, 11. See also Zimdars, *Masterclasses of Von Bülow*, 17.

diences have been reluctant to follow them—stylistic awareness, fidelity to the score, and structural grasp being the most obvious.

Some claim that the romantic striving for a beautiful tone was based on false premises: a pianist can certainly control the volume but can hardly affect the tone of an instrument at all; differences in sound are owed largely to differences between instruments, rather than whether the performer "kneads" the keys from close position or strikes them from a great height, to name just two of the approaches the romantics believed changed the quality of tone. This view is usually supported by the observation that it is difficult to discern any change in tone quality when striking a single unpedaled note in isolation no matter how one plays it, although the dynamic level is easily changed depending on the force of the stroke. It seems to me that this argument rather misses the point. It is transparently true that isolated notes are resistant to tonal manipulation, unless one strikes with such power as to force the instrument well beyond its comfortable dynamic range, producing what is usually described as a "hard," or plain ugly, tone. The situation, however, is completely different with regard to balance within and between chords and to the performance of melody and harmony. Music offers a wealth of opportunity for tonal manipulation. Here the *relative* volume of each note and the skilled or unskilled use of the pedals can produce vast differences in sound quality and variety. The proof of the pudding, as they say, is in the eating: when auditioning performers one cannot avoid noticing that some can produce a much more beautiful or more flexible sonority than others, even when they are playing the same piece on the same instrument. Admittedly, some pianos make the production of an attractive tone a tough, even impossible task, while others can sound beautiful in the hands of even inept performers.[7] But the majority of instruments fall somewhere between these two categories. They reward sensitive and imaginative handling while punishing carelessness. Unfortunately, the audience then gets punished too—"collateral damage," in current military parlance.

The romantic concern with the way one struck the keys was not naiveté. It simply recognized that some approaches to the keyboard produce a generally different sonority compared with others, because they encourage or discourage certain types of tonal and dynamic balance. (Other techniques, such as the much-mocked "pseudo-vibrato" of continuing to press the finger backward and forward

---

[7] I once asked a colleague who had played in a certain recital hall a few weeks before my own concert what the piano was like. "Well, you know," he replied, "it sounds like violently broken glass." "What if you use the *una corda*?" I hazarded. He had a quick answer: "Then it sounds like softly broken glass."

on an already depressed key, is indeed ludicrous if the player really imagines he is changing the sonority of the note that has just been played, but perfectly viable if the purpose is to relax the wrist, or even just to give the audience something "artistic" to look at.) Many pianists spent intense effort on working out tonal manipulations in the highest degree of detail, especially as regards touch and the treatment of the pedal. Teresa Carreño entitled the manual of pedal technique she was working on at her death (1917) "Possibilites of Tone Colour by Artistic Use of the Pedals,"[8] and "The Secret of a Beautiful Tone" is one of the largest sections of Josef Lhévinne's *Basic Principles in Pianoforte Playing*,[9] to take just two examples among many. When Paderewski felt he was performing under par, his first worry was not producing too many wrong notes (these were merely "un-invited guests," in Rubinstein's terminology) or failing to elucidate the formal structure of the work, but not being able to produce "the tone."[10]

It is, however, fair to say that some of the means adopted by earlier per-formers to promote tonal beauty and variety have been not just neglected, but positively vilified by modern pianists—even, ironically, some of those who play on nineteenth-century instruments—for they include restrained to copious use of techniques now regarded as in the worse possible taste: dislocation of the hands, the staggering of melodic entries, and the (unmarked) arpeggiation of chords. My purpose here is not to write yet another manual of piano technique designed to foster a fine tone or to exhaustively catalog types of rubato (though, as I will discuss later, rubato is an inevitable consequence of some of these approaches).[11] Rather, it is to investigate the much-maligned asynchronization and related pedal effects used by romantic musicians to sing at the piano.[12]

Paderewski is normally thought of as representing the ne plus ultra of rubato and indulgence in asynchronization ("the license of his tempo rubato goes

[8] Reprinted in Joseph Banowetz, ed., *The Art of Piano Pedaling: Two Classic Guides; Anton Rubinstein and Teresa Carreño* (Mineola, N.Y.: Dover, 2003), 49–77.

[9] Josef Lhévinne, *Basic Principles in Pianoforte Playing* (1924; reprint, Mineola, N.Y.: Dover, 1974).

[10] Paderewski, 367. The young Paderewski was, however, like so many less than mature artists, frequently taken to task by critics for forcing the tone of his instrument. Shaw declared, "He goes to the point at which a piano huddles itself up and lets itself be beaten instead of unfolding the richness and colour of its tone." Shaw, *London Music in 1888–89, as Heard by Corno di Bassetto* (New York: Dodd, Mead, 1961), 393.

[11] For rubato in general see Hudson.

[12] Here defined as the deliberate avoidance of playing the hands, or individual notes in the texture, exactly together.

beyond all reasonable limits," remarked Shaw in 1890),[13] but his style is actually very similar to that of his teacher and scarcely the isolated aberration (a "late mannerism," according to Hudson)[14] that some imply it is and surely would wish it to be. The young Brahms was criticized for the "unremitting spreading of chords in slower tempi" as early as 1865, but he apparently maintained the habit to the end of his life.[15] Although Paderewski's master Leschetizky did not record, he made twelve piano rolls for the Welte-Mignon company in 1906, including performances of Mozart's Fantasy in C Minor, K. 475, and Chopin's Nocturne in Db, op. 27 no. 2, in addition to a few of his own pieces. There has been much debate over the inadequacy of piano rolls as a method of reproduction. They were often edited to produce results just as deceptively faultless as are our contemporary recordings spliced together from multiple takes (needless to say, players loved this aspect of them), and they are quite incapable of reproducing dynamics with any finesse at all, let alone a carefully layered tonal balance. But one thing they do show is a performer's use of asynchronization and arpeggiation. In fact, it is their robotic failure to reproduce tone colorings and dynamics adequately that makes this feature much easier to hear on rolls than in early recordings. It is immediately obvious, for example, which left-hand octaves Paderewski is arpeggiating and which he isn't in his piano roll of the first movement of the *Moonlight* Sonata. Identifying this accurately on his acoustic and even electric recordings requires much more careful listening, because the subtleties of Paderewski's approach are here more faithfully reproduced. Paderewski did not intend the details of his technique to be clinically laid bare. Leschetizky's piano rolls duly show a liberal application of procedures familiar from his pupil's playing, especially in the Chopin Db Nocturne, where the left hand regularly comes in with its bass note before the right-hand tune begins, and where the double thirds and sixths of the melody in the first episode are consistently arpeggiated.

It is perhaps more than just coincidence that this nocturne should be one of the examples of the asynchronization technique given by Leschetizky's assistant

---

[13] Shaw, *Music in London*, 15.

[14] Hudson, 213. Paderewski himself claimed that he was not a typical Leschetizky product, having come to the master rather late in his training. Nevertheless, there seem to be large stylistic similarities between their general approach to the piano, on the evidence of Leschetizky's piano rolls and Paderewski's recordings.

[15] Bernard D. Sherman, "How Different Was Brahms's Playing Style from Our Own?," in Musgrave and Sherman, 2.

Malwine Brée in *Die Grundlage der Methode Leschetizky* (1903).[16] There has been some discussion about the value of Brée's treatise and whether or not it gives a true representation of the thought of the master. It has often been rightly remarked that Leschetizky adapted his teaching very skillfully to the individual pupil (Schnabel and Ignaz Friedman, to name just two, must have had very different requirements) and to this extent can hardly be said to have had a "method" at all. Nevertheless, the evidence that Brée's book is a fair account of Leschetizky's principles is so overwhelming as to be sufficient even before the most skeptical court. It was published not only with Leschtizky's full authorization, but even with his fulsome prefatory letter, printed in facsimile in his own handwriting. This is no routine vote of thanks.[17] He tells Brée, "I am in principle no friend of theoretical piano schools; however, your splendid work, which I have carefully looked through, corresponds in such an astonishing way to my personal views, that I sign my name to everything that you expound in your book, word for word." Leschetizky was so pleased with Brée's book that he allowed her to use pictures of his hands to demonstrate the various positions recommended. The treatise is consequently graced by forty-eight photographs of the fingers that wrote the preface. All in all, Brée tells us plainly much that we could have expected from recordings by Paderewski, Hambourg, Benno Moiseiwitch, Friedman, and many others.

The first bars of the Chopin D♭ Nocturne are used for illustration in the section entitled "Arpeggiation," and the comments could well be a description of Leschetizky's piano roll recorded a few years later. We are told:

> The fundamental bass note and the melody note must also not always be taken at the same time; rather, the melody note should be struck quite shortly after the bass, by which method the melody rings out more clearly and sounds softer. Nevertheless, this may happen only at the beginning of a phrase, and mostly only with important notes and strong beats of the bar. (Weak beats are better struck precisely together.) The melody note must be brought in so quickly after the bass that this is hardly noticeable for lay listeners, for example Chopin's Nocturne:[18]

---

[16] An English translation was published in 1907. The quoted excerpts are, however, my own translation of the original edition.

[17] It is worth noting that Leschetizky's "testimonial" preface for Marie Prentner's *Fundamental Principles of the Leschetizky Method* (1903) is much more vague and noncommittal than his enthusiastic effusions for Brée's treatise.

[18] Brée, 73. Examples 5.1 to 5.5 are from Brée's treatise.

EXAMPLE 5.1. Frédéric Chopin, Nocturne in D♭, theme

The important thing to note here is that such dislocation is not regarded, as it would be later, as sloppy technique, but as a deliberate effect designed to emphasize the melody and to vary the tone color. The approach should also be used with a subtlety that prevents it from being immediately obvious. If the bass note is struck first, with open pedal, the melody note gets the benefit of the sympathetic vibrations thus set up and is more effectively "floated" over the bass. This is no mere pianistic myth. There is a genuine difference in sonority that will be evident to anyone experimenting with such effects at the keyboard. The consequent dislocation is also a type of rubato, for it is clear here and elsewhere that the fundamental bass note should usually be struck on the beat, with the melody following in slight syncopation. Rubato is the inevitable result of many of the other types of chordal arpeggiation also advocated, for most romantic (and earlier) treatises insist on beginning arpeggiations on the beat with the lowest note of the chord, the melody note following slightly later.[19] Many pianists nowadays are reluctant to do this because it causes syncopation of the melodic line and prevents the crisp rhythmic attack we so often favor. This, however, was part of the point.

Brée goes into some detail about the appropriateness of arpeggiation, advice worth quoting in detail because it is so contrary to much present-day practice. We learn that

one must not always only arpeggiate where a chord is too widely spaced to allow simultaneous attack. Arpeggiation is also suitable where a softer expression needs to be brought out. Here the right hand arpeggiates, while the left strikes the chord:

[19] For just two examples, see Brée, 59, and S. Lebert and L. Stark, *Klavierschule* (Stuttgart: Cotta, 1883), Teil 3, pp. 62–63, on arpeggiation.

EXAMPLE 5.2. Ignacy Jan Paderewski, *Legende*, excerpt

The other way round, the chord sounds energetic and yet not hard, when the right hand strikes the notes together and the left hand arpeggiates. But this must be a quick flourish[*ein schneller Riss*], for example:

EXAMPLE 5.3. Frédéric Chopin, First Scherzo in B Minor, excerpt

Arpeggiation is further to be used, where the polyphony ought to be made more clear to the ear, but only in important moments, when, for example, one voice ends and another begins at the same time:

EXAMPLE 5.4. Robert Schumann, Romance in F♯ Major, excerpt

and in the same way in a canon, for example:

EXAMPLE 5.5.  Ignacy Jan Paderewski, Variations in A Major, excerpt

Of course, the two examples from Paderewski's compositions are especially apt because this master's own playing made such prolific use of the relevant techniques. But to confine this approach to Leschetizky and some of his most famous pupils would be a gross underestimation of how prevalent it was. Bauer, who was more or less self-taught as a pianist and whose recordings show frequent use of dislocation, had noticed when making piano rolls that "it was best, in accentuating a single tone contained within a chord, to allow this tone to precede the other tones by a fraction of a second, instead of insisting that all tones be played simultaneously. . . . The illusion of simultaneity was perfect, and it sounded better that way, so I introduced this method into my technical practice."[20] As far as polyphonic playing is concerned, the displacement of parts in order to emphasize the voice leading was a standard method of performance, intriguingly (and unusually) notated in detail in the so-called *facilité* to the fugal section in Alkan's "Quasi Faust," the second movement of his ambitious programmatic sonata *The Four Ages* (1848).

Far from being a straightforward simplification for use by the technically less adept, this alternative version is in fact absolutely necessary for even the most gifted. It is a feasible version of the unplayable (except perhaps for those with Rachmaninoff-size hands) principal text, which has—typically for Alkan—been composed more with an eye to strict counterpoint than to practicality. Alkan, fine pianist that he was, knew in his heart of hearts that the text was preposterous as it stood. It is not the quite unexceptional arpeggiation of wide stretches that concerns us here, but the bringing out of the main voices by means of rhythmic displacement indicated in the *facilité*:

[20] Bauer, 176.

EXAMPLE 5.6.   Charles Valentin Alkan, *Grande sonate*, second movement, "Quasi Faust," excerpt

Such rhythmic displacement can, of course, also be achieved by arpeggiation of a chord from the top down, with the bottom or middle note emphasized. We can hear this now and again in Alfred Grünfeld's recording of the Wagner-Liszt "Liebestod" from *Tristan*. It was especially pervasive in Pachmann's playing and features in the Chopin editions following his method produced by his ex-wife, "Madame Pachmann-Labori" (see, for example, that of the Etude op. 10 no. 11). These and other techniques mentioned by Brée were common features of pianism up until the Second World War. Pachmann recorded Chopin's D♭ Nocturne for Columbia around 1916 and performed the opening bars in a way that would have met with Leschetizky's complete approval, although he was rather more circumspect about arpeggiating the thirds and sixths in the right hand that come later.[21] In a 1936 recording Moriz Rosenthal also plays the opening in a similarly dislocated manner, uses frequent arpeggiation later in the right hand and a subtle but thorough left-before-right style in the whole piece.[22] These are beautiful performances, very individual in their expressive effects, and both are marked by wonderfully varied tone colors. If we turn to the several recordings of this nocturne by Josef Hofmann,[23] we hear a rather

---

[21] OPAL CD 9840.

[22] Pearl Gemm CD 9963.

[23] All on Marston MR52004-2. Two recordings exist from 1935, one of which is missing the last few bars. A short section of another is extant as a test pressing from 1940, and a radio broadcast from 1942 makes a fourth.

different approach, with virtually no dislocation between the hands (there is a—probably accidental—slight syncopation between bass and the very first melody note in the incomplete 1935 performance) but several arpeggiated thirds and sixths.

This would at least superficially seem to bear out Hofmann's oft-quoted opinion on dislocation that "this 'limping' as it is called, is the worst habit you can have in piano playing,"[24] but an examination Hofmann's entire recorded output shows that he did use the technique, albeit relatively seldom compared with most recorded players of his generation (see, for example, the 1916 disc of Chopin's Waltz in C♯ Minor, op. 64 no. 2).[25] It is partly this rather ascetic aspect of his playing that can make him seem among the most "modern" of late-romantic pianists. But he was certainly far from it in many other ways. His blanket condemnation of "limping" was cautious advice written in a book confidently called *Piano Questions Answered* and intended for tyro pianists. They would undoubtedly have been far better avoiding asynchronization altogether than indulging in it regularly and crudely. Certainly Hofmann's vast admiration for Rosenthal's playing seems to have been in no way affected by the older performer's frequent recourse to such devices.

Other warnings against abuse of asynchronization can easily be found. Godowski, for example, asserted "one thing is unendurable—to hear the left hand before the right, constantly appoggiating."[26] Comments like these have been seized upon by those who wish to isolate the technique as some bizarre late-romantic malady, without previous solid precedent and now happily cured. Most of these criticisms, however, like Hofmann's, occur in didactic literature. They cannot be taken as accurately representing the actual practice of mature musicians, especially because the recorded legacy so definitely declares the opposite. Moreover, one must decide in a quote like that from Godowski how much emphasis to put on the word "constantly." Is he recommending an outright ban or simply cautioning against overuse? Given the fact that Godowski himself can be heard to use asynchronization in his recordings—albeit subtly—the latter is likely to be correct. Mark Hambourg represents a similar case. In his *How to Play the Piano* (a wonderfully brusque and businesslike title for a complicated undertaking, rather like "How to Achieve World Peace") we find the chapter "Some Common Mistakes and How to Avoid Them." Sure enough, dislocation

---

[24] Hofmann, 25 in "Piano Questions Answered."

[25] VAI Audio/IPA 1036-2.

[26] Jeffrey Johnson, *Piano Mastery*, 95.

is here condemned as "another blunder...like drawling in speech or even stuttering."[27] Hambourg even rewrites the opening of Rachmaninoff's C♯-Minor Prelude in the condemned style, when it turns out thus:

EXAMPLE 5.7. Mark Hambourg, parody of Rachmaninoff's Prelude in C♯ Minor, from *How to Play the Piano*

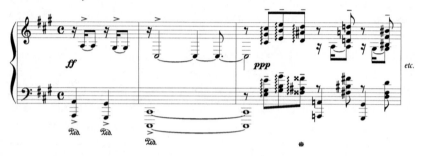

Can we conclude from this that Hambourg's own playing religiously avoided these techniques? Of course not. His recordings show their liberal application (see, for example, his discs of the Chopin Nocturnes op. 9 no. 2 and op. 55 no. 1).[28] As a good student of Leschetizky, he used them as one of his main means of expression. It is simply their exaggerated, routine, and tasteless use that he is parodying. Unfortunately, to many modern pianists the only application of these techniques within the boundaries of taste is no application at all, and Hambourg's remarks, like Godowsky's, can easily now be read tendentiously as a condemnation of the entire approach, rather than a caution to students against its misuse. It is highly unlikely that his comments would have been so interpreted on their publication in 1923, when Hambourg's own playing was still regularly heard and Paderewski and Rosenthal were among the most lauded performers on the concert circuit. I would argue that Chopin's advice to his pupil Carl Mikuli that he ought to strike chords "strictly simultaneously" and avoid unmarked arpeggiation should also be considered in this context,[29] that is, as an injunction against abuse to a student performer, and not as a blanket ban intended to apply to mature artists. After all, Chopin sometimes told his students to imitate the sound of guitars in certain chordal passages (like the opening of the B-Major

---

[27] Mark Hambourg, *How to Play the Piano* (London: Arthur Pearson, 1923), 56–57.
[28] Pearl GEMM CD 9147.
[29] Eigeldinger, *Chopin: Pianist and Teacher*, 41.

Mazurka, op. 41 no. 3),[30] which certainly implies an arpeggiation that is unmarked in the text. Tausig used the same analogy for the accompanying chords in the op. 9 no. 2 Nocturne (also for the opening movement of Beethoven's Sonata op. 101, which according to Wilhelm von Lenz he played "so that I could hear the guitars"!).[31] Most romantic pianists on record certainly arpeggiated some, and some almost all, of the chords in this Chopin nocturne.

One should be similarly circumspect in drawing hasty conclusions from Saint-Saëns's description of what he learned from Pauline Viardot about Chopin's rubato. This too condemns "limping," but does recommend a more subtle asynchronization:

> The accompaniment holds its rhythm undisturbed while the melody wavers capriciously, rushes or lingers, sooner or later to fall back upon its axis. This way of playing is very difficult since it requires complete independence of the two hands; and those lacking this give both themselves and others the illusion of it by playing the melody in time and dislocating the accompaniment so that it falls beside the beat; or else—worst of all—content themselves with simply playing one hand after the other. It would be a hundred times better just to play in time, with both hands together, but then they would not have the artistic air.[32]

Again it is over-regularity and predictability of asynchronization that is criticized here, not the basic practice itself, for the "rushing or lingering" actually advocated is evidently only a more varied and imaginative type of dislocation than the one condemned. "Playing in time with both hands together" is here simply the best refuge for those unable properly to master a flexible dislocated rubato, not the ideal style of performance as it would be today.[33]

---

[30] Eigeldinger, *Chopin: Pianist and Teacher*, 76.

[31] Wilhelm von Lenz, *The Great Piano Virtuosos of Our Time* (1872; reprint, London: Kahn and Averill, 1983), 65.

[32] Eigeldinger, *Chopin: Pianist and Teacher*, 49; Hudson, 194–95. I have slightly conflated the translations given by these two authors.

[33] I am afraid I must beg to differ from Jean-Jacques Eigeldinger here, who comments: "This practice, criticised by Saint-Saëns, is clearly recognisable in the recordings of 'renowned' Chopin players of the time, notably Leschetizky, Pugno, Pachmann, Friedman, and, to a lesser extent, Paderewski and Maurycy [Moriz] Rosenthal" (*Chopin: Pianist and Teacher*, 118). As I mention in the main text, it seems to me that Saint-Saëns is not criticizing the practice itself at all, merely its inept abuse. Furthermore, the fact that asynchronization was extensively used by this long roll call of great performers, whose renown as Chopin players deserves more respect than to be placed in quotation marks, should tell us that it is maybe not the technique, but our evaluation of it that is at fault. Finally, I should reiterate that Paderewski and Rosenthal seem to me from their recordings to be among the most dedicated followers of this practice, rather than adherents "to a lesser extent."

One could easily go through the entire surviving collection of early recordings and pick out individual uses of asynchronization—Leopold Godowski's *Raindrop* Prelude from 1913,[34] where the initial return of the main melody is emphasized by a dislocation not present on its first playing, or Alfred Grünfeld's Chopin Ab Nocturne, op. 32 no. 2, from 1911,[35] where the variable speed of separation between bass and treble gives a striking rhetorical quality to some turns of phrase. But in the end the general conclusion would simply be that virtually all players of the era used this approach sometimes, and many very frequently indeed. At its worst it can be like Arthur Friedheim's Trio from the Chopin Funeral March (1912),[36] where the bass is plonked down before the melody far too predictably and overemphatically (to be fair to Friedheim, this is more likely to be a miscalculation of the bass balance required for the acoustic recording process than an accurate representation of his normal playing), or Paderewski's Chopin Eb Nocturne (1930),[37] in which the sheer regularity of the bass and treble dislocation, despite the gorgeous sonority, is indeed verging on the constantly syncopated "limping" abhorred by Hofmann. Yet at its best, as in Paderewski's (1922) and Rosenthal's (1929) recordings of the Chopin-Liszt "Meine Freuden," or Pachmann's gorgeous *Raindrop* Prelude (where the melody note often arrives on the beat but a split second *before* the supporting harmony—a feature frequently heard in Pachmann's playing),[38] the technique really does yield a glorious flexibility of tone color and a pliant variety of melodic emphasis.

Leschetizky, though originally a pupil of Czerny in Vienna, had first acquired his fascination with the possibilities of varying tone color from listening in the 1840s to Julius Schulhoff (1825–1898), a pianist from Chopin's circle in Paris who was relatively well-known as a composer of salon music.[39] Schulhoff had made the constant production of a beautiful sound the chief goal of his labors, no doubt inspired by Chopin's own example. Chopin's pupil George Mathias (1826–1910) told his own student Isidor Philipp that for his master, "beauty of tone was the immediate object of study."[40] Czerny believed that it

---

[34] Marston 52046-2.

[35] OPAL CD 9850.

[36] Pearl GEMM CD 9993.

[37] Pearl GEMM CD 9397.

[38] Paderewski, Pearl GEMM CD 9397; Rosenthal, Pearl GEMM CD 9339; Pachmann, OPAL CD 9840.

[39] As a student, Rachmaninoff played some pieces by Schulhoff in concert; see Martyn, 366.

[40] Jeffrey Johnson, ed., *Piano Lessons in the Grand Style* (New York: Dover, 2003), 27. See also Eigeldinger, *Chopin: Pianist and Teacher*, passim.

was only in his own day that methods of piano construction had advanced far enough for the player to have a really wide variety of tone color and dynamics at his disposal (whatever modern advocates of the fortepiano might argue), and it is therefore not entirely unexpected that sonority from this point on should have become an increasing preoccupation, along with a yet more intense focus on "singing."[41] On first hearing Schulhoff, the slightly younger Leschetizky was bowled over: "The melody standing out in bold relief, that wonderful sonority. All this must be due to a new and entirely different touch. And that cantabile, a legato such as I had not dreamed possible on the piano, a human voice arising above the sustaining harmonies! I could hear the shepherd sing, and see him."[42]

Schulhoff's sound must indeed have been remarkable, although from this distance in time it is impossible to judge how "new" it was compared with that of Chopin or others, or indeed what exactly that implied in a technical sense. William Mason had also been impressed with Schulhoff when he later heard him, though less so with other aspects of his performance:

I remember on one occasion Schulhoff came to Weimar and played in the drawing room of the Altenburg house. His playing and Liszt's were in marked contrast. He has been mentioned in an earlier chapter [of Mason's memoirs] as a parlor pianist of high excellence. His compositions, exclusively in the smaller forms, were in great favor and universally played by the ladies. Liszt played his own "Bénédiction de Dieu dans la Solitude," as pathetic a piece as, perhaps, he ever composed, and of which he was very fond. Afterward Schulhoff, with his exquisitely beautiful touch, produced a quality of tone more beautiful than Liszt's; but about the latter's performance there was intellectuality and the indescribable impressiveness of genius, which made Schulhoff's playing, with all its beauty, seem tame by contrast.[43]

Though initially inspired by Schulhoff's tone, Leschetizky was not a monomaniac: he learned what he could where he could. He was well acquainted with most of the preeminent pianists of his era, had heard and admired both Liszt and Thalberg in their prime, and was later a colleague of Anton Rubinstein's at the

---

[41] Czerny, *Complete Theoretical and Practical Pianoforte School, Op. 500: Supplement* (London: Cocks, 1846), 3.

[42] Angele Potocka, *Theodore Leschetizky*, trans. Henry Lincoln (New York, 1903), 90. See also Hullah, 5–6.

[43] Mason, 112–13.

St. Petersburg Conservatory.[44] Leschetizky's methods of tone production were evidently influenced by the playing of all of these, and indeed the specific techniques he recommended had a very long pedigree indeed.

Asynchronization and arpeggiation had been standard aspects of tonal enhancement and melodic emphasis in harpsichord and clavichord playing for centuries. They remain so today for players of these instruments. Girolamo Frescobaldi (1583–1664) had advised players of his *Toccate e partite d'intavolatura* (1614) that "chordal harmonies should be broken with both hands so that the instrument does not sound hollow."[45] Similar comments can be found regularly throughout the seventeenth and eighteenth centuries. For the first hundred years of its existence the piano shared the affections of keyboard players with the much older harpsichord, clavichord, and organ. It would have been very surprising, therefore, if performers did not begin to play the new instrument using the approaches they were familiar with from the earlier ones, in particular the first two, which shared the piano's short decay of tone. The organ, which could also have been taken as a model—and indeed seems later to have partially informed the legato keyboard approach of figures as diverse as Beethoven (who had played the organ frequently during his early years in Bonn), Mendelssohn, and Busoni—was significantly different in that it was genuinely capable of a sustained tone.

The relevance of the harpsichord and its playing techniques to the developing piano was further enhanced by the fact that the thin, penetrating sonority of the eighteenth-century piano approximates the harpsichord rather closely—certainly much more than it does our concert grand of today. Even in the early nineteenth century, by which time the piano had achieved almost complete ascendancy, the attitudes to asynchronization and arpeggiation of the harpsichord era had remained alive in many quarters and were to continue in rude health for a long time afterward.

The writings of P. A. Corri are a case in point. In the *Complete Guide to Preluding on the Pianoforte* quoted in chapter 4, he gives general instructions how to play the chords of his specimen preludes:

> The chords that are long and which conclude the prelude [reproduced as ex. 4.4 of the present volume] ... should not be struck together, but by a long extended appoggiando.... These chords that begin any run or passage (as the chord marked *sf* in the same prelude ... ) should have emphasis, and should be played

---

[44] Like so many others, Leschetizky was full of praise for Liszt the pianist but deeply skeptical about the worth of his original compositions.

[45] From the preface (Rome, 1614 and 1637).

more together, and with more firmness; When there are several chords together (as at the beginning of the same prelude ...) they should be played almost together and not appoggiando.[46]

Rather comically to us, Corri's chordal performance style thus ranges from "not together" to "almost together," totally omitting the modern default option—completely together except where otherwise indicated.

Czerny too was quite well aware of the expressive possibilites of added arpeggiation, although it is difficult to tell the amount that he would have regarded as advisable (it would probably shock us if we knew). At any rate, his discussion of the topic in his op. 500 *Pianoforte School*—"On the Situations Most Suitable to the Arpeggioing of Chords"[47] treats the arpeggiation of unmarked chords as a perfectly normal weapon in the pianist's expressive armory, especially helpful in softening or otherwise making distinctive the top note of a melody—again a usage partly rhetorical, and partly concerned with sonority. Evidently, even in his day unmarked arpeggiation was widespread, to such an extent that he felt compelled to caution against overuse of the technique. He complained that many pianists "accustom themselves so much to arpeggio chords, that they at last become quite unable to strike full chords or even double notes firmly and at once."[48] This from the teacher of Leschetizky! It is, however, Thalberg who gives us by far the most detailed nineteenth-century account of the topic, and what he tells us is both generally similar to Chopin's ideal in its concentration on singing at the piano, and in detail startlingly like Brée's "Leschetizky Method" of fifty years later. It also adumbrates comments in lesser-known works such as Adolph Christiani's *Principles of Expression in Pianoforte Playing*, published in 1885 and, significantly, dedicated to Liszt. Here asynchronization is advocated as a type of artistic rubato, accompanied by the usual foaming denunciations against its abuse.[49]

## Thalberg and *L'art du chant*

If Christiani has usually been ignored,[50] hats have been formally doffed to Thalberg in passing. Little attention, however, has been paid to what he actually

[46] Corri, 4.

[47] Czerny, *Complete Theoretical and Practical Pianoforte School* (1838), 3:55–56.

[48] Czerny, *Complete Theoretical and Practical Pianoforte School* (1838), 3:55–56.

[49] Adolph Friedrich Christiani, *The Principles of Expression in Pianoforte Playing* (New York: Harper and Brothers, 1885).

[50] Not by Hudson, who discusses some parts of his work, 324–25.

had to say, and his opinions (when noted at all) have been distorted by misleading quotation. His importance has also been underestimated owing to our emphasis on Chopin and Liszt, who certainly were much finer composers.[51] Thalberg and Liszt were nevertheless commonly regarded as evenly matched as virtuoso pianists in the late 1830s and early 1840s. Chopin's delicate style was effectively *hors de concours* in the public brawl. In some quarters Thalberg was even considered more inventive than Liszt—"the creator of a new school," according to Fétis in 1837,[52] in a response to Berlioz's extolling of his friend Liszt as "the pianist of the future"—and several of Thalberg's signature keyboard features soon turned up in Liszt's works (notably the *Norma Fantasy*, which was intended to out-Thalberg Thalberg) and in those of lesser luminaries such as Döhler. Mendelssohn also adopted them (in the D-Minor Piano Concerto, for example)—significantly so, for he otherwise showed little interest in trendy keyboard advances.

The indefatigable Czerny gave a vivid firsthand account of the unprecedented impact Thalberg had on musicians and audiences, particularly in his use of the pedals to produce his famous "three-handed" effect, in which a melody was sustained in the middle ("tenor") register while a profusion of figuration was scattered over and under it:

> Thalberg who, about the year 1830, completed his musical studies in Vienna, therefore conceived the idea of extending these pedal effects [holding on a bass note by means of the pedal] which (as we have seen in the example from Beethoven's Bagatelles) formerly occurred only in bass notes, to the notes of the middle and higher octaves, and thereby produce entirely new effects, which had hitherto never been imagined.... From this period may be dated the invention of the modern style of Pianoforte playing, which has now become general. While the notes of a melody are struck with energy in a middle position and their sound continued by skilful use of the pedal, the fingers can also perform brilliant passages *piano*, with a delicate touch; and thus arises the remarkable effect, as if the melody were played by another person, or on another instrument.... When, therefore, Thalberg first publicly performed his *Don Juan Fantasia* in Vienna, about the period here alluded to, the new effects therein developed justly excited the greatest astonishment, and in passages such as the following:

---

[51] I plead guilty to this myself in some of my other writings.
[52] Lina Ramann, ed., *Franz Liszt: Gesammelte Schriften* (Leipzig, 1880–83), 2:87.

EXAMPLE 5.8. Sigismond Thalberg, *Don Juan* Fantasia, excerpt

even the most experienced pianists could not understand the possibility of these effects. For the powerful octaves, being sustained by means of the pedal, sounded in the following manner:

EXAMPLE 5.9. Sigismond Thalberg, *Don Juan* Fantasia, score reduction

and the intermediate brilliant figure seemed to be performed by other hands.[53]

"The most experienced pianists" no doubt included the unperturbable Czerny himself, for once duly perturbed. Czerny was insistent that Thalberg's pianistic innovations were of lasting value, and not simply ephemeral tricks: "It would be very wrong to regard this new style of playing as of mere singular effect. An actual extension of the means of art is always a true gain."[54] His view was similar

[53] Czerny, *Complete Theoretical and Practical Pianoforte School, Op. 500: Supplement*, 3.
[54] Czerny, *Complete Theoretical and Practical Pianoforte School, Op. 500: Supplement*, 4.

to that promoted in Moscheles and Fétis's extensive treatise on piano playing *Méthode des méthodes (Die Vollständigste Pianoforte-Schule).*[55] This consists of a summary and evaluation of the advice given in previous treatises, with new material added to ensure contemporary relevance. (It is also the first case known to me of the modern academic plague of "footnote-itis," for in many pages the footnotes are ludicrously more extensive than the supposed "main" text itself.) Moscheles and Fétis were in no doubt of Thalberg's lasting importance: "Through this style of piano playing art has won a completely new shape, it has been enriched with new advantages and techniques."[56] Time has proved the correctness of this view. Not only did Thalbergian textures, and the concomitant style of pedaling, feature extensively in later romantic keyboard writing, but his inheritance is still with us today, as anyone will testify who has ever heard a cocktail-bar pianist wreath a slow popular tune in elegant arpeggios.[57]

But we do not have to rely on commentators to assess Thalberg's playing style. As well as numerous compositions (more impressive, admittedly, in their keyboard command than in other aspects of their inspiration), we also have an extensive preface to his magnum opus, *L'art du chant appliqué au piano,* op. 70 (1853–63).[58] The title is itself an indication of a familiar stance (compare Friedrich Wieck's *Klavier und Gesang* of 1853), and the ensuing collection consists

---

[55] Ignaz Moscheles and F.-J. Fétis, *Méthode des méthodes* (Paris: Schlesinger, 1840).

[56] Moscheles and Fétis, 20. Moscheles had been one of Thalberg's early piano teachers.

[57] See also chapter 1, p. 18.

[58] The first two of the four "series" of *L'art du chant* appeared toward the end of 1853, the second series at this point containing only four numbers. Two additional Weber transcriptions were published in 1854 that supplemented the second series. There was then a considerable break before the next two series, which came out respectively in 1861 and 1863. In its final form, *L'art du chant* consisted of: First series, (1) "A te, o cara," quartet from Bellini's *I puritani;* (2) "Tre giorni," aria by Pergolesi; (3) "Adelaide" by Beethoven; (4) "Pietà, signore" by Stradella; (5) Lachrymosa from the Requiem and a duet from *Le nozze di Figaro* by Mozart; (6) "Perché mi guardi e piangi" from Rossini's *Zelmira.* Second series, (1) "Bella adorata incognita" from Mercadante's *Il giuramento;* (2) "Nel silenzio fra l'orror" from Meyerbeer's *Il crociato;* (3) Ballad from Weber's *Preciosa;* (4) Lied from Schubert's *Schöne Müllerin;* (5) Duet from Weber's *Der Freischütz;* (6) "Il mio tesoro" from Mozart's *Don Giovanni.* Third series, (1) Serenata from Rossini's *Barber of Seville;* (2) Duet from Mozart's *Magic Flute;* (3) Barcarolle from Donizetti's *Gianni di Calais;* (4) "Protegga il giusto cielo" and "Là ci darem la mano" from Mozart's *Don Giovanni;* (5) Serenata from Grétry's *L'amant jaloux;* (6) Romanza from Rossini's *Otello.* Fourth series, (1) "Casta diva" from Bellini's *Norma;* (2) "Voi che sapete" from Mozart's *Le nozze di Figaro;* (3) Quartet from Weber's *Euryanthe;* (4) "Dafyyd garrey wen [David sur le rocher blanche]," ancient bardic aria; (5) Aria and chorus from Haydn's *Seasons;* (6) "Fenesta vascia," Neapolitan folk song.

of piano transcriptions of vocal numbers (mostly taken from opera, but including lieder, religious music, and even a Welsh folk song) designed to showcase Thalberg's ability to produce a singing melodic line and for the instruction of other players in this art.

The preface goes into more explicit detail on the techniques required to "sing" on the piano. It is worth treating this at some length here, because Thalberg's comments have mostly been either ignored or edited in such a way as drastically to distort their meaning. (Busoni, as we shall see, stands in the dock on this charge.) Thalberg was not a naive romantic. He realized full well that the piano is basically a percussion instrument. All cantabile playing, he averred, attempts more or less effectively to disguise this: "The art of fine singing . . . always remains the same no matter what instrument it is practiced on. . . . Since the pianoforte, looked at rationally, is not in a condition to be able to reproduce the beautiful art of singing in the greatest perfection, especially in prolonging a note, so one must by skill and artistic means ameliorate this imperfection to the extent of being able deceptively to imitate not just sustained and prolonged tones, but even a crescendo on a single note. . . . The singing part, the melody, should dominate in our transcriptions and we have paid especial attention to this. . . . The melody, and not the harmony, has proved itself to be triumphal throughout the ages."[59] Then follow eleven rules for performance, which I give here in a mixture of summary and direct quotation. (The need for hefty passages of direct quotation will become apparent when we subsequently discuss Busoni's use of Thalberg's text.) Thalberg's main points are:

1. Cultivate freedom from stiffness in the forearm, wrist, etc.
2. In order to produce a full sonority from the instrument, do not strike the keys hard, but sink into them deeply from a close position with strength, decisiveness, and warmth. In simple tender melodies, "knead the keys as if with silken fingers."
3. The melody must always be intoned clearly and distinctly, and must separate itself from the accompaniment in the same way as a human voice from a gentle orchestral accompaniment (in order to aid the apprehension of this, Thalberg always prints the melodic line—as Liszt occasionally did, and Grainger would do frequently—in larger notes). *Chords that have the melody in the upper note can be played in very close arpeggio* [my italics]. The dynamic levels indicated for the melody are only relative, and even at pianissimo it should always dominate the accompaniment.
4. The left hand must be subordinate to the right hand when the latter has the melody.

---

[59] Thalberg, preface to *L'art du chant*; my translation.

5. "Avoid absolutely that ridiculous and tasteless manner, playing the melody notes at an exaggeratedly long interval after those of the accompaniment, and thus from the beginning to the end of the piece giving the impression of a continuous syncopation. *With a melody that moves along in slow tempo and in notes of a longer duration, it is certainly of good effect, particularly at the beginning of each bar or at the beginning of each section of the melody, if one lets the singing part come in after the bass, however only with an almost imperceptible delay"* [my italics].

6. It is very important to hold onto notes for their absolute value (except when otherwise indicated) to avoid a dry and insufficient melodic line. Especially in multivoiced pieces is finger substitution very useful. One should study fugues to practice this technique.

7. Young artists should pay close attention to variety of dynamics, tone color, and sonority, otherwise their playing will be boring through lack of shading. The longer a note is, the more powerfully it should be struck (Thalberg marks these notes in *L'art du chant* with accents). *"The chords which have their melody in the upper voice are to be constantly broken (arpeggiated), but very swiftly, almost laid on top of one another, and the singing note more stressed than the other notes of the chord"* [my italics].

8. "The use of both pedals (singly or together) is necessary throughout, in order to bring fullness to the performance, to let consonant harmonies sound out together, and through their judicious use to bring out the imitation of sustained and swelling notes. *To this end one must often use the pedal first after striking a long-lasting melody note"* [my italics; what we now refer to as syncopated pedaling]. He adds— recalling Czerny—a warning to avoid misusing the pedals, for there are artists who have in this way lost "their feeling for pure harmony."

9. Too many people play too quickly—and place too much stress on finger agility. It is more difficult to avoid hurrying and to play slowly than one thinks.

10. To promote beauty of tone the pianist should play in a relaxed manner and avoid striking the keys from above. [This is really a repeat of points 1 and 2.] Normally one works too much with the fingers and too little with the mind [a very common observation: compare Liszt's "technique comes from the mind(*Geist*), not the fingers," or Busoni's "the greatest technique has its seat in the brain"].[60]

11. Listen to good singers, and learn to sing yourself [as Chopin also advised].

Thalberg closes by pointing out that himself studied singing for five years with one of the most famous leaders of the Italian school (Manuel Garcia the younger), and recommends this course to all pianists.

Some of these precepts are of course more quickly grasped by looking at the arrangements in *L'art du chant*. In the following excerpt from Thalberg's transcription of the Lacrimosa from Mozart's Requiem:

[60] Busoni, *Wesen und Einheit*, 113.

EXAMPLE 5.10. Sigismond Thalberg, *L'art du chant appliqué au piano*, Lacrimosa from Mozart's Requiem, opening

we can see a thoughtful and varied alternation between arpeggiated and block chords depending on the expression required. It might also be noted that despite what Thalberg says in point 8 of the preface, the pedaling marked here (and elsewhere in the collection) is distinctly of the non-syncopated variety. I shall focus on this topic more thoroughly later, but suffice it to say here that this is one more piece of evidence that syncopated pedaling was in routine use long before it was normally indicated in scores.

None of Thalberg's advice is discordant with the general practice in early recordings. Leschetizky (and possibly Chopin too)[61] could no doubt have

---

[61] Chopin's opinion of Thalberg in 1830 is well-known: "Thalberg plays famously, but is not my man: he is younger than I, popular with the ladies, writes pot-pourris on themes from Masaniello, produces piano with the pedal instead of with the hand, takes 10ths as easily as I do octaves, and wears diamond shirt-studs." Hedley, 76. It seems to me that too much stress is sometimes put on the critical (even simply bitchy) remarks here, and not enough on the general evaluation: "he plays famously." Moreover, in 1830, both Chopin or Thalberg were very young and by no means completely mature in their traits or judgments. I therefore cannot quite agree with Eigeldinger, who writes of Chopin's "low esteem" for Thalberg (*Chopin: Pianist and Teacher*, 104).

subscribed to his rules word for word as he did with the Brée treatise, for they are largely the same, even down to the close attack to the keys and the deep "kneading" action. Thalberg's dictums that the melody should predominate and should always be brought out by dynamics and tone color, and sometimes by arpeggiation and asynchronization as well, can also be illustrated by so many early recordings that it is hardly worth mentioning specific ones. From some pianists (such as Paderewski or Rosenthal) one rarely hears the modern organlike approach, with every note in the chord including the melody equally weighted and played strictly together. When they play chords together, the melodic note is still usually stressed. It seems to me highly likely (absolute proof, of course, we will never have) that many, probably most, pianists before the recording era played in a broadly similar way, although there will inevitably have been a spectrum of styles. Leschetizky's student Mark Hambourg believed that his master's general approach to performance derived from Liszt and Rubinstein (he did not mention Schulhoff or Thalberg), but that his specific teaching was tailored to the hands of the pupil before him. Leschetizky had come to the conclusion that Liszt's slender hands were more suited to agility, Rubinstein's shorter but massive paws to producing a full tone. The pupil with the former type of hand would thus be advised to cultivate the deep-pressure technique, the one with the latter encouraged to minimize the hands' natural weight and develop flexibility.[62]

I am in the business here of tracing the arpeggiated, asynchronized singing tone back to Thalberg and his predecessors. I am not trying surreptitiously to reinstate the concept of an uncorrupted "continuous tradition" of performance. After all, if traditions were so continuous, performance practice would change but little over time. Liszt plus Rubinstein with a dash of Schulhoff thrown in is not a recipe for Leschetizky. All great players have their own individuality, and none play exactly like their teachers, though some certainly come closer than others—Paderewski and Leschetizky, and perhaps also Friedheim and Liszt. It is sometimes not possible even to identify a main teacher (Rosenthal, for example was a pupil of Mikuli, Rafael Joseffy, and Liszt, and was also heavily influenced by Anton Rubinstein; Sauer was similarly impressed by Anton Rubinstein, but a pupil of Deppe, Nikolas Rubinstein, and Liszt). Nevertheless, Hambourg, a pupil of Leschetizky, had no trouble in identifying a general Leschetizky "style" among some of the master's students (where someone like

---

[62] Mark Hambourg, *From Piano to Forte: A Thousand and One Notes* (London: Cassell, 1931), 49–50.

Schnabel fitted in was left in slightly awkward silence).[63] Hambourg was also closely acquainted with many of the other great players of the era, and he could not avoid noticing that some had developed remarkably divergent techniques: "Busoni . . . who had a large following, developed a school of playing in quite a different style, as also has Leopold Godowski. Godowski's elaborate polyphonic system of technique necessitates a light sound on the keyboard, as against Leschetizky's teaching that pressure on the keys obtained the most satisfactory sonority."[64]

One only has to play a few bars of a Godowski "symphonic metamorphosis" like that on Johann Strauss's *Künstlerleben* Waltz to realize that it would be impossible to get through it at all, let alone make the tangled counterpoint audible to the audience, with anything but a fleet and superficial touch—no kneading of the keys here. But despite the survival of Godowski's music on the fringes of the virtuoso repertoire, it is undoubtedly Busoni's style and precepts of piano playing—he was almost alone in being "universally appreciated by his fellow pianists," in the experience of HMV recording maestro Fred Gaisberg[65]—that have had the bigger influence on the approaches to keyboard sonority customary today. Now the Leschetizky-Paderewski style seems to be from a time warp, and Godowski is a cult rather than a mainstream figure. Busoni's monumental approach to piano tone is, however, still with us, shorn to some extent of its individuality, and transplanted into a much more respectful interpretative context.

### Busoni versus Thalberg (or Not)

Busoni was almost as eloquent verbally as musically. His 1894 edition of the first book of Bach's *Well-Tempered Clavier* was specifically intended to be his

---

[63] George Bernard Shaw, on the other hand, blamed Leschetizky for some of the forced tone and liberty with the text that he heard at Paderewski's early concerts and regarded his influence on pianists as largely harmful: "Leschetizky seems to me to have done more to dehumanise pianoforte playing than any other leading teacher in Europe. When I hear pianists with fingers turned into steel hammers, deliberately murdering Beethoven by putting all sorts of accellerandos [*sic*] and crescendos into his noblest and most steadfast passages, I promptly put them down without further inquiry as pupils of Leschetizky." Shaw, *Music in London*, 3:219. One might take leave to doubt how much Shaw knew about Leschetizky's actual teaching.

[64] Hambourg, *From Piano to Forte*, 175. Arrau's comment (chapter 1, p. 15) that Godowski never played very loudly supports Hambourg's remarks here.

[65] Gaisberg, 187.

"pianistic testament" and a vehicle for his ideas on performance.[66] He was, in prose at least, both an admirer and an opponent of the "singing tone." The sheer inconsistency of many of his remarks, even in a single volume like Book I of *The Well-Tempered Clavier*, makes it difficult to draw a coherent thread through all his convoluted, if ever fascinating thought. But the gist is usually clear, even if a summary reveals something of a precarious balancing act. Busoni took his initial stance on cantabile playing in a footnote to the Bach D-Minor Prelude:

> The chase after an ideal legato is a relic of that period in which Spohr's violin method and the Italian art of song held despotic sway over the style of execution. There obtained (and still obtains) among musicians the erroneous notion, that the instrumental technic ought to be modeled after the rules of singing, and that it more nearly approaches perfection, the more closely it approaches this model so arbitrarily set up for imitation. But the conditions—the taking [of] breath, the necessary joining and dividing of syllables, words and sentences, the difference in the registers—on which the art of singing is based, lose greatly in importance even when applied to the violin, and are not in the least binding to the pianoforte. Other laws, however, produce other—characteristic—effects. These latter, therefore, are to be cherished and developed by preference, in order that the native character of the instrument may make itself duly felt. In proof of the staccato nature of the pianoforte, we instance the enormous development which has come about, within a few decades, in wrist technics and octave playing.[67]

One might here briefly remark that early- to mid-nineteenth-century pianos did indeed sound quite different from register to register, and that one can play octaves legato as well as staccato, but at least here Busoni's comments are internally coherent.

We would be unwise to assume from these remarks that Busoni was actually a complete opponent of the striving after cantabile effects—although that is more or less what he says—because when he reaches the soulful and songful Eb-Minor Prelude we are told "the soprano ought fairly to 'sing.'"[68] Busoni was certainly aware of the apparent contradiction here—hence the embarrassed inverted commas—and felt the need to explain himself a little more fully. He first waxes

---

[66] Busoni, *Well-Tempered Clavichord*. Busoni's edition is, alas, often ignored today.

[67] Busoni, *Well-Tempered Clavichord*, 1:35.

[68] Busoni, *Well-Tempered Clavichord*, 1:48.

lyrical and mystical, then returns to his earlier argument with a few significant modifications:

> This deeply emotional movement, emanating from the inspiration of a devout dreamer, is Bach's prophetic forecast that in the fullness of time a Chopin would arise. . . . The execution of long-breathed melodies on the pianoforte is not only difficult, but positively unnatural. In no case can a tone be evenly sustained, and a swell is still less possible; yet these are the two indispensable conditions for the rendering of cantabile passages, and impossible of fulfillment on the piano. The connection of one sustained tone with a following tone is perfect to a certain extent only when the second tone is struck with a softness precisely corresponding to the natural decrease in tone of the first. . . . While the tone of the pianoforte, by reason of the instrument's mechanism, naturally increases in power and sonorousness in the descending scale, the melody requires, on the other hand, that intensifications as a general rule, shall be accompanied by an increase in tone power when ascending:—but beyond a certain pitch the duration of the piano tone becomes so short, that pauses and breaks in the melodic continuity are absolutely unavoidable. It is the function of the touch to overcome these difficulties and to counteract these defects as far as may be. To avoid plagiarism of various remarks made by Thalberg on this point, I quote literally a few passages from the preface to his *L'art du chant appliqué au piano.* This course appears to be the best, in view of the fact that these remarks are noteworthy, and yet already forgotten.[69]

So, although the piano is not really suited to cantabile playing, we can sometimes create the illusion that it is. This is more or less what Thalberg himself says at the beginning of *L'art du chant.* But Busoni is willing to go along with Thalberg only to a certain extent. He quotes Thalberg's rules 1 and 2 (listed earlier), then skips to no. 5, from which he cites only "Avoid absolutely that ridiculous and tasteless manner, playing the melody notes at an exaggeratedly long interval after those of the accompaniment, and thus from the beginning to the end of the piece giving the impression of a continuous syncopation." There Busoni stops, without any indication that Thalberg carries on to significantly qualify his statement—"it is certainly a good effect . . . if one lets the singing part come in after the bass, etc." Busoni's silent editing, first omitting rule no. 3 entirely (which includes the comment that chords with the melody note at the top can be played in close arpeggiation), then selectively and deceptively

---

[69] Busoni, *Well-Tempered Clavichord,* vol. 1.

quoting only part of rule no. 5, gives the false impression that Thalberg adamantly opposed arpeggiation and asynchronization, whereas he in fact advocated its judicious use. He condemned—as did so many others—only its inept employment.[70]

This was not the only time in his published output that Busoni misled by omission. His edition of Liszt's *Fantasy on Themes from Mozart's "Marriage of Figaro"* claims on the title page to have been "completed [*ergänzt*] from the manuscript," but Busoni somehow forgot to mention that in the process of "completion" he left out nearly one-third of the original score.[71] He had transparent reasons for molding Thalberg as well as Liszt in his own image. In his playing Busoni used dislocation between bass and melody relatively rarely, for his basic conception of piano tone was conceived as a partial imitation of the sonorities of the organ. One might, of course, expect this in his magnificent transcriptions of Bach's organ works, but even his majestic arrangement of Bach's Chaconne in D Minor for solo violin was bizarrely made "from the standpoint of organ tone."[72] The concept suffused his playing approach as a whole. Busoni was well aware of the peculiarity, not to say eccentricity, of transcribing a violin piece for piano in imitation of the organ, for his efforts had met with a very mixed response.[73] Josef Hofmann was openly dismissive of the idea of imitating any other keyboard

---

[70] Daniel Hitchock's otherwise precise summary of Thalberg's *L'art du chant* on the Italian "Centro Thalberg" website at http://www.centrothalberg.it/Artduchantinglese.htm (accessed May 2006) is equally misleading on this point. Like Busoni, he only quotes the opening of Thalberg's fifth rule and omits the subsequent qualifications. The most recent published mention of Thalberg's *L'art du chant* that I know—in Ates Orga, "The Piano Music," in Colin Scott-Sutherland, ed., *Ronald Stevenson: The Man and His Music* (London: Toccata Press, 2005), 103—also selectively quotes Thalberg in the same way as Busoni does. There is evidently a very deceptive "Busoni tradition" here. Richard Hudson, on the other hand, gives a fairer selection from Thalberg's remarks in *Stolen Time*, 196.

[71] See Kenneth Hamilton, "Liszt Fantasises—Busoni Excises: The Liszt/Busoni Figaro Fantasy," *Journal of the American Liszt Society* 30 (1991): 21–27.

[72] Busoni, *Well-Tempered Clavichord*, Appendix "On the Transcription of Bach's Organ Works for Piano," 167. Bülow, in the preface to his edition of Bach's Chromatic Fantasy and Fuge (Berlin: Bote und Bock, 1859), shared Busoni's subsequent ideas on the grandeur and suitability of organ tone: "It appeared more suited to Bach to have the fantasy recall the sound of the organ than to diminish it by an imitation of the spinet or clavichord." It may well be that Bülow had little direct knowledge of the capabilities of the clavichord at this time (see chapter 6, p. 214).

[73] Indeed, even his organ transcriptions were not universally admired: "a ridiculous travesty" was the *Musical Times*'s restrained description in 1897 after Busoni's performance of one of them. Scholes, 2:318.

instrument at all, arguing that "to transform the modern pianoforte, which has distinctly specific tonal attributes, into a clavichord or into an organ must result in tonal abuse." He subsequently put it more succinctly: "Why not make a piano sound like a piano?"[74]

Even Eugen d'Albert, the chaconne transcription's dedicatee, had severe doubts about its validity, feeling that it was overloaded and far too distant from its original model.[75] He told Busoni candidly that he much preferred Brahms's modestly restrained arrangement for piano left-hand alone, which more closely copied the restrictions of the setting for solo violin. Busoni's defense was made on grounds both of aesthetics and of historical precedent: "This procedure, which has been variously attacked, was justified, firstly, by the breadth of conception, which is not fully displayed by the violin; and secondly by the example set by Bach himself in the transcription for organ of his own violin fugue in G-minor."[76]

In retrospect, Busoni's chaconne transcription has proved itself by its popularity in the concert hall. Its noble and magisterial sonorities make it the most effective of opening recital pieces, while Brahms's overly ascetic version has never gained even a foothold in the repertoire. The cyclopean concept of piano-organ tone that resounds from the chaconne arrangement and from Busoni's other Bach transcriptions has also proved enormously influential on modern pianism. It is a keyboard approach that is rigorously unsentimental, necessarily avoids spreading of chords ("all chords, even those of the widest span, are to be played together and not arpeggiated," Busoni directs in a footnote to his arrangement of the *St. Anne* Prelude and Fugue—rather impractically for the majority of players, who are unlikely to be able to stretch certain major tenths),[77] and has little place for asynchronization of the hands. It was partly this treatment of piano tone that made Busoni's Chopin interpretations

[74] Hofmann, 85, 86.

[75] The relevant letter of d'Albert to Busoni, and the latter's response, is printed in the preface to Paul Bank's pioneering edition of the Chaconne (Edition Peters). This admirable publication is one of the few to take seriously what Busoni actually played (in his piano roll of the piece), rather than treating the printed sources as the sole source of wisdom.

[76] Busoni, *Well-Tempered Clavichord*, 1:167.

[77] Amusingly, Busoni's own printed score of this piece (now part of the Busoni Nachlass in the Staatsbibliothek zu Berlin) has a rearrangement of the first two bars added in pencil in what seems to be Busoni's writing. This variant eliminates the major tenth originally spanned by the left hand. Perhaps Busoni was beginning to realize that he had previously restricted the possible pool of players a trifle too severely.

unusually controversial, for he felt compelled to rescue the composer from the aspects of "elegant sentimentality" that he found in his style to allow his affinity to Bach to shine through.[78] Listeners used to a different, "singing" Chopin (i.e., almost all of them) found these radical interpretive ideas difficult to accept. "In the name of Chopin, I protest!" muttered an outraged—and departing— audience member at a concert in Paris.[79]

Busoni's pianistic influence was spread not just by his own tireless touring and phenomenal reputation, but also by the wide scope of his teaching activities. Yet we must once more be careful not to exaggerate just how "modern" his playing was. Certainly in his attitude to textual fidelity it was anything but (see the next chapter). Even the idea of a relatively sober, unarpeggiated, organlike tone has, naturally enough, a history. In the late 1850s Bülow had declared that the imitation of an organ sonority was the ideal in playing pieces like Bach's Chromatic Fantasy and Fugue.[80] Far earlier than that, Beethoven's cultivation of a more sonorous legato touch in contrast to Mozart's "choppy" style was sometimes attributed to his experience as an organ player in Bonn.[81] Descriptions of the playing of Mendelssohn, who was as successful an organist as he was a pianist, also stress the influence of the former instrument. His style was characterized by the critic Henry Chorley, in an item that actually made the front page of the *Philadelphia National Gazette* of 20 August 1841 (it must have been a slow day for news), as exhibiting "solidity, in which the organ-touch is given to the piano without the organ ponderosity; spirit (witness his execution of the finale of the D Minor Concerto); animating, but never intoxicating to the ear; expression, which making every tone sink deep, requiring not the garnishing of trills and appogiaturi, or the aid of changes of time." He might have been talking

---

[78] Busoni, *Well-Tempered Clavichord*, vol. 1., preface. Busoni first complains of about the "femininity" of Hummel's style and its baleful influence. He then goes on to talk of Chopin in this connection. The relevant passage reads in its entirety, "The unhappy leaning towards 'elegant sentimentality,' then spreading wider and wider (with ramifications into our own time), reaches its climax in Field, Henselt, Thalberg and Chopin [modified in a footnote: 'Chopin's puissant inspiration, however, forced its way through the slough of enervating, melodious phrase-writing and the dazzling euphony of mere virtuoso sleight-of-hand, to the height of teeming individuality. In harmonic insight he makes a long stride towards the mighty Sebastian'], attaining, by its peculiar brilliancy of style and tone, to almost independent importance in the history of pianoforte literature." For the skeptical reaction to Busoni's Chopin interpretations, see Dent, 108–9, 267.

[79] Bauer, 65.

[80] See n. 72.

[81] See Rosenblum, 23–24.

about Busoni fifty years later—apart, of course, from the bit about the changes of time.

Some other aspects of Busoni's pianism, as one would expect, were very much of their era, and we can hear these clearly on his recordings. Like many of his fellow artists, he found the practicalities, and even the concept, of recording an unpleasant trial—"a devilish invention *which lacks the demonic nuance*," he called it[82]—so we must accept that his surviving discs are unlikely to represent him at his best (as his associates acknowledged at the time). It was, after all, an era where the medium was treated as of doubtful value even by recording producers and engineers themselves. Fred Gaisberg of HMV once explained the scanty representation of Brahms's more ambitious music in the catalogue by commenting—amazingly—that "for the average virtuoso, its preparation would require too much effort for mere recording."[83] Busoni wrote irritably to his wife in 1919 after one session complaining of the "cutting, patching and improvising" necessary to fit pieces onto 78-rpm disks that could only hold around four and a half minutes of music, the alien approach to pedaling and accentuation demanded by the recording process, and the immense pressure on the pianist of knowing that "every note was going to be there for eternity." "How can there be any question of inspiration, freedom, swing and poetry?" he asked, rhetorically.[84] Similar despair was voiced to his recording producer, and it is not surprising that many pieces set down in this and other sessions (including a Mozart-Busoni Andantino, a transcription of the slow movement from the Piano Concerto K. 271; Liszt's Third *Petrarch Sonnet*, Fifth *Paganini Study*, and First *Valse oubliée*; the Gounod-Liszt Waltz from *Faust*; and Weber's *Perpetuum mobile*) were found to be so unsatisfactory that they were never issued. (This was a not uncommon event—virtually every early pianist tempted into the studio ended up with a sizable number of unreleased recordings.) Of the recordings that were issued, the F♯ Nocturne, op. 15 no. 2 (1922), gives us a fairly good idea of Busoni's unsentimental Chopin. Not only is there scarcely any use of dislocation and unmarked arpeggiation, but even one of the chords Chopin marks as an arpeggio (bar 10) is played together. This is not the whole story, however, and we should not generalize too widely. Although in Busoni's perfunctory, almost flippant performance of Chopin's Prelude in A, op. 28 no. 7 (1922) there is also precious little arpeggiation, the piano roll of the D♭ *Raindrop* Prelude (1923) features, in

---

[82] Beaumont, *Busoni: Selected Letters*, 350.
[83] Gaisberg, 182.
[84] Busoni, *Letters to His Wife*, trans. Rosamond Ley (London: Arnold, 1938), 287.

the opening and closing sections, frequent spread chords in the typically romantic style.[85] Even for Busoni there were places where a granite sonority was
inappropriate.


## The Soul of the Piano

The tried and trusted sustaining pedal—"the soul of the piano," in Rubinstein's
oft-quoted phrase—remained for the late romantics an indispensable method of
cultivating not only a singing legato in cantabile playing, but an appropriately
warm harmonic cushion in the background. Few aspects of piano performance
had changed so much over the nineteenth century as pedal usage, but the changes
were for a long time hardly reflected in notation.[86] In particular syncopated
pedaling (regularly pedaling slightly after each note has been struck to aid a
continuous legato) and various types of half-pedaling (partially lowering or
fluttering the dampers to suppress treble notes, but allowing the heavier bass
strings to carry on sounding) appear to have been used by performers with
increasing frequency throughout the nineteenth century before becoming a
common feature in scores. In fact, although syncopated pedaling appears regularly in works (and editions of earlier music) from the 1870s onward, half-
pedaling to this day is rarely marked (with the major exception of Percy
Grainger's scores). It is nevertheless used universally by professional performers.
    The lag between practice and consistent documentation has led to a belief in
some quarters that more sophisticated pedaling techniques were only invented in
the later part of the century (in other words, if they weren't written down, they
can't have existed). Rosenthal, still smarting from the feeling that he had never
been given adequate training in pedal technique by any of his teachers (Mikuli,
Joseffy or Liszt), even went so far as to claim that Liszt himself had had no
inkling of the use of syncopated pedal until it was introduced to him by the
*Technische Künstler-Studien* sent for his approval by their author, Louis Köhler, in
1875.

---

[85] The Prelude and Nocturne recordings are on Pearl GEMM CD9347, the piano roll on
Nimbus NI 8810.
    [86] A fine, detailed treatment of this general topic for a slightly earlier period can be found in
Rosenblum, 102–43, and, carrying on to the later era, David Rowland, *A History of Pianoforte
Pedalling* (Cambridge: Cambridge University Press, 1993). The latter's "Beethoven's Pianoforte
Pedalling," in Stowell, 49–69, is also relevant.

By 1875 Köhler (1820–1886) had been involved with the Liszt circle in Weimar for decades, and his attitude to piano performance had been greatly influenced by the older master. In acknowledgment of this, he had dedicated his two-volume *Systematische Lehrmethode für Clavier-Spiel und Musik* (1st ed. 1858–59) to Liszt and had been instrumental in forming the Allgemeiner Deutscher Musikverein in 1859, with Liszt as the first president. Rosenthal's only evidence for his remarkable assertion about Liszt's pedaling was a letter to Köhler of 1875 in which Liszt expressed admiration at the way Köhler consistently indicated the syncopation of the pedal in the *Künstler Studien*. It is noteworthy that Liszt here did not react as if the scales had suddenly fallen from his eyes. He does not congratulate Köhler for having invented syncopated pedaling itself, or indeed say that he himself was unfamiliar with its use. Even Rosenthal does not assert that Liszt was not performing with syncopated pedaling when he first personally heard him play only a year later in 1876. But he nevertheless stuck firmly to his belief that Anton Rubinstein must have been the first to use a syncopated technique. He assumed that it was also unknown to Chopin, because Mikuli (Chopin's pupil) never mentioned it to him during his studies.[87]

Rosenthal's chain of inferences is easily disproved, but the development of more advanced pedaling is indeed a murky subject. There is a very good reason for this, namely that the piano was developing rapidly throughout most of the nineteenth century, and pedaling requirements were developing just as quickly. Liszt lived through many of these changes, and his technique, like that of any good musician, necessarily responded to the new instruments. It is evident that from the early years of the nineteenth century, the sustaining pedal was being used in some quarters much more frequently than it was actually notated, particularly by Dussek and other members of the so-called London School. On the other hand, Hummel famously used little pedal, and in Vienna his crisp, dry playing was explicitly contrasted with Beethoven's much more lavish application of washes of pedal. Czerny commented that Beethoven used the pedal far more than marked in his scores, and also remarked (in 1838) that "modern composers

---

[87] Mitchell and Evans, "The Old and New School of Piano Playing," 26, 76–77. In Joseph Banowetz's very useful *The Pianist's Guide to Pedaling* (Bloomington: Indiana University Press, 1985), an excerpt from Rosenthal's comments on syncopated pedaling is quoted in the chapter on Liszt (206), though Rosenthal's remarks are here used simply to support the conclusion that Liszt was well aware of syncopated pedaling in his later years. Banowetz underplays Rosenthal's bizarre claim that Liszt did not know of syncopated pedaling during his virtuoso years—and that Chopin had no idea of it at all—perhaps because he (understandably) can hardly believe it.

by no means always indicate where the pedal is necessary"[88] It was around the same time that frequent complaints appeared about players who used the una corda, rather than their fingers, to achieve a soft tone. The idea that this is somehow "cheating" persists to this day.[89] In their piano treatise, Moscheles and Fétis described the pedaling of "the present-day school" (Thalberg, Chopin, Liszt, et al.) in terms similar to those used by Czerny, claiming that it "modulates in an unheard-of manner, puts the foot almost in an unbroken movement, which in the initial/early practice of this exercise gives students difficulties, but soon becomes an easy habit."[90] Obviously this does not specifically mention syncopated pedaling, but the "unbroken movement" of the foot is certainly suggestive of it. Yet more so is Czerny's remark (while discussing Henselt's compositions) "the raising and re-employment of the pedal must be effected as quickly as possible, in order that no loss of sound may be discoverable between."[91]

As we have seen, Thalberg was directly advocating syncopated pedaling in the preface to L'art du chant of 1853, although it is not notated in the actual music. What Thalberg actually did in performance was described, long after the event, in Lavignac's treatise L'école de la pédale (1889). As a young man Lavignac had heard Thalberg play in the Salle Érard in Paris, and initially he thought the performer a bundle of nerves owing to the shaking of his foot on the sustaining pedal. However,

> Thalberg was not afraid, but he used the pedal admirably with very brief touches brilliantly distributed just at the required moment and with such frequent repetition that at first, a little naively, I had though it trembling. . . . Attention once drawn to the subject, I have never neglected to observe the way in which great pianists use the pedal on every occasion I have been able to—I have never seen any take it on the beat on purpose, to beat time, but almost always a little before or a little after, depending on the circumstances. . . . All use rapid movements of half-pedaling.[92]

[88] Czerny, *Complete Theoretical and Practical Pianoforte School, Op. 500* (1838), 3:2 and 14.

[89] See n. 59. Also C. Moscheles, *Life of Moscheles*, 2:176, for Moscheles's grumble that "such a thing as a pianissimo can be obtained without a soft pedal." Elsewhere (51) he talked about "the new school" of piano playing that produced "piquant effects by the most rapid changes from the soft to the loud pedal."

[90] Moscheles and Fétis, 118. This is adumbratory of a much later review describing Busoni as "trilling with his feet" (Couling, 185).

[91] Czerny, *Complete Theoretical and Practical Pianoforte School, Op. 500: Supplement* (1846), 13.

[92] Quoted from Rowland, *History of Piano Pedalling*, 115–16. Rowland also reproduces (117) Lavignac's detailed notation of Thalberg's pedaling in performance.

But why, if Thalberg's pedaling was so sophisticated in practice (and we have no reason not to believe the same thing of Chopin, Liszt, and several others), was this complexity so rarely reflected in the notation, which is not only inadequate, but sometimes positively misleading? Two answers suggest themselves. The first is prompted by Liszt's open astonishment that Chopin should have indicated pedaling in great detail in his Barcarolle.[93] Trying to write down syncopated pedaling simply took too much time. Moreover, since the exact placing of the pedal markings was usually subject to the vagaries of careless engravers, it was easier just to indicate pedaling on the beat. A good pianist would make all necessary adjustments according to taste and necessity. Liszt cared so little about this that in 1846 he did not even get round to indicating the pedal in his transcriptions of Weber's overtures and asked Theodore Kullak to add the markings for him onto the proofs as he saw fit.[94]

The second answer to my question is that pedal usage is heavily dependent on the instrument being played. Some nineteenth-century pianos suit syncopated pedaling more than others. Érards in particular, with their peculiar system of under-damping (i.e., dampers that are pushed up onto the string from below rather than designed to fall from above), often do not damp cleanly in the bass, especially during forte playing. After a good amount of experience performing on several early- to mid-century Érards (that is, instruments known to Chopin, Liszt, and Mendelssohn), I have noticed that the piano can produce its own syncopated pedaling. Strike an octave strongly in the bass, and it will likely still be resounding noticeably for a few seconds after the dampers have been fully engaged. Syncopated pedaling here must be used with great caution, and sometimes not at all. As dampers on grand pianos from the late 1850s onward became bigger, heavier, and more effective, syncopation of the pedal became routinely necessary to ensure a fine legato tone. According to Lina Ramann's *Liszt Pädagogium*, Liszt was regularly advising the use of both syncopated pedaling and half-pedaling to his students in the 1870s and 1880s.[95] Carl Lachmund reported that in 1882, Liszt told a pupil "one should change the pedal an instant *after* the beat; otherwise you will be apt to catch the notes of the previous beat and blur the clearness. Furthermore you can thus get a perfect legato on distant notes or chords."[96] Amy Fay claimed that she personally only learned how to use the

---

[93] Zimdars, *Masterclasses of Liszt*, 30.

[94] Short, 46.

[95] Lina Ramann, *Liszt Pädagogium* (Wiesbaden: Breitkopf und Härtel, 1986), virtually passim, but see especially 2nd ser., 5 and 11.

[96] Walker, *Living with Liszt*, 158.

technique in 1873 from Ludwig Deppe, at which point she suddenly realized that this was actually how Liszt had been pedaling when she attended his master classes earlier in the year.[97] For Deppe, just as for Leschetizky and many others, the pedaling was only a means to an end, and that was the achievement of a beautiful tone—"one of his grand hobbies," as Fay ingenuously remarked.[98] "All my attention is now bent upon tone,"[99] she later added. Although she herself never seems to have come near membership of the pianistic pantheon, the recordings of Emil von Sauer, another Deppe student before he went to Liszt in Weimar, show that Deppe's strictures on the cultivation of a fine tone and subtle pedaling sometimes fell on fertile ground. Sauer's performances of pieces such as Schubert's Impromptu op. 90 no. 3 (1940),[100] or Liszt's *Consolation* in Db (1938),[101] have, quite simply, a gorgeous sound.

In Busoni's recordings, because the technology of the day did not allow him to use his normal approach to pedaling, we hear little of his subtleties in that regard, especially his fondness for the middle pedal,[102] which he used extensively and with magisterial disregard for the vintage of the music. Liszt, after all, had embraced the new invention eagerly (it was featured on a grand piano that Steinway and Sons had sent him as a gift). He was keen to suggest appropriate places for its use in his earlier works even though it hadn't been around when they were composed.[103] The middle pedal was a normal part of American Steinways from the late 1870s (it had been patented in 1874) but was rarely found on European instruments until after the turn of the century. Voices of caution at the Hamburg Steinway factory delayed introducing the new feature to their own pianos, perhaps realizing it had many detractors among European pianists.

[97] Fay, 276–77.

[98] Fay, 297.

[99] Fay, 315.

[100] Arbiter CD 114.

[101] Pearl GEMM CD 9403.

[102] This allows the pianist freedom in sustaining only certain notes while leaving others unaffected. It is particularly useful in producing clean, long-held notes in the deep bass underneath rapid changes of harmony in the treble. As a result, it goes a little way toward imitating the effect of the organ pedal board. The sostenuto pedal also allows the player to raise the dampers on unstruck notes of his choosing. The open strings of the undamped notes then create a haze of sympathetic vibrations.

[103] It is quite true that Boisselot of Marseilles, a piano manufacturer with whom Liszt was closely associated, patented a version of the sostenuto pedal in the 1840s, but it was received at this stage with apathy. Boisselot did not include the device on his instruments for very long.

Busoni first had the opportunity to experiment with the middle pedal extensively during his time in Boston and New York from 1891 to 1894, and he was soon convinced of its value in further increasing the instrument's variety of sonority. Percy Grainger, for a short time a Busoni pupil, became if anything an even more fanatical advocate than his master, declaring in 1920 with typical hyperbole that "in the near future a pianist not availing himself of the advantages of this truly wonderful American invention will be as much out of date as the dodo."[104] But Mark Hambourg and Moriz Rosenthal were quite happy to be dodos, thinking the new pedal a largely pointless addition.[105] Benno Moisewitsch was of a similar opinion. One suspects that this view may have been common to most of the Leschetizky pupils—in their Viennese student days, few pianos with a third pedal would have been available, and Leschetizky himself never seems to have owned one. Rosenthal steered a middle course in his publications, if not in his performances. In his edition (Ullstein Verlag) of Liszt's Pastorale from the first *Année de pèlerinage*, he suggests experimenting with either the middle pedal or, alternatively, a more normal half-pedal to sustain the opening ostinato E in the bass.

Percy Grainger had no time for Rosenthal's ambivalence; he was a positive proselyte for the new pedal. His scores contain numerous directions for its obligatory use, some even intended to produce a reverberant background of sympathetic harmonies by silently lifting the dampers of certain notes and holding them up:

EXAMPLE 5.11. Percy Grainger, *Rosenkavalier Ramble*, excerpt

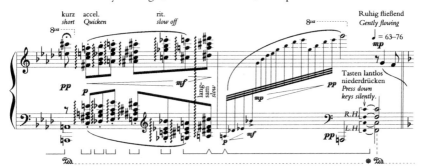

---

[104] Jeffrey Johnson, *Piano Lessons*, 55.

[105] Hambourg, *Eighth Octave*, 10: "I think that skilful use of the existing loud pedal can produce all essential effects of tone sustaining." See also Rosenthal, "If Franz Liszt Should Come Back Again," 224: "I rarely use the middle pedal on the grand piano. In fact, I find that very few pianists employ it. Very much the same effect can be obtained by depressing the damper pedal a short distance."

EXAMPLE 5.11. (*continued*)

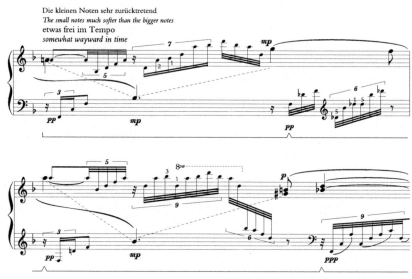

The middle pedal was, in this way, effectively brought to the aid of the cushion of sound that would help to float the singing tone. Grainger called the romantically arpeggiated, Paderewskified approach of pieces like *Rosenkavalier Ramble* or the touching *Colonial Song* the "harped" style. They contrast strikingly with the aspects of his technique that cultivated an energetically percussive edge (he was one of the first composers to suggest striking certain notes with a clenched fist).[106] Busoni, on the other hand, was largely drawn to the middle pedal because it allowed the pianist to approximate certain organ effects "which can be obtained only by the combined action of the three pedals."[107]

These effects naturally tend to act as a limited substitute for the organ pedal board, which, like the sostenuto pedal, can hold certain notes down in the bass without affecting the clarity of the rest of the texture. In his appendix to his edition of Bach's *Well-Tempered Clavier*, which deals with piano transcriptions of Bach's organ music, he gives several examples of middle-pedal usage, including the proto-Grainger initial silent depression of held chords (one wonders whether Grainger actually learned this technique from Busoni), and even an arrangement

---

[106] As at the end of the celebrated *Country Gardens*, or his arrangement of Stanford's *Maguire's Kick*.

[107] Busoni, *Well-Tempered Clavichord*, 1:178.

EXAMPLE 5.12. J. S. Bach–Ferruccio Busoni, Prelude in E♭ (*St. Anne*), excerpt

of the opening of Beethoven's Fourth Symphony where the long octave B♭s are sustained by the new pedal.[108] Ironically, his indications for middle pedal and *una corda* usage in his transcription of Bach's *St. Anne* Prelude did not actually appear in the final edition of the piece itself, and as a result remain little known by performers. Busoni used the new pedal in many other contexts—the last of his *Seven Short Pieces for the Cultivation of Polyphonic Playing* is a study for it. In his performances of the Chopin Third Scherzo, for example, the chords of the chorale in the central section were sustained in this way, allowing a drier performance of the surrounding figuration and no doubt encouraging more accusations of abuse of Chopin's music.

What caused the moderating of the obsession with the singing tone? Why did pianists' priorities shift? Styles naturally evolve, and subsequent generations (as every parent knows) have interests and enthusiasms that may be very different from those of their elders. Some of the care that had been spent developing a fine cantabile began to be directed not toward achieving the soulless swift scales and octaves so despised by Leschetizky, but rather toward a concern for the clear delineation of formal structure, stylistic suitability, and respect for the score that Leschetizky may well have derided as sterile academicism. Moreover, it was very difficult for the early recording methods to capture the subtleties of sonority so lovingly cultivated by the romantics. Asynchronization techniques often sounded simply inept (witness Friedheim's unfortunate recording of the Chopin Funeral March), and a good recording piano, according to Mark Hambourg, was one that produced the most penetrating tone, rather than the most beautiful. By the

---

[108] Busoni, *Well-Tempered Clavichord*, 1:179. The Beethoven example is, strangely, not identified by Busoni. He must have thought, like Brahms, that "any ass" could tell what it was.

time recording technology was equal to reproducing an adequate range of tone color, many pianists seemed to regard ostentatious variety here as unnecessary window dressing for "the music," even a tawdry distraction from more weighty concerns. One notable exception was Horowitz, always in command of a quite breathtaking tonal palette. In this he was indeed, if not "the last romantic," then at least a true one.

# 6

# The Letter of the Score

> The letter killeth, but the spirit giveth life.
> —II Corinthians 3:6

## Pianist-Composer/Composer-Pianist

"The left hand of this etude is entirely altered from Chopin, it's better, modernized, more melodic you know. And then the last part—Godowsky was the author." We hear this, with some bemusement no doubt, from pianist extraordinaire Vladimir de Pachmann (or, as he with disarming honesty usually described himself, "The Great Pachmann!") at the beginning of one of the most remarkable discs to come out of the early recording era—or indeed any era. This rendition (1927) of Chopin's *Black Key* Etude, op. 10 no. 5, with modifications by Godowsky, has Pachmann intermittently chattering, harrumphing, or mumbling in the background throughout the performance.[1] To whom was Pachmann addressing his remarks? Certainly himself, in part, for his recitals, like François Planté's, were often accompanied by a stream-of-consciousness verbal commentary on his own playing (including the truly priceless "Bravo, Pachmann!" after any few bars handled with special deftness). Many members of the public sitting close enough to hear found this vastly entertaining, and at Pachmann's recitals places near the piano were eagerly sought after. But for the recording under discussion, Pachmann had a small captive audience of typists from the neighboring offices, who had been dragged into the studio in order to create a

---

[1] OPAL CD 9840. Additionally on Arbiter 129 (a much clearer transfer, in my view). In François Planté's recording of the Chopin op. 10 no. 7 study we also hear something spoken at the end. In his case it is only one word: "Merde!" (The world of recording really became much more boring with the advent of editing technology.)

suitably adulatory atmosphere for the great maestro's effusions.[2] After enunci-
ating his artistic credo—"better, modernized"—he begins the etude, only to get
into a dreadful tangle a few bars later. With the words "I start again . . . ," he
starts again. This time things go fine, and he makes it to the end of the piece
without major mishap, pointing out along the way certain passages that he felt
should give the audience a special thrill. After a final flourish in contrary-motion
octaves (as it happens, Chopin wrote descending octaves in conjunct motion),
Pachmann closes the disk decisively with the emphatic words "Godowsky was
the author!" before the background crackles of the recording fade and we sadly
find ourselves once more in our own more respectful, more accurate, but certainly
duller urtext-obsessed modern era.

　　Pachmann may at times have been an eccentric buffoon, but he was also a
genuinely splendid pianist, regarded by many as one of the very greatest of
Chopin players. It would be a great mistake to let his antics obscure this for us.
After all, if amusing eccentricity had been completely banished from the musical
world, nineteenth-century concert stages would have remained largely deserted.
Talent need not always sport an unsmiling face. Pachmann's voluble equation of
"modernized" with "better" and his advocacy of the Godowsky rearrangements
of Chopin's etudes (he made a fine recording of the Godowski-Chopin *Revolutionary* Etude for left hand alone) were quite unexceptional views for his era.
Indeed, he was regarded by some as among the most faithful Chopin interpreters
before the public, as was the now much-maligned Paderewski. Percy Grainger
contrasted both these players with Busoni, who certainly had never been accused
by anyone of a preoccupation with the letter of the score: "Busoni . . . was not a
'normal' player as Paderewski was, and even de Pachmann was, unfolding the
music straightly and faithfully. Busoni was a twisted genius making the music
sound unlike itself, but grander than itself, more super-human."[3]

　　Grainger's view presents us with a clear spectrum of interpretative fidelity.
Unfortunately for us, at its most faithful end are players—Paderewski and
Pachmann—who seem now from their recordings to be enormously self-indulgent. Yet Pachmann did indeed make one of the most "faithful" early disks of
the Chopin Funeral March,[4] free of the popular Anton Rubinstein "processional" approach (apart perhaps from a slightly more extended diminuendo at
the end). Paderewski rarely indulged in extensive recomposing of his repertoire

---

[2] See Gaisberg, 189.
[3] Bird, 2nd ed., 89.
[4] Arbiter 141.

(asynchronization notwithstanding), although he did play the brilliant Leschetizky ending for Liszt's *La leggierezza* (as did Moiseiwitsch). On Busoni's piano roll of Liszt's E-Major Polonaise, on the other hand, most of the greatly extended coda is by the performer.[5] Pachmann was content to record Liszt's original coda. His enormous drive and panache show how stirring it can be, even without the rambling hyperbole added by Busoni.[6] In fact, we hardly have an interpretative category for Busoni now, so extreme were his liberties. In the same way, Philip Corri's advice on how to play chords in preludes (discussed in the previous chapter) completely omits our normal manner of performance, with the notes played rigorously together. Corri evidently didn't have a category for us. We therefore have to tread very warily indeed when discussing the attitudes to interpretation of the great players of the past who lived before the recording era, for we do not have any direct aural evidence of their playing to act as a control, and what they and their contemporaries meant by the term "strict adherence to the letter of the score" was likely rather different—to put it mildly—from our automatic assumptions.

A fundamental facet of the romantic attitude to interpretation was that virtually all pianists were composers as well as performers. (Pachmann was one of the few who, although he had composed in his earlier days, never included his own music in his recital programs.) Our present era has largely abandoned this tradition and often segregates conservatory students into separate performance, composition, and musicology streams. Of course, even today there are few performers who do not have some attempts at composition guiltily hidden in their attic, and being a composer as well as a performer does not necessarily imply great talent in either field, or that the two areas have to openly interact on stage. Liszt, who was well placed to comment on the general situation in 1854, singled out Rubinstein as "conspicuously different from the opaque mass of self-styled composer-pianists who do not even know what it is to play the piano, still less with what fuel it is necessary to heat one's self in order to compose, so that what they lack in talent for composition they fancy themselves pianists, and vice-versa."[7] There were indeed many signs in the later nineteenth century of increasing specialization, but for many of the romantic virtuosi, composition remained an integral part of performance, as it had been for Bach, Handel, Mozart, and Beethoven in their day. Naturally, the performers' creative

---

[5] Busoni also published this coda. His piano roll can be heard on Nimbus CD 8810.
[6] Arbiter 129.
[7] Williams, *Letters of Franz Liszt*, 180.

personalities as *composers* tended to seep into their playing and often turned what we now think should be acts of interpretation into acts of more or less free re-creation.

Busoni was an extreme example. A towering virtuoso but also a questing composer, the two sides of his musicianship were in a slightly uneasy symbiosis. "While the virtuoso in me still abides by older habits," he mused in 1917, "I believe that I have, as a composer, stripped myself of all superficiality and 'inevitability' in the practice of my profession. Where the performer has, after all, to reach a compromise between his originality and that of his programme, the composer is free of such binding agreements."[8] Yet the compromise Busoni achieved as a performer was, by our standards, massively weighted toward his composing side, and few pieces he played remained unaffected by his sometimes extreme intervention. Just what this sort of intervention might entail will be the subject of by far the largest part of this chapter.

## A Question of Fidelity

It is fairly simple for us to survey the nineteenth-century battleground of in-terpretative fidelity, at least from reputation, however hazardous it might be to map it directly onto our own. After all, critics then were just as quick as critics today to seize on what they regarded as undue liberty, especially in the music of the emergent "great masters." Beethoven was a particular object of reverence, and an attitude of respect for his scores was persistently encouraged from Czerny onward. In 1845 Czerny had published an item in the *Allgemeine Wiener Musik-Zeitung* recalling Beethoven's fury when he heard him make a spontaneous and unauthorized adaptation of the piano part of the Quintet op. 16 for piano, oboe, clarinet, horn, and bassoon at a concert in 1816. Beethoven had written to Czerny with some contrition the next day, but in doing so had further clarified his views: "I burst out with that remark yesterday and was very sorry after I had done so. But you must forgive a composer who would rather have heard his work performed exactly as it was written, however beautifully you played it in other respects."[9] A penitent Czerny remarked: "I permitted myself, in the spirit of youthful carelessness, many changes, in the way of adding difficulties to the music, the use of the higher octave, etc. Beethoven quite rightly took me severely

[8] Beaumont, *Busoni: Selected Letters*, 253.
[9] Emily Anderson, ed., *The Letters of Beethoven* (London: Macmillan, 1961), 2:560.

to task. . . . This letter did more than anything else to cure me of the desire to make changes in the performance of his works, and I wish that it might have the same influence on all pianists."[10] The Viennese public, rendered thus suitably receptive, would no doubt have been more than usually grateful for Czerny's *Über den richtigen Vortrag der saemmtlichen Werke für das Piano allein* (*On the Proper Performance of Beethoven's Pianoforte Works*), which just happened to appear the following year.

But on closer examination, Czerny's noble professions of fidelity to the letter of the master's scores ring a trifle hollow—at any rate by our more exacting standards. *Proper Performance* was intended to codify a Beethoven interpretation stamped with the authority of his most celebrated pupil, but some of the advice therein, alas, directly contradicts the only scores printed in Beethoven's lifetime. As discussed perceptively by George Barth, many of Czerny's specific musical examples, too, are different in detail from any published editions known to the composer and seem more likely to derive from Czerny's tastes than Beethoven's.[11] We might argue that Czerny may have been privy to advice from his master that superseded the score, at least for a few pieces—but that would only be another way of affirming that, for Czerny, proper performance was not always quite the same as performance according to the letter of the original scores.

"Faithful" performance of Beethoven, whatever that meant in practice, would nevertheless continue to maintain its prestige throughout the century, even if as much honored in the breach as in the observance. George Bernard Shaw contrasted Rubinstein's cavalier manner in Beethoven with Charles Hallé's more sober approach, leaving his readers in no doubt of where his sympathies lay:

> Sir Charles is not a sensational player; but nobody who has heard him play the largo of this sonata [op. 10 no. 3] has ever accepted the notion that his playing is "icy and mechanical." Is there any audience in the world that would come to hear Rubinstein play a Beethoven sonata for the twentieth time? Yet Hallé . . . is always sure of his audience, no matter how often he has repeated the sonata he chooses. The secret is that he gives you as little as possible of Hallé, and as much as possible of Beethoven, of whom people do not easily tire. When Beethoven is made a mere cheval de bataille for a Rubinstein, the interest is more volatile. The "classical" players have the best of it in the long run.[12]

[10] Forbes, 2:640–41.
[11] Barth, 81–103. See also chapter 4, p. 110.
[12] Shaw, *London Music in 1888–9*, 42.

Taking our cue from Shaw, on a broad spectrum of romantic interpretative fidelity we can roughly place each pianist according to his or her reputation among their peers. We might have, for instance, a notional group consisting of Charles Hallé, Mendelssohn, Moscheles, and Clara Schumann in one corner of the ring as examples of generally acknowledged "faithful" performers (as Shaw quipped, "the sort of artist you praise when you want to disparage the other sort"),[13] and the usual suspects of Liszt, Rubinstein, Busoni, and their ilk in the other corner—all intermittently egotistical vandals bent on turning interpretation into transcription. Perhaps Bülow is hovering somewhere in the middle as an abrasive referee—vicious insults, potentially directed at both parties, constantly on the tip of his tongue. One can hardly fail to note in passing that those huddled defiantly in the libertarian section, despite Bernard Shaw's deprecations, were the most celebrated virtuosi of the entire era—after all, the names of Liszt and Rubinstein fall easily from the lips of pianists today who have scarcely heard of Hallé and Moscheles, and think of Mendelssohn as the fellow who wrote all these Songs Without Words.

But this nineteenth-century fidelity was not the far greater rigor of later eras, and should not be casually confused with it, however enticing this might seem. A typical twentieth-century view was articulated by Sviatoslav Richter, who believed that "the interpreter is really an executant, carrying out the composer's intentions to the letter. He doesn't add anything that isn't already in the work."[14] Richter, accordingly, was appalled when he heard pianists ignoring repeats (a particular bugbear of his) or introducing dramatic tempo modifications. A century before, while it would have been simple enough to find a few musicians who paid lip service to an attitude like Richter's, it would have been difficult to find many who would have met his standards in practice. The contrast between practice and preaching in this field was particularly marked. Eduard Hanslick, no friend of excessive liberties, could not help noting that the generous doses of tempo modification, *Luftpausen*,[15] and other expressive nuances favored by Hans von Bülow as a conductor were very similar to those he used as a pianist. He remarked, seemingly without irony, "It would be unjust to call these tempo changes 'liberties,' since conscientious adherence to the score is a primary and

---

[13] Shaw, *Music in London*, 2:84.

[14] Monsaingeon, 153.

[15] Literally "pauses for breath," frequently used by Bülow to add expression to melodies or underline especially significant chords. Even Liszt felt that Bülow went a little too far with these; see Zimdars, *Masterclasses of Liszt*, 167.

inviolable rule with Bülow. It is hard to draw the line."[16] When Wagner, ironically Bülow's model in this regard, adopted a similar approach on conducting Beethoven's *Eroica* Symphony in 1872, he seems to have crossed the aforementioned line. Were this free style to be universally adopted, Hanslick warned, "tempo rubato, that musical seasickness which so afflicts the performances of many singers and instrumentalists, would soon infect our orchestras, and that would be the end of the last healthy element of our musical life."[17]

Bülow, enviably, seems to have pulled off the next-to-impossible—retaining a reputation for an invigorating strictness while simultaneously allowing himself whatever freedoms he regarded as necessary. Once his reputation for fidelity (acquired partly by talking very loudly about respect for the score) had been established, whatever he did must, by definition, have been faithful. It is, to say the least, unlikely that Bülow would retain this reputation intact today as a performer, just as he demonstrably would fail as a faithful editor. The liberties of his editing, in fact, give us a fair idea of what we might have heard from Bülow the player. But for nineteenth-century audiences and critics, he was a scholastic, severe, even at times cold pianist far distant from the recklessness of Rubinstein.[18]

Some treatises can give us a more specific idea of the range of unnotated performance strategies that were expected to be read between the lines of a text in the nineteenth century. Hummel, for example, was by reputation also a precise and disciplined pianist. In his lifetime his playing was often contrasted with Beethoven's wild, almost chaotic intensity. Yet he himself, in his *Ausführliche theoretisch-practische Anweisung zum Piano-Forte-Spiel*, printed an edition of his A-Minor Piano Concerto (then a very popular piece) with numerous indications for modifications of tempo and other nuances that did not appear in the original score. These additions do not represent second thoughts, but are simply an illustration for the student of the sort of musical freedom any good performer might be expected to enjoy in order to secure an expressive performance. Appropriate liberty would, obviously, have varied from composer to composer and from genre to genre, but few composers, one might guess, would have expected the rigorously reverential attitude to the text characteristic of the modern era. It

---

[16] Henry Pleasants, ed., *Eduard Hanslick: Vienna's Golden Years of Music* (New York: Simon and Schuster, 1950), 273.

[17] Pleasants, *Eduard Hanslick*, 108.

[18] Stradal characterized Bülow as an objective, Rubinstein as a subjective player. Liszt, he felt, kept both qualities in balance. See Stradal, 161.

was simply not the mainstream view. Brahms, for example, seems to have welcomed a certain flexibility in the interpretation of his works. "Elastic tempo," he commented, was hardly a recent invention.[19] In contrast, Alkan's now amusingly authoritarian direction "Allegretto without any license whatever" in the *Aesop's Feast Variations*, op. 39 no. 12, was likely an essential warning in an era when license could be lavish. Yet even in this piece by this notoriously unbending artist, every variation can hardly be fitted comfortably into the prescribed metronome marking without a little give and take.

If we therefore adhere strictly to the letter of the score, as usually defined nowadays, we may in fact end up with a performance rather different from any a nineteenth-century composer could have imagined. Our reading of the text itself simply proceeds from more literal assumptions. To take the question of rhythmic "accuracy": the characteristic clipping of rhythms in agitated music (what in baroque parlance would be called over- or double-dotting), and their dragging in more languid pieces, which we hear frequently on early recordings, was a perfectly routine part of romantic performance practice. Some players, as ever, seem to have taken the effect too far. In the 1890s Bernard Shaw claimed that Josef von Slivinski had "contracted the habit of slurring over—indeed all but dropping—the unaccented notes in rapid passages. . . . When he came to Liszt's transcription of Schubert's *Auf dem Wasser zu singen*, with its exquisite accompaniment of repeated semiquavers, the ticking of the second semiquavers was not heard until they were played as chords instead of single notes."[20] But Liszt sometimes advised his students to play in this manner—although he may still have regarded Slivinski's version of it as an abuse.

Liszt also recommended agogic accents to bring out a melody over accompanying figuration. "One should in such places give the first note of each group a little more than the exact time," he told a student playing the central part of the slow movement of Chopin's B-Minor Sonata.[21] A rhetorical emphasis on the main beats, and a consequent slighting of the weak ones, can radically change the rhythmic outline, as indeed happens in Moriz Rosenthal's recording of the first movement of the same Chopin sonata. Here the second-subject tune is delivered in a flexible manner that does not always coincide with Chopin's notation. By

---

[19] George Henschel, *Personal Recollections of Johannes Brahms* (Boston: Gorham, 1907), 78–79.

[20] Shaw, *Music in London*, 2:185–86. See also chapter 8, p. 277. Slivinsky, a Polish pupil of Leschetizky, was for a time in the 1890s touted as a serious rival to Paderewski. His impact was, however, less enduring. He is almost forgotten today.

[21] For Liszt's advice on rhythm, see chapter 7, p. 245. The quote is from Lachmund, in Walker, *Living with Liszt*, 129.

modern standards, Rosenthal's rendition is simply a misreading; by the standards of his generation, and probably of Chopin's time too, it was an allowable rhetorical license. We may regard the effect as free and inspired, or irritating and mannered. Chopin may have loved it or hated it, but he is unlikely to have been surprised by it.

A century after Hummel's death, and a few decades after Alkan's, the change in attitudes to textual fidelity was well under way, but not at all universally accepted. The famously draconian statements of Ravel ("I do not ask for my music to be interpreted, only to be played")[22] and Stravinsky ("Music should be transmitted and not interpreted, because interpretation reveals the personality of the interpreter rather than that of the author")[23] were still very extreme views for the first half of the twentieth century, and not entirely realizable in practice (as Stravinsky's very different recordings of his own pieces unintentionally succeed in demonstrating). For many composers and performers, the idea of even trying completely to remove "the personality of the interpreter" would have been a puzzling aim that might well have impoverished rather than enriched a performance. Busoni went so far as to claim that any notation of music is a transcription of an originally abstract sonic idea, and every performance of this inevitably inexact notation is, like it or not, a further transcription[24]—a view explicitly supported by Arnold Schoenberg, who used it to defend Mahler's retouching of the orchestration of Beethoven's symphonies.[25]

By 1948, when tempo modifications à la Bülow had largely fallen out of fashion, Schoenberg expressed himself against the new trend with his usual dyspeptic forcefulness:

> Today's manner of performing classical music of the so-called "Romantic" type, suppressing all emotional qualities and all unnotated changes of tempo and expression, derives from the style of playing primitive dance music. This style came to Europe by way of America, where no old culture regulated presentation, but where a certain frigidity of feeling reduced all musical expression. . . . All were suddenly afraid to be called Romantic, ashamed of being called sentimental . . . to change tempo, to express musical feelings, to make a ritardando or Luftpause. A change of character, a strong contrast, will often require a modification of tempo. . . . It must be admitted that in the period around 1900 many

[22] Marguerite Long, *At the Piano with Maurice Ravel* (London: Dent, 1973), 16.

[23] Igor Stravinsky, *Autobiography* (1936; reprint, New York: Norton, 1962), 75.

[24] Busoni, *Wesen und Einheit*, 125.

[25] See the letter of 1909 from Schoenberg to Busoni in Beaumont, *Busoni: Selected Letters*, 394.

artists overdid themselves in exhibiting the power of the emotion they were capable of feeling. . . . Nothing can be more wrong than both these extremes.[26]

We do not have to agree with all aspects of Schoenberg's rather simplistic reasoning here, his abomination of dance music, or his condemnation of American culture to accept that the stylistic changes he had witnessed were both real and vivid—the history of recordings tells us much the same thing. Fidelity to the score had, by the middle of the twentieth century, come to mean the eschewing of overt tempo modifications and a host of other unnotated expressive devices that would have scarcely raised an eyebrow a hundred years before. Schoenberg's hated "primitive dance bands" were hardly necessary to this process, whether they contributed to it or not. Decades of urtext editing had created urtext playing.

## "Get Thee to a Conservatory!"

Textual fidelity may be to a large extent in the eye of the beholder, but we can look in more detail at how at least a reputation for it, or its opposite, could be gained in the romantic era. Respective proponents of a stricter and a more relaxed attitude to the letter of the score were heavily involved both in private teaching and in the establishment of institutions that still play an important role in the training of musicians. As is well known, Anton Rubinstein founded the St. Petersburg Conservatory and had intimate links with the one in Moscow through his brother Nikolas. Leschetizky too was on the piano faculty at St. Petersburg for many years before beginning the private classes in Vienna that would make his name. Busoni's teaching included series of Liszt-style master classes in Weimar in 1900–1901 (given at the personal invitation of Duke Karl Alexander), an (eventually abortive) class for advanced students at the Vienna Conservatory in 1907–8, and numerous private students, including such sterling successors as Egon Petri, Leo Sirota, Edward Weiss, and Guido Agosti. They would themselves go on to have intensive performing and teaching careers. Liszt, of course, taught extensively, but he roundly despised conservatories and conservatory training (as a child he had been refused admittance to the Paris Conservatory). He had little to do with most of them, apart from the institution

---

[26] Arnold Schoenberg, "Today's Manner of Performing Classical Music" (1948), in *Style and Idea: Selected Writings*, ed. Leonard Stein, trans. Leo Black (New York: St. Martin's Press, 1975), 320–21.

run in Nuremberg by his faithful disciple and biographer Lina Ramann and—more distantly—Lebert and Stark's establishment in Stuttgart. For Liszt, Bülow's Beethoven edition "outweighed a dozen conservatories in instructional value."[27]

Those players in the stricter section had strong associations with the conservatories at Leipzig (Mendelssohn and Moscheles) and Frankfurt (the head of the piano department at the Hoch Conservatory for many years was none other than the venerable Clara Schumann herself). Liszt's abomination of music schools was cordially reciprocated. Clara Schumann avoided teaching his compositions in Frankfurt (though she had played a few of them herself in her younger days), and his—supposedly worthless—music was banned outright in the Berlin Hochschule. But through their teaching, compositions, and concert performances, the influence of all these musicians would be strongly felt for many decades after their deaths, and even to this day some pianists proudly claim to be pupils of pupils of pupils in an attempt to ordain their playing with the authority of apostolic succession.

What then, in the romantic era, constituted a conscientious detective, faithfully ferreting out clues to interpretation contained in composers' scores, and what constituted a self-indulgent libertine? We can take Mendelssohn (the "ideal artist-virtuoso," according to Friedrich Wieck)[28] as a suitable case study for the former and Liszt as the latter—for the main part of his virtuoso career he was a true Moriarty to Mendelssohn's Holmes. They are particularly useful examples, too, in that their own music (unlike that of Moscheles or Rubinstein) has remained firmly part of the repertoire. Their attitudes to performance can be regarded as having a certain unimpeachable authority at least for this, whether we wish to follow it nowadays or not. We shall leave a more detailed discussion of Liszt's own pianism until the next chapter, for its development was unusually complex and its influence unusually important, but looking here at Liszt's view of Mendelssohn, and vice versa, should shed some light on both musicians.

All firsthand accounts of Mendelssohn's playing agree that he was a serious, conscientious, and intensely musical performer, an opponent of affectation and sentimentality, who favored brisk tempi, minimal rubato, and what was then regarded as a highly strict adherence to the letter of the score. He was quite clear-eyed about the contrast between his own playing and that of some of his

[27] La Mara, *Franz Liszts Briefe*, 8 vols. (Leipzig, 1893–1905), 2:176–77 .
[28] Wieck, 149.

other contemporaries, thinking in 1834 that Chopin and Ferdinand Hiller "both labor somewhat under the desperate Parisian addiction to despair and search for passion [*Verzweiflungssucht und Leidenschaftssucherei*], and have often turned their eyes away from correct timekeeping [*Tact und Ruhe*] and the truly musical." He added, with a self-awareness unusual among performers, "I, on the other hand, have perhaps done this too little."[29] The widening reputation of the Leipzig Conservatory, which Mendelssohn had helped to found, and in which he had taught both piano and composition, almost turned his sober performance style into caricature after his death in 1847. This center of learning supposedly fostered— at least to those avant-garde artists such as Liszt who were disaffected with its aims—a dry, pedantic, and conservative approach, hopelessly devoid of inspiration or spontaneity. The joke ran that the absence of windows in the Leipzig Gewandhaus was designed to "preserve the same air that Mendelssohn had breathed."[30] It was not for nothing that one could read on the Gewandhaus wall a frowning motto from Seneca, "res severa ist gaudium verum" (a serious thing is a true joy). Definitely no giggling à la Pachmann welcome here.

Although Liszt's personal relations with the considerably more straitlaced Mendelssohn had ranged from the overeffusively cordial to the extremely uneasy, he retained both a vast respect for him as a musician and keen memories of his playing. Instructing his pupils in 1883 on the approach required for the principal romantic piano composers, Liszt gave a summary that is even more useful today: "Schumann especially must be phrased well in details; and played very compact—rhythmically well articulated. With him ritenutos should be very great, as with Mendelssohn the accelerandos and animatos are great; Mendelssohn dashes out bright and quickly. Schumann has breadth, but Chopin has greater height."[31] Remembering Mendelssohn's reputation for swift performances, he added on a later occasion: "I am not in favour of extreme tempi, as often heard done by virtuosos of today. It is justifiable only in a few exceptions—perhaps with Mendelssohn."[32] Liszt's student Hans von Bülow had not only frequently heard Mendelssohn play, but even received a lesson from him. As he put it: "I had the honour of being Mendelssohn's pupil for exactly two hours,"[33] and his comments on the distortions of what sometimes passed for performance style in

---

[29] Paul Mendelssohn Bartholdy, ed., *Mendelssohn Briefe aus den Jahren 1830 bis 1847* (Leipzig: Hermann Mendelssohn, 1863–64), 41.

[30] Stanford, 143.

[31] Walker, *Living with Liszt*, 231.

[32] Walker, *Living with Liszt*, 275. See chapter 8, pp. 271–72, for more on tempi.

[33] Zimdars, *Masterclasses of Von Bülow*, 84.

Mendelssohn's own music were typically trenchant: "The ritardandos which are added to Mendelssohn have given him an undeserved reputation for lemonade-like sentimentality. It is, however, noble wine, not lemonade."[34] A Mendelssohn *Lied ohne Worte* was, according to Bülow, "as Classical as a Goethe poem" and should be played as such.[35]

Although Liszt enjoyed a well-deserved reputation for benevolence and graciousness, certainly in comparison with the often acerbic Bülow, the Leipzig Conservatory and occasionally others were habitually referred to with humorous contempt and sarcasm during his master classes. Overcorrect, dull playing was "Leipzigerisch," and Clara Schumann was regularly "Die Göttliche Clara" (the divine Clara). In general, he far preferred the playing of the dashing Sophie Menter to the aged Frau Schumann. A student playing Liszt's *Liebestraum* no. 1 in 1884 was instructed: "You must play that totally carried away as if you were not even seated at the piano, completely lost to the world, not 1, 2, 3, 4 as in the Leipzig Conservatory!"[36] while a performer of the *Mephisto* Polka was told sarcastically: "This piece is composed especially for the Leipzig Conservatory. Play it only paying attention to yourself, and not at all brilliantly."[37] Liszt's most withering comments, however, were occasioned by some inept attempts at performing Chopin's C-Minor Nocturne, op. 48 no. 1, when his criticism extended far beyond the unfortunate performers to take in both Frankfurt and Leipzig, in the shape of Clara Schumann and Moscheles:

> The first lady played the theme at the beginning extremely sentimentally and fragmented, whereupon the master sat down and played the theme in an extremely broad and expansive manner. The young lady continually swayed along back and forth, to which Liszt said[,] "Keep perfectly calm, child. This tottering is 'frankfurtisch,' just do not totter so." He sat down and said: "Even the wonderful [Clara] Schumann sways like that," and he humorously imitated it. Then he came to speak about the fashionable fragmenting of all themes and said: "Disgusting! I thank you, that is certainly the opposite of all good manners." . . . Then in an extremely droll manner he imitated Moscheles playing one of his etudes. . . . Then he said, "Yes, in Leipzig, or Frankfurt, or Cologne or Berlin at the 'great conservatories,' there you will make a success with that. One can say to you as to Ophelia: 'Get thee to a nunnery'—get thee to a conservatory."[38]

---

[34] Zimdars, *Masterclasses of von Bülow*, 84.

[35] Zimdars, *Masterclasses of von Bülow*, 84.

[36] Zimdars, *Masterclasses of Liszt*, 47.

[37] Zimdars, *Masterclasses of Liszt*, 48.

[38] Zimdars, *Masterclasses of Liszt*, 22.

But what of the other side of the coin—what did Mendelssohn, Moscheles, and their circle think of Liszt in his virtuoso days? In 1837 in a letter to his mother, Mendelssohn had reacted indignantly to his sister Fanny's admiration of contemporary virtuoso playing while conveniently summarizing his own views:

> I was annoyed, however, to hear that Fanny says the new school of piano-playing has left her behind . . . but there is absolutely nothing to that. She really plays all the little fellows such as Döhler into the ground; they can manage a couple of variations and party tricks nicely, and then everything becomes terribly boring, and that never happens when Fanny plays the piano. Then there is something other than party-tricks. Thalberg and Henselt are a rather different matter, for they are supposed to be true virtuosi in the manner of Liszt (who outclasses them all); and yet it all amounts to nothing more than a Kalkbrenner in his heyday, and blows over during their lifetime if there is not some spirit and life in it, and something more than mere dexterity. . . . For my part I believe that Chopin is by far the most inspired of them all, although Liszt's fingers are yet more amazing and supple than his.[39]

However much the tone of these comments was colored by family solidarity, they are of a piece with views that Mendelssohn expressed on other occasions. He later grew to admire Thalberg more and more for his "composure and restraint."[40] As far as the notably unrestrained Liszt was concerned, he wrote: "I have seen no musician whose musical sensitivity . . . courses straight into his fingertips and then flows directly out from there. And with this immediacy and his enormous technique and skill, he would leave all others far behind him, if it were not that his own ideas always predominate in whatever he is playing, and at least up to now these seem to have been denied him by nature."[41] In other words, Liszt's playing exhibited too much of his own creativity, and since this creativity was weak, his performances suffered. Later, Mendelssohn's pleasure in some of Liszt's concerts in Berlin in 1842 was marred by what he regarded as an inappropriately cavalier license in the music of the great classical masters, in accordance with his almost fanatical comment to Joachim that it is "inartistic, nay barbaric, to alter anything they have ever written, even by a single note":[42]

---

[39] Letter of 15 May 1837, quoted from Peter Ward Jones, *The Mendelssohns on Honeymoon* (Oxford: Clarendon Press, 1997), 156.

[40] Little, 118.

[41] Little, 118.

[42] C. Brown, 223.

Even Liszt doesn't please me here half as much as he did elsewhere. He has forfeited a large degree of my respect for him through the ridiculous pranks he plays, not only on the public (that didn't do any damage) but rather on the music itself. He has played here works by Beethoven, Bach, Handel and Weber so wretchedly and unsatisfactorily, so impurely and so unknowledgeably, that I would have heard them played by mediocre performers with more pleasure: here six measures added in, there seven omitted; here he plays false harmonies, and then later these are cancelled out by others. Then he makes a horrible fortissimo out of the softest passages, and goodness knows what other kinds of dreadful mischief. That may be all well and good for the public at large, but not for me, and that it was good enough for Liszt himself, that lowers my respect for him by a very great deal. At the same time my respect for him was so great, that there is still enough left."[43]

Not surprisingly, when a pupil arrived at Leipzig sporting long Lisztian locks, Mendelssohn's first instruction to him was, "You must get your hair cut!"[44]

It was not only Mendelssohn who abominated Liszt's taking such liberties with the score. Glinka made similar criticisms in 1842, claiming that "sometimes Liszt played magnificently, like no-one else in the world, but at other times intolerably, in a highly affected manner, dragging tempi and adding to the works of others, even to those of Chopin, Beethoven, Weber and Bach a lot of embellishments of his own that were often tasteless, worthless, and meaningless."[45] When Charles Hallé, during his early years in Paris, rehearsed Beethoven's *Emperor* Concerto with the conservatory orchestra, he was promptly upbraided by one of the players—the eccentric violist Chretian Urhan[46]—for making changes to the text. Hallé subsequently regretted his lax approach, claiming that he had been "misled by the example of Liszt," although he noted that Liszt's own *Emperor* performance a few years afterward at the Beethoven festival in Bonn had been a surprisingly faithful one.[47] Nevertheless, Liszt's reputation for playing fast and loose with the score was so well established by then that several critics castigated even this performance for its disrespect to Beethoven.

---

[43] Little, 122.

[44] Nichols, 75.

[45] Vladimir Stasov, *Selected Essays on Music*, trans. Florence Jonas (New York: Praeger, 1968), 121.

[46] When playing in the opera orchestra, Urhan was famous for turning his back when the girls from the ballet came on stage. His religious convictions forbade his exposing himself to such devilish temptations.

[47] Hallé, 102.

On the general question of interpretative fidelity, some thinly veiled strictures appeared around this time in the section "On Style in Performance" of the Moscheles and Fétis *Méthode des méthodes*:

> There are certain cases when artists of the first rank, through mood and will-fulness, let themselves be seduced into altering the character of the piece of music in the performance of compositions of the great masters, which they take now faster, now slower, according to how they feel prompted themselves; they add in a few additions, instead of playing what is written; without attention to the beautiful thoughts therein, which they perhaps don't understand, they denature them, and effectively only make an improvisation over given themes. Such an abuse [*Missbrauch*] is the most deserving of condemnation that can be, however great the talent should be of the person guilty of it.[48]

It is difficult to believe that they did not have a certain celebrated Hungarian virtuoso in mind here—one who happened to be famed for his improvisations.

In vast contrast to Liszt, Mendelssohn was known for his strictness in performing the music of the masters he most admired. His concert programs were relatively severe for the times (see chapter 2), and several accounts testify to a passion for adherence to the letter of the score that would have given Moscheles and Fétis no grounds for complaint. What could count as zealotry in the nineteenth century, however, often falls far short of the even greater fanaticism of our age. We must not forget that even Friedrich Wieck, Clara's teacher and an abominator of many virtuoso liberties, regarded the "new, brilliant manner of playing" as an advance over that of earlier eras and thought it inevitable that compositions by Mozart and others should be updated to some extent in the modern style.[49] The upright Mendelssohn's famous revival of Bach's *St. Matthew Passion* also took—quite deliberately, and for quite understandable practical reasons—what would now be regarded as liberties with the score, including extensive cuts and radical reorchestration. It was effectively a modernization, though much more restrained than the Godowski versions of the Chopin etudes so loved by Pachmann.[50] Additionally, Mendelssohn was perfectly happy to

[48] Moscheles and Fétis, 119.
[49] Wieck, 146.
[50] A more extreme revision of the *St. Matthew Passion* was mulled over in 1919 by Busoni, which would have turned it entirely into a choral work: "The aria is the crippling, desanctifying

compose a piano accompaniment filling out the harmony to Bach's D-Minor Chaconne, originally written for unaccompanied violin. Yet, there can be little doubt that by the standards of his time he was an unusually faithful, even puritanical performer. A pupil adding simply an extra note to a chord was apt to be met with the disapproving "Es steht nicht da!" (That's not how it's written!), while he preferred any tempo fluctuations within a piece to be restrained and unobtrusive (see his comments on Chopin and Hiller quoted earlier), an attitude that, in conducting, contrasted strikingly with Wagner's ostentatiously flexible approach. It might reasonably be argued that Mendelssohn's resistance to his pupils' unlicensed liberties and additions could well have stemmed as much from their ineptitude ("Quod licet Jovi non licet bovi," or "What suits the gods doesn't suit clods") than from an outright opposition in principle, but this is to ignore what indubitably was a streak of fundamentalism in his nature.

When performing his own music Mendelssohn not only reportedly adopted an especially straightforward style, but even played in a deliberately withdrawn manner, as if trying to avoid anything approaching a flashy or affected execution. Friends attributed this to his essential modesty—he did not wish his composition to gain in effect from any unworthily superficial technical brilliance. This directness of approach went with an abomination of anything bordering on sentimental playing. Bülow put it with typical bluntness in the introduction to his edition of the "Andante and Rondo capriccioso": "Whoever plays Schumann tolerably well will play Mendelssohn rather intolerably. . . . Schumann is a sentimental poet; Mendelssohn a naive one." These adjectives cannot be taken at face value. Bülow is here alluding to Schiller's famous distinction between naive and sentimental poetry: the sentimental poet was the reflective writer, seeking by thought to reproduce what the naive author produces naturally. In this context, Mendelssohn, with his astonishing musical precocity, was undoubtedly a "naive" musician, in contrast to what seemed to be Schumann's more tortuous struggle as an adult toward musical mastery. For Bülow, the fact that Mendelssohn's musical style was fully formed at a relatively young age meant that, in performance, even the slightest hint of affectation must be avoided. Warming to his theme, he went

---

moment, the pedantic bigot's passing comment, and indeed, so offensive is the disharmony between these texts and that of the Gospel, that I am amazed at the absence of any protest against them. . . . As I see it, a complete performance of the Passion without the arias would have a striking effect, a dramatic saga with great expressive power and a theatrical heartbeat." Beaumont, *Busoni: Selected Letters*, 286–87.

on in an authoritative manner that succinctly summarizes his view of the essence
of Mendelssohn's performance style and deserves extended quotation:

> If one wants to play Mendelssohn correctly, one should first play Mozart, for
> example. Above all, one should renounce all Empfindsamkeit of conception,
> despite the temptations that are provided by certain frequently recurring me-
> lismas peculiar to Mendelssohn. One should try, for example, to play passages of
> this apparent character simply and naturally in rhythm, with a beautiful and
> regular attack, and one will surely find that they sound, in this fashion, much
> nobler and more graceful than in a passionately excited rubato. The master was
> committed, above all, to the strict observance of meter. He categorically denied
> himself every ritardando that was not prescribed, and wanted to see the pre-
> scribed ritards restricted to their least possible extent. He despised, furthermore,
> all arbitrary arpeggiation (chords that could not be played without breaking
> them, à la Schumann, he did not write, or only when he wanted successive
> chords—see the introduction to op. 22). In op. 14 there is not a single arpeggio
> mark, despite the "brilliant" style. He permitted the use of the pedal only for
> certain tonal effects. What subtle caution was to be exercised in this matter can
> be gleaned from his specification of the appropriate symbols throughout. Finally,
> he also protested against that "thrilling" haste, against the rushing and forcing of
> his pieces by players who believed that the best way they could meet the charge
> of "sentimental" interpretation was through this kind of speeded-up, summary
> behavior. Here we must nonetheless observe very decisively that his most fre-
> quent comments while teaching were "lively, briskly, keep going."[51]

Although one should not infer from this that the ideal Mendelssohn performance should resemble that of a pianola, or that his own playing was lacking
in feeling (Liszt's opinion of Mendelssohn's pianism was that it showed "more
warmth than Thalberg, but less technique"),[52] Bülow's basic meaning could
hardly be clearer.

Mendelssohn's approach was on the stricter, and swifter, end of the argument,
but he was far from an isolated prophet in the wilderness, and he had powerful
supporters, both as a pianist and a conductor. His no-nonsense performance
style was—unsurprisingly—particularly admired in England, and Wagner's
slower, enormously flexible conducting was accordingly abominated when the
preacher of endless melody was engaged as a guest artist in London in 1855. It

---

[51] R. Larry Todd, *Mendelssohn and His World* (Princeton, N.J.: Princeton University Press,
1991), 392–93.
[52] Göllerich, 20.

was to be a few decades before the tide would turn and the passionate Wagnerian George Bernard Shaw could begin to fulminate against the "Mendelssohnic curse of speed for speed's sake."[53] Clara Schumann shared Mendelssohn's general attitude to interpretation ("Play what is written. Play it as it is written. It all stands there," she told her pupil Fanny Davies),[54] although she did offer the opinion, in private, that his performances had often been too hurried. Her "strict conformity of measure" was duly noted by Hanslick. Although it took him somewhat by surprise when applied even in a performance of Chopin's Fantasy-Impromptu, he was content to contrast it to 'the common misuse of rubato.' "[55] The implication was that such an unbending style was less than idiomatic for Chopin, but it might nevertheless be preferred as a healthy option. Many felt that the liberties taken by the more headstrong of the virtuosi owed more to egotism than inspiration. These performers might be counseled to develop a little more humility in the face of the score. But what sort of score, exactly, would deserve such reverential treatment?

## The Letter of Which Score?

The exhortation to play any piece accurately according to the score assumes an edition concordant with the composer's intentions. Fidelity to the opinions of editors is, in theory, rarely required (despite the dogmatic tone of publications by Bülow and Busoni). In practice, however, fidelity to the score before the fashion for urtext editions became established must have often resulted in exactly that.

The idea that the composer's urtext is the ultimate arbiter of performance decisions is a useful one for conservatories, whose examination systems are keen to find any means possible to make evaluation of performances more objective, and for musicologists, to whose scholarly skills are entrusted the important role of deciding what the urtext should actually be. Performers, so favored as editors in the romantic era, are now often regarded as not having the appropriate training (with a few honorable exceptions such as Alfred Brendel and Paul Badura-Skoda), or, perhaps, a suitably meticulous attitude. One result has been a profusion of laudably "clean" texts, but with ludicrously impractical fingering uselessly added

---

[53] Shaw, *Music in London*, 3:313.

[54] Reich, 295.

[55] Henry Pleasants, ed. and trans., *Eduard Hanslick: Vienna's Golden Years of Music, 1850–1900* (New York: Simon and Schuster, 1950), 42.

by editors whose academic skills are far more advanced than their executive. At the time of Bülow's master classes in the 1880s and 1890s the problem was reversed: it was often difficult for pianists to obtain publications free of greater or lesser editorial interference, but at least the text would be suitable for practical performance. The fingering would work, and the suggested pedaling would sound good on most instruments students would likely encounter. Of course, this ease of access was frequently achieved only through drastic intervention. When Harold Bauer, in the early twentieth century, wanted to check the accuracy of a questionable bar in an edition of Beethoven's *Moonlight* Sonata, what would now probably involve little more than turning to the critical notes of an urtext turned out to be a time-consuming rigmarole. Eventually he found what he was seeking, and discovered that the text he had known for years was unlikely to have been entirely Beethoven's.[56] Even to this day it can be difficult to locate editions of Chopin that accurately reflect the multifarious readings of the original publications, especially in terms of phrasing and pedaling (Paul Badura-Skoda's superb Wiener Urtext edition of the etudes is a welcome exception).[57] Much of the text in the widely used "Paderewski" edition, for example, represents conflations of several distinct sources and is identical to no score that appeared during Chopin's lifetime. The pedaling, especially, is extensively, and often silently, modified.

Pedaling was a natural target for later editors, given its often haphazard treatment in original publications (though not those of Chopin, who was extremely precise in this respect) and changes in the resonance of the piano. In late-nineteenth-century Mendelssohn scores edited by Kullak and others, it was routinely altered to bring it in line with later practices. As Bülow implied, the sustaining pedal had been, for the naturally conservative Mendelssohn, still to some extent a special effect designed to change the tone color and increase the volume of sound as much as to guarantee a perfect legato. The score of the early G-Minor Sonata even contains a very Beethovenian (and by the 1820s, distinctly old-fashioned) effect of pedaling straight through soft tonic and dominant harmonies for several bars (as in the opening of the last movement of the *Waldstein* Sonata).[58] The piano-duet arrangement of the *Hebrides* Overture at

---

[56] Bauer, 268–70.

[57] See Jeffrey Kallberg, *Chopin at the Boundaries: Sex, History, and Musical Genre* (Cambridge, Mass.: Harvard University Press, 1996), 215–28.

[58] Beethovenian to us, that is, and likely also to Mendelssohn. Yet this gentle mingling of tonic and dominant harmonies seems to have been one of the most common ways of treating the sustaining pedal at the end of the eighteenth and the beginning of the nineteenth century. It is found in pieces by Steibelt, Dussek, and Louis Adam, to name but a few.

times indicates similarly lengthy pedalings, seemingly to create an appropriately stormy sonority, but at other points is remarkably free from any pedal markings at all. Although Mendelssohn's "Thalberg-style" writing, as found in the prelude to the E-minor fugue, obviously demanded a copious application of the pedal, some pianists would have been surprised at the reticence with which it was actually indicated in the original printings of most of Mendelssohn's works, especially if they were accustomed to the numerous editions in which swaths of extra pedaling, usually accompanied by extended phrase markings, were generously provided.

Much of the pedaling added by editors was of the syncopated variety. Later on in the century this technique was regarded as indispensable for performing pieces such as the very first *Lied ohne Worte* op. 19 no. 1. Indispensable it may indeed be for more modern pianos, with their impressively effective damping systems, but it is not so necessary on some of the instruments known to the composer.[59] Nevertheless, despite our present skepticism about "unauthorized" alterations to a composer's text, most interventionist editors were certainly not careless vandals, but often—like Theodor Kullak, who edited all the *Lieder ohne Worte*—fine pianists whose intentions were simply to fit the music, as they saw it, to the instruments of the day. The famous "Spring Song" is an instructive example of Mendelssohn's sparing approach to pedaling and careful marking of phrasing. In the original edition of this work, the main tune is performed first without pedal, then with dabs of sustaining pedal later at the recapitulation for a subtle variation in the sonority. The initial presentation of the celebrated melody is obviously intended to have a crisp, unpedaled, staccato accompaniment (indeed Mendelssohn's piquant staccato was especially remarked upon in his own performances), with the required melodic legato to be achieved as far as possible by the fingers alone. This is made easier if Mendelssohn's relatively short original phrase lengths are printed and observed. Several editors, however, lengthened the phrasing and (necessarily) added copious pedal to the opening pages, creating a late-romantic broad legato that completely eliminated the contrasts of tone color between unpedaled exposition and pedaled recapitulation seemingly intended by the composer. We can hear this super-legato style of interpretation on the pellucid-toned recordings by Josef Hofmann and Vladimir de Pachmann, for a long-breathed, pedaled legato became for many years the "standard" interpretation of this piece, and to some extent it is still with us. So used have we become

---

[59] See chapter 5, pp. 170–74.

to it, in fact, that a drier approach with shorter phrases and much less pedal can sound almost trivial, unless presented with subtlety and discretion.

But will just playing Mendelssohn's text as written on a modern concert grand produce the effect the composer presumably desired? The present-day performer has to keep in mind that his instrument may react rather differently to any known to the early nineteenth century. This could well necessitate sensitive adaptation to express the likely intention, if not the letter, of the score. When the "Spring Song" is played on a modern instrument, we may have to very slightly extend, without pedal or with only short dabs, the length of the bass octaves supporting the tune during its first presentation. In this way we can imitate the short overhang of bass sound produced by Mendelssohn's instruments, avoid an over-flippant staccato in the lower register, and yet still maintain a largely unpedaled sonority. Bülow's seemingly straightforward advice—"in Mendelssohn you do not need to interpret, he wrote everything scrupulously and exactly as he wanted to have it"—presupposes not only an accurate edition,[60] but also (although Bülow himself may have disputed this) a piano of Mendelssohn's own era.

Even some of the most liberal of romantic interpreters counseled beginning work on a piece with close attention to the original text, although the final performance might well depart radically from it. Anton Rubinstein's advice to Josef Hofmann may be taken as axiomatic for many players of the romantic generation: "Just play first exactly what is written; if you have done full justice to it, and still feel like adding or changing anything, why, do so."[61] A prevalent modern attitude, ably promoted by Ravel and Stravinsky, would embrace the first point, but abominate the second. In other words: if you can't make it effective as the composer wrote it, don't play it at all. Ironically, Rubinstein's insistence on first mastering the original score was if anything a rather rigorous point of view for his era, and Hofmann felt that his master adopted a slightly hypocritical "do as I say, not do as I do" approach:

> He always compelled me to bring the pieces along, insisting that I should play everything just as it was written! He would follow every note of my playing with his eyes riveted on the printed pages. A pedant he certainly was, a stickler for the letter—incredibly so, especially when one considered the liberties he took when playing the same works! Once I called his attention modestly to this seeming

---

[60] Zimdars, *Masterclasses of von Bülow*, 61.
[61] Hofmann, 55.

paradox, and he answered: "When you are as old as I am now you may do as I do—if you can."[62]

To be sure, even Liszt seemed to adopt a radically more severe approach (judged by the standards of the time) when teaching later in life—especially for the works of Beethoven and Chopin—than he evinced during his own performing heyday.

We can get an idea of the young Liszt's willful approach to interpretation from an account of Wilhelm von Lenz (1809–1883), a biographer of Beethoven and something of a piano groupie. He sought out lessons from many of the day's celebrated performers, among them Chopin, Liszt, Henselt, and later Tausig. In 1828 von Lenz visited Liszt, mightily impressed after having seen a poster advertising a performance of Beethoven's *Emperor* Concerto with the young virtuoso as soloist. Whether he knew it or not, the performance had been canceled when Liszt less impressively fell ill. Lenz had been studying the piano works of Weber (of the existence of which Liszt professed not even to be aware, though he had certainly played the *Momento capriccioso* as a lad) and in his first lesson played the *Invitation to the Dance*. Liszt "could hardly tear himself away from the piece. He played through the different parts over and over again. He tried various reinforcements. He played the second part of the minor movement in octaves, and was inexhaustible in his praise of Weber."[63] His reaction to the A♭ Sonata was equally enthusiastic: "He played the first part over and over again in various ways. At the section (in the dominant) in E♭ at the close of the first part he said[,] 'It is marked legato there. Would it not be better to make it pianissimo and staccato? Leggermente is indicated there, too.' He experimented in every direction. So I had the experience of observing how one genius looks upon the work of another, and turns it to his own account."[64] Liszt carried on with the lesson in a similar fashion, adding and altering as he saw fit—rather a contrast (though not a complete one) to the more severe elderly Liszt, and an even greater one to Mendelssohn. A few years later, in 1832, although he was expressing sentiments of "profound humility" toward Weber and Beethoven to his pupil Valerie Boissier, he was also adding complications of octaves, thirds, and sixths to the Weber sonatas and filling out the *Konzertstück* because he found the texture "a bit thin."[65] A bewildered Charles Hallé in 1836 famously heard him play his

[62] Hofmann, 59–60.
[63] Von Lenz, 19.
[64] Von Lenz, 20–21.
[65] Mach, xv.

transcription of the Scherzo from Beethoven's Sixth Symphony in which "the peculiarity, the oddity of the performance consisted in his playing the first eight bars . . . rather quicker than they are usually taken, and the following eight bars, the B-major phrase [Halle must have meant D-major], in a slow andante time. 'Ce sont les vieux' [these are the old folk], he said to me on one occasion."[66] Liszt's practice and his professions could obviously diverge somewhat.

The Weber scores that von Lenz brought to Liszt in 1828 were probably those that had appeared during the composer's lifetime (Weber had died only two years before) and were thus free from the enormous amount of editorial intervention of later publications (including an edition by Liszt himself). But many of the scores that Hofmann brought to Rubinstein toward the end of the century were in all likelihood far distant from the original publications, and it could well be that the letter of the score Rubinstein taught Hofmann initially to observe derived, as I have noted, largely from the editor rather than the composer. An urtext edition might even have been positively unwelcome to some, were one available. Liszt gave a dusty reception to a scholarly edition of Palestrina that he felt was useless for practical performance,[67] and the reason that so many nineteenth-century scores were edited by performers rather than musicologists was that the scores were intended to be placed on the piano music stand and simply played, not to be used as stepping-stones toward further scholarly study. Performing musicians generally had little interest in the niceties of source studies (not much has changed), and part of an editor's duty was to update pedal markings and phrasings to make them more concordant with contemporary instruments and tastes. If the editor was also a great performer, the score might authoritatively embody his interpretative ideas in a manner stimulating to other professionals and helpful to the student. Editors could also, if they were so minded, rescue the composers of the past from the embarrassing ignorance necessitated by their benighted historical milieu. For Godowski, phrasing was not a question of taste, but (somehow) of advancing knowledge: "In the matter of phrasing, Beethoven was considered very particular, Chopin also, but neither knew as much about the subject as we do now."[68] Bauer went even further, believing that Chopin had little idea what he was doing when he wrote the etude op. 10, no. 3: "the dynamic markings are questionable

---

[66] Hallé, 58.
[67] See chapter 1, p. 23.
[68] Jeffrey Johnson, *Piano Mastery*, 94.

throughout, the slurs are inadmissible from the standpoint of musical phrasing, and it is hardly too much to say that none of these markings are of value in building up an artistic interpretation of this piece, while on the other hand there is unfortunately much which, if strictly followed, will distort its musical contour."[69] Godowski and Bauer felt they had not just the opportunity to save composers from themselves, but a positive duty to improve the music of the past in the light of modern advances.

Finding out what the composer, rather than the editor, wrote was not always an easy task in an era that frequently saw no need to differentiate the markings of the one from those of the other. In the case of Beethoven—surely the great master most likely to be treated with respect—there were a profusion of editions available toward the end of the century, most of them more or less heavily edited. Ironically, one of the least invasively edited was the 1857 edition of Beethoven sonatas by the very same Liszt whose reckless ways with the classics so appalled Mendelssohn and Moscheles. Published by Holle (and later reissued by Bosworth and Hachette), this had the pedagogical peculiarity that the pieces were ordered not by opus number, but by difficulty, with the *Hammerklavier* Sonata naturally appearing last. The surprisingly "clean" text of this edition cannot, alas, be attributed to Liszt's having intended a visionary urtext approach (as has occasionally been claimed), but more likely is due to his lack of time for, and perhaps interest in, such a major editing job. He was more than usually busy (which for Liszt really is saying something) in 1856–57 with the completion of the *Dante* Symphony and other pieces, and numerous first performances of major works, including the *Missa Solemnis*, the Second Piano Concerto, and the *Faust* Symphony. It is perhaps surprising in the light of this that he agreed to take on this editing task at all. He seems really to have only paid much attention to the Sonatas opp. 109, 110, and 111, which have many changes in dynamics, phrasing, and articulation. The other pieces were largely ignored, hence the almost modern-style noninterventionist editing (the superficial appearance of which, after all, can be achieved even more easily by lack of effort than by assiduous industry). In the *Tempest* Sonata Beethoven's notoriously long first-movement pedal indications were modified, and a few metronome marks were added to other pieces, but otherwise Liszt was mostly content to leave the text initially sent to him by the publisher (based on original editions) well alone. He had his own fish to fry.

[69] Bauer, 271.

This minimalist Beethoven edition made relatively little impact on the musical world and even less on Liszt himself, who in his later years always taught from the famous Beethoven sonata volumes edited by Bülow (Cotta, 1871).[70] Liszt had the highest admiration for this publication, which was used by many subsequent generations of performers. Most of the early sonatas in this edition were entrusted to Sigmund Lebert. Bülow's contribution was the Sonatas op. 13, op. 26, op. 27 no. 2, and op. 31 no. 3, and everything from op. 53 onward. This he generously dedicated to Liszt as "the fruits of his teaching," while the latter's gracious reaction was, "Here the master learns from the pupil." Although other Liszt pupils, such as Frederick Lamond and Karl Klindworth, also edited the Beethoven sonatas (Bülow later claimed to prefer the 1884 Klindworth edition to his own)[71], and Schnabel's if anything even more interventionist version gained wide circulation,[72] the Bülow edition has been outstandingly influential—it is in print to this day.

Bülow's editing gives a good idea of just how far removed the nineteenth-century spectrum of attitudes to textual fidelity was from our assumptions. He was universally regarded then as a rather strict, cerebral performer, but his Beethoven edition appears now to be lavish in its liberties; flabbergastingly dogmatic, and amusingly arrogant to boot. At one point he openly complains about the ineptitude of his co-editor for countenancing an "amateurish error" in his earlier edition of the *Moonlight* Sonata—no hypocritical collegiality for Bülow. Numerous silent changes are made to Beethoven's phrase markings; dynamics and signs for articulation are altered and supplemented. Changing the order of the movements in op. 26 is recommended as "more effective." "Modern" versions of certain passages (for example in the last movement of op. 101), reflecting Bülow's own performances, are suggested in footnotes. On the last page of the *Hammerklavier* Sonata, for example, we read, "To give the closing measures the requisite brilliancy, we recommend the modern transcription employed by Franz Liszt in performance":

---

[70] See Fay, 218. For a detailed discussion of von Bülow's editing, see Hinrichsen, 156–204. Hinrichsen also reproduces (516–47) the lengthy exchange of letters between Bülow and his publishers, Cotta.

[71] Zimdars, *Masterclasses of von Bülow*, 40.

[72] Berlin: Ullstein Verlag; English edition, New York: Simon and Schuster (1935). According to the publisher's preface, Schnabel was "the greatest living master of Beethoven, and possibly the greatest exponent of all time of his works. It is therefore a signal honour to be entrusted with the publication of this memorial edition"—a claim that might well have sold a few extra copies. It is cheering to see commerce and art striding hand in hand toward a common goal.

EXAMPLE 6.1. Ludwig van Beethoven, *Hammerklavier* Sonata, excerpt, ed. Hans von Bülow

Bülow also recommends a double repeat of the Scherzo and Trio in Sonatas opp. 106 and 110 when performing in public, to aid comprehensibility—"if one is aiming at an effect satisfactory to the hearer, this liberty on the editor's part will hardly meet with disapproval"— although he simultaneously advised ignoring many repeats actually indicated by the composer. He later told a student playing the first movement of the F♯ Sonata, op. 78: "One should not repeat . . . aesthetically, it would not be beautiful; Beethoven wrote the repetition just as one often writes 'respectfully yours' at the end of a letter without thinking further about it."[73] So now we know.

Whatever we think of Bülow's Beethoven edition as a piece of editing—and there is a lot in it, as we might expect from such a fine musician, that is stimulating and imaginative—it indubitably tells us as much about the performance practice of the time as about Beethoven's sonatas. Sometimes we almost feel we can hear Bülow himself playing as we try to cope with his copious additional markings, or raise our eyebrows at the enormously cocksure comments laying down the law for almost every detail of interpretation. His general performance approach was far from unique, although the level of sarcasm probably was. Students attending Bülow's master classes were also given detailed advice on Beethoven interpretation that supplements the instructions in his editions, such as a rewriting of parts of the first movement of the *Emperor* Concerto, and even the extension of the solo part in the last movement so that it plays right up to the close of the piece—none of this nonsense about letting the orchestra end on its own when Bülow was at the keyboard. Those appalled by this last addition should note that recent research has indicated that Beethoven in fact intended both a continuo and a solo role for the piano in this concerto and may well have expected the piano to play during the

[73] Zimdars, *Masterclasses of Von Bülow*, 37. Contrast this with Rosenblum's comment: "Casual disregard of Beethoven's repeats would seem an affront to his formal designs" (73).

closing orchestral tutti.[74] Bülow ironically may have been closer to the composer's own practice here than many an urtext edition. Apparently Leschetizky too felt himself the inheritor of a weighty tradition in this concerto and used a score that had belonged to his teacher Czerny, with comments in Beethoven's hand. According to his assistant Ethel Newcomb: "Over some heavy chords and some passages in the first movement Beethoven had written the word 'free.' In one of the introductory passages there was a mordent written in also in Beethoven's own hand. He had many other interesting copies handed down to him by Czerny with marks by Beethoven. In several of these was advice to put in a cadenza ad libitum—notes which are never seen in any edition."[75]

Bülow's practice of introducing new repeats of certain sections "to aid comprehension," while sometimes ignoring others written by the composer, was widespread and is heard on early recordings, despite the space limitations of the disks. Liszt told his pupils to play the central part of his *Au lac de Wallenstadt* twice

FIGURE 6.1. Hans Schliessmann's silhouette of Hans von Bülow at the piano. Something of von Bülow's precise, punctilious, and pontificating style certainly comes over here, especially in contrast with the "inspired" Anton Rubinstein of figure 1.1.

[74] See Leon Plantinga, *Beethoven's Concertos: History, Style, Performance* (New York: Norton, 1990), 279–304, and Tibor Szász, "Beethoven's Basso Continuo: Notation and Performance," in Stowell, 1–22.

[75] E. Newcomb, 165.

and regularly repeated parts of certain Chopin etudes and preludes. The first prelude, for example, he usually went through two times, the second as a faint echo of the first.[76] We can hear similar repeats in Busoni's piano rolls of the Chopin preludes.[77] Eugen d'Albert even made three separate, and very different, recordings of Chopin's *Butterfly* Etude, which partly function as examples of how to make a short piece longer. One is played as in the score, while the other two have an added repeat. In the last recording the repeat is very extensive indeed (sounding, it must be admitted, not entirely intentional), for the piece now takes two minutes and thirty-seven seconds compared with one minute and three seconds for the shortest version (the one of middle length is one minute and forty-three seconds), and d'Albert's tempi are not substantially different in any of the performances.[78] When the longest recording approaches a conclusion, d'Albert plays an emphatic extra chord to finish up—presumably out of sheer relief—to bring the etude to a definite halt before it potentially circles on ad infinitum. For d'Albert, the work was obviously not substantial enough as it stood, and he was determined to keep playing until it was.

Again, it would not be entirely fair to treat the romantic tendency to play free and easy with repeats as mere willfulness. Audience attention and audience comprehension were uppermost in the minds of players before the recording era. As the standard repertoire solidified and certain works began to be performed ad nauseam, there was a natural tendency to omit some repeats in well-known pieces and, ironically, a concomitant trend to extend short popular ones. After all, when Beethoven wrote the repeats in his sonatas, he did not know quite how ubiquitous they were to become in concert halls. Brahms appears to have held a rather flexible attitude to the written repeats in his own works, believing that they were necessary when a piece was unfamiliar, less so when it was well-known. Many players today omit repeats for the same reason, despite the strictures of musicologists. How often, for example, do we hear the repeat of the second half of sonata-form movements played? That we now rarely add repeats that are not indicated has surely something to do with our greater reluctance actively to "tamper" with scores. Silently ignoring a repeat sign seems more passive and less invasive than adding one of our own. In a similar fashion, we are very reluctant to cut music actually written out in the score, even if it too is simply a repeat.

[76] Zimdars, *Masterclasses of Liszt*, 120.
[77] Nimbus NI 8810.
[78] All can be heard on Arbiter CD 147.

## The Protean Piano

Just as phrasing, in Godowski's view, naturally evolved toward a state of per-fection, so did the piano, and the concomitant duty to adapt earlier music to the requirements of the developing instrument was rarely denied. After all, what is the point of playing something according to the letter of the score when this produces an effect on a modern instrument very different from that on the old? There have been so few changes in the basic construction of the piano for so many years now that it is easy to lose sight of the instrument's fluid state for most of the nineteenth century. Our reluctance to make adaptations of the text of a masterwork to suit the piano in front of us is an aversion that would hardly have seemed viable in the past (and indeed is scarcely viable now, whatever some might think). As is well-known, in the early part of the nineteenth century Viennese and English instruments were so different as to have fostered radically disparate playing styles, and even some decades later the pianos produced by Érard and Pleyel in Paris alone were distinct enough to encourage a different approach to fingering and certainly a characteristic use of the pedal (as anyone who has played, for example, the Chopin etudes on Érards and Pleyels of the 1830s will readily confirm). Czerny regarded it as blindingly obvious that Beethoven's original pedal markings had to be modified for pianos of a later vintage. All good performers would certainly have been prepared for potential surprises from an unfamiliar piano and would have adapted their playing style accordingly.

It was not until 1857 that Bülow inaugurated an iron-framed Bechstein in a recital in Berlin (playing, among other things, the Liszt Sonata), and another decade before Steinway scored an overwhelming success at the 1867 Paris In-ternational Exhibition with its iron-framed, overstrung concert grand. This set the template for the modern instrument. The pianos available previously were mostly of a more modest size and volume, and of a quite bewildering variety of tone and touch. Again, we can use the cosmopolitan Mendelssohn and Liszt, with their extensive European travels, as case studies to discuss the diversity of instruments with which any touring performers would have been faced.

Mendelssohn's early and occasional piano teacher, Marie Bigot, probably prompted the initial purchase of an English Broadwood piano for the Men-delssohn family during a sojourn in Paris in 1816.[79] Bigot had been admired as a player by Haydn and had enjoyed a close friendship in Vienna with Beethoven.

---

[79] Christian Lambour, "Fanny Hensel: Die Pianistin," in *Mendelssohn Studien* 12 (Berlin: Duncker und Humblot, 2001), 235 n. 50.

She herself had initially owned an Érard but subsequently changed to a Broadwood. Mendelssohn's father therefore purchased one of the latter pianos (which he later had taken to Germany) rather than the expected French model. This was one of the main instruments that Mendelssohn would have practiced on as an adolescent. By the 1830s the Broadwood was still in the family home in Berlin, if, one might imagine, somewhat the worse for wear. Nevertheless, according to Mendelssohn's mother (admittedly not an unbiased witness), he could still make it produce a "heavenly" tone.[80] A drawing by William Hensel from 1821 shows the juvenile Felix seated at the other piano in the Mendelssohn household, a more slender Austrian instrument dating from around 1810.[81]

Partly owing to his traditional musical schooling by Carl Friedrich Zelter, Mendelssohn developed fluency in a variety of older keyboard styles and was well acquainted with a range of historical keyboard instruments and their capabilities. At home he had access to a Silbermann clavichord, an instrument that he later kept in the study of his Leipzig apartment. Although he was greatly feted as an organ player, particularly in England, the majority of his time at the keyboard was spent at the pianoforte, and both he and his sister Fanny were accordingly eager to try out the wide variety of instruments produced by renowned makers in England, France, Germany, and Austria. By the mid-1830s he had traveled widely enough to be familiar with examples of pianos from virtually every major European manufacturer. At Goethe's house in Weimar, for instance, he performed frequently on the poet's Viennese grand piano, made by Nannette Streicher. This instrument, which still exists, had a span of five octaves and featured four pedals ("harp" and "bassoon" in addition to the now usual two).[82] Few serious composers—and certainly not Mendelssohn—wrote explicit directions for the extra pedals, and many influential pedagogues such as Czerny regarded them with distaste. Nevertheless these and some even more extravagant examples could be found on pianos well into the 1830s.

Soon after Mendelssohn had begun to establish a European reputation as a pianist, conductor, and composer, the first gifts appeared at his doorstep. The English branch of Érard presented him with one of their instruments on 22 June

[80] Hensel, 360.

[81] Lambour, 234.

[82] Both these pedals uncannily adumbrate features of the twentieth-century "prepared" piano familiar from the works of John Cage and others. The bassoon pedal caused the bass strings to produce a remarkably unbassoonlike dull buzz by laying a piece of parchment (sometimes silk) over them. The harp pedal worked in a rather similar fashion, but there the idea was to create a plucked string effect.

1832. Moscheles, residing at the time in London, had already given a concert there on it before it was shipped to the Continent. Mendelssohn enthusiastically wrote to him in English on the piano's arrival, paraphrasing a Byron poem he would set to music the next year: "there be none of beauty's daughters with a magic like Érard."[83] Although Fanny Mendelssohn found at least one Érard piano she encountered a little too heavy, despite what she admitted was its magnificent tone, her brother seems to have been less troubled by this. Lest Fanny's opinion be regarded as merely a reflection of her own lack of strength, we should remember that by the 1840s even Liszt considered some Érards to have actions that were rather too heavy for comfort.[84] There can indeed be a remarkable difference of action weight in restored Érards from the same period and the same factory, although most are significantly lighter than modern pianos, and all have a noticeably shallower fall of key.

On many occasions Mendelssohn simply had to play on whatever piano was available, but he seems to have considered only Broadwood instruments to be serious rivals to the Érards, even if the family's first Broadwood—according to his sister—had the fault that "one hears in playing something besides the note, which sounds very unpleasant."[85] We know of Mendelssohn performing without complaint on an Érard in London (from the local factory), on a Broadwood he happened to come across on a steamer anchored off Liverpool in 1826 (not much choice in that particular venue), and on a Parisian Érard in 1832, an occasion where his performance received especially warm praise from the critics.[86] When, however, he was explicitly given the choice between a Broadwood and an Érard for the Birmingham premiere of his D-Minor Concerto in 1837, he decided in favor of the latter.[87] In fact, so thoroughly impressed was he by the instruments of this company that he had a new Érard grand delivered to his Leipzig home in 1839. A little while later he performed Beethoven's *Moonlight* Sonata, an improvisation on the same composer's "Adelaide," and his own Rondo op. 29 at Gewandhaus concerts on this piano. Nevertheless, in a final twist that prevents an easy summary of his preferences, the Broadwood company sent a new piano to Leipzig for Mendelssohn shortly before his death in 1847, an instrument he seems to have greatly admired.

[83] Lambour, 236.

[84] An opinion also shared by Moscheles, who was concerned about the weight of the Érard action as far back as 1828. See C. Moscheles, *Life of Moscheles*, 1:219.

[85] Lambour, 239.

[86] Todd, *Mendelssohn: A Life in Music*, 207, 254.

[87] Todd, *Mendelssohn: A Life in Music*, 357.

Liszt shared Mendelssohn's admiration for Érard pianos and was for many years both personally and professionally associated with the Érard piano company. He also had close contacts with Boisselot in Marseilles (who provided him with the pianos for his Iberian tour of 1844–45), and Streicher, Graf, and later Bösendorfer in Vienna. (For his famous Viennese appearances of the 1870s, he specifically requested pianos from Bösendorfer.) Ever the diplomat, Liszt often used pianos provided by local manufacturers during his concert tours across Europe and seems to have been remarkably adaptable in his needs. There can be little doubt, however, that his favored instrument from his early to middle years was indeed an Érard grand. The situation for his last decades is more complex. In the 1850s, during his residence in the Altenburg in Weimar, his Érard piano took center stage in the reception room, which also doubled as a music library. The Érard nestled together with the Broadwood grand that had once been Beethoven's—a visual symbol of Liszt's musical inheritance rather than an instrument for regular performance (to make the point clearer, Beethoven's death mask was also on display). Upstairs, in the "official" music room, a Boisselot piano was available, and two Viennese grands (a Streicher and a Bösendorfer) shared space with Mozart's spinet. By July 1854 the spinet, and indeed all other instruments, had been dwarfed by a gargantuan contraption called a piano-organ, made especially for Liszt by the organ and harmonium manufacturer Alexandre et Fils of Paris in collaboration with Érard. This was a relative of the pedal piano (of the type favored by Alkan) mutated as if by some unfortunate dose of radiation to enormous size and complexity. Its three keyboards and pedal board struck strings and also operated harmonium pipes in imitation of wind instruments. Liszt had intended the piano-organ as an aid in working out orchestration, but it also took an active role in his domestic musical performances. Richard Pohl heard him play on it the Funeral March from Beethoven's op. 26 Sonata, his transcription of Berlioz's "Danse des sylphes," and the "Ave Maria" from *Harmonies poétiques et religieuses*.[88] Those interested in musical curiosities can now see it in the Kunsthistorisches Museum in Vienna.

The piano-organ was the most grotesque outcome of Liszt's continuing interest in the development of keyboard instruments. In the late 1840s he had gone so far as to produce a version of his arrangement of "Salve Maria" from Verdi's *I Lombardi* for the Armonipiano. By peculiar coincidence, the arrangement was published by his friend Ricordi, who also owned the patent for the

---

[88] Kunsthistorisches Museum, Wien, *Katalog der Sammlung Alter Musikinstrumente*, Teil 1, Saitenklaviere (Wien, 1966), 89–92. See also Legany, 150–51.

Armonipiano. Liszt added a note: "A new invention which the house of Ricordi and Finzi have just adapted to their pianos will have a happy effect here. It is an invention by which one can obtain, without moving the fingers, a tremolo like Aeolian harps. . . . Such a poetic sonority is impossible to achieve on pianos unequipped with the tremolo pedal, and I recommend the restrained employment of it to pianists." Other musicians found the sonority less "poetic," and the Armonipiano was buried in the graveyard of forgotten novelties. Liszt apparently never owned one himself. Nevertheless, he had written publicly as far back as the 1830s of the need for an improvement in the tonal capabilities of the piano, which he then felt confident would soon be forthcoming. He was, of course, more aware than most of the constant development of the instrument. He could hardly fail to be, because many piano makers of the day insisted on sending him instruments as gifts in the hope of a valuable endorsement. More than a century later Steinway and Sons was still using a letter of Liszt from the 1880s praising its pianos in its promotional literature. The type of Steinway that Liszt admired toward the end of his life—such as that in Wagner's Bayreuth home Wahnfried, which Liszt played frequently—was not substantially different from the modern variety, although the warm and supple tone quality of surviving examples is particularly noteworthy.

During his Weimar years, if we leave aside the monstrous piano-organ mentioned earlier and Beethoven's Broadwood, Liszt's grand pianos represented a contrasted selection of the concert instruments of the day: the Érard with its double-escapement action and penetrating tone, and the two Viennese instruments with their simpler action and more intimate sound. Decades later, Leschetizky's house in Vienna would also have a selection of instruments, a Bösendorfer and Bechstein in the main music room and a Steinway and Blüthner upstairs.[89] Unlike Leschetizky's pianos, however, none of Liszt's Weimar instruments were overstrung, which meant they were capable of less volume but had greater purity of tone. The harshly metallic sound of some of today's pianos—especially in the upper registers—was not so evident, lending a delicate flavor to the high treble passagework. This more restrained sound quality (even on the Érard) had also to do with the design and composition of the hammers— much smaller than on a modern instrument—and of the piano frame itself. Of Liszt's pianos, only the Érard would have produced a sound anything like the thunderous bass notes today's grand is capable of. Though Liszt may have

---

[89] E. Newcomb, 21–22.

welcomed increased sonority in this register, he is hardly likely to have applauded the modern overbearing treble, for pupils reported that he played high filigree passagework *una corda* even on his own instruments. Moriz Rosenthal, his only pupil at Tivoli in the autumn of 1878, recalled "the marvellous delicacy and finish of his touch. The embellishments were like a cobweb—so fine—of costliest lace."[90]

Despite the major differences between Érard's double-escapement action and the Viennese action of the 1850s, both demanded a lighter touch and featured a shallower fall of key than the usual modern piano, making virtuoso playing far less arduous. This was a significant difference between most nineteenth-century instruments and those of today, whether we are talking about Liszt's Érards, Chopin's Pleyels, Robert Schumann's Graf, or Brahms's Streicher.[91] Brahms's *PaganiniVariations* are certainly a less daunting prospect when played on most contemporary Viennese instruments, despite Brahms's enthusiastic admiration for Steinways. Liszt, his technical wizardry notwithstanding, found the gradual increase in action weight as the piano became larger and more sonorous something of a problem and was complaining to Érard about it as early as the late 1840s.[92] Many subsequent pianists have had similar difficulties, which have prompted them to request adaptations to suit their own technique. When touring America, Paderewski demanded modifications to lighten the action of his Steinway and had the hammers of the Érards he used most often in Europe specially hardened to produce a more penetrating sound with less effort. Josef Hofmann, whose hands were able to stretch only an octave on a normal keyboard, had Steinway construct for him a novel instrument with keys of slightly narrower dimensions, on which he could manage a ninth. Horowitz's "signature" Steinway was voiced very peculiarly, to allow him to play *una corda* as the normal sonority (he took off the soft pedal when he wanted a particularly thunderous sound). These artists were, however, exceptional in having enough prestige and influence to insist on pianos fully customized to their demands. Most musicians, then and now, had to play on what was available and trust in the skill of the local technician to make whatever adjustments they might need.

[90] Williams, *Portrait of Liszt,* 561–62.

[91] For Brahms's pianos, see Camilla Cai, "Brahms's Pianos and the Performance of His Late Piano Works," in *Performance-Practice Review* 2, no. 1 (Spring 1989): 58–72, and, for a rather different view, Styra Avins, "Performing Brahms's Music: Clues from His Letters," in Musgrave and Sherman, 11–14.

[92] Williams, *Liszt: Selected Letters,* 256.

## The Thoroughly Modern Musician

We should not exaggerate too much the standardization of pianos even in the twentieth century, although we are usually confronted with a smaller variety of instruments and rarely have to cope with such differences as between a Graf and a Broadwood, or between Érard and Pleyel. Every piano requires its own adaptation, but it is easy to forget just what astonishing changes a Liszt or a Rubinstein would have personally witnessed in the power, durability, and reliability of his chosen instrument. This realization could hardly fail to prompt the outright rewriting of many pieces to take into account new, "modern" pianistic possibilities, especially because developments in piano building were mostly welcomed with enthusiasm by contemporaries. The advantages of the new instruments did encourage the forgetting of the best qualities of the older ones, even when it was quite arguable that there were losses as well as gains in modernization. We should also, alas, not underestimate the sheer ignorance some performers managed to maintain about the instruments of the past. According to A. J. Hipkins, tuner for Chopin during his visit to Britain and keyboard antiquarian extraordinaire, when he showed a clavichord to Bülow, Hallé, and Clara Schumann, none of them had ever come across one before.[93] This had, of course, not prevented them from playing (in Bülow's case even editing) a few pieces originally intended for the instrument. Slightly later players of the generation born around the 1870s, such as Bauer and Godowski, often seemed simply to have ignored the possibility that the phrasing and dynamic markings they so condemned in Beethoven and Chopin might have worked well on pianos of the composers' own eras. Busoni, to take just one other striking example, was grandly dismissive of early instruments and explicit in his intention to give at least one great master of the past—Bach—the full benefit of the modern keyboard. In doing so he effortlessly surpassed Bülow's Beethoven edition in freedom and even matched it in pontificating arrogance (no easy task).

In the preface to his edition (1894) of Book I of Bach's *Well-Tempered Clavier*, Busoni ringingly declared:

> Outsoaring his time by generations, [Bach's] thoughts and feelings reached proportions for whose expression the means then at command were inadequate. This alone can explain the fact, that the broader arrangement, the "modernizing" of certain of his works (by Liszt, Tausig, and others) does not violate the "Bach style"—indeed, rather seems to bring it into full perfection; it explains how

---

[93] Scholes, 2:778.

ventures like that undertaken by Raff, for instance, with the Chaconne [from the violin partita in D-Minor, arranged for full orchestra] are possible without degenerating into caricature. Bach's successors, Haydn and Mozart, are actually more remote from us, and belong wholly to their period. Rearrangements of any of their works in the sense of the Bach transcriptions just noticed, would be sad blunders. The clavier-compositions of Mozart and Haydn permit in no way of adaptation to our pianoforte style; to their *entire* conception the original setting is the only fit and appropriate one.... The attainments of modern pianoforte-making, and our command of their wide resources, at length render it possible for us to give full and perfect expression to Bach's undoubted intentions.

Poor Mozart and Haydn. But the spirit of Mozart at least had only to wait for a few years before Busoni's modernizing ethos embraced his music as well. Among several other works, the G-Major Gigue was extensively rewritten to become part of *An die Jugend*, the finale from the K.482 piano concerto ("a piece which I originally disparaged")[94] was produced in a "concert-edition," and the finale of the K. 459 piano concerto was updated into the *Duettino concertante* for two pianos in 1919.

But Bach was Busoni's chief concern, and his editions show a quite astonishing fertility of invention that is impressive and admirable on its own terms, even if it produces a result that has as much to do with Busoni as Bach. Pianistic variants are regularly suggested, as with the First Prelude in C Major:

EXAMPLE 6.2. J. S. Bach–Ferruccio Busoni, Prelude in C Major, *The Well-Tempered Clavier*, Book I, alternative version

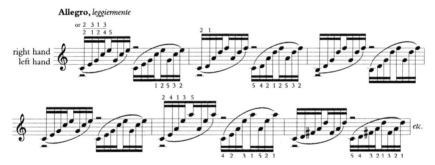

New contrapuntal combinations are cobbled together, as in the D-Major Prelude, and even Bach's delicate *Goldberg Variations* theme is turned into a suitable peroration for the end of the mighty work (replacing Bach's unaccountably anticlimactic repeat of the modest original setting):

[94] Beaumont, *Busoni: Selected Letters*, 296 (letter of 1919).

EXAMPLE 6.3. J. S. Bach–Ferruccio Busoni, *Goldberg Variations*, recapitulation of theme

In a procedure recalling Liszt's joining together movements from different Beethoven sonatas, or Clara Schumann's grouping of disparate pieces into a unit linked by (improvised) preludes, Busoni also suggests that series of Bach preludes could be arranged to form short suites, for example the B-Major (as the suite's prelude), the A-Minor (as a fughetta), the B-Minor (as an andante), and the B♭-Major (as a toccata finale). All numbers, he claims, would have to be transposed into the one key, probably B♭, "an aesthetic transgression over which—presumably—a very unaesthetic uproar would be raised."[95] Indeed.

Busoni was evidently well aware of the objections his free editing attracted in some quarters. In response to criticism of his alterations to the score in a 1902 performance of Franck's Prelude, Chorale and Fugue, he wrote to Marcel Remy:

> You start from false premises in thinking it is my *intention* to 'modernize" the works. On the contrary, by cleaning them of the dust of tradition, I try to restore their youth, to present them as they sounded to people at the moment when they first sprang from the head and pen of the composer. The *Pathétique* was an almost revolutionary sonata in its own day, and ought to sound revolutionary. One could never put enough passion into the *Appassionata*, which was the culmination of passionate expression of its epoch. When I play Beethoven, I try to approach the liberty, the nervous energy and the humanity which are the signature of his compositions, in contrast to those of his predecessors. Recalling the character of the man Beethoven and what is related of his own playing, I built up an ideal

---

[95] Busoni, *Well-Tempered Clavichord*, 1:143.

which has been wrongly called "modern" but is really no more than "live." I do
the same with Liszt; and oddly people approve in this case, though they condemn
me in the other.[96]

Busoni thought of himself as a translator who needed to change the literal
meaning of the words in order to make the general meaning of the work as a
whole clear to a new generation. His rejection of the term "modernization"
nevertheless seems rather disingenuous considering his open embrace of it in his
Bach edition. We are really just quibbling over semantics here.

Liszt had no such qualms over terminology. For his Schubert edition of 1868
he introduced "variants which I find rather *appropriate*. Several passages, and the
whole conclusion of the C-Major [*Wanderer*] Fantasy, I have rewritten in the
modern piano style, and flatter myself that Schubert would not be displeased
with it."[97] Busoni and several other virtuosi toward the end of the century duly
disseminated Liszt's version of the *Wanderer* Fantasy in their own concerts (we are
speaking here of the solo version, not the arrangement for piano and orchestra
that Liszt also made). If we also remember that Liszt was one of the very first to
play this piece in public (when he performed it in March 1846 in Schubert's
hometown of Vienna, at least one critic had never heard it in concert before),[98]
we can see how influential his manner of performing it must have been. In Liszt's
version, the first movement is little changed, but alterations accumulate during
the slow section, and the finale is almost totally rewritten. Liszt, however, had a
certain modesty, and in at least one respect was ahead of his time. He usually
tried to include a clean version of the original text along with his suggested
adaptations. As he himself put it: "My responsibility . . . I hold to be: fully and
carefully to retain the original text together with provisory suggestions of *my* way
of rendering it, by means of *distinguishing* letters, notes and signs."[99] His reproduction of the original text often did not meet modern standards of scholarship,
but he did at least allow the performer a choice between original and improved,
which by no means all editors of the time gave. The same was true for his Weber
edition. This of course included the *Konzertstück*, a work that Liszt had performed
in his young days with more than usual freedom (and frequent censure from
critics). Although the variants added seem to have been relatively restrained
compared to accounts of his earlier performances, they are still extensive. Liszt

---

[96] Dent, 110.
[97] Williams, *Liszt: Selected Letters*, 693 (to Prof. Dr. S. Lebert in Stuttgart), 2 December 1868.
[98] Legany, 88.
[99] La Mara, *Liszts Briefe*, trans. Bache, 2:160–61.

hoped not only to improve Weber's piano writing but also to stimulate imagination: "I flatter myself that I have thus given performers greater license, and have increased the effect without damaging or overloading Weber's style."[100] As with his Schubert, Liszt's Weber edition was not without influence. Yet again it was taken up by Busoni, whose performances of the *Konzertstück* (no doubt with his own variants included as well as Liszt's) were duly criticized in turn for his cavalier approach.[101]

In Practice . . .

What, then, might modernizing a score involve? Though there are here transparently as many answers as there were pianists, it is easy to detect general trends. Some players, after no doubt decades playing the same pieces again and again, revived their interest by emphasizing inner voices that possibly even the composer had hardly noticed were there, and indeed occasionally were not there at all. We hear such an approach especially emphatically on Hofmann's live Casimir Hall recording of the Chopin Fourth Ballade, and on the discs of the Chopin C♯-Minor Waltz by Rachmaninoff and Godowski. Godowski goes as far as to rewrite Chopin's figuration in order to complete an inner line that he found particularly piquant. It is clear that he could well have carried on from there to end up with a complete rearrangement, like his version of the Schubert F-Minor *Moment musical*, transposed to F♯ minor, to ease the playing of his new inner voices. Not everybody approved. Arrau remarked cuttingly: "You know, Hofmann and his pupil Shura Cherkassky, and others—at a certain moment they *discovered* inner voices. As if nobody had ever noticed them before. . . . I always got so angry when I heard Hofmann or Shura bringing out so-called inner voices that didn't have much importance. I thought, Why are they doing it? Just to amaze. Just to attract attention."[102] It is true that while the effect can impress and entertain, it can also sound forced, and nowhere more so than on the two Horowitz recordings of Schubert's late B♭ Sonata. Here peculiar inner parts are woven in and out of the texture in a manner that would likely have stunned Schubert. It sounds as if Horowitz would far rather have been playing Rachmaninoff.

Unsurprisingly, repeated passages were fair game for inner-voice hunters when they came around for the second or third time (the second variation in

[100] La Mara, *Liszts Briefe*, trans. Bache, 2:194 (letter to Lebert of 1870).
[101] Dent, 108.
[102] Horowitz, 40.

Brahms's *Handel Variations*, with its suave inner part, was an obvious target). Romantic pianists disliked literal repetition as much as nature abhors a vacuum. Recapitulations and similar sections were therefore likely to be rewritten in some way. Emil von Sauer, in his recording of Schubert's Impromptu op. 90 no. 3, used the Liszt edition (which follows the early published versions by being in G major, not Gb major). In it we can hear the complete rewriting of the return of the main theme (which in Schubert's original is exactly the same as its first appearance) in luxuriously spread chords with an extended, arpeggiated bass. Liszt was obviously unwilling to give the audience a chance to get bored (like Busoni with the repeat of the theme of the *Goldberg Variations*; see ex. 6.4).[103] This avoidance of unvaried repetition extended to dynamics: when Josef Hofmann repeated a sonata exposition, he often played it entirely differently. In general, when a composer instructed the literal repeat of a section, there was a good chance that some later pianist would give his flagging imagination a helping hand. If in doing so they could make use of the extended dynamic range of the late-nineteenth-century piano, all the better.

Rubinstein's widely copied fondness for varying the dynamics at the repeat of Chopin's Funeral March turned the whole movement into a processional that gradually approached in crescendo for the first section, stood at the graveside for the trio (sometimes played with copious asynchronization of hands), then marched away into the distance. The impression was fostered by beginning the repeat after the trio fortissimo, then introducing a gradual diminuendo—totally at variance, naturally, with Chopin's dynamic markings. For good measure, certain notes in the bass at the beginning of the repeat of the march were sometimes played an octave lower, for an appropriately doom-laden sonority. Rubinstein's approach here was, astonishingly, condemned by the elderly Liszt, for whom age had cast a veil over his own sins. In terms almost identical to Mendelssohn's criticisms of the virtuoso Liszt forty years before, he grumbled that "for the sake of an effect the player must never do the exact contrary of what the composer wrote."[104]

Rubinstein's cinematic interpretation was adopted by many performers, Busoni and Rosenthal among them,[105] and can be heard in outline on the

---

[103] Stradal commented: "Owing to frequent repeats, even the most beautiful things in Schubert often become boring. In the G-major[i.e., Gb-major] Impromptu he [Liszt] therefore added some variants to the accompaniment in the left hand" (75). Liszt's changes do, however, have a habit of extending to the right hand as well.

[104] Stradal, 89.

[105] Thus played by Busoni in Berlin in 1895. See Dent, 106.

recordings by Rachmaninoff and Raoul Pugno.[106] Although Paderewski does not adopt this approach on his recording, that is not to say he follows Chopin's score either. He too was anxious to avoid a literal repeat, and on the return of the march section plays what sounds remarkably like a chord cluster pianississimo in the deep bass, giving the impression of distant thunder. He then gradually increases the volume to thrilling (if not exactly Chopinesque) effect. We cannot tell what Arthur Friedheim did in the repeat of the march in his performances, for no room was found on his recording for it. But the most faithful to the text of the early players? Step forward the much-mocked Pachmann. His rendition of the trio is, on top of this, utterly exquisite.

Almost needless to say, a prime candidate for the Rubinsteinian gradual crescendo effect was the famous octave passage in Chopin's A♭ Polonaise, originally written in two repeated sections, with identical crescendi separated by a few chords, during which the octaves momentarily stop. Busoni regarded this as a wasted opportunity on Chopin's part, for he could so easily have had one enormous crescendo encompassing the entire section, as Liszt wrote for a very similar passage of his "Funérailles." Taking the procedure in "Funérailles" (which paradoxically had been originally inspired by the self-same Chopin polonaise) as a model, Busoni recomposed the whole section, continuing the octaves underneath the repeated chords in the central measure and producing a gargantuan crescendo encompassing the entire passage. This made full use of the sheer volume the late-nineteenth-century instrument was capable of:

EXAMPLE 6.4. Frédéric Chopin, Polonaise in A♭ Major, excerpt, arr. Busoni

[106] OPAL CD 9836.

At the climax Busoni sometimes also played the octaves an octave lower, depending on the sonority of the piano. Well handled, the impact of this is certainly overwhelming, but unfortunately the modest succeeding episode now becomes something of an anticlimax. Chopin, after all, had never intended it to follow such a stunt (which he would probably have hated, to judge by his abomination of all excess). When Liszt wrote the enormous crescendo in "Funérailles" he topped it quite appropriately with a fortissimo recapitulation of the main theme rather than a subsidiary lyrical section. The Busoni version of the Ab Polonaise is unquestionably thrilling, but the balance of the piece is skewed by one stunning effect.

In a less melodramatic way, Busoni also played the central section of Chopin's *Raindrop* Prelude on his piano roll recording as a gradual crescendo.[107] Schubert's F-Minor *Moment musicale* was performed by others as a gradual dynamic intensification followed by a diminuendo carried to the point of inaudibility (the justification for this was seemingly that the piece should sound—or could sound—like a gypsy caravan passing by), and Moiseiwitsch even recorded the "music box" variation of Brahms's *Variations on a Theme of Handel* in a similar fade-in/fade-out manner. What all these pieces or sections of pieces have in common is ostinati, whether of rhythm, melody, or harmony. With this in mind it is not difficult to pick out other works that might have been regarded as fair game.

Adapting pieces to the late-romantic piano, or to programmatic ideas, frequently involved that Lisztian technique par excellence, "blind" or alternating octaves. Almost any scalar passage, especially if chromatic, could be rewritten in double alternating octaves, and many were. The entire last two pages of the third movement of Chopin's First Concerto (originally in octave unison divided between the hands) were so played by Tausig and several others after him. (Shaw declared tastelessly, "I am now more than ever convinced that Tausig's early death was . . . the result of supernatural interposition for the extermination of a sacrilegious meddler.")[108] Such an adaptation also of the final scale of the Chopin B-Minor Scherzo was recommended by Liszt to his students (qualifying the idea that in later life he always treated Chopin with the utmost respect—after all, he was also delighted with Rosenthal's rewriting in thirds and sixths of the *Minute* Waltz).[109] Stojowski suggested filling out the trills in the middle section

[107] Nimbus CD NI 8810.

[108] Shaw, *Music in London*, 2:279.

[109] And often so played by Horowitz. Claudio Arrau cuttingly remarked about this modification, "It's ten times easier that way than to play the chromatic scale with the accents as they are written, and the power." Horowitz, 122.

of the *Military* Polonaise likewise with octaves.[110] Liszt's pupils were additionally directed to add octaves to the main theme at the opening of Schumann's D-Major *Novelette*, op. 21 no. 5, which necessitated the playing of a few of the relevant bars an octave higher in order to have space on the keyboard for the right-hand octaves.[111] Busoni, ever the extremist, in his edition of Book I of Bach's *Well-Tempered Clavier*, even suggests playing as a study both parts of the entire E-Minor Fugue in octaves throughout and doubling the bass of the B-Minor Prelude.[112] This type of addition is also a standard feature of Henselt's versions of many pieces (published as "interpretations"), which were very popular with virtuosi toward the end of the century. Among them were Weber's *Invitation to the Dance* (played in the Henselt version by Pachmann), all four sonatas, and the so-called fragment of the opening movement of Chopin's First Concerto, arranged and cut for piano solo. As well as other reinforcements, bass notes were regularly taken down an octave or doubled, chords were filled out, and the range of figuration was extended. Fascinatingly in the Chopin fragment, Henselt rewrote part of the second subject by specifically adding the sort of asynchronised rubato (discussed in chapter 5) that was so often played by the Romantics, but so rarely notated. More contentiously, he also bolstered Chopin's chances of passing a harmony exam by "correcting" a certain sequence in the bass that threatens to create parallel octaves with the treble. (Liszt too had noticed the offending progression, but simply remarked that because it was Chopin, it still sounded good.)

The increasing use of the lower bass was a natural consequence not of the extension of the piano's range (most of the notes had been available since the late 1830s), but of a new evenness between the registers. As the treble and mid-ranges were strengthened, the deep bass was not so in danger of overbalancing the entire texture in the way it can easily do in an Érard of the 1840s or 1850s. In the first of Liszt's *Transcendental Studies* (the Preludio discussed extensively in chapter 4), the lowest C on the piano is used for the opening flourishes but thereafter conspicuously avoided, even in the grand final cadence. I remained

---

[110] Jeffrey Johnson, *Piano Lessons*, 40.

[111] Zimdars, *Masterclasses of Liszt*, 116.

[112] Playing Bach's two-part inventions and two-voiced fugues in octaves throughout seems to have been a common method of octave study. Bülow's early teacher Louis Plaidy (1810–74), hired by Mendelssohn to teach at the Leipzig Conservatory, also recommended such an approach to his pupils (see Haas, 12). It is likely that such things were more frequent in the practice studio than on the concert platform, though Alexander Dreyschock did indeed publicly perform his stunt of Chopin's *Revolutionary* Study with the left-hand part largely in octaves.

curious about the reason for this—for it is certainly not necessary on most modern Steinways—until I had the opportunity of performing these studies on a contemporary Érard. All became clear. The upper registers of the instrument were simply too weak to cope with a fortissimo low C ringing out in the bass.

Rubinstein was especially addicted to bulking out the bass once it became feasible, and Busoni carried on the practice. In performing the Chopin Etudes op. 25, Busoni extended the final scale of no. 11 in A minor and strengthened the melody with octaves and chords in no. 12 in C minor.[113] Von Sauer also added some doubling in his recording of this last work.[114] In d'Albert's recording of the Chopin Berceuse, one cannot help noticing a deep D♭ reinforcing the bass right at the beginning of the piece.[115] Additions to the bass were married to extensions of figuration in the treble, partly in imitation of bel canto improvised ornaments in singing. Liszt seemed especially fond of such amplifications, advising von Lenz to make a lavish extension to one of the runs in Chopin's B♭ Mazurka. When von Lenz played it this way to Chopin, the latter remarked wryly: "*He* showed you that. *He* must have a hand in everything."[116] It was a comment that could also have been made about Rubinstein, Busoni, and a host of other performers. It is, in fact, just this personal input (applauded by some, abominated by others) that characterized many of the most celebrated pianists of the time and marked their playing out from the practices of our more cautious, work-centered era.

[113] Couling, 185.

[114] Arbiter CD 114.

[115] Arbiter CD 147.

[116] Von Lenz, 42. We should not forget that Chopin too was in the habit of improvising extensions and variants to the ornaments in his own compositions.

# 7

# Lisztiana

Auch Liszt taucht wieder auf, der Franz.
[Even Liszt turns up once again, our Franz.]
—Heinrich Heine, "Im Oktober," 1849

## Myth and Reality

As a wellspring of romantic pianism and the fount of the legendary great tradition, Liszt is of fundamental importance to any discussion of nineteenth-century performance style. To his contemporaries, he represented the archetype of the piano virtuoso, as Paganini did that of the violin—an unavoidable point of reference in assessments of other pianists. Yet discussions of Liszt as a player often seem like *Hamlet* without the prince. We can read myriad reviews and accounts of his performances, absorb reminiscences of his teaching, hear recordings of his pupils, and study scores of his own music, but Liszt died before the art of recording was properly established: the actual sound of his own playing is, frustratingly, as lost as that of Mozart or Beethoven. It also matters more how Liszt played than some of the other great virtuosi mentioned in this book—even those as influential as Anton Rubinstein or Ignacy Paderewski—for Liszt's piano music has retained a not exactly unchallenged but still comfortable place in the standard repertoire.[1] Moreover, as Lina Ramann, Liszt's first major biographer, already suggested during his final years, "With no other of our masters does the effect of the composition depend so much on the performance.... So few

---

[1] The "struggle for acceptance" of Liszt's music can easily be exaggerated. While it is transparently true that the orchestral and choral music has never entirely established itself in the repertoire (the success of *Les préludes* and a few other pieces notwithstanding), large swaths of Liszt's output for piano have been standard concert fare for over a century. A glance at the programs in Kehler's *The Piano in Concert* is enough to verify this. It does not mean, of course, that the quality of this music has gone unchallenged by critics; it simply means that the music has been regularly played. Liszt's piano music never needed "rediscovery" like Alkan's.

players can really get to the heart of his style."[2] This can really be no surprise—Liszt himself was a supreme performer, and his scores demand the same sort of creative panache that he brought to his own playing. The *Transcendental Studies*, for example, which can be so dull in some renditions, were utterly thrilling when performed by Sviatoslav Richter. On another level, things are somewhat more problematic. Extreme performer dependency has often been produced as "exhibit A" to make a case against the value of Liszt's music "in itself."[3] But if performance style is such an unusually essential part of Liszt's message, then we would be well advised to take more pains than usual to uncover his intentions in this regard, should we wish to play the music at all.

This is not the place to discuss Liszt the composer's exact rank in the pantheon of genius, but the truly vast amount of contemporary material on Liszt as a player allows us to make some attempt at reconstruction of his performance approach, even if the sheer charisma of his character was buried with him. With Liszt, perhaps even more than with Paderewski, we do seem to have to talk about charisma—even, as many said, "magic"—to explain his effect on listeners. His student Arthur Friedheim believed that Liszt as a man had quite literally a hypnotic ability that transcended music—the audience was captivated by the force of his presence and personality.[4] For this reason, Friedheim suggested, Liszt would have had the same unparalleled success in whatever century he had been born. This quasi-mystical evaluation was echoed by Friedheim's fellow student Alexander Siloti, who wrote with awe, "A pianist myself, I am still completely unable to give an idea of how he played."[5] No doubt Liszt's overwhelming fame and authority toward the end of his life—when both Friedheim and Siloti studied with him—had reinforced the impact of his live playing. Nevertheless, such comments cannot be totally dismissed as the naiveté of awestruck youth, especially because they came from students who themselves were outstanding performers. We might think it possible that they exaggerated, but few would deny that such a personal quality as charisma exists, however difficult it is to explain or explain away.

Busoni believed more mundanely that the master had made his initial effect in the 1830s and 1840s largely through his superiority to the players who had

---

[2] Ramann, *Lisztiana*, 250. Ramann's comments were prompted by hearing Siloti perform the Third *Petrarch Sonnet* and the First *Mephisto* Waltz in 1884.

[3] Although anyone ever involved in auditioning pianists will confirm that it is possible to make any composer's music sound boring if one tries hard enough.

[4] Arthur Friedheim, "Life and Liszt," in Bullock, 159.

[5] Alexander Siloti, "Memories of Liszt," in Bullock, 355. Carl Lachmund and others also remarked upon the hypnotic quality of the aged Liszt's presence.

preceded him. This had also been suggested by those who directly experienced Liszt's youthful triumphs. Moscheles and Fétis remarked on how distant his style was from those currently familiar to audiences in 1840: "His talent differs from the school of Hummel in a scarcely believable manner. Tenderness in playing is not his main aim; his goal is rather to increase the tonal capabilities of the pianoforte and to bring it as near as possible to the power of the orchestra."[6] They additionally noted his frequent use of the pedals and his eschewing of any fixed sitting position before the keyboard, for he noticeably moved to the right or the left as the range of the music demanded, adding to the restless visual impression of his performances. A greater contrast to the restrained dynamics and statuesque demeanor of the elderly Liszt could hardly be imagined. We must therefore not forget that there was more than one "Liszt the pianist," just as Liszt the composer adopted a protean number of styles, from almost hysterical romantic effusiveness to restrained religious devotion.

Busoni's own Liszt performances had such a convincing mastery and aplomb that it was widely believed he himself had been a Liszt pupil. This was not so, although he did play through some of his Liszt repertoire to Arthur Friedheim, who passed on some hints from the master at second hand. What Friedheim was passing on, of course, was Liszt's teaching and performance practice from the last years of his life, when his interpretative attitudes had hardened. Previous chapters of this book have chronicled considerable contemporary discontent with the restless bodily movements, interpretative willfulness, and even piano smashing of the Liszt of the "glory days." It was, however, with such playing that he mostly made his stellar reputation, not with that of his ascetic old age. The strict elder statesman was as capable as any of us of remolding the past according to the image of the present. He even declared querulously (and a tad hypocritically) in 1885, "Today they don't play the piano, they hit the piano. Then it's said—that's Liszt, that's his school . . . but I have always loved my piano."[7] Too violent and too noisy—it could well have been a review of his own concerts from the 1830s or 1840s. But Liszt was charting a typical course from the effusiveness of youth to the more contemplative virtues of old age. Even for those who age gracefully, aural awareness changes with advancing years—excessive volume often becomes increasingly distasteful and occasionally painful. Not entirely without medical justification does one modern T-shirt sport the grossly insulting motto "If it's too loud, you're too old!"

---

[6] Moscheles and Fétis, 19.
[7] Ramann, *Lisztiana*, 292. Similar remarks can be found in Stradal, 160.

The diminishing dash of the aged Liszt's playing was counterbalanced by a more vivid stylistic awareness and a greater respect for some aspects of the letter of the score (scores by a handful of favored composers, at least). In 1875 Lina Ramann heard him play a selection of music from the eighteenth century onward, and admired the way he adjusted his touch to imitate the tone of the harpsichord in Bach, broadened the sonority a little for Haydn, then completely let rip for Beethoven in a much more generous style.[8] Similarly, an observer at one of Liszt's Rome master classes in 1877 described his careful treatment of the music he most admired:

> It was interesting to note the varied degrees of tension that he brought to the different composers. When Chopin was being played, only the most delicate precision would satisfy him. The *rubatos* had to be done with exquisite restraint, and only when Chopin had marked them, never *ad libitum*. Nothing was quite good enough to interpret such perfection. A student played one of Liszt's own Rhapsodies; it had been practiced conscientiously, but did not satisfy the master. There were splashy arpeggios and rockets of rapidly ascending chromatic diminished sevenths. "Why don't you play it this way?" asked Liszt, sitting at the second piano and playing the passage with more careless bravura. "It was not written so in my copy," objected the youth. "Oh, you need not take that so literally[,]" answered the composer.[9]

We should not overemphasize this newfound fidelity; it bore little resemblance to a vision on the road to Damascus. Liszt continued to interpret virtuoso music—by himself and others—with great liberty, and he remained quite capable of making minor additions to Beethoven or restructuring pieces by Chopin by means of newly interpolated repetitions. Appallingly to those who regard the composer as the final interpretative arbiter, he steadfastly argued that the declamatory style of his own bravura transcription of Schumann's *Widmung* was preferable to the original, believing the piece lost effect if the final lines were intoned intimately, whatever Clara and Robert Schumann might think. (Clara never forgave him for this, he told his pupils with more amusement than regret.)[10] But he did at least occasionally attempt interpretative fidelity toward the end of his life in a way that seems rarely, in practice if not in prose, to have preoccupied him earlier. By studying surviving written sources, and recordings by his pupils,

---

[8] Ramann, *Lisztiana*, 55. Liszt, of course, regarded Beethoven as a romantic suited to an almost contemporary playing style.

[9] Mrs. W. Chanler, *Roman Spring* (Boston, 1934), quoted from Williams, *Portrait of Liszt*, 552.

[10] Ramann, *Lisztiana*, 215.

we can get what is probably a fairly accurate general picture of Liszt's performance practice and its development. It also allows us to get some way toward discovering how Liszt expected his own music to sound, and what interpretative approach present-day pianists should adopt if they wish to respect this.

To talk about "fidelity to the score" in the case of Liszt's oeuvre is especially problematical, because many pieces exist in a multiplicity of versions with differences ranging from minor nuances to major reworkings. Liszt may have had some sort of ideal form distantly before his eye, but he often never quite attained it, even by his own admission. He himself put it succinctly in 1863: "The fact is that the passion for variants, and for what seems to me to be ameliorations of style, has got a particular grip on me and gets stronger with age."[11] Variable attitudes to textual fidelity and stylistic improvement also affected his performances of other composers' music. Some of these approaches were propagated far beyond the grave by such means as Hans von Bülow's edition of Beethoven's piano sonatas—"the fruits of Liszt's teaching"—or Liszt's own concert reworkings of pieces such as Schubert's *Wanderer* Fantasy.[12]

But with Liszt we have to deal not just with a commanding legacy—we also have the myth. In the accounts of some biographers/hagiographers, Liszt emerges as pianistic god, infallible as a sight reader, completely unaffected by too little sleep or too much cognac, simply incapable of a poor performance. We are asked to believe in more than Liszt's superb talent or even genius. Supposedly even as an old man he possessed a never-to-be-matched digital proficiency at the keyboard (something that he himself did not assert—"Virtuosity," he said to Hanslick, "requires youth").[13] In the last few decades of his life he supposedly maintained a superhuman technique without having to practice, thanks to some sort of Platonic communion with the essence of pianism itself—"Technique creates itself from the mind [*Geist*], not from mechanics," as he was often quoted as saying (interestingly, Moscheles, Thalberg, and Chopin said much the same thing—it was obviously what you told students in those days).[14] Nevertheless, Liszt himself was more realistic than his eulogizers. He was well aware that what happened to his playing when he did not get the chance to practice was the same as what happens to everyone's. This was as true for the young Liszt as for the old. Toward the end of his life, he reminisced about the 1840s: "In those days I did not practice very much. I was always on the go. In fact I did most of my practising

---

[11] La Mara, *Franz Liszts Briefe*, 8:161.

[12] In versions both for piano solo (performed widely by Busoni) and for piano and orchestra.

[13] Pleasants, *Hanslick's Music Criticisms*, 107.

[14] C. Moscheles, *Life of Moscheles*, 1:53. For Thalberg and Chopin, see chapter 5.

at my concerts, and necessarily the first few times I played a new piece it was somewhat of a failure."[15] One only has to glance at the itinerary of Liszt's tours of that era—undertaken before the full development of the railway system—to realize that practice time must often have been impossible to find.

The fantasy view of Liszt's performances has been buttressed by the usual technique of selective quotation—a favoring of the positive comments over the negative, and an assumption that if something remarkable was done at all, it must have been done well. Emil von Sauer's admiration of Liszt's playing of Beetho-ven's *Kreutzer* Sonata in the 1880s is sometimes mentioned, but we less often hear about his disappointment when he heard the old man play solo. Sauer—a student at the same time as Friedheim and Siloti—described Liszt's performance of the Chopin B♭-Minor Nocturne, a *Consolation* of his own composition, and the Weber *Perpetuum mobile* (the finale of the C-Major Sonata) as "zu dürftig" ("too sketchy" or "insufficient" is a possible translation). He was far more impressed by the way Liszt looked while playing—"the silent performance of face and eyes"— than the way he sounded. It was "not a pianistic, but certainly a theatrical [*schauspielerisch*] achievement of the first rank."[16]

That Liszt's playing had its ups and downs even when he was in his prime will be of no surprise to musicians, though the idea seems to be resisted by some biographers. Alan Walker, for instance, claims that at a Leipzig Gewandhaus concert in 1840 "the musical highlight ... was Liszt publicly sight-reading Mendelssohn's piano concerto in D minor," and that this and his relatively unprepared performance of some pieces by Schumann and Hiller that same evening were "a musical tour-de-force which those in the know were quick to admire." It was in fact not sight reading at all, though hardly a practiced per-formance. Liszt had been given the score of the concerto a few days before and had no doubt read it on the train journeys between Leipzig and Dresden. A friend in Dresden had even heard him play it through. It was quite an achievement that he managed to play the piece in public at such short notice, but he did not cover himself with glory. The consensus of several musicians present—Robert and Clara Schumann among them—was that his playing, far from being a "highlight," unavoidably reflected his sketchy knowledge of the work. One reviewer com-mented, "Herr Liszt did not play the concerto very well, in fact not even satis-factorily even in a technical regard,"[17] and Clara Schumann later wrote: "He felt

---

[15] Walker, *Living with Liszt*, 43.

[16] Von Sauer, 175.

[17] *Allgemeine musikalische Zeitung* 42 (1840). Quoted in Little, 118. For Walker's comments, see Walker, *Franz Liszt: The Virtuoso Years*, 347, 351.

most at his ease in the *Hexameron* [the last piece in the program], one could hear and see that. He did not play the things by Mendelssohn and Hiller so freely, and it was distracting to see him looking at the notes all the time."[18] Robert Schumann summarized the situation succinctly: "No man is a God."[19] Bringing Liszt down to earth is not to belittle him, but rather to try and evaluate his obviously exceptional talents in a way that allows us to fit him practically and credibly, rather than mythically, into a history of performance. Yes, Liszt too had to practice—it should come as no surprise.

If Thalberg established new ways of handling a singing melody on the piano, Liszt brought octave and chordal technique center stage, making it a touchstone of romantic virtuosity. The keyboard writing of Tchaikovsky and Rachmaninoff, as well as a host of lesser luminaries, would have been unthinkable without his example. Even the famous majestic parade of chords in D♭ up and down the piano that opens Tchaikovsky's First Piano Concerto is obviously derived from a similar D♭-major passage in Liszt's Second Concerto. Liszt himself claimed not just the popularization, but the invention of blind octaves[20]—the fantasy on Halévy's *La Juive* of 1835 contains their earliest appearance in his music:

EXAMPLE 7.1. Franz Liszt, *Réminiscences de La Juive*, excerpt

[18] Berthold Litzmann, *Clara Schumann: An Artist's Life*, trans. and abridged Grace Hadow (London: Macmillan, 1913), 1:290.

[19] Robert Schumann, *Music and Musicians*, trans. Fanny Raymond Ritter, 2 vols. (London: W. Reeves, 1877), 153.

[20] Liszt said to Amy Fay, "'Oh, I've invented a great many things . . . this, for instance': and he began playing a double roll of octaves in chromatics in the bass of the piano." Fay, 220.

EXAMPLE 7.1. (*continued*)

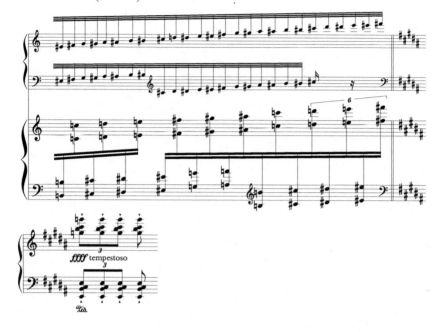

Within a decade these had turned up with such frequency in other virtuoso works that Czerny, in the supplement to op. 500 (1846), advised every performer with pretensions to mastering the "modern" style to practice them rigorously (strangely, he mentions them in a section devoted to Thalberg). According to Moscheles and Fétis, Liszt played "chromatic octave scales with a speed that bordered on the miraculous."[21]

Liszt did not invent all of the tricks of digital dexterity sometimes credited to him. The idea of routinely dividing passagework between the hands for increased velocity—as seen, for example, with the decorative scales in the first variation in *Réminiscences de Don Juan*—was inspired by Ernst Haberbier (1813–1869),[22] while the technique of chromatic glissando was an innovation of Carl Tausig in his piano ballade *Das Geisterschiff*.[23] According to the composer Wendelin Weiss-

[21] Moscheles and Fétis, 93.

[22] See Lachmund's account in Walker, *Living with Liszt*, 131.

[23] A chromatic glissando is achieved simply enough by playing a standard glissando on the white notes with one hand, and simultaneously on the black with the other. (Sometimes for ease of rendition, the black notes are fingered in a swift 1–2–3–4–5 pattern rather than glissandoed.) One of the few examples of this in the (almost) standard repertoire can be found in Godowsky's *Die*

heimer, an associate of the Liszt circle in Weimar, Liszt first came across the chromatic glissando when he heard Tausig perform the *Geisterschiff* (Weissheimer called it the *Gespensterschiff*):

> A piece containing an incredible passage which put even Liszt in difficulties. It was an ascending chromatic glissando ending shrilly on a top black note! After a few vain attempts, Liszt eventually said to Tausig: "Junge, wie machst du das?" [My lad, how do you do that?] Tausig sat down, performed a glissando on the white keys with the middle finger of his right hand, while simultaneously making the fingers of his left fly so skilfully over the black keys that a chromatic scale could clearly be heard streaking like lightening up the entire length of the keyboard, ending on high with a shrill "bip." Then Liszt had a go again, and after some half a dozen practice runs he too finally achieved the desired high "bip" without accident.[24]

These and other erroneous attributions helped to add to the Liszt myth. But it was not really necessary—his reputation would have been high enough without them.

## Once More the Letter of the Score

Our view of Liszt's performance aesthetics will differ radically depending on whether we look at what he wrote and taught, or at what he actually did. In 1837, under some pressure from the success of Thalberg, he had turned his thoughts publicly to the role of the performing musician in re-creating works of art. His philosophical ruminations, he hoped, would mark him out as a serious artist, in contrast to his less articulate rivals:

---

*Fledermaus* paraphrase. It also features at the close of what was possibly the original piano version (not the slightly later edition usually played) of Grainger's *Colonial Song* (published by Schott). Alan Walker attributes this innovation to Liszt (*Franz Liszt*, 1:298), although he notably fails to give an example from Liszt's works, possibly because there isn't one. Comically, in the film *Impromptu* (1991)—the German title of which, *Verliebt in Chopin*, gives a more distinct idea of its subject—Liszt is shown demonstrating how to perform a chromatic glissando to a bewildered Chopin. This scene is as historically incorrect as the quasi-Hungarian accent that Liszt (played by Julian Sands) is here endowed with, but one does wonder how the film's writers heard about chromatic glissandos in the first place.

[24] Quoted from Williams, *Portrait of Liszt*, 357–58.

The poet, painter or sculptor left to himself in his study or studio, completes the task he has set himself; and once his work is done, he has bookshops to distribute it or museums to exhibit it. There is no intermediary between himself and his judges, whereas the composer is necessarily forced to have recourse to inept or indifferent interpreters who make him suffer through interpretations that are often literal, it is true, but which are quite imperfect when it comes to presenting the work's ideas or the composer's genius. If on the other hand the musician is himself a performer, how many times, compared to these rare occasions when he is understood, must he prostitute himself to an unresponsive audience.[25]

In other words, written music is only the transcription of an idea that requires an inspired performer for realization. The inevitably inexact and lifeless notation can never delineate every aspect of music adequately—indeed might even mislead—leaving its fate substantially at the mercy of the performer's talent or understanding. A "literal" rendition is here implicitly contrasted with a "spiritual" one that communicates the artistic core of the work. Can an interpretation be both literal and spiritual at the same time? The question is left open, but we are left in no doubt that if a choice must be made, then the decision is obvious. As Paderewski later said, "It is not a question of what is written, but of musical effect."[26] Liszt even went so far in his fantasy on Paganini's *La clochette* to print a radically simplified (and much more effective) *ossia* to the principal text, subscribed "as played by the composer." Here we have the composer/performer dichotomy embodied in the one individual.

During his principal years as a performer Liszt took more than his fair share of license. He later said that it was chiefly his performances of Weber's *Konzertstück* that gave him a reputation as a pianist who indulged in extreme interpretative liberties, but by 1837 he had already admitted in print the problem was more extensive than this. Like a penitent sinner he confessed:

> During that time [1829–37], both at public concerts and in private salons (where people never failed to observe that I had selected my pieces very badly), I often performed the works of Beethoven, Weber and Hummel, and let me confess to my shame that in order to wring bravos from the public that is always slow, in its awesome simplicity, to comprehend beautiful things, I had no qualms about changing the tempos of the pieces or the composers' intentions. In my arrogance

[25] Franz Liszt, *An Artist's Journey: Lettres d'un bachelier ès musique*, trans. and annotated Charles Suttoni (Chicago: University of Chicago Press, 1989), 31.

[26] Bauer, 272.

I even went so far as to add a host of rapid runs and cadenzas, which, by securing ignorant applause for me, sent me off in the wrong direction—one that I fortunately knew enough to abandon quickly. You cannot believe, dear friend, how much I deplore those concessions to bad taste, those sacrilegious violations of the SPIRIT and the LETTER, because the most profound respect for the masterpieces of great composers has, for me, replaced the need that a young man barely out of childhood once felt for novelty and individuality. Now I no longer divorce a composition from the era in which it was written, and any claim to embellish or modernize the works of earlier periods seems just as absurd for a musician to make as it would be for an architect, for example, to place a Corinthian capital on the columns of an Egyptian temple.[27]

Written around the time of his groundbreaking performance of Beethoven's *Hammerklavier* Sonata, which according to Berlioz was a model of textual fidelity, Liszt's contrition must have, temporarily at least, seemed sincere. In this passage there can be no doubt that he believed the spirit of the score was compatible with the letter—indeed, both appeared interlinked, and any violations of them by the author were attributed to naiveté. Liszt's penitence was, however, distinctly temporary. Numerous reviews of his concert tours of the 1840s indicate that he cultivated an attitude akin to St. Augustine's famous exhortation, "Oh Lord, grant me chastity—but not yet!" Charles Hallé, whose testimony as a fine performer himself is certainly more immediately trustworthy than that of many reviewers, was surprised by some of Liszt's capricious interpretative decisions. He mentioned in particular a sudden, drastic slowing down during a performance of his transcription of the Scherzo of Beethoven's Sixth Symphony (the "Peasants' Dance"). Halle later asked Liszt why he had performed the relevant passage in this jarring manner. "That," said the latter, "is the old men." As Carl Reinecke commented, when Liszt got it into his head to "dazzle the ignorant throng" there was no telling what one would hear.[28] The necessity of pleasing the crowds and earning a living indubitably accounted for much of Liszt's libertarian approach, though it must be remembered once more that the interpretative customs of the era permitted a large degree of freedom anyway. For Liszt's interpretative license to be specially remarked upon, it must have been pretty extreme.

The older Liszt was more sober. Though he habitually played virtuoso works and character pieces with a large degree of freedom, the major masterpieces of

[27] Suttoni, 17–18.
[28] Williams, *Portrait of Liszt*, 145. See also chapter 6, pp. 201–2.

great composers were interpreted with a fidelity that contrasted notably with the playing of his earlier years. A student at an 1882 master class drove Liszt into a rage by playing the closing few chords of Chopin's Ballade no. 3 in A♭ staccato on the grounds that it made "the ending more brilliant." Pacing the floor angrily, Liszt replied, "Chopin knew how he wanted that piece to end, and I do not propose to argue with anyone about such matters!"[29] As far as his own music was concerned, Liszt encouraged the more talented pupils to put their own ideas into his virtuoso pieces like the operatic fantasies or Hungarian rhapsodies. Sophie Menter was told in 1880, "Alter, cut and improve the 'Huguenots' Fantasy at your discretion. Such pieces are only to be performed by extraordinary virtuosi— *thus* Sophie Menter."[30] Alexander Siloti was given similar license, which resulted in his versions of, among other pieces, the *Totentanz* and the study *Unsospiro*. These may be somewhat closer to the composer's own performances in his later years than the original editions are. At any rate, Liszt's own permissive attitude exposes the contradictions of the cultivation of an urtext mentality for his virtuoso music. Those who can master it have earned the right to make any changes they wish.

Liszt habitually gave his pupils advice on oft-played works such as "St. Francis Walking on the Waves" that mildly contradicted any score printed during his lifetime. He also improvised new endings, which were then adopted by favored students. Alternate versions heard in the recordings or editions of Liszt pupils are therefore worth taking more seriously than some modern editorial practice allows, with its preference for written rather than aural evidence and its dismissal of anything not directly published by the composer. The alternate—and much more convincing—conclusion of the second *Légende* used by Arthur Friedheim on his piano-roll recording appeared in the notes of the relevant Liszt-Stiftung volume of piano music,[31] edited by another Liszt student, José Vianna da Motta. It conspicuously fails to make an appearance in the New Liszt Edition. Yet visitors to the house in Bayreuth where Liszt died will notice on display an original edition of this very piece. The conclusion has been scored out, replaced by the ending played by Friedheim. The handwriting is seemingly that of Liszt himself.

Several other thought-provoking variant readings have been passed down by Liszt pupils. They have likewise largely been ignored by modern performers and editors. An extract from Siloti's edition of the *Sospiro* study is a good example of the sort of changes involved:

---

[29] Walker, *Living with Liszt*, 134–35.

[30] Short, 220.

[31] Now reprinted by Dover.

EXAMPLE 7.2. Franz Liszt, *Un sospiro*, excerpt, ed. Alexander Siloti

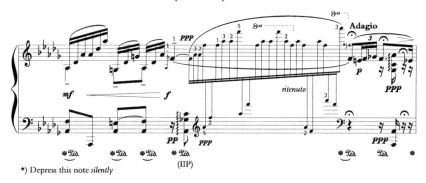

\*) Depress this note *silently*

EXAMPLE 7.3. Franz Liszt, *Un sospiro*, excerpt, original version

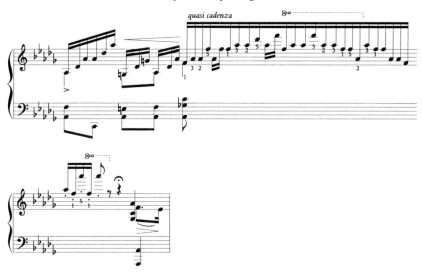

Siloti's alterations agree to a significant extent with those recommended in the 1902 *Liszt-Pädagogium*,[32] a collection of notes assembled by Lina Ramann containing Liszt's comments on his own works, itself based on contemporary notes taken by pianists present at master classes. Unfortunately, the *Liszt-Pädagogium* appears to have slumbered undisturbed by most modern performers and its

---

[32] Reprinted for the centenary of Liszt's death with a new foreword by Alfred Brendel (Wiesbaden: Breitkopf und Härtel, 1986).

advice treated as irrelevant for many urtext publications,[33] although brief excerpts have appeared in the New Liszt Edition. The whole volume was reprinted in 1986, so it is scarcely difficult to obtain. It covers works of varying degrees of importance in varying degrees of depth, but the relationship of these two aspects is not what we might think it ought to be, and the criterion for a work's inclusion is random indeed: namely, that at some point a pupil brought a certain piece to a master class, and Ramann either chanced to be present or happened later to have access to students' notes. (Of these students, her most important sources were Stradal, Berthold Kellermann, Göllerich, Heinrich Porges, Ida Volckmann, and Auguste Rennebaum.) Although some works now in the standard repertoire, like the Sonata, "Funérailles," the *Sospiro* study, and the *Bénédiction de Dieu dans la solitude* are treated in some detail, a far greater number of important pieces are conspicuous by their absence, and we might be forgiven for wishing that we had Liszt's recommendations for the performance of, for example, the *Dante* Sonata or the first *Mephisto* Waltz rather than an extended disquisition on the nuances required for *Slavimo, Slava Slaveni!* and some other not-too-interesting chips from the floor of the master's studio.[34] As well as performance notes, the *Pädagogium* also contains additions and revisions to certain pieces, for example, a slightly extended ending to *Ricordanza* and major alterations to *Réminiscences de Robert le diable*, intended to form the basis of a new edition of the piece (a plan thwarted by Liszt's death).

The *Pädagogium* itself must, of course, be used with common sense, for it is sometimes unclear what the exact status was of the sources that Ramann relied upon. We do not know for certain whether her notes, or those of the contributing students, were written up during the master classes or soon afterward, or are simply "reminiscences of a master class" recalled—accurately or not—at a later date. Fortunately, we do not have to rely on the *Pädagogium* alone for information on Liszt's teaching, but can also turn to other writings, such as the diaries and memoirs mentioned earlier. Several of Liszt's students, too, were later involved in editing extensive collections of his works (most prominently von Sauer, Vianna da Motta, d'Albert, Rosenthal, and Joseffy). From an earlier period we even have a remarkable edition by Liszt's fellow virtuoso Adolf Henselt of *Réminiscences de*

---

[33] For example the new Henle urtext of the *Transcendental Studies*, edited by Ernst-Günter Heinemann. In the preface (by Maria Eckhardt), the extended ending to "Ricordanza" found in the *Pädagogium* is referred to but—frustratingly—nowhere printed in the score itself. The effect is akin to saying to the performer, "I know what Liszt's last thoughts on this piece were—but I'm not going to tell *you*."

[34] Stradal does give some detailed comments concerning his lessons with Liszt on the *Dante* Sonata: see Stradal, 49.

*Lucia di Lammermoor* which, though published as Henselt's own "interpretation," supposedly reflects the considerable liberties—and they are great indeed, especially in the introduction—Liszt allowed himself in the performance of this piece. Liszt was given the opportunity to correct the proofs of this publication but declined to make any alterations because "all the variants are admirably suitable."[35] In 1886 he advised his students to use this score, saying, "I have always played these pieces [the opera fantasies] completely freely, not as printed. Henselt heard me play it [*Réminiscences de Lucia de Lammermoor*] once and included much of what he learned in his edition."[36]

EXAMPLE 7.4. Franz Liszt, *Réminiscences de Lucia de Lammermoor*, ed. Adolf Henselt, excerpt

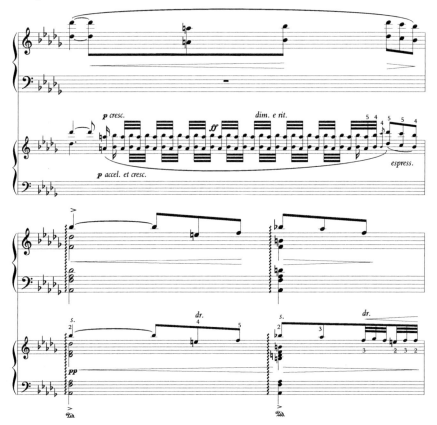

[35] Walker, *Living with Liszt*, 224.
[36] Zimdars, *Masterclasses of Liszt*, 140.

EXAMPLE 7.4. (*continued*)

We must, however, sound another commonsense warning when considering the value of editions by Liszt's pupils. The broad agreement between the advice in the *Liszt-Pädagogium* and Siloti's edition of the *Sospiro* study, for example, helps to confirm that—as Siloti states in his preface—the variants come from Liszt himself. But it is obvious, especially with the more extensive of these pupils' editions—for example, Sauer's many volumes for Peters, da Motta's for the Franz Liszt-Stiftung, or Rosenthal's for Ullstein Verlag—that the editors could hardly have received personal guidance from Liszt on every piece they edited. We should therefore beware lest we imbue all their work with too much authority on account of their status as famous Liszt students. To take just one instance: in d'Albert's edition of the Sonata in B Minor we read that the opening octaves are to be played "wie Pizzicato," an interpretation that has been very popular in the twentieth century (see the two recordings by Horowitz). It is no surprise to find that d'Albert neither himself studied the sonata with Liszt nor appears to have been present at a performance by a pupil who did, for his advice is directly contradicted by the *Pädagogium* (using notes taken by Stradal after a lesson on the piece), where a sound like "muffled timpani" is recommended. Liszt even gave technical instructions as to how this was to be achieved—namely, by striking the keys toward the back in order to lessen the force of the attack. Liszt admired d'Albert's playing tremendously, and all his annotations make cogent musical sense. They do not, however, necessarily derive from Liszt's own practice. We may, in the end, decide we want to play the sonata *d'après d'Albert*, but we ought to be clear that this is what we are doing.

Finally, we should beware of some entrenched exaggerations concerning Liszt's teaching: namely, that after his middle years he never gave private lessons, and that he was not interested at all in technical matters but concentrated idealistically only on "the music" while leaving students to work out for themselves how exactly it should be produced. Specific technical advice is indeed thin on the ground, but it does exist, as will be discussed a little later. As for the question of private instruction, it is certainly true that in the final two decades of his life Liszt's most frequent teaching forum was the master class, but even then certain favored pupils—for example Siloti, Stradal, and Friedheim—were asked to stay after class for extra instruction, and in earlier years many pianists—Mason, Tausig, Bache, and more—were fortunate enough to receive individual lessons.

The *Pädagogium* and associated writings show that Liszt's principal concern was always with musical characterization and communication, rather with pedantic adherence to the score. His performance directions have to be interpreted in the context of the specific piece and its intended musical effect. The direction "Andante con moto," for instance, in "Invocation" from *Harmonies poétiques et religieuses* might seem to indicate a fairly placid albeit flowing tempo. The instruction in the Göllerich diaries is a counterintuitive "fast and fiery."[37] There is unfortunately not yet an equivalent of Eigeldinger's indispensable *Chopin: Pianist and Teacher* for Liszt, drawing together all the various sources of performance information for each piece. Such a volume would be very large indeed, but it at least would save pianists a trawl through many different works, several of them difficult to obtain, for information on Liszt's intentions.

[37] Zimdars, *Masterclasses of Liszt*, 116.

The following is a necessarily crude summary of some points that featured frequently in Liszt's teaching. Written information like this is often only fully understood by musicians who already play in this manner anyway. I give it nevertheless; most of it is simply good musicianship.

1. The music must flow in large phrases, not chopped up with overaccentuation. In lyrical works such as *Bénédiction de Dieu* this does not imply particularly fast speeds, or alla breve tempi, but rather manipulation of tone and articulation to produce a breathing, singing melody.
2. The musical sense must continue through the frequent rhetorical pauses in Liszt's music. In Liszt's words: "Don't mince it up."
3. *Expression should always avoid the sentimental.* Liszt was emphatic about this, and often parodied what he regarded as excessively affected playing, even if it was by Anton Rubinstein, whose energy and drive he otherwise greatly admired. (After a particularly overcautious performance he advised a student: "Das müssen Sie mehr Rubensteinisieren" [You have to Rubinsteinize it more].)[38] The common idea of Liszt as a performer prone to lapses of precious sentimentality is far from the truth, for the aged Liszt at least. This should extend to posture—no swaying around or nodding of the head ("The divine Clara [Schumann] has this soulful head-wagging on her conscience");[39] sit upright, and don't look at the keys, rather straight ahead. This advice, of course, is characteristic of the old Liszt rather than the young, for in earlier days he had been notorious for his animation at the keyboard. Even with the elderly Liszt, the visual impact of the performance was an important part of the act, but attention increasingly centered on his face rather than the entire body.
4. Piano tone is usually to be imagined in orchestra terms—for example, clarinet in the central A♭ melody of "Funérailles." According to Friedheim, even in Liszt's advanced years, when some other aspects of his technique had deteriorated, he was still unrivaled in building up an orchestral-style climax on the keyboard.
5. Figuration in melodic sections of Liszt's music should frequently be slow, not brilliant. He had a fondness for adding mordents and other embellishments, sometimes of an Italianate or even Hungarian character, to emphasize parts of the melodic line.
6. A certain flexibility of tempo is in order in most of Liszt's music, however inadequate the directions in the score; metronomic playing will not suffice. When discussing his Weber edition, Liszt claimed: "A metronomical performance is certainly tiresome and nonsensical; time and rhythm must be adapted to and identified with the melody, the harmony, the accent and the poetry. . . . But how to

[38] Walker, *Living with Liszt*, 149.
[39] Zimdars, *Masterclasses of Liszt*, 58.

indicate all this? I shudder at the thought of it."[40] In some of his earlier works (such as the 1838 *Grandes études*), Liszt had tried to indicate fluctuations of tempo and rhetorical pauses more accurately by means of special signs. These were likely modeled after similar indications in Türk's *Clavierschule*,[41] but were soon abandoned, probably owing to their overprescriptive effect. Nevertheless, comparison between the *Grandes études* and their later incarnation as the *Transcendental Studies* (where the extra signs were omitted) can tell us much about the more minute nuances of tempo expected by Liszt. They also tell us that—contrary to much modern Liszt playing—*rinforzando* can imply a speeding up rather than an invitation to slow down.

EXAMPLE 7.5. Franz Liszt, *Transcendental Study* in A Minor, 1838 version

7. Liszt's rubato was, according to Lachmund, "quite different from the Chopin hastening and tarrying *rubato* . . . more like a momentary halting of the time, by a slight pause here or there on some significant note, and when done rightly brings out the phrasing in a way that is declamatory and remarkably convincing. . . . Liszt seemed unmindful of time, yet the aesthetic symmetry of rhythm did not seem disturbed."[42]

8. The wrong notes of a d'Albert or a Rubinstein did not matter; their inaccuracies were insignificant compared with their panache. Splashy playing unaccompanied by musical insight, however, brought Liszt's wrath upon the perpetrator. In a moving 1946 BBC radio broadcast, Frederick Lamond talked about Liszt's surprising strictness and concern for musical cleanliness. Awe of Liszt's censure is still apparent in Lamond's voice after nearly sixty years.

---

[40] La Mara, *Liszt's Briefe*, trans. Bache, 2:194 (letter to Lebert of 1870).

[41] Daniel Gottlob Türk, *Klavierschule, oder Anweisung zum Klavierspielen fuer Lehrer und Lernende* (1789; neue vermehrte und verbesserte Ausgabe, Leipzig und Halle: Schwickert, 1802). Türk's indications include, for instance, three parallel horizontal lines, meaning a gradual slowing down.

[42] Walker, *Living with Liszt*, 53. For Chopin's rubato, see chapter 5, p. 151.

Concerning what the later pupils learned from their lessons and classes with Liszt, we have an invaluable—and for once, aural—source in recordings, including stimulating performances by Rosenthal, von Sauer, Lamond, d'Albert, Friedheim, Siloti, and others. Although it is certainly true that the individuality of these artists renders it unlikely that we can hear in their performances a slavish rendering of their master's wishes (and anyway, pianists such as Rosenthal were also taught by other major figures of the day), with a performer such as Arthur Friedheim we may get as close to this as is possible with a genuinely mature player. Liszt famously remarked that Friedheim's performance of the B-Minor Sonata was "the way I imagined it when I was writing it," and although Friedheim was deeply unhappy with both his acoustic recordings and piano rolls, his idolatry of his teacher was such that we might expect to find specific aspects of Liszt's performance style copied in his own playing. In fact we do indeed come across features that echo comments in the *Pädagogium* and other memoirs.

In Friedheim's piano roll of *Harmonies du soir* (the lead-in to the E-major section) he inserts a turn similar to that suggested by the *Pädagogium* for inclusion before the recapitulation of *Un sospiro*. On the previously mentioned piano roll of the second *Légende* we hear a performance that corresponds closely to Liszt's advice as preserved in Göllerich's diaries, with a loud and stately opening that modifies the dynamic and tempo indications in the score, and an extension and repetition of the "waves" figuration into upper and lower octaves. (Suggestions for extensions such as these are found throughout the *Pädagogium*, especially concerning *Réminiscences de Robert le diable*, where long sections of passagework are treated in a similar fashion). It should be pointed out that such amplifications of the figuration were by no means always prompted by extensions of the piano's range. This *Légende* could easily have been played on a piano of the 1860s as Friedheim recorded it decades later. Liszt suggested similar modifications for other pieces, such as his two polonaises.[43]

Why Liszt had not simply written things thus in the first place is an interesting question, harking back to the "as played by the composer" *ossia* in the *Clochette* Fantasy. Some changes were probably genuine afterthoughts, and some were made in response to a belated realization of just how difficult his virtuoso music was. Of *La campanella* he remarked mischievously, "The difficult octave accompaniment in the left hand on the last page may be simplified. . . . When I wrote that I did not teach as much as I do now."[44] A few were no doubt the sort of alterations that any

[43] Walker, *Living with Liszt*, 210, 271.
[44] Walker, *Living with Liszt*, 33.

accomplished virtuoso would consider making and should not be confined to Liszt's own music. Even with Chopin, Liszt advised the occasional modification (for example repeating the introduction to the A-major section of the F♯ Polonaise).[45] When telling a pupil to alternate the direction of the spread of certain chords in his transcription of Saint-Saëns's *Danse macabre*, he added as an aside: "I did not write it so—it takes too much time."[46] He also suggested changes in several other pieces, for example: a repetition of the introduction before playing the second stanza of his transcription of "Gretchen am Spinnrade"[47] and the repeat of the middle part of *Au lac de Wallenstadt* "to enhance its effect."[48] For bars 276–78 and 284–86 of *Scherzo and March* he recommended increasing the demonic clangor by crossing the right hand over the left to "hit a few low A's."[49] Just the sort of disrespectful striving after sonorous effect that would no doubt be abhorred by urtext fetishists.

All this is of course in addition to the improvised prelude that any competent pianist could be expected to play before beginning a piece, and to the liberties that could be taken with endings. When a student failed to prelude before a performance of the third *Liebestraum*, Liszt pointed out the omission and made a short one one up himself (consisting of only three chords).[50] For his *Ave Maria* (written for Lebert and Stark's *Grosse Klavierschule*) he instructed, "At the end, so that the people know that it is over, play the *Lohengrin* Chord [i.e., a chord of A major in the treble, as at the opening of the prelude to act 1 of Wagner's opera]."[51]

Other aspects of Liszt's interpretative legacy are more surprising for the modern performer. The *Pädagogium* indicates that the performance of the main theme of "Funérailles" should be "not rhythmical!" and that a dragging, mournful articulation is needed here, in contrast to the clipped and precise interpretation that we hear in many recordings. According to Lachmund, Liszt expected the performance of rhythmic figures to vary depending on the mood of the music: "In quiet music the sixteenth-note should be played a little slower, and in lively time a bit later and faster than the exact value."[52] This was absolutely standard practice for the time, though it is now usually decried as inaccurate score reading.

[45] Walker, *Living with Liszt*, 324.
[46] Walker, *Living with Liszt*, 194.
[47] Walker, *Living with Liszt*, 14.
[48] Walker, *Living with Liszt*, 214.
[49] Zimdars, *Masterclasses of Liszt*, 134. Stradal claimed that "the more demonically one played, the happier Liszt was" (160).
[50] Zimdars, *Masterclasses of Liszt*, 87.
[51] Zimdars, *Masterclasses of Liszt*, 140.
[52] Walker, *Living with Liszt*, 271.

The more general comments on "Funérailles" are also relevant to other pieces. The opening left-hand ostinato is to be doubled in duration, with the right hand entering in a "when ready" fashion (similar instructions are given for *Un sospiro*). A more difficult recommendation is the injunction that the bass of the later D♭ ostinato section is to be played with clarity in every note. This is an especially frequent type of admonition in Liszt's pupils' memoirs (see, for example, Göllerich's notes concerning the master's irritation at a sloppy performance of Tausig's *Ungarische Zigeunerweisen*)[53] and recalls admiring critiques of the lucidity of Liszt's own playing. Exactly how this clarity is to be achieved while also observing the long pedal markings is a problem aptly raised by Alfred Brendel in his preface to the *Pädagogium* reprint, and certainly a consistent solution is not possible here: even on Liszt's instruments, either the pedal markings are altered, or clarity is replaced by an indistinct rumble in the bass.

## Liszt's Pedaling

Indeed, the whole question of pedaling in Liszt is a contentious issue. Exact adherence to the score is rarely advisable or even possible on today's pianos (with the exception of the *Tannhäuser* Overture transcription, which simply says that use of the pedal "is left to the discretion of the performer"). It appears that Liszt used the *una corda* more frequently than is indicated in his scores, and that in particular soft filigree passagework was sometimes played with the *una corda* depressed. In the Sonata, a dash of *una corda* for just one bar is recommended in the *Pädagogium* for the second group to give a distant, mystical tone color to an unexpected harmonization. Liszt was, however, alive to the muffling effect of the *una corda* and felt that it could often hinder the production of a singing tone. He insisted, said Stradal, that his students "sing as much as possible on the keys."[54]

Liszt's indications for the sustaining pedal are not just scanty, but inconsistent. In the G-minor study of the *Grandesétudes* (later titled "Vision"), he marked no pedal until nearly halfway through the piece, despite the fact that the first page is to be played with the left hand alone—quite impossible without constant pedal. When the pedal is actually indicated, at the climatic turn to G minor, it seems to be there merely to underscore the increased volume required. A bar after that, specific pedal markings disappear. This is a piece deliberately written in Thalberg's legato arpeggio style, and some pedal is required virtually throughout. Of

[53] Zimdars, *Masterclasses of Liszt*, 19.
[54] Stradal, 159.

course, there were differences in the pedal and damping mechanism of Liszt's pianos in the 1830s compared to those of today, but none of these would affect our general conclusions here. The paucity of indications in the G-minor study is all the more puzzling because other pieces in the set, such as the C-minor, have a detailed range of pedal markings. Indeed, pedal is indicated in the C-minor study even where we would not expect it. At "animato il tempo," the bar-by-bar pedal seems to contradict (as in "Funérailles") the instruction "sempre staccato e distintamente il basso" [the bass to be played staccato and distinctly throughout], which would be more easily achieved with no pedal at all.

The implication is that Liszt, during the period of the *Grandes études* at least, tended to indicate the use of the sustaining pedal only when the pedaling was not immediately obvious or in order to underline a dramatic increase in volume. This would explain, for example, why the F-minor study has no pedal marked at all, despite the long passages of passionate legato melody over extended bass figuration. In the G-minor study, the pedal markings at the climax might actually have been designed to prevent overpedaling, by requesting a change at each new harmony, rather than to initiate the use of the pedal. Liszt's attitude appears to have been, "Any fool can see you need pedal here." In the transcription of Wagner's *Tannhäuser* Overture (published in 1849), he simply carried through this attitude consistently, giving no pedal indications at all.

Even during the Weimar period Liszt's approach was unreliable. All the pieces in *Harmonies poétiques et religieuses*, published in 1853, contain detailed pedalings—except one. The Andante lagrimoso has pedal marked for only four bars—again, the climax of the piece—though all pianists would use pedal in this work at least as frequently as in the others of the set. Significantly, the marked pedal here extends the bass note much further than its written value to provide a warm cushion of sound for the melody above. Liszt must have feared that otherwise this type of passage might be played in a cold and dry manner. Similar inconsistency can be seen in the six *Consolations* (1850). The famous no. 3, in D♭, is heavily pedaled, but the others are pedaled not at all, though no. 6 requires nearly as much pedal and the rest certainly some.

Of the larger Weimar piano pieces, the First Ballade has no pedaling, as might be expected in a piece published the same year as the *Tannhäuser* Overture. The Concert Solo (published in 1851) has frequent markings, perhaps partly resulting from its genesis as a conservatory competition piece. The Second Ballade (published in 1854) begins as if the pedal markings are going to be as extensive as in the Concert Solo, but they disappear after three pages. The opposite applies to the *Scherzo and March* (1854), where pedaling suddenly puts in an appearance on the very last page of a twenty-four-page piece. The Sonata, not that unusually for a work published in 1854, contains miserly pedal indications. From the late 1850s onward, however, Liszt, chastened by the experience of listening to ineptly pedaled performances of his music, took more care to indicate the basic requirements for each piece.

Liszt's cancellation instructions for the *una corda* pedal are equally variable. He was chary with writing "tre corde," perhaps assuming that any decent pianist would use his judgment as to the right moment. In the sonata, for example, the "una corda" and "sempre una corda" indications in the Andante sostenuto are Liszt's own, but the "tre corde" cancellation that we find in the New Liszt Edition at bar 363 is an editorial addition. Unquestionably the *una corda* will have to be abandoned somewhere around here, for the intense central section can hardly be given an adequate rendering with the *una corda* depressed. Perhaps after the triple-forte climax the *una corda* should be retaken—certainly for the triple-piano passage a few bars later.

Liszt was well aware that use of both pedals would vary in each separate performance according to the acoustics of the hall and the characteristics of the piano. It was this consideration that prompted him sometimes to abandon pedal markings in the first place. Accounts of Liszt's playing and teaching show that his pedaling was subtle, sophisticated, and at variance with his own published indications. As discussed in chapter 6, the *Pädagogium* contains many references to Liszt's use of various types of half-pedal—here described as "a momentary half-damping of the strings"[55]—and tremolo pedal effects, demonstrating what should be obvious, namely that his pedaling was too complex in practice to be easily accommodated within standard musical notation. Any composer who would recoil from setting down the profusion of markings found in Chopin's Barcarolle (which naturally does not even try to indicate half-pedalings) would certainly have rolled his eyes at the idea of Graingeresque delineation of the minutiae of such things. When pedaling Liszt's music, we are best off ensuring that our ears, even more than our eyes, are open.

## Tempo and Technique

Liszt claimed he was not in favor of extreme tempi—except for Mendelssohn.[56] This was not a sarcastic joke. Liszt, like Bülow, had heard Mendelssohn play many times and noted his fondness for brisk speeds. The *Pädagogium* gives several specific metronome marks for Liszt's works. Although typographical errors are

[55] Ramann, *Liszt Pädagogium*, ser. 2, 3.
[56] Walker, *Living with Liszt*, 275.

frequent here, and Liszt was as much a proponent of the "elastic" tempo as Brahms,[57] we should be grateful that the marks are there at all for general guidance. There are few things more pointless than advice such as that in the Göllerich diaries (for *Harmonies du soir*)—"not too slow"—when we have no idea how slow that is. As for the numerous misprinted *Pädagogium* markings, they are luckily so extreme as to make it obvious that something is wrong. The marking of quarter note = 96 for the central Andante of the sonata seems preposterously rushed until we remember that one of the *Pädagogium*'s favorite misprints involves reversing the order of the numerals, and quarter note = 69 does indeed feel about right for this section. In faster passages, however, Liszt often appeared to favor tempos that would be considered slightly on the speedy side by modern standards. Stradal claimed that *St. Francis Walking on the Waves* (the *Wasserstiefellegende* [Water-Boots Legend], its composer called it) was normally played too slowly. Liszt strode vigorously around the room one day at a tempo of quarter note = 92 to indicate the right speed.[58] When, on another occasion, a student played *Eroica*, Liszt let the tempo be taken "much faster" than the diarist Göllerich would have imagined.[59]

The reminiscences of Charles Hallé, among others, suggest that as a young man, Liszt sometimes took tempos very fast indeed, which contributed to his reputation for technical wizardry. The *Pädagogium* tempos for the Fantasy on *Robert le diable*, however, do give us some pause for thought, because Liszt apparently intended the long octave section in the middle to be played at a moderate tempo (no faster than in the ballet at this point!), rather than the sprint it has since become (when it is played at all). Liszt claimed that this section constituted "the point of rest" in the fantasy and criticized Anton Rubinstein for his excessive speed here. Interestingly, another piece that has nowadays become a test of rapid fingerwork—*Feux follets*—was also described as requiring a "sehr bequem" performance by Göllerich.[60] It is probably too late to do much about the standard treatment of *Feux follets* as a hectic race to the finish (usually aided by judicious simplifications of the treacherous double-note passages here and there).[61] Velocity

---

[57] See Henschel, 78–79. See also chapter 6, p. 186.

[58] Stradal, 137.

[59] Zimdars, *Masterclasses of Liszt*, 22.

[60] Zimdars, *Masterclasses of Liszt*, 21.

[61] *Feux follets* is now, of course, much more difficult than it was when it was written: the increasing action weight of pianos has seen to that. Even such sterling technicians as Horowitz found it advisable to make some simplifications to this study, though such rearrangements usually go unnoticed by audiences and critics. Late in life, Horowitz demonstrated his modifications ("which would ease its difficulty") to David Dubal. David Dubal, *Evenings with Horowitz* (Pompton Plains, N.J.: Amadeus Press, 2004), 262.

in this piece has become a sign of pianistic virility not willingly abandoned, but those considering learning the Fantasy on *Robert le diable* should at least be aware of Liszt's original intentions. The slower speed allows the thematic combination at the climax of the central section to be managed without an awkwardly massive ritardando (which raises a smile, at least from this listener, on Earl Wild's otherwise spendid recording).[62]

William Mason reported that Liszt felt that he himself was not a good technical model to follow. Despite his studies with Czerny, he believed that his early training had been mostly haphazard and that he had reached his goals mainly "by force of personality"—a path that he did not recommend to Mason, because, as he told him honestly, if perhaps too frankly, "You lack my personality." Those students who came to Liszt's 1880s classes certainly did not hear him at his technical best, for old age and ill health had by that time taken their toll. According to Brahms, the playing of Liszt in his prime was quite incomparable, and even as late as his Vienna concert of 1874 Hanslick was amazed that he had retained such a complete technical command. As we have remarked, three years later the sheer bravura was less pronounced. Friedheim recalled that in Liszt's final years, although his technique was still astonishing, it was not unsurpassable. Godowsky, he claimed, had finer octaves, and Rosenthal was more adept in the handling of complex passagework. He did concede that he had never since heard anyone build up an orchestral climax on the keyboard like Liszt, and it is not surprising that most of the technical advice in the *Pädagogium* and elsewhere concerns the manipulation of piano sonorities, rather than the achievement of accuracy or speed. According to Lamond, the aged Liszt responded to one pupil's technical display (in Chopin's Polonaise op. 53) with the scathing "Do you think I care how fast you can play octaves?" Rather unfair, perhaps, as he undoubtedly would have cared forty years earlier, and the three volumes of exercises composed in the late 1870s show that Liszt had a more than casual interest in the codification of technical difficulties.

According to Stradal and others, Liszt's basic technique all his life remained centered on wrist and finger action. He eschewed many of the experiments with

---

[62] In this recording we also hear an entire page in the major instead of the minor mode, turning what should be a fierce and proud "Hungarian" variation into something rather like a can-can. This was a misprint in the original Schlesinger edition and was corrected in most later ones (but not, alas, the one Earl Wild was evidently using). For those obsessed with textual accuracy, it is worth pondering why, despite one radically "wrong" tempo, and one rather massive misreading, the performance is nevertheless quite superb.

arm weight essayed by some younger performers.[63] Octaves, Liszt claimed, should be played from a light wrist; otherwise they will sound hard and jabbed (*spitzig*).[64] Other technical advice includes several remarks on the way one should hold the hand in certain circumstances (when playing a melody using both thumbs, the wrists should be held higher than normal),[65] and advice toward the achieving of certain sonorous effects akin to tone clusters in the *Grande solo de concert* and *Réminiscences de Robert le diable*. In the opening of the latter piece and the "funeral march" section of the former, the player is directed to hold on to each note of (and pedal through) the ornament in the bass, creating a threatening, tenebrous fog of sound in the lower register of the keyboard that is hardly implied by the notation, and contrary to the modern manner of playing such passages crisply and cleanly. For *Un sospiro* Liszt made some recommendations on the dividing of octave passages between the hands, and similar advice appears in the Göllerich diaries for the opening of the Fantasy on *Rigoletto*,[66] which could no doubt apply in many other pieces, like the central climax of *Waldesrauschen*. Of as much a visual as an aural nature is the comment in Lachmund's diaries that when playing the opening of the B-Minor Ballade, Liszt lifted his right hand up to twelve inches in the air before striking each note, while at the same time sitting upright and looking straight ahead, saying, "One should not play for the people who sit in the front row—they are usually 'dead-heads,' but play for those up in the gallery that pay ten pfennigs for their tickets; they should not only hear, but they should see."[67] It must have been quite a sight.

What is the main point that we can take away from an overview of the *Pädagogium* and related material? Liszt was obviously very concerned with what he described in the preface to his *Symphonic Poems* as a *periodischer Vortrag*, in other words the maintenance of a musical line in performance, by, among other things, carefully regulating the weight of accents within and between bars. The numerous rhetorical pauses (not a sign of "creative poverty," according to Ramann) should not break up the flow—rather, the music was to "carry on through the silence." The

---

[63] See chapter 1, p. 17.

[64] Stradal, 159. Ironically, playing octaves with a loose wrist was a novel technique in the 1820s, when Liszt himself was a student. When Moscheles heard Kalkbrenner using this technique in 1821, he described it, with a mastery of tautology, as "a bad method, and not a sound one." C. Moscheles, *Life of Moscheles*, 1:53.

[65] Walker, *Living with Liszt*, 151.

[66] Zimdars, *Masterclasses of Liszt*, 141.

[67] Walker, *Living with Liszt*, 308.

exact speed of a performance was of much less importance than fluidity and a singing tone. This is one of the most striking disjunctions with modern practice, where a *sempre tenuto* style of playing occurs frequently. It is illustrative in this regard to compare Moriz Rosenthal's recording of Liszt's Chopin song transcription "Meine Freuden" with some modern performances. Rosenthal's limpid and plastic delineation of the melody is evidently inspired by the desire to "sing" on the piano in the same way as Liszt seems to have taught his pupils. The speed is not particularly fast, but the music moves flexibly forward unhindered by overaccentuation, or the desire to impose a weighty profundity often indistinguishable from boredom.

The same points can be illustrated in the recordings of other Liszt pupils, in particular Emil von Sauer's beautifully shaped performance of *Ricordanza*. Problems with the early recording process, which allowed only a little more than four minutes of music to be recorded continuously, meant that few long works were recorded in the early decades of the twentieth century. We do have a profusion of shorter pieces recorded by Liszt students and a performance of the two concertos by von Sauer, with the orchestra conducted by Felix Weingartner, another Lisztian. Friedheim was famously unhappy with his recordings, and they are unlikely to show him at his best, yet his rigorously unsentimental, even "modern" performance of the first movement of the *Moonlight* Sonata perhaps reflects something of Liszt's later approach to Beethoven, even if his tempo is faster than the quarter note = 58 that Stradal noted as Liszt's speed for this movement.[68] Liszt once parodied what he regarded as Rubinstein's hasty and wayward tempo changes in this sonata. According to both Stradal and Siloti, Liszt's own mature interpretation was understated (an adjective rarely used in connection with the young Liszt), but unforgettable.

And finally, what of Liszt's attitude to the arpeggiation and asynchronization that formed the core of the discussion in chapter 5? Here we have little direct evidence other than Liszt's occasional attempts to notate such things in his own scores,[69] but it seems highly unlikely that something that formed such a striking feature of his students' playing should have been absent from his own. We have also noticed previously how reluctant Liszt was to spend too much time marking details of arpeggiation and pedaling, and the same is likely too for subtle dislocations, which would anyway differ with each performance. Claudio Arrau was

---

[68] Stradal, 87.
[69] For example in the Valse-Impromptu (second version), where one passage is varied by introducing continuous dislocation between the left hand and the right.

given some idea of Liszt's flexible approach to arpeggiation by his teacher, the Liszt pupil Martin Krause: "He would speak of Liszt's way of breaking chords, and of trilling. He taught us several ways of breaking chords: to start slowly, and then accelerate toward the highest note; or to make a crescendo to the highest note; or to make a diminuendo; or to do it freely, with rubato. But always so that broken chords would have a meaning coming from what went before."[70] The message here, even at third hand, seems to be communication, imagination, and variety.

[70] Horowitz, 39.

# 8

# Postlude: Post-Liszt

You lack my personality!
—Franz Liszt to William Mason

### The Instrument of the Immortals

Liszt's superficially brutal but no doubt honest remark to William Mason homes in on a fundamental issue. At the heart of romantic pianism remains the idea that the performer, not the composer, is the center of interest. This is why the outstanding pianists of the era can sometimes seem to be part of a golden age and why it is tempting to think of them as part of a Great Tradition. Even if they all played differently, and even if their playing could hardly have been "better" than the best that came after them, they simply occupied a more important role in concert life than any pianist could achieve today.

Just how important their role was in the public imagination can be seen in commercial piano advertising. Advertisers are not usually renowned for their finely tuned artistic sensibility, but they can certainly be relied upon to know what will strike a chord with their market. In the 1920s Steinway and Sons produced a particularly quaint series of portraits for their products. Artists' impressions of great musical scenes of past and present appeared above the standard by-line "the instrument of the immortals." The musical scenes are varied indeed, and among the "immortals" the performers preside equally beside the composers. Josef Hofmann is shown giving a recital to a respectably attentive audience of conspicuously hat-wearing ladies. Berlioz (who famously couldn't play the piano at all)[1] appears misplaced in front of some distinctly non-piano-like orchestral instruments. Percy Grainger is evoked by a scene from the Australian bush, complete with copious kangaroos, while a long-suffering Paderewski looks out

---

[1] When Wagner was criticized for the inadequacy of his piano playing, he would reply that at least he played better than Berlioz.

255

with a resigned forebearance next to the rubric "The room in which we live and entertain our friends really is an index to the quality of our culture"—a reminder that though tastes may be ephemeral, snobbery remains timeless. Such a room would, of course, be incomplete without a good piano, even if Paderewski might not necessarily be on hand to play it. Liszt was famous enough to be featured in at least two of these ads. In the first he was depicted, with Wagner by his side, as a youngish man sitting at the keyboard. The instrument, surprisingly, looks suspiciously like the Érard it was likely to have been rather than a Steinway (the artist's honesty triumphing over base commercial considerations). The great men are obviously conferring about some weighty musical matter, aided by the presence of the piano, which can immediately translate their inspirations into sound. In the second, Liszt is a white-haired old abbé, playing an instrument that thankfully looks about right this time from the salesman's point of view. The most evocative picture is undoubtedly one of Ignaz Friedman "interpreting the overture to Tannhäuser":

Friedman's grand imaginary performance is surrounded by feverish images of chanting monks and blossoming staffs—the pianist can obviously conjure up the entire opera before his enraptured audience. He is not simply playing—as Ravel and Stravinsky would have wished—but "interpreting," surely a much more elevated exercise. He transmits the core of Wagner's four-hour-long masterpiece in the fifteen minutes it takes to play Liszt's transcription. The emphasis is not on Wagner, nor even on Liszt, but on Friedman and the potency of the piano— "the instrument of the immortals." No other instrument held such an all-encompassing position in the romantic imagination, and nothing else could take the place of voices, orchestra, and indeed the entire operatic stage. We cannot hear how Friedman is playing, but we can guess roughly what the effect might be—for this surely must be pianism in the Great Tradition.

The most potent explanation of the nostalgia for a pianistic golden era, for a Great Tradition of performers and performance style, is that the piano itself was more important then. It took a central position in both domestic and public musical life that it has irrevocably lost in our day. Our golden-age fantasies may also have something to do with a fond harking back to the freedom of some playing styles of the past, to memories of great talents and great imaginations, and to the human penchant for nostalgia, pure and simple. But however one evaluates the performance practices of the romantic era, the piano was simply a much more vital part of the musical world, and its performers consequently invested with more authority, charisma, and freedom than we pianists would dare to hope for today. If the awed adulation with which Paderewski is treated in the film *Moonlight Sonata* seems naive, almost embarrassing to us, it is partly because we cannot share

*Friedman at his Steinway interpreting the Liszt arrangement of the Tannhäuser Overture*

# STEINWAY
## THE INSTRUMENT OF THE IMMORTALS

FIGURE 8.1. Steinway and Sons advertisement: Ignaz Friedman interpreting the Liszt arrangement of Wagner's *Tannhäuser* Overture

the values of an era when being a great pianist meant a lot more than being a great pianist today. It meant having a priestly role—in Paderewski's case, almost a papal one—in the "religion of the pianoforte" that George Bernard Shaw so wittily dissected in his eponymous essay.[2] And of course, when the authority of the performer reaches that of a hierophant, it vies with that of the composer. A much larger degree of interpretative, even re-creative, freedom must be expected and allowed.

[2] George Bernard Shaw, "The Religion of the Pianoforte," originally printed in the *Fortnightly Review* (February 1894); reprinted in Dan H. Laurence, ed., *Bernard Shaw: How to Become a Musical Critic* (London: Rupert Hart-Davis, 1960), 213–28.

Romantic pianists were fully conscious of the important role granted them and sought to make music genuinely communicative to contemporary audiences, rather than an exercise in academic resuscitation. At their most extravagant, romantic interpretations such as Busoni's version of the Bach *Goldberg Variations* occupy a nebulous area between rendition and rearrangement. We can argue in each individual case whether interpretation shades into transcription, but we can be sure that our general viewpoint has shifted significantly toward a less liberal orthodoxy. In the preface to his 1862 edition of sonatas by C. P. E. Bach, Hans von Bülow drew a telling analogy with literature. He described his work not as anything approaching an urtext, but as "a translation from the keyboard-language of the eighteenth century, from that of the clavichord to the piano."[3] Bülow's knowledge of early keyboard instruments was probably sketchy at best, and he offered a C. P. E. Bach for a new era according to how he personally thought the music ought to go—how he felt its spirit. To help the piece speak directly to his audience—to make it effective, in other words—he allowed himself all manner of creative adaptations. At its best, the result could be something as unfaithfully successful as Edward FitzGerald's magnificent *Rubaiyat of Omar Khayyam* (1859), one of the most popular English poems of Bülow's era. Although purporting to be a translation, it would hardly satisfy even the most relaxed scholar of medieval Persian:

Awake! for Morning in the Bowl of Night
Has flung the Stone that puts the Stars to Flight
And Lo! the Hunter of the East has caught
The Sultan's Turret in a Noose of Light.

Dreaming when Dawn's Left Hand was in the Sky,
I heard a Voice within the Tavern cry,
"Awake, my Little ones, and fill the Cup,
Before life's Liquor in its Cup be dry."

Wonderful stuff—and we know it's supposed to be old Persian because of the bit about the sultan, in the same way that we know that Bülow's C. P. E. Bach or Busoni's *Goldberg Variations* are supposed to be baroque because of the odd eighteenth-century ornamental twiddle allowed in here and there. Apart from that, the whole poem is resolutely nineteenth century, a creative adaptation that is effectively a new work in its own right, and none the worse for it unless our

[3] My translation. See also Haas, 37, and Hinrichsen, 145–50.

demands are more literal. A rather more exact version (an attempt at an urtext translation, if one might stretch the analogy a little) by Peter Avery and John Heath-Stubbs, reveals such vast differences that it is often difficult to tell exactly which stanzas match with the FitzGerald. The following two seem to be possibilities:

> Get up lad, it is dawn.
> Fill the crystal goblet with the ruby wine;
> In this hole and corner of transience you will seek this borrowed moment
> Long and never find it.

> Get up my sweetest, it is dawn,
> Gently, gently sip the wine and twang the harp,
> For not a soul will remain of those here,
> And of those gone none will return.[4]

The scholarly version is surely a more accurate representation of the Persian. But many, I would hazard, will be less stirred by "Get up lad, it is dawn" than FitzGerald's more ornate, if less faithful exhortation to awake to "Morning in the Bowl of Night."

Romantic pianism was not simply a matter of creative translation, of free rearrangement. Virtually the entire spectrum of playing styles were heard and applauded somewhere, from our standard sober renditions of pieces to versions which we would without hesitation classify as transcriptions. The key word is variety—the fascinating variety of approaches one finds on early recordings, which always leave open the possibility that with each new disk transferred to CD we will hear something quite thrilling, or something quite appalling. Modern pianism is no less full of talent, but it is often more uniform and straitlaced, a mirror of our stiffer concert etiquette.

## The Cult of the Artist

Despite the establishing of a canonic repertoire, despite the increasing focus on "the work" rather than the performance, Liszt, Rubinstein, Busoni, and the others remained bigger than the pieces on their programs, if not for future generations,

---

[4] Peter Avery and John Heath-Stubbs, trans., *The Rubáiyat of Omar Khayyam* (London: Penguin, 1981), 97, 75. The Fitzgerald excerpt was from the first edition (1859, printed privately).

then at least for their contemporaries. The repertoire and "the work" have long since taken over, except with players like Glenn Gould or Vladimir Horowitz, whose talents and eccentricities were among the most mesmeric of the later twentieth century. Their individual musical approach tended to overshadow the repertoire they played, crashing headlong through modern notions of fidelity and polarizing critical opinion in the way that only genuinely interesting artists can. The notoriously damning article on Horowitz by Michael Steinberg in the 1980 edition of *The New Grove Dictionary of Music and Musicians* graphically showed how little his playing squared with some present-day values.

"Horowitz is an extraordinary pianist," admitted Steinberg. But his caveats were severe: "He conceives of interpretation not as the reification of the composer's ideas, but as an essentially independent activity; in Schumann's *Träumerei*, for example, he places the high points anywhere except where Schumann placed them. It is nearly impossible for him to play simply, and where simplicity is wanted, he is apt to offer a teasing *affetuoso* manner, or to steamroller the line into perfect flatness.... Horowitz illustrates that an astounding instrumental gift carries no guarantee of musical understanding."[5] A clash of cultures indeed.

Although Steinberg had many supporters in condemning interpretation that chose not to aim at "the reification of the composer's ideal," the performance decisions of players from Liszt to "the last romantic" can be a potent source of inspiration for pianists. After all, these players were the first to encounter "our" piano, and the first to try out our repertoire on it. They tried to find new meanings in ever more well-worn texts and came up with viable solutions to technical problems that can still cause headaches today. These new meanings were, of course, often not those intended by the composer, and here lies the source of a significant divergence between performers and musicologists. Many pianists are quite happy to treat the performance history of a work as representing a fascinating catalog of ideas, valid on its own terms and informing their own performances. Hence we can have Liszt's First *Mephisto* Waltz advertised on a recording as composed by Liszt-Busoni-Horowitz, or Chopin's op. 10 no. 3 Etude played demonstrably, but unrepentantly, much more slowly than Chopin probably intended.[6] Once a piece of music is released into the world, it can take on a life of its

---

[5] Michael Sternberg, "Horowitz, Vladimir," in Sadie, *New Grove Dictionary* (1980), 8:723. For a discussion of other, similar reactions to Horowitz, see Schonberg, 166–67.

[6] Horowitz's recording of Liszt's *Mephisto* Waltz no.1 was listed thus. He played partly the Liszt original, and partly the Busoni rearrangement (Busoni was convinced—mistakenly—that the Liszt version had surreptitiously been arranged by Tausig), but with his own further alterations on top of all this. For Chopin's op. 10 no. 3, see pp. 272–73.

own rather different from any its creator could have expected. Musicologists, on the other hand, tend to ignore performance ideas not derived from or associated with the composer. They regard them as at best irrelevant or at worse corrupting. These performance approaches are sidelined in modern scholarly editions and often treated in books and articles as so much detritus to be cleared away before the composer's conception can once more be revealed to the world in its pristine form. Of course, urtext-based research is of essential value. It helps us to see clearly what does belong to the composer and his era and what is of later provenance. But the latter might seem just as interesting, might even speak to us more compellingly. We may simply prefer an "unauthorized" performance style.

The concert conditions of the past were, too, predicated on the personal interaction between performer and audience in a manner that is today regarded as a distraction from "the music," rather than an essential part of the concert experience itself. Concert etiquette now also approaches the urtext ideal. Liszt's solo concerts, in contrast, were held together as much by the force of his own personality as by any particular musical coherence. The point was brought home personally to the present author a few years ago. I had been asked to "re-create" for the Istanbul International Festival some of Liszt's famous 1847 concerts in that city. Because most of the pieces Liszt had played there were in my repertoire already, I initially and naively thought that it would be a fairly straightforward task to adapt his programs to a modern evening recital structure, allowing two acceptably varied continuous halves of around forty-five minutes playing time, with the customary break between them. But it wasn't quite as easy as that. Each of the several programs Liszt performed in the city lasted around an hour in actual playing time, without a specific interval in the middle. Moreover, every concert consisted of what would now be regarded as a breathlessly unbroken string of virtuoso encores or end-of-concert pieces (the *William Tell* Overture, *Réminiscences de Norma*, *Réminiscences de Lucia di Lammermoor*, Schubert's "Erlkönig," *Hexameron*, etc.). Only an unspecified "Mazurka by Chopin," played in one program, looked as if it might provide a short opportunity to rest both audience and performer in an oasis of gentle lyricism before the bravura onslaught re-started. But I was judging Liszt's programs too much by our own concert practice. In smaller venues at least, Liszt's pieces would not have been performed unin-terruptedly one after the other. There would have been pauses in which he chatted to friends in the audience or even addressed the entire public. The programmed works would have been further separated by improvised preludes (no doubt designed to offer some contrast with what had gone before). In other words, Liszt's recitals were structured by improvisation and social activity, all bound together by the magnetism of the performer.

Music, then, was only one part of Liszt's act, albeit (usually) the most important one. In larger halls, which necessarily distanced the performer from the audience and prevented easy social interaction, he thought up other ways of making a theatrical impact. According to Vladimir Stasov, who was present for his 1842 concerts in the vast Hall of the Nobility in St. Petersburg, Liszt had "this idea of having a small stage erected in the very centre of the hall like an islet in the middle of the ocean, a throne high above the heads of the crowd."[7] On this stage two grand pianos had been placed, facing opposite directions. His frock coat bedecked with orders and decorations, Liszt entered the hall for the first recital on the arm of one of the most prominent of the Russian noblemen, made his way through the chattering audience, then positively leapt up onto the platform, deliberately ignoring steps that had been set up to make his ascent easier (and to take him directly past the view of the royal box). He then took off his white gloves and threw them theatrically under one of the pianos. The stunned silence that ensued after this bolt of energy and breach of etiquette allowed him to begin his first number, the *William Tell* Overture, "without any preliminaries" (that is, without a prelude—itself a surprising event at the time).[8] For the subsequent pieces, Liszt alternated between the two pianos on stage, not entirely for musical reasons, but to allow both halves of the hall an equal view of the play of passions on his face.

Liszt's concerts in Istanbul had taken place in more modest venues, and there had been consequently little opportunity for theatricality on the scale of the Russian recitals. For my own "re-creation" concerts, a fairly compact venue was chosen (most of the original ones no longer exist), the ornately intimate Yildiz Palace Theatre. This allowed me easily to talk to the audience between pieces (not during pieces, like Pachmann). In order to give some relief from an exclusive diet of virtuoso music, I replaced the Schubert-Liszt "Erlkönig" transcription with the more intimate "Ständchen" ("Leise flehen meine Lieder"). To increase the novelty value of the program, I included two rarely performed pieces that Liszt actually wrote in Istanbul but apparently never played publicly there—the first version of the Fantasy on Verdi's *Ernani* and his transcription of Giuseppi Donizetti's *March for the Sultan Abdul-Mecid*. A few bars of improvised prelude introduced some pieces. An example of the resultant compromise program was: first half: Bellini-Liszt, *Réminiscences de Norma*; Donizetti-Liszt, *Réminiscences de Lucia de Lammermoor* (in the Henselt edition, which Liszt claimed enshrined his own

[7] Stasov, 120.
[8] Stasov, 121.

performing variants);[9] a Chopin mazurka; Rossini-Liszt, Overture to *William Tell*; second half: Verdi-Liszt, Fantasy on *Ernani*; Donizetti-Liszt, *March for Sultan Abdul-Mecid*; Schubert-Liszt, "Ständchen"; Liszt et al., *Hexameron*. Contrary to my fears, the audience did not seem to feel that there was too much bravura music here, but the lesson I personally learned was twofold. Firstly, the concert structure of every era has its own rationale and logic, but one that is inseparable from the venues, etiquette, and audience expectations of the time. One cannot simply play exactly the same program in the same order, modern style, to a modern audience, and expect it to work.[10] Secondly, recitals such as Liszt's were given variety and coherence by the performer and his interaction with the public as much as by the programmed music itself. The personality of the performer, not the pieces played, had the central role.

For the immediately succeeding generations, concert programs and etiquette began to change, but the crucial significance of the performer as personality retained much of its power, reinforced by the improvised preluding that, as we have seen, remained a part of musical life well into the twentieth century. The scowling seriousness of Anton Rubinstein (with his oft-noticed physical similarity to Beethoven),[11] the mystical impact of Busoni (a counterpart of the striking passages marked "visionario" in his scores),[12] and the undeniable personal authority of Paderewski ("pianist, statesman, and philanthropist," as the posters for his later concerts reminded anyone in danger of thinking he was only a musician) gave an unmistakable extramusical glamour and focus to a recital. These performers were indeed personalities—mesmeric orators through which music was channeled. Sometimes, it is true, the composer's voice might be smothered by the eccentricity of their delivery, but it could equally well be enhanced. The fame of these pianists and the allure of their characters could at any rate rival or surpass that of the music they played. In contrast, those players

[9] See chapter 7, pp. 238–40.

[10] Most ridiculous, it seems to me, are "authentic" performances of Mozart et al. advertised as being given on period instruments, with candlelit performers in eighteenth-century dress. The actual programs, and their venues, are for the most part distinctly modern. Performing on modern instruments in modern dress would, for us, more closely replicate the original impact of such events on an eighteenth-century audience.

[11] This was more than just a trick of iconography. It struck even people such as Moscheles who had known Beethoven. See C. Moscheles, *Life of Moscheles*, 2:252.

[12] Antony Beaumont commented, "Some accounts of his recitals read more like descriptions of séances." Beaumont, *Busoni the Composer*, 307. Busoni himself believed that "the entrance to a concert-hall must promise the most extraordinary experience, and lead completely from mundane daily life into the essence of things." Busoni, *Wesen und Einheit*, 222.

who built their reputation on a more sober rendition of the music they admired had little "added value" to offer that would compete with the excitement of the larger-than-life figures. Moscheles and Hallé may have been fine pianists, but they failed to become names to conjure with in the piano world. "The great tradition of strict fidelity to the score" remains a phrase rarely heard. Of the more sober school, only Clara Schumann achieved a celebrity as a performer that could match that of the more flamboyant virtuosi, helped by the fact that the colorful, almost cinematic story of her own life—child prodigy under the thumb of tyrannical father, struggle for marriage with Robert Schumann, Schumann's madness and death—gave her image the enticing superficial sheen that she deliberately avoided in her playing. It was natural, then, that when the movies finally arrived, a rather bizarre version of the Schumann story should appear as *Song of Love* (1947). Here an unlikely Katharine Hepburn as Clara Wieck makes her concerto debut in the 1830s with—of all things—the First Piano Concerto (premiered in 1855) by the very same Franz Liszt whose music the real Clara came to despise.

The idea of a golden age of pianism, which implicitly treats the performers of the time as musical heroes, sometimes underestimates the extramusical glamour of their personalities. The individualism of their performances is certainly recognized, but it is assumed to arise from (or at least go hand in hand with) genuine "musical" or technical superiority. We accordingly abominate the dull routines of much music making today, the naked commercialism of modern marketing, and the frequent emphasis on peripheral advertising gimmicks (is the performer a young prodigy? a recent competition winner? pretty? battling with insanity? all of the above?). But things were always thus.

For all his astonishing musical talent, Liszt achieved his remarkable impact partly through his striking physical appearance, not forgetting the fascination, even scandal, of his very public private life. If Liszt were to perform behind a curtain, said Schumann, much of the poetry of his playing would be lost.[13] Substitute "on a recording" for "behind a curtain" and we might wonder whether Liszt's visually flamboyant style (unlike that of the unostentatious Thalberg) would suit us today. Those jealous of Paderewski's early successes attributed it largely to female admiration for his hair and the ludicrously inflated publicity that eventually succeeded in enthroning the phrase "He's no Paderewski" as a common byword for a pianist of modest abilities. ("Paderewski plays well enough," quipped Rosenthal, "but he's no Paderewski.") Pachmann openly admitted that one of the reasons he kept on talking to audiences during his performances was

---

[13] R. Schumann, 1:146.

that some people liked to hear the talking more than the playing. This is not to deny the talents of the famed players of the past, but simply to point out that some of their success can be attributed to reasons that are less than exclusively musical. It is so today, and was so even more so then, when all music was live music, and hearing an artist demanded his hopefully charismatic physical presence.

Despite the furor surrounding their performances, it is highly unlikely that Liszt, Rubinstein, and their immediate successors were members of some unique pianistic species whose musical achievements must forever remain unmatched by subsequent generations. In a 1924 interview for *Etude* magazine titled "If Franz Liszt Should Come Back Again," Moriz Rosenthal commented:

> Liszt, if he lived today, would probably be the greatest of living pianists. His powers and genius would make him that. But the Liszt that I heard, in 1876 and thereafter . . . has been surely equaled, if not surpassed, in technic and tone by several pianists of the present. If Liszt were living now, he, with his broad grasp, would be among the first to recognise this; and he would immediately set about to place himself at the top.[14]

Liszt, in other words, would have been able to match himself to the requirements of any age he found himself in—even the age of recordings. But it would have implicitly required modifications to his style and, in his later years, perhaps a bit more practice.

The stylistic markers of romantic pianism that have been touched on in previous chapter would no doubt be evident in Liszt's playing were he to come back again. Some of these were notated in conscientious detail by Percy Grainger in scores such as *Rosenkavalier Ramble* or *Colonial Song*, where the layered voicings and minute changes of tempo reach a complexity unlikely to be scrupulously observed in performance.[15] Grainger himself did not come anywhere near their exact realization in his own recordings of *Rosenkavalier Ramble*, though he did produce performances of pellucid flexibility. Paderewski, on the other hand, actually played in the style notated by Grainger, but this was hardly reflected at all in his own scores. Compare, for instance, his wonderfully poetic recordings of his own Nocturne in B♭ with the prosaic published edition. Here the letter of the score is more than usually deceptive.

---

[14] Rosenthal, "If Franz Liszt Should Come Back Again," 223. It is likely that the title and general thrust of this interview, with its almost messianic overtones (or, for Scots, its covert allusion to a famous song about Bonnie Prince Charlie: "Will ye no come back again? Better loved ye canna be . . .") was devised by the editor/interviewer rather than Rosenthal.

[15] See exx. 4.12 and 5.11 for these aspects of Grainger's scores.

Occasionally we seem to hear a living romanticism not only in early recordings, but in more recent discs, like the extraordinary CDs of the elderly
eccentric Ervin Nyiregyházi (1903–1987), which sound like a throwback to an
earlier, more willful era.[16] It is Nyiregyházi's distinctive hands, incidentally, we
occasionally see standing in for Liszt's in *Song of Love*,[17] and for Chopin's in *A Song
to Remember*, though his performances did not feature on the sound tracks. The
hands, but not their owner, became famous. Although his recordings will hardly
be to everyone's taste (which is part of the point), they do retain much of the
emotionally generous pre–First World War style in which the child prodigy
Nyiregyházi was trained, with a large palette of color, sporadic emphases on
inner voices, extreme fluctuations of tempo, and a heedlessness of wrong notes.
The overall impression—whether one likes the playing or not—is spontaneity,
something that is often lost with modern performers who are all too worried
about control and accuracy.

## Tracing the Traditions

Our age often demands pianistic cleanliness and fidelity to the score; previous
ages seemed less concerned with both. Yet many of the adaptations to the score
routinely made by pianists of the past were actually designed to enhance security
in live performance, even if a few wrong notes here and there would hardly
matter. Retakes, after all, are not advisable in front of an audience, although Liszt
did occasionally—and histrionically—repeat an item when he felt he could do
better a second time.[18] The irascible Bülow, on the other hand, had been known
to throw the piano stool at the audience and storm off stage when a piece went
badly.[19] Some influential players also had the security of performing on their
own specially customized pianos—Paderewski with his hardened-hammer
Érards or light-actioned Steinways, Horowitz with his uniquely voiced instrument, or Hofmann with his narrower keyboard suitable for small hands. In
adapting the music to their own technique and instruments, performers such as
these were able to display themselves at their absolute best. For the vast majority

[16] I am grateful to Jonathan Bellman for introducing me to these remarkable recordings.
Nyiregyházi divided opinion even in his younger days: some believed him grippingly inspired,
others merely a willful eccentric.
[17] Not for Clara Schumann's: they were presumably considered too obviously masculine.
[18] See chapter 2, p. 90.
[19] Haas, 21.

of artists forced to play on standard instruments, the increasing action weight and deeper fall of key made several passages that were a tough enough task in the first half of the nineteenth century next to impossible by the end of the second without some judicious rewriting or modifications of tempo. Changing performance traditions, after all, are not just a matter of changing tastes, but are decisively influenced by developments in instrument manufacture.

I have already traced in earlier chapters some traditions that seem to represent a late-romantic fondness for programmatic interpretations—Anton Rubinstein's highly influential approach to Chopin's Funeral March, for instance. There is no doubt that audiences in the few decades after Rubinstein's death were almost as likely to hear the piece played in this manner as to hear a straightforward rendition of Chopin's score, although there was no essentially pianistic reason—apart, perhaps, from the tempting volume of tone allowed by the cast-iron-framed piano—to perform it à la Rubinstein rather than à la Chopin. With a piece like Schubert's *Wanderer* Fantasy, or the Liszt transcription of Schubert's "Erlkönig," however, the heavier keyboard made already severe difficulties formidable indeed. The notoriously awkward sixteenth-note octaves in the first movement of the fantasy are simply rewritten as much more practical triplets in Liszt's version,[20] but the perennial problems in "Erlkönig" are not so easily solved. In some respects, Liszt's vivid transcription is ironically a little less tiring than the original, because the greater variety of texture ensures that the player at least gets sporadic respite from the purgatorial repeated octaves. Nevertheless, most players are forced to redistribute certain passages between the hands in order to ease the strain on the right wrist while maintaining the desired speed and fire, and there is no doubt that a degree of overt virtuosity and sheer volume is required in the transcription that would be out of place in as accompaniment to a singer. Even Sviatoslav Richter found it a tough nut to crack: "In *Erlkönig*, Schubert's original accompaniment is already taxing enough, but in Liszt's version the difficulties are practically insurmountable. I've always been afraid of it, even if I sometimes emerged from performances unscathed, so I didn't risk it for long. Technical difficulties of this order are harmful to your health."[21]

---

[20] These octaves, only slightly more approachable on a piano of Schubert's era, seem to represent a technical miscalculation on Schubert's part rather than a deliberate attempt to extend the boundaries of virtuosity. An almost exactly identical miscalculation can be found in Elgar's *Concert Allegro*, where the sixteenth-note octaves in the left hand that suddenly appear in the second half of the piece are largely impractical in the fairly vigorous tempo the music otherwise seems to demand. Neither Schubert nor Elgar, of course, could have claimed to be expert pianists.

[21] Monsaingeon, 114.

Liszt's lavishly spread chords in the B♭-major section are particularly treacherous in live performance on a modern piano without either a little adaptation, or
what might in some quarters be regarded as an inadvisably exaggerated slowing
down:[22]

EXAMPLE 8.1.  Franz Schubert–Franz Liszt, "Erlkönig," excerpt

The tempo needs to be relaxed here even on the lighter pianos of Liszt's era,
and to some extent the keyboard writing assumes such a strategy, as does the
"tranquillo" marking a few bars earlier. Liszt's original fingering, repeating the
fifth finger of the right hand for the suave triplet in the middle of the passage,

---

[22] At a recital I recently attended, I was curious to hear how a certain pianist—who will
remain anonymous—allegedly famed for his technique, would deal with the elaborate arpeggios.
When the eagerly anticipated moment came, he simply cut the arpeggios out entirely: what we
heard were straightforward block chords spanning an octave. As the cliché goes, for this player
difficulties really didn't exist.

indeed hints at a much slower tempo, while the luxuriant arpeggiation at the final cadence of the section implies a hefty rallentando. The problems arise when we wish to maintain a more consistently fast tempo throughout the entire piece, as many later players did, and as most modern performers seem to consider essential. We can hear a changing interpretative approach to this piece in the 1903 and 1916 recordings by Josef Hofmann.[23] The earlier rendition has only a slightly longer overall timing than the later—four minutes and fifty-five seconds as against four minutes and thirty-one seconds—but this small difference hides the much greater amount of tempo flexibility in the 1903 recording. Hofmann in 1903 radically slowed down the B♭ section and other passages compared to his procedure in the 1916 disc, which maintains a much greater uniformity of tempo. I am not trying to claim that Hofmann consciously incarnated twentieth-century performing trends—he may well just have felt like playing the piece a bit differently in 1916. Perhaps a third recording would have been different again. Even his 1916 recording hardly shows the modern striving to make any tempo changes as unobtrusive as possible, for such an unbending approach renders the extended arpeggios a challenge indeed. The Herculean technician Busoni was no doubt as happy as Hofmann to modify a tempo when it suited him, but he nevertheless found it safer radically to rewrite the B♭ passage for his own performances (adding the characteristic rubric "visionario").[24] Most present-day solutions to the technical problems here are akin to his—a pruning of the arpeggios, rather than a very noticeable deceleration:

EXAMPLE 8.2. Franz Schubert–Ferruccio Busoni, "Erlkönig," excerpt

[23] VAI/IPA 1036-2.

[24] Busoni's version can be found in his *Klavierübung* (discussed in more detail later on in the chapter), 2nd ed., book 2, extract f: "nach Schubert."

EXAMPLE 8.2. (*continued*)

It happens to be just this section that is so often lauded by scholars as demonstrating Liszt's unerring sensitivity to characterization in this transcription. One cannot help wondering how many of them have ever tried playing it in public.

The later "traditions," then, of performing the "Erlkönig" transcription partly include strategies for the alleviation of those difficulties that became greater and greater as piano actions became heavier, and as a fondness for a consistently fast speed increasingly held sway. It is highly probable that this trend does not reflect Liszt's own performances. Not only did he have a lighter piano, but the performance practices of the era would scarcely have prevented him from decelerating the Bb-section considerably, as Hofmann did in 1903 and as the score implies. He could even have cut the Gordian knot clean through by playing the whole piece rather more slowly. Suggestively, Moriz Rosenthal claimed in 1924 that Liszt had been accustomed to perform his virtuoso works at a more moderate speed than was coming into fashion by the late nineteenth century. He would be "astonished at the tempo that certain of his compositions are ordinarily played in our concert halls." At any rate, he had "marveled" in the 1880s at Rosenthal's speedy delivery of the Champagne Aria from *Réminiscences de Don Juan*.[25] Ro-

[25] Rosenthal, "If Franz Liszt Should Come Back Again," 223.

senthal's edition of this piece for Ullstein Verlag (1925) in fact shows some of the rewriting of chordal figuration and ornaments that made such a speed possible.

Rosenthal's remarks are not unsupported and do not appear to apply simply to Liszt in his less vigorous old age. At the turn of the century, William Mason devoted several pages of his reminiscences to tell his readers that current tempos in rapid movements—especially in Chopin "and, in fact, in all composers not of the extreme modern type"—were considerably quicker than those he had heard from Liszt, Dreyschock, and others in the 1840s and 1850s, when these players were in their prime.[26] In Mason's opinion, these tempos were not just quicker, but simply "too fast," and he also deplored the beginning of a concomitant tendency to play slow movements too slowly.[27] We have mentioned in the previous chapter that that Liszt's *Feux follets*, among other pieces, likely falls into the "speeded-up" category.[28] Even Arthur Friedheim's recording of this piece (1912) is on the swift side, despite his otherwise close identification with Liszt's interpretative style, clocking in at a slightly breathless three minutes and forty-four seconds.[29] I suspect that once a piece such as *Feux follets* became a race to the finish, few pianists were willing to court criticism of their technique by adopting Liszt's moderate, "sehr bequem" tempo, especially since a slower speed also exposes rather too painfully whether the player has made a few judicious simplifications to the double-note figuration.

Admittedly, it is very unlikely that the situation regarding speeding up and slowing down can be quite as simple as Mason makes out (how could it be?), even if his general assessment is correct, and even if the flexible attitudes to tempo modification in the nineteenth century are taken into account.[30] For instance, Chopin's original metronome marks for the Etudes opp. 10 and 25 are very much on the fast side, both in the quicker and the slower etudes. Such tempos are quite suitable for pianos of the 1830s but became increasingly problematic on heavier and more sonorous instruments of even twenty years later. We also do not know how usual it was to try to play the studies at these speeds, for it is probable that

---

[26] Mason, 243–47.

[27] Mason, 244–45.

[28] See chapter 7, p. 249. Compare with Leslie Howard's more leisurely four minutes and five seconds on Hyperion CDA66357. Howard certainly knows that Liszt did not intend this piece to go as fast as possible.

[29] On Pearl GEMM 9993. One could speculate whether Friedheim's tempo was in any way conditioned by worries over the limited record side length.

[30] See chapter 6, pp. 185–88.

the metronome markings were normally taken as merely very rough guides. In the preface to his intriguing Schirmer edition of the Chopin etudes, Arthur Friedheim claimed that Chopin's original metronome marks were largely based on Liszt's early performances. He does not give a source for this. It could represent what Liszt himself told him, or some "legend" (of which there are many in the piano world). At any rate, the new metronome markings Friedheim supplies are mostly rather slower than Chopin's originals (for instance, op. 10 no. 1 is marked at quarter note = 144, as opposed to Chopin's 176) and were derived—according to Friedheim's preface—from the elderly Liszt's performance practice. Friedheim additionally mentions that he heard Anton Rubinstein play many of the works in question and implies that the slower metronomizations also accord with his approach.

The less hectic speeds broadly fit the heavier action weight and expansive sound of later pianos in the more lively etudes and have a relatively neutral effect on the works' character. But the same treatment tends to change radically the atmosphere of the slower ones. For the famous op. 10 no. 3, Chopin appears to have intended a fairly flowing two beats to the bar tempo (he had initially written "vivace ma non troppo" in the manuscript, only to score it out and replace it with "allegretto"). Many later performances intoned the outer sections of this piece in an intensely elegiac slow four beats to the bar (which necessitates, incidentally, a conspicuous increase in speed for the middle section, rather than Chopin's subtler "poco piu mosso"). We frequently hear this languid–lively–languid style of interpretation on recordings—from Wilhelm Backhaus in the 1920s to Earl Wild in the 1980s.

The tradition seems to have started fairly early. Carl Lachmund tells us that in the 1880s, Liszt was recommending a slow speed for op. 10 no. 3 and "was sarcastic with a young lady who started . . . too rapidly."[31] She may well have just been observing the score. By the time Lachmund himself came to play the work for Liszt, he had taken the earlier advice a bit too much to heart, and was now upbraided for being too slow.[32] Nevertheless, in 1884 Liszt told his students explicitly that the printed metronome mark for this piece was "completely wrong" and proceeded to play it himself "very slowly and broadly" while singing along at the same time.[33] The image of this etude as a langourous elegy was further reinforced in the middle of the twentieth century by the popular song

[31] Walker, *Living with Liszt*, 159. The original metronome marking is eighth-note = 100.
[32] Walker, *Living with Liszt*, 232.
[33] Zimdars, *Masterclasses of Liszt*, 58.

"So Deep Is the Night," an extremely lethargic and sentimentalized arrangement of the etude's main melody sung to great acclaim by the tenor Richard Tauber. The result of all this accumulated tradition is that present-day auditors (especially older ones who remember the song) can be slightly nonplussed to hear a genuinely allegretto performance of the etude close to Chopin's metronome mark.[34] We can perhaps expect this reaction to continue, because yet another rendition of "So Deep Is the Night" has recently (2003) been released by the popular soprano Lesley Garrett.[35]

Tracing of performance traditions may therefore not always get us closer to the composer's own interpretation, but at the very least it illuminates what the piece has turned into after decades of performance. And it may be the heretical later style of interpretation that we prefer. "I see with approval the better course, and choose to follow the worse one," as Ovid, with uncommon self-awareness, declared.[36] Just because Chopin probably envisioned a fairly flowing op. 10 no. 3 or Liszt recommended a gentle *Feux follets* does not mean that other approaches are not possible or effective. For players who adopt a consistently fast tempo in *Feux follets* or in "Erlkönig," it is useful to know that some solutions to the resultant technical problems have already been sought out by the virtuosi of the past; for players who wish to understand how the tempo relationships were originally envisaged by the composer in op. 10 no. 3, it is useful to have an urtext edition.[37] Both traditions and source studies have their role to play.

Practicing a piece for public performance does automatically give sudden insights into traditional technical solutions and why certain passages were so

[34] Tauber was, of course, not the only singer to showcase "So Deep Is the Night." It turns up, for example, in the film *Demobbed* (1944), sung by Anne Ziegler and Webster Booth. (This movie also features the wonderfully named "Felix Mendelssohn and His Hawaiian Serenaders": he really was multitalented, that Mendelssohn.) I have rarely played the Chopin op. 10 etudes in concert without someone asking me after the performance why I took op. 10 no. 3 "so quickly." This is despite the fact that I think my playing of it is getting slower with the years: my performance too is gradually beginning to turn into four to the bar.

[35] On EMI Classics.

[36] "Video meliora proboque, deteriora sequor." Ovid, *Metamorphoses* VII, 20.

[37] A little more attention to the practicality—or lack of it—of some extreme textures in the piano repertoire might also benefit scholars who extol the brilliance of certain passages that are either simply unplayable at common modern tempi as they stand or not entirely effective. Liszt's revisions to his transcription of Berlioz's "March to the Scaffold" (from the *Symphonie fantastique*) are instructive in this regard. Some clear-sighted comments on the mind-boggling impracticality of the odd bar or two in Alkan's works can be found in Hugh Macdonald, "La voix de l'instrument," in Brigitte Françoise Sappey, ed., *Charles Valentin Alkan* (Paris: Fayard, 1991), 129–40.

often modified in the recordings of even the finest players before the era of routine editing. Liszt's Second Hungarian Rhapsody is a case in point. At one time seemingly in the repertoire of almost every virtuoso, there can be few works that were so extensively rewritten (an astonished Busoni once heard a performance of it in 1915 from a hotel orchestra in Chicago with the cadenza from the Grieg Piano Concerto interpolated in the middle).[38] Composed as it was in 1847, shortly before Liszt's official cessation of his concert tours, the rhapsody (as printed at least) never featured in his own regular repertoire—a rather important point, for he was in the habit of revising and tidying up technically problematic passages of works he played frequently, customarily issuing the fruits of his experience as a second—or even third or fourth—edition. (Indeed, the fact that he subjected his oft-played "Erlkönig" transcription to only very minor revisions—there are three slightly different versions—is one of the signs that he found it practical in his own tempos as it stood.) Although some "Hungarian style" variants for the rhapsody were given in the *Liszt-Pädagogium* and two alternative cadenzas suggested (all largely ignored by subsequent performers), no advice is found on how to tackle the specifically pianistic problems of the piece. Judging from early recordings, one passage in particular was found to be all too tricky:

EXAMPLE 8.3. Franz Liszt, Hungarian Rhapsody no. 2, excerpt

[38] Beaumont, *Busoni: Selected Letters*, 195.

At this climactic moment, combining accuracy in the widely leaping left hand with suitably swift scales in the right is a tough problem indeed. Pianists playing the text as written often either strike the odd false note in the bass or simply take a moderate tempo. Yet the passage absolutely demands a hectic, heedless panache. Accordingly the left hand was somewhat simplified by Josef Hofmann on his two recordings (1922 and 1923), although Liszt's basic texture was retained.[39] Moriz Rosenthal undertook a more radical revision for his disk, made in 1929–30.[40] Noticing that it was easy enough to use the chromatic tag-end of one of the other themes as a (pianistically much less dangerous) bass for the right-hand scales, he replaced the leaping bass with thunderous, but thankfully more secure, octaves. Finally, Horowitz adopted a more percussive variant of Rosenthal's approach in his celebrated rewriting of the "Friska" section:

EXAMPLE 8.4. Franz Liszt–Vladimir Horowitz, Hungarian Rhapsody no. 2, excerpt

It is important to note here that these rewritings make a stunning effect, seem more complicated (especially given the thematic combination), but are paradoxically easier to play accurately. The same holds true for much of Horowitz's brilliant recomposition, which is a lot less tiring for the wrists than Liszt's original, though certainly trickier in some other ways. Predictably, Horowitz multiplied figuration that suited his technique (he was particularly adept at bringing out inner voices) and rewrote passages that didn't (his wrists and arms tended to stiffen up rather quickly).[41] There is no reason to think that Liszt

[39] VAI/IPA 1047. Only one of Hofmann's recordings is more or less complete. The other is a radically abridged version designed to fit on one side of a 78-rpm disc. He nevertheless plays the passage under discussion in both performances. We can also hear Jorge Bolet simplifying the left-hand writing of the Rhapsody on the soundtrack of the Liszt biopic *Song without End*.

[40] Pearl GEMM CD9963. This does not, interestingly enough, feature in his edition of the piece. Here not the passage in question but the subsequent few bars were the subject of his rewriting.

[41] See Horowitz, 90.

would have disapproved (though he may have raised an eyebrow at some of Horowitz's Godowskian harmonies). A few of Horowitz's other revisions are obviously derived from d'Albert's cadenza (it includes another amusingly slick thematic combination), with which Liszt was greatly pleased when he heard its author's dashing performance.

Many such performance traditions have retained a current place in virtuoso music, albeit oft unacknowledged. For instance, Marc-André Hamelin's exciting recording of Liszt's *Réminiscences de Don Juan* appears to feature a handful of adaptations possibly derived from the Busoni version (1917) of the piece. Yet I could not find this mentioned anywhere in the accompanying booklet.[42] Busoni considered his edition "the first *instructive* edition of Liszt, and hence [it] assumes the significance—for us pianists—of the 'classicalisation' of Liszt's pianistic style."[43] Inevitably, it closely reflects Busoni's own manner of performing the work: among other features, figuration is redistributed or reinforced for ease of execution, variant passages are borrowed from the two-piano version of the piece,[44] and the entire second variation of "Là ci darem la mano" is cut, rendering the whole significantly shorter.[45] It is a thought-provoking adaptation that is certainly easier to play on a modern instrument, allows faster tempos in places (the sort of tempo that, according to Rosenthal, astonished Liszt), and intensifies the bravura dazzle of the original. "Technical achievement," Busoni writes in the preface, "is nothing other than the adaptation of any given difficulty to one's own capabilities." There are no universal answers, but there are undeniably more or less stimulating ones.

Busoni remains among the most intelligent and imaginative of all contributors to traditions of late-romantic performance and has been oft quoted in this book.

[42] On Hyperion. This also has gone unremarked in the reviews of the recording that I have come across. Hamelin may have taken his cue from Busoni in the rewriting of some of the passages involving double thirds toward the middle of the piece. He does not seem to follow Busoni's suggestions in other respects, as far as I can hear. Hamelin is one of the pianists who give the lie to any idea that players today are necessary inferior to those of some earlier golden age, combining as he does a remarkable range of tone color with an inquisitive musical intelligence. His Alkan recordings, especially, are quite breathtaking.

[43] Beaumont, *Busoni: Selected Letters*, 263.

[44] Whether Busoni knew it or not, Liszt suggested to Sophie Menter that she use one of the same variants from the two-piano version when performing *Réminiscences de Don Juan*. He wrote this variant out for her in an unpublished manuscript now in the Library of Congress, which also contains alterations intended for the sixth *Soirée de Vienne*. The Tarantella from *La muette* was also rewritten for Menter's use.

[45] This omission puzzled Rosenthal, who argued strongly against it in his own edition of the piece.

His approach is also one of the best-documented, for he took pains to pro-
mulgate it in printed form, either in editions such as those of Bach or Liszt, or in
his remarkable *Klavierübung*, a collection (or rather, two different collections) of
arrangements, exercises, and variants assembled toward the end of his life that
enshrine his personal brand of pianism.

The *Klavierübung* has received disappointingly little attention. Not only has it
never been reprinted, but it has suffered mightily, like Busoni's editions, from the
present orthodoxy that any performance suggestions not ultimately derived from
the appropriate composer are of scant interest. The first edition appeared between 1918 and 1922; the second, somewhat expanded version was among the
last projects Busoni worked upon and was published in 1925, just after his
death.[46] Busoni had originally intended a pianistic magnum opus of general
validity but came to realize the impossibility of such an aim.[47] Nevertheless his
individual approach to common pianistic problems is always fascinating. It is
here that we find, along with his version of some Cramer studies and the Liszt
*Paganini Studies*, his rewritten B♭-major passage from the "Erlkönig" transcription
(see ex. 8.2), a redistributed version of the fairies' music from the Mendelssohn-
Liszt *Midsummer Night's Dream* arrangement, and short studies based on the Auber-
Liszt *La muette* Tarantella, the first version of the Liszt *Venezia and Napoli*, and the
Schubert-Liszt "Auf dem Wasser zu singen" (the same tricky passage that Josef
von Slivinski failed to play to Shaw's satisfaction in the 1890s).[48] Busoni's own
transcriptions of the Barcarolle from Offenbach's *Tales of Hoffmann* and the
Serenade from Mozart's *Don Giovanni* form pleasant oases among the exercises
based on scales, arpeggios, and trills. The whole compendium is astonishingly
inventive and stimulating—thought-provoking even when we do not wish to
follow its advice, or when we simply find that Busoni's facilitation seems more
awkward than the original (technique being, as he acknowledged, a personal
matter).

But not even the *Klavierübung*, the editions, and the recordings exhaust Busoni's
contribution to the art of the piano. We find intriguing suggestions in his letters
that never found their way into any score (a rewriting of the climax of the Liszt
"Mazeppa" study, for instance).[49] Penciled annotations in his own performing
copies (now in the Busoni Nachlass of the Berlin Staatsbibliothek) would allow

---

[46] A detailed summary of the contents of both editions can be found in Larry Sitsky, *Busoni and the
Piano: The Works, the Writings, and the Recordings* (Westport, Conn.: Greenwood Press, 1986), 163–73.

[47] Beaumont, *Busoni: Selected Letters*, 272.

[48] See chapter 6, p. 186.

[49] Beaumont, *Busoni: Selected Letters*, 160. This includes a music example.

us, among other things, to reconstruct his version of the complete Auber-Liszt Tarantella from *La muette*,[50] or make a revised edition of his superb transcription of Liszt's *Fantasy and Fugue on "Ad nos."*[51]

Finally, the manuscripts of his 1909 "concert interpretation" (*Konzertmässige Interpretation*) of Schoenberg's *Klavierstück* op. 11 no. 2 would form a fascinating study in themselves, peppered as one of them is with Schoenberg's own anguished criticisms in a tiny, crabbed hand that contrasts markedly with Busoni's elegant, commanding script.[52] The difference between their handwriting mirrors their musical divergence. Busoni had made Schoenberg's textures more pianistic, had "expanded the excessively laconic moments to enable the listener *to assimilate them*, and to make the instrument sound well."[53] Schoenberg was fearful of the consequences of this interference and argued against its validity, partly because transcribing his piano piece for the piano, so to speak, implied vast deficiencies in his command of keyboard writing, even ineptitude. He pleaded, if the piece were to be published, that Busoni "at least *once* give the original version" of his motifs before varying them,[54] and he was especially skeptical about the recomposition of the last few bars (see exx. 8.5 and 8.6): "I also find regrettable the repetitions at the end. My piece does not end, it only stops, and one would like to give the idea with this that it really still carries on."[55]

EXAMPLE 8.5. Arnold Schoenberg, *Klavierstück* op. 11 no. 2, conclusion

[50] Staatsbibliothek zu Berlin, N.Mus Nachlass 4, 88.

[51] Staatsbibliothek zu Berlin, N.Mus Nachlass 4, 366.

[52] Staatsbibliothek zu Berlin, N.Mus Nachlass 4, 243 and 244. The correspondence between Schoenberg and Busoni that relates to these manuscripts can be found in Beaumont, *Busoni: Selected Letters*.

[53] Beaumont, *Busoni: Selected Letters*, 401.

[54] N.Mus Nachlass 4, 243, p. 1, m. 7: "wenigstens *einmal* das Original."

[55] N.Mus. Nachlass 4, 243, p. 6: "Auch die Wiederholungen an Schluss finde ich bedauerlich. Mein Stück schliesst nicht, es hört nur auf; man möchte die Vorstellung geben, dass es eigentlich noch lange weiter geht."

EXAMPLE 8.6. Arnold Schoenberg–Ferruccio Busoni, *Klavierstück* op. 11 no. 2, conclusion

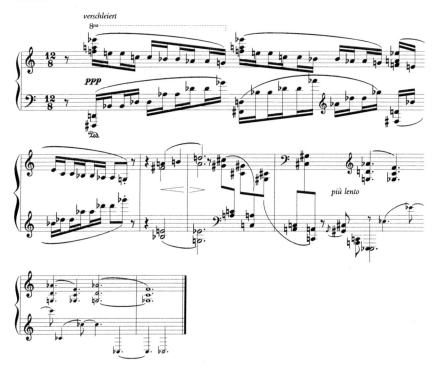

But audiences, as Busoni well knew, prefer more obvious punctuation. They
are more comfortable with endings that sound like endings. Liszt even told his
students to add definitive conclusions to a few of his late epigrammatic pieces if
playing them in public.[56] For him, as for Busoni, indecision did not belong on the
concert stage. Busoni's version of Schoenberg does indeed seem more transparent,
more easily comprehensible. It certainly sits better under the fingers. But in
making his alterations, Busoni shifted the work decisively toward his own aesthetic, and the more he did so, the less Schoenberg liked it. Busoni had the
pianist's typical concern for effectiveness in live performance, for variety of
keyboard texture, and for ease of execution. As Paderewski said in a similar
context, "It is not a question of what is written, but what the musical effect should
be."[57] In the Schoenberg-Busoni *Klavierstück*, romantic pianism clashed vividly

[56] Zimdars, *Liszt Masterclasses*, 87.
[57] Bauer, 272. Paderewski was rehearsing a Brahms trio when he made this remark.

and articulately with the standard-bearer of musical modernism; the egotism of the performer with that of the composer. To acclaim an outright winner would be invidious. It is all, as so often, a matter of taste.

## Codetta

Should we wish to, we could trace the multifarious performance history of most standard piano pieces by means of their editions and recordings, not in order to revive the chimera of a single great tradition, but to document many traditions and their development. Such exercises have sometimes been undertaken, but usually the purpose is to show how later scores or performances have diverged from a supposedly pristine original conception, for the restoration of which we should all be striving. Each piece, in this view, had its own golden age, which became tarnished with time. Few would wish to return to an era when it was normally next to impossible to tell which parts of a score were written by the editor and which by the composer. Nowadays we need not try to grasp Beethoven's meaning while being verbally bullied by Bülow, or Bach's while being harangued by Busoni. But we could, while not denying the indispensable value of the urtext back-to-basics approach, also embrace a tolerant position and treat the later performance history of music as offering viable options to present and future players, rather than simply constituting a sad catalog of corruption. This would refocus some attention on those fascinating old editions by great performers now treated in scholarly quarters with embarrassment or derision. We can be thankful that they are now not the only options available, while acknowledging that they also have much to offer.

A more liberal attitude would additionally give a wider choice of acceptable cadenzas for those performers who remain resistant to improvising their own.[58] Cadenzas by Clara Schumann and Busoni to Mozart's concertos, for instance, or by Liszt and Brahms to Beethoven's might be performed without having to read routine bleatings about "stylistic discrepancies." Can we not forget our recently acquired porcelain sensitivity to such discrepancies long enough to enjoy the skill and imagination of the offending interpolations in their own right? Does such a fertile and febrile—if gloriously preposterous—offering as Alkan's gargantuan

---

[58] "Self-reliant artists have no need for cadenzas," said Moscheles. C. Moscheles, *Life of Moscheles*, 2:249. He himself only published cadenzas to help those who were unable to write their own.

cadenza to Beethoven's Third Concerto (at the climax of which the main theme of the first movement is transformed into the finale theme from the Fifth Symphony) deserve to be considered an unspeakable solecism because it does not fit standards of taste that Alkan would not have recognized?[59] A cadenza of this fashion takes on the characteristics of a musical panorama, joining together originally separate pieces in a new idiom, just like Bülow's preludes derived from other works by the same composer.[60] The juxtaposition certainly can be jarring, but this in itself can be uniquely illuminating, like the modernistic pyramid in front of the Louvre.

The fundamental question might be: is the composer's voice the only one worth listening to when devising performance approaches? Should Busoni's ingeniously thrilling, if totally un-Chopinesque, rewriting of the A♭ Polonaise or Liszt's updated *Wanderer* Fantasy be quietly buried as impure aberrations of performance history, or should the ideas they enshrine be treated as acceptable options for modern performers? We surely have a lot to gain from adopting a more liberal attitude to our performance traditions—from taking seriously what players fashioned from the repertoire as well as what its composers envisaged— just as we have from loosening concert etiquette with entertainment as much as education in mind. Traditions, great or merely different, tell us not just about the potentialities in the music, but about the limitations of our own taste. Let us not treat them like embarrassingly garrulous elderly relatives, to be shunted off to the old-folks' home of anachronistic attitudes by the forward march of musicology.

[59] Taking his cue from Alkan, Busoni included part of the fugato from the last movement of Mozart's *Jupiter* Symphony in his cadenza (1922) for the concerto K. 503, and themes from the Symphony no. 41 in G Minor in that for the concerto K. 491. See also Beaumont, *Busoni: Selected Letters*, 352.

[60] See chapter 4, p. 107.

# Bibliography

Anderson, Emily, trans. and ed. *The Letters of Beethoven.* 3 vols. London: Macmillan, 1961.
———, trans. and ed. *The Letters of Mozart and His Family.* 3 vols. London: Macmillan, 1938.
Avery, Peter, and John Heath-Stubbs, trans. *The Rubáiyat of Omar Khayyam.* London: Penguin, 1981.
Avins, Styra. "Performing Brahms's Music: Clues from His Letters." In Michael Musgrave and Bernard D. Sherman, eds., *Performing Brahms: Early Evidence of Performance Style,* pp. 11–47. Cambridge: Cambridge University Press, 2003.
Bache, Constance. *Brother Musicians: Reminiscences of Edward and Walter Bache.* London: Methuen, 1901.
Banowetz, Joseph. *The Pianist's Guide to Pedaling.* Bloomington: Indiana University Press, 1985.
———, ed. *The Art of Piano Pedaling: Two Classic Guides; Anton Rubinstein and Teresa Carreño.* Mineola, N.Y.: Dover, 2003.
Barber, Charles. *Lost in the Stars: The Forgotten Musical Life of Alexander Siloti.* Lanham, Md.: Scarecrow Press, 2002.
Barth, George. *The Pianist as Orator: Beethoven and the Transformation of Keyboard Style.* Ithaca, N.Y.: Cornell University Press, 1992.
Bates, Nellie R. Cameron. "A Country Girl at a Paderewski Concert." *Musician* 19 (February 1914): 125–26.
Bauer, Harold. *His Book.* New York: Norton, 1948.
Beaumont, Antony. *Busoni the Composer.* Bloomington: Indiana University Press, 1985.
———, trans. and ed. *Ferruccio Busoni: Selected Letters.* New York: Columbia University Press, 1987.
Beirao, Christine Weismann. *Ferruccio Busoni–Jose Vianna da Motta: Briefwechsel, 1898 bis 1921.* Wilhelmshaven: Florian Noetzel Verlag, 2004.
Bellman, Jonathan. "Chopin and the Cantabile Style in Historical Performance." *Historical Performance,* no. 2 (Winter 1989): 63–71.
———. "Chopin and His Imitators: Notated Emulations of the 'True Style' of Performance." *Nineteenth Century Music* 24, no. 2 (Fall 2000): 149–60.
———. "Improvised Ornamentation in Chopin's Paris." *Early Keyboard Studies Newsletter* 8, no. 2 (April 1994): 1–7.

————. "Toward a Well-Tempered Chopin." In Artur Szklener, ed., *Chopin in Performance: History, Theory, Practice*, pp. 25–38. Warsaw: Narodowy Instytut Fryderyka Chopina, 2005.

Bird, John. *Percy Grainger*. 1st ed., London: Paul Elek, 1976; 2nd ed., New York: Oxford University Press, 1999.

Brée, Malvine. *Die Grundlage der Methode Leschetizky, mit Autorisation des Meisters herausgegeben von seiner Assistentin*. Mainz: Schott, 1903.

Brown, Clive. *Classical and Romantic Performing Practice*. Oxford: Clarendon Press, 1999.

————. *A Portrait of Mendelssohn*. New Haven, Conn.: Yale University Press, 2003.

Brown, Howard Mayer. "Performing Practice." In Stanley Sadie, ed., *The New Grove Dictionary of Music and Musicians*, 14:370–93. London: Macmillan, 1980.

Bullock, Theodore, ed. *Remembering Franz Liszt: Including "My Memories of Liszt" by Alexander Siloti and "Life and Liszt" by Arthur Friedheim*. Introd. Mark N. Grant. New York: Limelight Editions, 1986.

Busoni, Ferruccio. *The Essence of Music*. Trans. Rosamond Ley. London: Rockliff, 1957.

————. *Wesen und Einheit der Musik*. Ed. Joachim Hermann. Berlin: Max Hesses Verlag, 1956.

————, ed. *The Well-Tempered Clavichord by Johann Sebastian Bach: Revised, Annotated, and Provided with Parallel Examples and Suggestions for the Study of Modern Pianoforte Technique*. New York: Schirmer, 1894.

Cai, Camilla. "Brahms's Pianos and the Performance of His Late Piano Works." *Performance Practice Review* 2, no. 1 (Spring 1989): 58–72.

Chantavoine, J., ed. *Franz Liszt: Pages romantiques*. Paris: Félix Alcan, 1912.

Chasins, Abram. *Speaking of Pianists*. New York: Knopf, 1961–62.

Chorley, Henry. *Modern German Music*. 2 vols. 1854; reprint, New York: Da Capo Press, 1973.

Christiani, Adolph Friedrich. *The Principles of Expression in Pianoforte Playing*. New York: Harper and Brothers, 1885.

Cooper, John Michael. "Felix Mendelssohn-Bartholdy, Ferdinand David, und Johann Sebastian Bach. Mendelssohns Bach-Auffassung im Spiegel der Wiederentdeckung der 'Chaconne.'" *Mendelssohn Studien: Beitrage zur neueren deutschen Kultur- und Wirtschaftsgeschichte* 10, pp. 157–79. Berlin: Duncker und Humblot, 1997.

Corri, P. A. *Original System of Preluding*. London: Chappell, [1813?].

Couling, Della. *Ferruccio Busoni: A Musical Ishmael*. Lanham, Md.: Scarecrow Press, 2005.

Czerny, Carl. *Complete Theoretical and Practical Pianoforte School, Op. 500*. 3 vols. London: Cocks, 1838.

————. *Complete Theoretical and Practical Pianoforte School, Op. 500: Supplement*. London: Cocks, 1846.

————. *A Systematic Introduction to Improvisation on the Pianoforte*. Trans. Alice Mitchell. New York: Longman, 1983.

————. *Beethoven, Über den richtigen Vortrag der saemmtlichen Werke für das Piano-allein*. Ed. Paul Badura-Skoda. Universal ed., Vienna: 1963.

Day, Timothy. *A Century of Recorded Music: Listening to Musical History*. New Haven, Conn.: Yale University Press, 2002.

Dent, Edward. *Ferruccio Busoni: A Biography*. London: Eulenberg, 1974.

Dubal, David. *Evenings with Horowitz*. Pompton Plains, N.J.: Amadeus Press, 2004.

Dürr, Walther. "Schubert and Johann Michael Vogl: A Reappraisal." *Nineteenth Century Music* 3, no. 2 (November 1979): 126–40.

Eigeldinger, Jean-Jacques. *Chopin: Pianist and Teacher*. Cambridge: Cambridge University Press, 1986.

———. "Chopin and 'La note bleue': An Interpretation of the Prelude, Op. 45." *Music and Letters* 78, issue 2 (May 1997): 233–53.

———. "Twenty-four Preludes, Op. 28: Genre, Structure, Significance." In Jim Samson, ed., *Chopin Studies*, pp. 167–93. Cambridge: Cambridge University Press, 1988.

Eigeldinger, Jean-Jacques, and Jean-Michel Nectoux, eds. *F. Chopin: Oeuvres pour piano; Facsimile de l'exemplaire de Jane W. Stirling*. Paris: Bibliothèque Nationale, 1982.

Ellis, Katharine. "Female Pianists and Their Male Critics in Nineteenth-Century Paris." *Journal of the American Musicological Society* 50, nos. 2–3 (Summer–Fall 1997): 353–85.

———. "Liszt: The Romantic Artist." In Kenneth Hamilton, ed., *The Cambridge Companion to Liszt*, pp. 1–13. Cambridge: Cambridge University Press, 2005.

Elvers, Rudolph, ed. *Mendelssohn Bartholdy Briefe*. Frankfurt: Fischer Verlag, 1984.

Fay, Amy. *Music Study in Germany*. London: Macmillan, 1893.

Ferguson, Howard. "Prelude." In Stanley Sadie, ed., *The New Grove Dictionary of Music and Musicians*, 15:210–12. London: Macmillan, 1980.

Ferris, David. "Public Performance and Private Understanding: Clara Wieck's Concerts in Berlin." *Journal of the American Musicological Society* 56, no. 2 (Summer 2003): 351–408.

Finscher, Ludwig, ed. *Die Musik in Geschichte und Gegenwart*. Sachteil 1. Kassel: Bärenreiter, 1994.

Fleishmann, Tilly. *Aspects of the Liszt Tradition*. Cork, 1986.

Forbes, Eliot, ed. *Thayer's Life of Beethoven*. 2 vols. Princeton, N.J.: Princeton University Press, 1964.

Friedheim, Arthur. "Life and Liszt." In *Remembering Franz Liszt: Including "My Memories of Liszt" by Alexander Siloti and "Life and Liszt" by Arthur Freidheim*, pp. 1–335. New York: Limelight Editions, 1986.

Gaisberg, Fred. *Music on Record*. London: Robert Hale, 1946.

Goehr, Lydia. *The Imaginary Museum of Musical Works: An Essay in the Philosophy of Music*. New York: Oxford University Press, 1992.

Goertzen, Valerie Woodring. "By Way of Introduction: Preluding by Eighteenth- and Early Nineteenth-Century Pianists." *Journal of Musicology* 14, no. 3 (Summer 1996): 299–337.

———. "Setting the Stage: Clara Schumann's Preludes." In Bruno Nettl, ed., *In the Course of Performance: Studies in the World of Musical Improvisation*. Chicago: University of Chicago Press, 1998.

Goldmark, Daniel. *Tunes for "Toons": Music and the Hollywood Cartoon*. Berkeley: University of California Press, 2005.

Göllerich, August. *Franz Liszt*. Berlin: Marquardt Verlag, 1908.

Good, Edwin. *Giraffes, Black Dragons and Other Pianos: A Technological History from Cristofori to the Modern Concert Grand*. Stanford: Stanford University Press, 2002.

Gooley, Dana. *The Virtuoso Liszt*. Cambridge: Cambridge University Press, 2004.

Grove, George. "Mendelssohn." In *Dictionary of Music and Musicians*, 1st ed., 2:253–310. London: Macmillan, 1882.

Gutknecht, Dieter. "Aufführungspraxis." In Ludwig Finscher, ed., *Die Musik in Geschichte und Gegenwart*, Sachteil 1, pp. 954–86. Kassel: Bärenreiter, 1994.

Haas, Frithjof. *Hans von Bülow: Leben und Wirken; Wegbereiter für Wagner, Liszt und Brahms*. Wilhelmshaven: Florian Noetzel Verlag, 2002.

Hallé, Charles. *Autobiography, with Correspondence and Diaries*, ed. Michael Kennedy. 1896. Reprint, London: Elek, 1972.

Hambourg, Mark. *The Eighth Octave*. London: Williams and Norgate, 1951.

———. *From Piano to Forte: A Thousand and One Notes*. London: Cassell, 1931.

———. *How to Play the Piano*. London: Arthur Pearson, 1923.

Hamilton, Kenneth. *Liszt: Sonata in B-minor*. Cambridge: Cambridge University Press, 1996.

———. "Liszt Fantasises—Busoni Excises: The Liszt/Busoni Figaro Fantasy." *Journal of the American Liszt Society* 30 (1991): 21–27.

———. "Liszt's Early and Weimar Piano Works." In Hamilton, ed., *The Cambridge Companion to Liszt*, pp. 57–85. Cambridge: Cambridge University Press, 2005.

———. "Reminiscences de la Scala—Reminiscences of a Scandal: Liszt's Fantasy on Mercadante's 'Il Giuramento.'" *Cambridge Opera Journal* 5, no. 3 (1993): 187–98.

———. "The Virtuoso Tradition." In David Rowland, ed., *The Cambridge Companion to the Piano*. Cambridge: Cambridge University Press, 1998. 57–74.

———, ed. *The Cambridge Companion to Liszt*. Cambridge: Cambridge University Press, 2005.

Hanslick, Eduard. *Concerte, Componisten and Virtuosen, 1870–1885*. Berlin: Allgemeiner Verein für Deutsche Literatur, 1886.

Hedley, Arthur, ed. *Fryderyck Chopin: Selected Correspondence*. New York: McGraw Hill, 1963.

Henschel, George. *Personal Recollections of Johannes Brahms*. Boston: Gorham, 1907.

Hensel, Sebastian. *Die Familie Mendelssohn, 1729–1847: Nach Briefen und Tagebüchern*. Berlin, 1879. Reprint, Frankfurt am Main: Insel Verlag, 1995.

Hinrichsen, Hans-Joachim. *Musikalische Interpretation Hans von Bülow*. Beihefte zum Archiv für Musikwissenschaft, herausgegeben von Hans Heinrich Eggebrecht, Band XLVI. Stuttgart: Franz Steiner Verlag, 1999.

Hofmann, Joseph. *Piano Playing with Piano Questions Answered*. Mineola, N.Y.: Dover, 1976.

Horowitz, Joseph. *Arrau on Music and Performance*. Mineola, N.Y.: Dover, 1999.

Hudson, Richard. *Stolen Time: A History of Tempo Rubato*. New York: Oxford University Press, 1995.

Hullah, Annette. *Theodore Leschetizky*. London: John Lane, 1906.

Hummel, J. N. *Ausführliche theoretisch-practische Anweisung zum Piano-Forte-Spiel*. Vienna: Haslinger, 1828.

Jacobs, Robert L., and Geoffrey Skelton, trans. *Wagner Writes from Paris*. London: Allen and Unwin, 1973.

Johnson, James H. *Listening in Paris: A Cultural History.* Berkeley: University of California Press, 1995.

Johnson, Jeffrey. *Piano Lessons in the Grand Style from the Golden Age of "The Etude" Music Magazine, 1913–1940.* Mineola, N.Y.: Dover, 2003.

———, ed. *Piano Mastery: The Harriet Brower Interviews, 1915–1926.* Mineola, N.Y.: Dover, 2003.

Jones, Peter Ward. *The Mendelssohns on Honeymoon.* New York: Oxford University Press, 1997.

Jones, Timothy. *Beethoven: The "Moonlight" and Other Sonatas, Op. 27 and Op. 31.* Cambridge: Cambridge University Press, 1999.

Kallberg, Jeffrey. *Chopin at the Boundaries: Sex, History and Musical Genre.* Cambridge, Mass.: Harvard University Press, 1996.

———. "Small 'Forms': In Defence of the Prelude." In Jim Samson, ed., *The Cambridge Companion to Liszt*, pp. 124–44. Cambridge: Cambridge University Press, 1992.

Kehler, George. *The Piano in Concert.* 2 vols. Metuchen, N.J.: Scarecrow Press, 1982.

Kennedy, Michael. *Richard Strauss.* New York: Oxford University Press, 1995.

Kunsthistorisches Museum, Wien. *Katalog der Sammlung Alter Musikinstrumente.* Teil 1, Saitenklaviere. Wien, 1966.

Lambour, Christian. "Fanny Hensel: Die Pianistin." *Mendelssohn Studien* 12, pp. 227–42. Berlin: Duncker und Humblot, 2001.

Laurence, Dan H., ed. *Bernard Shaw: How to Become a Musical Critic.* London: Rupert Hart-Davis, 1960.

Lawson, Colin, and Robin Stowell. *The Historical Performance of Music: An Introduction.* Cambridge: Cambridge University Press, 1999.

Leavis, F. R. *The Great Tradition: George Eliot, Henry James, Joseph Conrad.* London: Chatto and Windus, 1948.

Lebert, S., and L. Stark. *Klavierschule.* Stuttgart: Cotta, 1883.

Legany, Deszo. *Franz Liszt: Unbekannte Presse und Briefe aus Wien, 1822–86.* Vienna: Verlag Hermann Böhlaus, 1984.

von Lenz, Wilhelm. *The Great Piano Virtuosos of Our Time.* 1872. Reprint, London: Kahn and Averill, 1983.

Leppert, Richard. "Cultural Contradiction, Idolatry and the Piano Virtuoso, Franz Liszt." In James Parakilas, ed., *Piano Roles: Three Hundred Years of Life with the Piano*, pp. 252–81. New Haven, Conn.: Yale University Press, 1999.

Levine, Lawrence W. *Highbrow/Lowbrow: The Emergence of Cultural Hierarchy in America.* Cambridge, Mass.: Harvard University Press, 1988.

Lhévinne, Josef. *Basic Principles in Pianoforte Playing.* 1924. Reprint, Mineola, N.Y.: Dover, 1974.

Liszt, Franz. *An Artist's Journey: Lettres d'un bachelier ès musique, 1835–1841.* Trans. and annotated Charles Suttoni. Chicago: University of Chicago Press, 1989.

Little, William. "Mendelssohn and Liszt." In R. Larry Todd, ed., *Mendelssohn Studies*, pp. 106–25. Cambridge: Cambridge University Press, 1992.

Litzmann, Berthold. *Clara Schumann: An Artist's Life.* Trans. and abridged Grace Hadow. 2 vols. London: Macmillan, 1913.

Long, Marguerite. *At the Piano with Maurice Ravel*. London: Dent, 1973.

Lott, R. Allen. *From Paris to Peoria: How European Piano Virtuosos Brought Classical Music to the American Heartland*. New York: Oxford University Press, 2003.

Macdonald, Hugh. "La voix de l'instrument." In Brigitte Françoise Sappey, ed., *Charles Valentin Alkan*, pp. 129–40. Paris: Fayard, 1991.

Mach, Elyse, ed. *The Liszt Studies*. New York: Associated Music Publishers, 1973.

La Mara, ed. *Franz Liszts Briefe*. 8 vols. Leipzig, 1893–1905. Abridged English trans. (*Letters of Franz Liszt*) by Constance Bache, 2 vols. London, 1894.

Marmontel, A. F. *Les pianistes célèbres*. Paris: Heupel et Fils, 1878.

Martyn, Barry. *Rachmaninoff: Composer, Pianist, Conductor*. Aldershot: Scholar Press, 1990.

Mason, William. *Memories of a Musical Life*. New York: Century, 1902.

McCarthy, Margaret William. *Amy Fay: America's Notable Woman of Music*. Warren, Mich.: Harmonie Park Press, 1995.

Mendelssohn Bartholdy, Felix. *Reisebriefe aus den Jahren 1830 bis 1832*. Leipzig: Hermann Mendelssohn, 1863.

Mendelssohn Bartholdy, Paul, ed. *Mendelssohn Briefe aus den Jahren 1830 bis 1847*. Leipzig: Hermann Mendelssohn, 1863–64.

Mitchell, Mark. *Vladimir de Pachmann: A Piano Virtuoso's Life and Art*. Bloomington: Indiana University Press, 2002.

Mitchell, Mark, and Allan Evans, eds. *Moriz Rosenthal in Words and Music*. Bloomington: Indiana University Press, 2006.

Monsaingeon, Bruno. *Sviatoslav Richter: Notebooks and Conversations*. Trans. Stewart Spencer. London: Faber and Faber, 2001.

Morrow, Mary Sue. *Concert Life in Haydn's Vienna: Aspects of a Developing Musical and Social Institution*. Stuyvesant, N.Y.: Pendragon Press, 1989.

Moscheles, C. [Charlotte]. A. *Aus Moscheles Leben*. 2 vols. Leipzig: Duncker und Humblot, 1873. Translated into English by A. Coleridge as *Life of Moscheles: With Selections from His Diaries and Correspondence by His Wife*. 2 vols. London: Hurst and Blackett, 1873.

Moscheles, Felix, ed. *Letters of Felix Mendelssohn*. Boston: Ticknor, 1888.

Moscheles, Ignaz, and F.-J. Fétis. *Méthode des méthodes*. Paris: Schlesinger, 1840.

Musgrave, Michael, and Bernard D. Sherman, eds. *Performing Brahms: Early Evidence of Performance Style*. Cambridge: Cambridge University Press, 2003.

Newcomb, Anthony. "Schumann in the Marketplace." In R. Larry Todd, ed., *Nineteenth-Century Piano Music*, pp. 258–315. New York: Schirmer, 1994.

Newcomb, Ethel. *Leschetizky as I Knew Him*. 1921. Reprint, New York: Da Capo Press, 1967.

Nichols, Roger. *Mendelssohn Remembered*. London: Faber, 1997.

Ollivier, Daniel, ed. *Correspondance de Liszt et de la comtesse d'Agoult*. Vol. 1. Paris: Grasset, 1933.

Orga, Ates. "The Piano Music." In Colin Scott-Sutherland, ed., *Ronald Stevenson: The Man and His Music*, pp. 43–130. London: Toccata Press, 2005.

Ott, Bertrand. *Lisztian Keyboard Energy: An Essay on the Pianism of Franz Liszt*. Lewiston, N.Y.: Edwin Mellen Press, 1992.

Paderewski, Ignacy, with Mary Lawton. *The Paderewski Memoirs, Including Letter from Bernard Shaw.* London: Collins, 1939.

Parakilas, James, ed. *Piano Roles: Three Hundred Years of Life with the Piano.* New Haven, Conn.: Yale University Press, 1999.

Philip, Robert. *Early Recordings and Musical Style.* Cambridge: Cambridge University Press, 1992.

————. *Performing Music in the Age of Recordings.* New Haven, Conn.: Yale University Press, 2004.

Plantinga, Leon. *Beethoven's Concertos: History, Style, Performance.* New York: Norton, 1990.

Pleasants, Henry, ed. and trans. *Eduard Hanslick: Vienna's Golden Years of Music, 1850–1900.* New York: Simon and Schuster, 1950.

————, ed. and trans. *Hanslick's Music Criticisms.* Mineola, N.Y.: Dover, 1988.

Potocka, Angele. *Theodore Leschetizky.* Trans. Henry Lincoln. New York, 1903.

Prentner, Marie. *Leschetizky's Fundamental Principles of Piano Technique.* Mineola, N.Y.: Dover, 2005. Originally published as *Fundamental Principles of the Leschetizky Method*, 1903.

Ramann, Lina. *Lisztiana.* Ed. Arthur Seidl. Mainz: Schott, 1983.

————. *Liszt Pädagogium.* Wiesbaden: Breitkopf und Härtel, 1986.

————, ed. *Franz Liszt: Gesammelte Schriften.* 6 vols. Leipzig: Breitkopf und Härtel, 1880–83.

Reich, Nancy. *Clara Schumann: The Artist and the Woman.* Ithaca, N.Y.: Cornell University Press, 1985.

Rink, John, ed. *Musical Performance: A Guide to Understanding.* Cambridge: Cambridge University Press, 2002.

Rittermann, Janet. "On Teaching Performance." In John Rink, ed., *Musical Performance: A Guide to Understanding*, pp. 75–88. Cambridge: Cambridge University Press, 2002.

————. "Piano Music and the Public Concert, 1800–1850." In Jim Samson, ed., *The Cambridge Companion to Chopin*, pp. 11–31. Cambridge: Cambridge University Press, 1992.

Rockstro, William. *Felix Mendelssohn-Bartholdy.* London: Sampson, Lowe, Marston, 1884.

Rosenblum, Sandra. *Performance Practices in Classic Piano Music: Their Principles and Applications.* Bloomington: Indiana University Press, 1988.

Rosenthal, Moriz. "Anton Rubinstein's Concert in Pressburg." In Mark Mitchell and Allan Evans, eds., *Moriz Rosenthal in Words and Music*, pp. 97–103. Bloomington: Indiana University Press, 2006.

————. "If Franz Liszt Should Come Back Again." *Etude* 42, no. 4 (April 1924): 222–23.

————. "On the Question of Applause." In Mark Mitchell and Allan Evans, eds., *Moriz Rosenthal in Words and Music*, pp. 127–28. Bloomington: Indiana University Press, 2006.

Rosenthal, Moriz, and Ludwig Schytte. *Schule des höheren Klavierspiels: Technische Studien bis zur höchsten Ausbildung.* Berlin: Fürstner, 1892.

Rosenthal, Moriz, with R. H. Wollstein. "The 'Grand Manner' in Piano Playing." In Mark Mitchell and Allan Evans, eds., *Moriz Rosenthal in Words and Music*, p. 3. Bloomington: Indiana University Press, 2006.

Rosselli, John. *Singers of Italian Opera: The History of a Profession.* Cambridge: Cambridge University Press, 1992.

Rowland, David. "Beethoven's Pianoforte Pedalling." In Robin Stowell, ed., *Performing Beethoven*, pp. 49–69. Cambridge: Cambridge University Press, 1994; paperback ed., 2005.

———. *A History of Pianoforte Pedalling.* Cambridge: Cambridge University Press, 1993.

Rubinstein, Anton. *Autobiography.* Trans. Aline Delano. 1890. Reprint, Honolulu: University Press of the Pacific, 2005.

———. *My Young Years.* London: Jonathan Cape, 1973.

Sadie, Stanley, ed. *The New Grove Dictionary of Music and Musicians.* 29 vols. London: Macmillan, 2000.

Saffle, Michael. *Franz Liszt in Germany, 1840–45.* Stuyvesant, N.Y.: Pendragon Press, 1994.

Samson, Jim. "The Practice of Early Nineteenth-Century Pianism." In Michael Talbot, ed., *The Musical Work: Reality or Invention*, pp. 110–27. Liverpool: Liverpool University Press, 2000.

———. *Virtuosity and the Musical Work: The Transcendental Studies of Liszt.* Cambridge: Cambridge University Press, 2003.

Sappey, Brigitte Françoise, ed. *Charles Valentin Alkan.* Paris: Fayard, 1991.

von Sauer, Emil. *Meine Welt: Bilder aus dem Geheimfache meiner Kunst.* Stuttgart: Spemann Verlag, 1901.

Schnabel, Artur. *Aus dir wird nie ein Pianist.* Hofheim: Wolke Verlag, 1991.

Schnapp, Friedrich, ed. *Ferruccio Busoni: Briefe an seine Frau, 1895–1907.* Zurich: Rotapfel Verlag, 1934. Trans. by Rosamond Ley as *Ferruccio Busoni: Letters to His Wife.* London: Arnold, 1938.

Schoenberg, Arnold. *Style and Idea: Selected Writings.* Ed. Leonard Stein. Trans. Leo Black. New York: St. Martin's Press, 1975.

Scholes, Percy. *The Mirror of Music, 1844–1944: A Century of Musical Life in Britain as Reflected in the Pages of "The Musical Times."* 2 vols. London: Novello and Oxford University Press, 1947.

Schonberg, Harold. *Horowitz: His Life and Music.* New York: Simon and Schuster, 1992.

Schumann, Eugenie. *Robert Schumann: Ein Lebensbild meines Vaters.* Leipzig: Koehler und Amelang, 1931.

Schumann, Robert. *Music and Musicians.* Trans. Fanny Raymond Ritter. 2 vols. London: W. Reeves, 1877.

Scott-Sutherland, Colin, ed. *Ronald Stevenson: The Man and His Music.* London: Toccata Press, 2005.

Shaw, George Bernard. *The Great Composers: Reviews and Bombardments.* Ed. Louis Crompton. Berkeley: University of California Press, 1978.

———. *London Music in 1888–9 as Heard by Corno di Bassetto.* New York: Dodd, Mead, 1961.

———. *Music in London, 1890–94.* 3 vols. London: Constable, 1931.

Sherman, Bernard D. "How Different Was Brahms's Playing Style from Our Own?" In Michael Musgrave and Bernard D. Sherman, eds., *Performing Brahms: Early Evidence of Performance Style*, pp. 1–10. Cambridge: Cambridge University Press, 2003.

Short, Michael, ed. and trans. *Liszt Letters in the Library of Congress*. Hillside, N.Y.: Pendragon Press, 2003.

Siloti, Alexander. "Memories of Liszt." In Theodore Bullock, ed., *Remembering Franz Liszt: Including "My Memories of Liszt" by Alexander Siloti and "Life and Liszt" by Arthur Friedheim*, pp. 338–75. New York: Limelight Editions, 1986.

Sitsky, Larry. *Anton Rubinstein: An Annotated Catalogue of Piano Works and Biography*. Westport, Conn.: Greenwood Press, 1998.

————. *Busoni and the Piano: The Works, the Writings, and the Recordings*. New York: Greenwood Press, 1986.

Smidak, Emil F. *Ignaz Moscheles: The Life of the Composer and His Encounters with Beethoven, Liszt, Chopin and Mendelssohn*. Aldershot: Scholar Press, 1989.

Stanford, Charles Villiers. *Pages from an Unwritten Diary*. London: Edward Arnold, 1914.

Stasov, Vladimir. *Selected Essays on Music*. Trans. Florence Jonas. New York: Praeger, 1968.

Steane, J. B. *The Grand Tradition: Seventy Years of Singing on Record*. London: Duckworth, 1974.

Stojowski, Zygmunt. "Paderewski w świetle moich wspomnień i wierzeń." In Wieńczyslaw Brzostowski, ed., "Ignacy Jan Paderewski," special issue, *Życie muzyczne i teatralne* 2, nos. 5–6 (May–June 1935): 5. Translated in *Polish Music Journal* 5, no. 2 (Winter 2002). Accessed June 2006 at http://www.usc.edu/dept/polish_music/PMJ/issue/5.2.02.

Stowell, Robin, ed. *Performing Beethoven*. Cambridge: Cambridge University Press, 1994; paperback ed., 2005.

Stradal, August. *Erinnerungen an Franz Liszt*. Bern: Paul Haupt Verlag, 1929.

Stravinsky, Igor. *Autobiography*. 1936. Reprint, New York: Norton, 1962.

Sydow, B. E., ed. *Korespondencja Fryderyka Chopina*. 2 vols. Warsaw: Panstwowy Instytut Wydawniczy, 1955.

Szász, Tibor. "Beethoven's Basso Continuo: Notation and Performance." In Robin Stowell, ed., *Performing Beethoven*, pp. 1–22. Cambridge: Cambridge University Press, 1994; paperback ed., 2005.

Talbot, Michael, ed. *The Musical Work: Reality or Invention*. Liverpool: Liverpool University Press, 2000.

Taruskin, Richard. Review titled "Speed Bumps." *Nineteenth-Century Music* 29, no. 2 (Fall 2005): 185–207.

————. *Text and Act*. New York: Oxford University Press, 1995.

Taylor, David. "Paderewski's Piano." *Smithsonian* (March 1999), 1–3.

Todd, R. Larry. *Mendelssohn: A Life in Music*. New York: Oxford University Press, 2003.

————, ed. *Mendelssohn and His World*. Princeton, N.J.: Princeton University Press, 1991.

Tunley, David. *Salons, Singers and Songs: A Background to Romantic French Songs, 1830–70*. Aldershot: Ashgate, 2002.

Türk, Daniel Gottlob. *Klavierschule, oder Anweisung zum Klavierspielen fuer Lehrer und Lernende*. 1789. Neue vermehrte und verbesserte Ausgabe. Leipzig und Halle: Schwickert, 1802.

Ubber, Christian. *Liszt's Zwölf Etuden und ihre Fassungen.* Weimarer Liszt Studien 4. Regensburg: Laaber Verlag, 2002.

Walker, Alan. *Franz Liszt, Vol. 1: The Virtuoso Years.* London: Faber and Faber, 1988.

——, ed. *Living with Liszt: From the Diary of Carl Lachmund, an American Pupil of Liszt, 1882–84.* Stuyvesant, N.Y.: Pendragon Press, 1995.

Ward Jones, Peter. *The Mendelssohns on Honeymoon.* Oxford: Clarendon Press, 1997.

Watson, Derek. *Liszt.* London: Dent, 1989.

Weber, William. *The Great Transformation of Musical Taste: European Concert Programs, 1750–1875.* Cambridge: Cambridge University Press, forthcoming.

——. "The History of Musical Canons." In Mark Everist and Nicholas Cook, eds., *Rethinking Music*, pp. 340–59. Oxford: Oxford University Press, 1999.

——. *Music and the Middle Class: The Social Structure of Concert Life in London, Paris and Vienna between 1830 and 1848.* 2nd ed. London: Ashgate Press, 2003.

——. *The Rise of Musical Classics: A Study in Canon, Ritual and Ideology.* New York: Oxford University Press, 1992.

——, ed. *The Musician as Entrepreneur.* Bloomington: Indiana University Press, 2005.

Wehle, Gerhard F. *Die Kunst der Improvisation: Die technischen Grundlagen zum stilgerechten, künstlerischen Improvisieren nach den Prinzipien des Klaviersatzes unter besonderer Berücksichtigung des Volksliedes ausführlich erläutert.* 2 vols. Köln: Musik Verlag Ernest Bisping, 1940. Earlier editions 1925–27.

Weissweiler, Eva, ed. *Fanny und Felix Mendelssohn: Briefwechsel, 1821 bis 1846.* Berlin: Propyläen, 1997.

Weissweiler, Eva, with Susanna Ludwig, eds. *Clara Schumann and Robert Schumann: Briefwechsel.* Frankfurt: Stroemfeld/Roter Stern, 1984–2001.

Wieck, Friedrich. *Piano and Song: Didactic and Polemic.* Trans. Henry Pleasants. Stuyvesant, N.Y.: Pendragon Press, 1988.

Williamon, Aaron. "Memorising Music." In John Rink, ed., *Musical Performance: A Guide to Understanding*, pp. 113–26. Cambridge: Cambridge University Press, 2002.

Williams, Adrian. *Portrait of Liszt: By Himself and His Contemporaries.* Oxford: Clarendon Press, 1990.

——, trans. and ed. *Franz Liszt: Selected Letters.* Oxford: Clarendon Press, 1998.

Winter, Robert. "The Emperor's New Clothes: Nineteenth-Century Instruments Revisited." *Nineteenth Century Music* 7, no. 3 (April 1984): 251–65.

——. "Performing Nineteenth-Century Music on Nineteenth-Century Instruments." *Nineteenth Century Music* 1, no. 2 (November 1977): 163–75.

Wright, William, ed. *Herold-Herz-Liszt Cavatine de "Zampa."* Glasgow: William Wright, 2005.

Zamoyski, Adam. *Paderewski.* London: Collins, 1982.

Zimdars, Richard, trans. and ed. *The Piano Masterclasses of Franz Liszt: Diary Notes of August Göllerich.* Bloomington: Indiana University Press, 1996.

——, trans. and ed. *The Piano Masterclasses of Hans von Bülow: Two Participants' Accounts.* Bloomington: Indiana University Press, 1993.

# Index

Page numbers in bold indicate figures or music examples.

Czerny, Carl, 10, 13–14, 28–29, 35, 75,
    77–78, 80, 85, 102, 104–5, 108,
    108n22, 110–11, 110n25, 127,
    133–34, 152–53, 155–57, 171–72,
    182–83, 208, 232, 250
Czerny, Carl, works
    op. 500 Pianoforte School, 80
    On the Proper Performance of
        Beethoven's Pianoforte Works, 183

d'Agoult, Marie, 82, **83**, 85, 91–92
d'Albert, Eugen, 39, 97, 167, 167n75, 207,
    223, 238, 240–41, 244, 276
da Motta, José Vianna, 236, 238, 240
Danhauser, Josef, 82, **83**, 83n35
Davies, Fanny, 197
Davison, J. W., 76
Debussy, Claude, works performed, 70
*Demobbed* (film), 273n34
Deppe, Ludwig, 133–34, 162, 174
Dietrich, Anton, 84
Döhler, Theodor, 40, 88, 156
Döhler, Theodor, works performed
    by Marie Pleyel, 56
Dohnányi, Erno, 127
Donizetti, Giuseppi, works performed
    by Liszt, 51, 51n46, 262
Dreyschock, Alexander, 38
Dubal, David, 5n6, 249n61
Dumas, Alexandre, **83**
Dussek, Jan Ladislav, 13, 106, 113, 171
Dussek, Jan Ladislav, works performed
    by Moscheles, 54

Eckhardt, Maria, 238n33
Eigeldinger, Jean-Jacques, 27, 124,
    151n33, 241
Elgar, Edward, works
    *Concert allegro*, 267n20
English school of piano playing, 11–12
entracte music, 37

Érard pianos, 12, 17, 19, 90, 173, 208–10,
    222–23, 266
Ernst, Heinrich Wilhelm, 85
*Etude* magazine, 5–6, 265, 265n14
Evans, Allan, 5

Fay, Amy, 73–74, 98–99, 129, 133,
    133n61, 173–74
Felix Mendelssohn and His Hawaiian
    Serenaders, 273n34
Fétis, F. J., 18, 63, 156, 158, 172, 172n90,
    194, 227, 232
Field, John, **126–27**, 140
FitzGerald, Edward, 258–59
Fontaine, Mortier de, 42
footnote-itis, 158
Franck, César, works
    Prelude, Chorale and Fugue, 216
Franck, César, works performed
    by Horowitz, 69
French school, 11–12
Frescobaldi, Girolamo, 154
Friedheim, Arthur, 10, 30, 64, 162, 226,
    236, 241–42, 244, 250, 252, 271,
    271n29, 272
Friedman, Ignaz, 68–69, 144, 256, **257**

Gaisberg, Fred, 35, 163, 169
Garcia, Manuel, 160
Gilbert, W. S., 12
Gilels, Emil, 4
Glinka, Mikhail, 193
Glinka, Mikhail, works performed
    by Liszt, 51
Glover, Lawrence, 16n38
Goddard, Arabella, 78n21
Godowsky, Leopold, 53n48, 55, 149,
    163, 179, 202–3, 218
Godowsky, Leopold, works
    *Die Fledermaus*, Concert-Paraphrase,
        232–33n23